# LAUBACH WAY TO
# READING

*TEACHER'S*
*MANUAL FOR* **4**
*SKILL BOOK*

## OTHER VOWEL SOUNDS AND CONSONANT SPELLINGS

Frank C. Laubach

Elizabeth Mooney Kirk

Robert S. Laubach

ISBN 0-88336-914-1

© 1984, 1991

New Readers Press
Publishing Division of
Laubach Literacy International
Box 131, Syracuse, New York 13210

Printed in the United States
of America

Edited by Caroline Blakely and
Kay Koschnick

Illustrated by Cheri Bladholm

20  19  18  17  16  15  14  13  12  11
10   9   8   7   6   5   4   3

# Table of Contents

4    Contents

Contents 5

**SB** indicates the page in *Skill Book 4*.
**TM** indicates the page in this teacher's manual.

---

### Index of Teaching Techniques and Aids

# The Laubach Way to Reading

The Laubach Way to Reading is a basic reading and writing series developed primarily for adults with little or no reading ability. The series consists of four skill books and correlated readers for student use. The teacher's manual for each skill book gives detailed instructions and lesson plans.

The series provides a systematic development of basic reading and writing skills. Each lesson includes vocabulary development, phonic or structural analysis of words, the reading of a short story, comprehension checks, and writing practice. The lessons progress from the sounds and regular spellings of basic consonants to those of the short vowels, the long vowels, and finally to irregular spellings and more difficult reading, writing, and grammar skills.

The skills books and correlated readers may be used with both speakers of English and those who are learning English. A separate series of manuals, the Laubach Way to English, provides complete instructions for teaching the skills of listening, speaking, reading, and writing English to the non-English-speaking student.

Although designed primarily for adults, the Laubach Way to Reading may also be used successfully with high school dropouts or students in intermediate grades who need remedial work in basic reading, writing, or spelling. Classroom teachers, teacher aides, and volunteer tutors may all use the books effectively.

## Skill Book 1: Sounds and Names of Letters

Beginning on a zero level, *Skill Book 1* lays an essential foundation in word attack and comprehension skills. The names and one sound for each letter of the alphabet and the digraphs *ch, sh,* and *th* are introduced. Simple sentence patterns encourage fluency in reading. Blending of sounds, punctuation, silent reading, and manuscript writing are introduced. A total of 132 words is used.

## Skill Book 2: Short Vowel Sounds

Lessons are structured around the short vowel sounds, *y* as a vowel as in *city,* and the *r*-controlled vowel sounds for *er, ir, ur,* and *ar.* The digraphs *ng* and *wh* are introduced, as are beginning and ending consonant blends. Simple skills of punctuation, structural analysis, comprehension, and sentence writing are introduced. A total of 192 new words is introduced.

## Skill Book 3: Long Vowel Sounds

This book presents the long sounds for *a, e, i,* and *o* with their regular spellings, one regular spelling for long *u,* and the sound for *or* as in *York.* Comprehension skills include finding main ideas, summarizing content, recognizing implied meaning, developing opinions, and predicting outcome. Lessons include functional materials like ads, bills, menus, letters, and checks. A total of 399 new words is used. Cursive writing is taught at this level. For this, the student needs the separate cursive writing workbook, and the teacher's instruction book.

## Skill Book 4: Other Vowel Sounds and Consonant Spellings

This book continues with the regular spellings for the long *u* sound and goes on to the letter combinations *oo, ou, aw, oi,* and their variant spellings. The book also covers different sounds represented by the same consonant symbol, such as the *s* in *see* and *please,* and regular spellings for consonant sounds that may be spelled in more than one way, such as the /k/ sound in *keep* and *can.* A total of 708 new words is used.

Word analysis skills are strengthened by more work with contractions and compound words and by the student's becoming familiar with the most common prefixes and suffixes. Practice is given to increase reading speed.

Comprehension skills emphasized include making inferences, identifying cause and effect, drawing conclusions, and understanding the mood and setting of a story. Also, students are helped to interpret the authors' purpose and to evaluate their own reactions to what they read.

## Correlated Readers

The correlated reader for each skill book is a collection of stories or articles using much of the same vocabulary as the skill book. The correlated readers are an intrinsic part of the series as they provide opportunity for the student to gain confidence and independent reading habits.

## About the Authors

More than 50 years of continuous experience in literacy education lie behind the Laubach Way to Reading. In 1930 in the Philippines, the late Frank C. Laubach (1884-1970) originated a method of teaching adults to read and write in their own language. After Laubach lessons had been used in some 300 languages, the method was applied to teaching in English. *Streamlined English* was published in 1946. In the 1960s, a complete revision and expansion, the New Streamlined English series, was published. The current Laubach Way to Reading series thus represents the third generation of Laubach curricula in English.

Author Elizabeth Mooney Kirk started working with Frank Laubach in 1945, developing *Streamlined English.* Her background includes master's degrees in education and journalism, developing adult literacy programs in India and Kenya, teaching adults and children, and training tutors and writers. Mrs. Kirk was co-author with Frank C. Laubach and Robert S. Laubach of the New Streamlined English series.

Co-author Robert S. Laubach is past-president and a lifetime board member of Laubach Literacy International and founder of its New Readers Press division. He started his literacy work as a teenager in the Philippines and then assisted his father in literacy campaigns in some 50 countries. He has a doctorate in reading education and taught literacy journalism at the university level for 30 years.

# REGULAR SPELLING OF VOWEL SOUNDS

|  | Sound | Examples | Regular Spelling |
|---|---|---|---|
| **Short Vowels** | i | in | i |
|  | y | lily | y |
|  | u | up | u |
|  | e | egg | e |
|  | a | apple | a |
|  | o | olive | o |
|  | er | fern, burn, bird | er, ur, ir |
|  | ar | arms | ar |
| **Long Vowels** | $\bar{a}$ | paper, day, paint, cake | a, ay, ai, a-e |
|  | $\bar{e}$ | we, see, eat, key, Pete | e, ee, ea, ey, e-e |
|  | $\bar{i}, \bar{y}$ | I, my, tie, night, time | i, y, ie, igh, i-e |
|  | $\bar{o}$, or | go, boat, snow, York, home | o, oa, ow, or, o-e |
|  | $\bar{u}$ | music, cure, argue, few | u, u-e, ue, ew |
| **Other Vowels** | oo | food, June, blue, chew | oo, u-e, ue, ew |
|  | $\bar{u}$ or oo | student, Duke, Tuesday, news | u, u-e, ue, ew |
|  | uu | book | oo |
|  | ou | mouth, town | ou, ow |
|  | aw | lawn, Paul, ball, caught bought | aw, au, a(ll), augh(t), ough(t) |
|  | oy | boy, oil | oy, oi |

This chart shows the regular spelling of vowel sounds taught in the Laubach Way to Reading. Generally, the vowel sounds are taught in the order of frequency of their use. When vowel sounds are spelled in more than one way, the spellings that occur most frequently are taught first.

## Principles on Which Laubach Lessons are Based

**Establishing letter-sound relationships.** The letters of the alphabet and the sounds they stand for are taught in a systematic manner. This series uses existing phonetic regularities, emphasizes regular spellings, and provides aids to irregular spellings.

**Learning through association.** Letters and sounds are presented through key words with picture associations.

**Moving from the known to the unknown.** The student starts with the spoken word, which he knows, and moves in short steps to the written word, which he does not know.

**Familiar vocabulary.** Words used are in the spoken vocabulary of the adult. Vocabulary is controlled, with a limited number of new words in each lesson.

**Use of repetition to strengthen the visual image.** Each word and sentence pattern is repeated several times soon after it is taught.

**Use of meaningful content.** From the beginning, reading for meaning is stressed.

**Something new in each lesson.** Each lesson teaches something new in a familiar lesson pattern.

**Independence in learning.** Visual aids, phonic skills, consistent lesson patterns, and uniformity of format make it easy for the student to help himself.

**Lessons are easy to teach.** The lessons are planned for maximum self-help and minimum teacher help. The detailed manuals for teachers make it possible for inexperienced teachers to use the materials successfully.

# Introduction to Skill Book 4

*Skill Book 4,* with 23 lessons, completes the basic phonics foundation needed for independent reading. The first 16 lessons present regular spellings for the long *u* sound, which was introduced in *Skill Book 3,* and for the additional five vowel sounds as found in *food, book, mouth, lawn, boy.* Four lessons cover different sounds represented by the same consonant symbol plus regular spellings for consonant sounds that may be spelled in more than one way. One lesson introduces the use of the dictionary. The last two lessons provide study helps for the correlated reader.

More word recognition, comprehension, writing, and spelling skills are introduced. These are listed in detail in the chart called Skills Introduced or Reinforced in Skill Book 4 on pages 11-15. You may use this chart as a guide to your student's progress.

## Materials Needed for This Level

In *Skill Book 4,* the charts on vowel sounds are similar in format to those in *Skill Books 2* and *3.* The charts for the four lessons on consonant sounds and spellings have a different format; key words are used, but there are no pictures. Both known words and new words are used as examples of the consonant sound or spelling being taught. New words are marked with an asterisk (*). Lesson 21 is about how to use a dictionary and includes a sample dictionary page for reference instead of a chart.

Each chart is followed by a story. The stories in this skill book are longer, with longer sentences and more variation in sentence patterns. Some of the stories are printed in two columns.

Each story is followed by a written checkup. These checkups, along with discussion of the story, help the student progress in more advanced comprehension skills, such as making inferences, relating cause and effect, drawing conclusions, understanding the author's purpose, and interpreting the mood and setting of the story.

Each lesson has a section called Reading for Living with a short functional reading selection and usually a related written exercise. Selections include applications, maps, calendars, want ads, and other practical materials.

The student does the writing lesson in a separate notebook, as he did for *Skill Book 3.* Instructions for the writing lesson are given in each lesson of this manual. A few of the homework exercises are also done in the notebook.

After each group of lessons covering two vowel sounds comes a lesson called More Reading. This lesson serves both as a review and as an opportunity for independent reading. There are three such lessons.

*Skill Book 4* introduces 708 words and seven symbols, not counting variants formed by adding known endings. The correlated reader *People and Places* is introduced in Lesson 22. (Replicas are not included in this manual.) *People and Places* has four factual stories and introduces 174 additional new words.

The student is expected to use cursive writing for most of his written work at this level. He should complete the *Laubach Way to Cursive Writing* workbook (except for Lesson 10) before beginning *Skill Book 4.* This workbook and its teacher's guide should be available for reference as needed.

*Checkups for Skill Book 4,* a separate booklet, should be given after the student completes *Skill Book 4* to help evaluate his progress in reading. Directions for administering and scoring the *Checkups* follow the lesson plans in this manual. Directions are also given for a checkup on writing and spelling skills done on separate paper.

## Supplementary Materials

*Focus on Phonics-4* may be used as a supplement to meet individual needs. Suggestions for its use are in the lesson plans. Other supplementary readers on this level and *News for You,* an easy-to-read newspaper, can be ordered from New Readers Press.

## Schedule

In most cases, a student can cover a lesson in a session of one-and-a-half hours. He will probably need an additional half hour for the homework. If a lesson needs to be presented in two sessions, cover the chart, story, and story checkup in one session and the Reading for Living, skills practices, and writing lesson in the other. It is important to present something new in each class session. A student who has two or more sessions a week should be able to complete the skill book, correlated reader, and checkups in 15 to 18 weeks. Additional time may be needed for the use of supplementary material. It is important that the student cover each lesson and not skip through the skill book. The lessons are systematically organized to provide a foundation of reading skills.

## General Plan for the Lessons

The sequence for the presentation of most lessons in *Skill Book 4* is as follows:

| I. Reading | II. Skills Practice | III. Writing |
|---|---|---|
| Chart | Practice on | Check homework from |
| Story | phonics and | previous lesson |
| Story Checkup | word recognition | Writing lesson in |
| Reading for Living | skills | separate notebook |
| | | Practice exercise in |
| | | skill book |
| | | Homework assignment |
| | | in skill book |

The three review lessons follow the same sequence but without a Reading for Living section in the skill book. Two of the lessons, however, are designed to help the student read the newspaper, and other supplementary practical materials are suggested for you to collect.

Each lesson plan suggests ways of checking the student's progress and reinforcing skills in which he needs more practice. The student should not be slowed down unnecessarily, however, in order to cover supplementary material.

# RESPELLINGS

The self-help device of respelling new words continues in *Skill Book 4* in accordance with these policies:

• Beginning in Lesson 1, a stress mark is used in the respelling after the syllable with primary stress.

• Beginning in Lesson 8, the letters *uu* are used to indicate the vowel sound heard in *book*, usually spelled *oo*, to distinguish it from the vowel sound heard in *food*, also spelled *oo*.

• Beginning in Lesson 17, a word of more than one syllable is not divided into syllables unless it contains an irregular spelling. For example, in Lesson 20, *history* is not respelled, as it is regular. But *improvement* is respelled im proov' ment as the second syllable has an irregular spelling.

• In *Skill Book 4*, a new word is respelled for one or more of these reasons:

**1. The word contains a regular spelling that has not yet been taught.** For example, the regular spelling pattern *-tion = shun* is taught in Lesson 20. Before that lesson, *-tion* in a new word is respelled *shun*.

**2. The word contains an irregular spelling.** The irregular part of the word is respelled with the most similar regular spelling pattern that has been taught. For example, the verb *refuse* is respelled r̄e fuze' when the spelling *u-e* has been taught for the long *u* sound, but the *s* needs to be respelled. Only the part of the word that is irregular is changed; any part that has already been taught is left as it is.

**3. The word contains a spelling that is regular for more than one sound.** In the case of a long vowel sound spelled with the single letter *a,e,i,o,* or *u,* a macron is placed over the vowel letter to indicate that it stands for the long sound. Examples of this are *only* (ōn ly), *lion* (lī' un), and *human* (hū' mun).

When *ow* stands for the long *o* sound, the *o* will always be marked with a macron, as in *low* (lōw). To make sure that *ow* is not pronounced as it is in *town.*

An exception is made to this policy for words in which the vowel sound can be pronounced either /ū/ or /oo/. If *u-e, ue,* or *ew* is used to represent the vowel sound, this part of the word is not respelled. Examples are *knew* (new) and *Luke.* If *u* by itself is used for the sound, then the *u* is respelled with a macron, as in *stupid* (stū' pid). However, if the pronunciation of *u* is only /oo/, the respelling is *oo,* as in *Judy* (Joo' dy).

**4. The word contains a schwa sound that needs respelling to prevent a wrong pronunciation.** The schwa sound, which can be represented by any of the vowel letters, occurs often in unstressed syllables. It is not respelled when the short sound for the vowel is not very different from the schwa sound. When it is necessary to respell the schwa sound, the letter *u* is used because the short sound for *u* is nearly the same as the schwa sound. Examples are *about* (u bout'), *Africa* (Af' ric u).

**5. The word has more than one syllable and is divided into syllables to make it easier to read.** This policy is followed in Lessons 1-16. After that, the word is divided into syllables only if it has an irregular spelling.

A double consonant is respelled with one consonant, as in *opposite* (op' u zit) and *annoy* (u noy'). If these words were respelled with their double consonants as *op' pu zit* and *u nnoy'*, the student might try to pronounce two distinct sounds for *p* in *opposite* and might be confused by a syllable beginning with a double consonant (*nnoy*).

**6. The word is a compound word, made up of two smaller words.** In the respelling, a compound word made up of two known words is simply divided between the known words for easier recognition. The known words are not respelled nor divided into syllables, although the stress mark is shown. An example is *afternoon* (af' ter noon).

# NOTES ON STYLE

**Slash marks.** Slash marks around a letter or letters indicate the sound for which they stand. Thus, you say /b/ like the beginning consonant sound in *bird* and /a/ like the beginning vowel sound in *apple.*

**Italics.** Letters in italic are read by their letter names, as *a, b, c.*

**Abbreviations.** Many of the instructions for teaching the lessons are given in dialog form. To save space, the letter *T* indicates *Teacher* and *S* indicates *Student.*

**Brackets [ ] and parentheses ( ).** Brackets are used to enclose the expected student response. Within dialog, parentheses are used to enclose what the teacher is expected to *do* but not to *say.*

**Pronouns referring to *teacher* and *student*.** Although the authors recognize that there are teachers and students of both sexes, they have chosen for the sake of brevity to use the pronoun *she* to refer to the teacher and *he* to refer to the student. In the skill book, stories and illustrations show both sexes in a variety of roles and activites.

## SKILLS INTRODUCED OR REINFORCED IN SKILL BOOK 4

| Phonics skills | Lesson | 1 | 2 | 3 | 4 | 5 | 6 | 7 | 8 | 9 | 10 | 11 | 12 | 13 | 14 | 15 | 16 | 17 | 18 | 19 | 20 | 21 | 22 A | 22 B | 23 A | 23 B |
|---|---|---|---|---|---|---|---|---|---|---|---|---|---|---|---|---|---|---|---|---|---|---|---|---|---|---|
| 1. Recognize the | *u* as in *music* | ● | | | | | ● | ● | | | | ● | | | | | ● | | | | | | | | | |
| long vowel sound /ū/ | *u-e* as in *cure* | ● | | | | | ● | ● | | | | ● | | | | | ● | | | | | | | | | |
| and its regular spellings: | *ue* as in *argue* | | ● | | | | ● | ● | | | | ● | | | | | ● | | | | | | | | | |
| | *ew* as in *few* | | ● | | | | ● | ● | | | | ● | | | | | ● | | | | | | | | | |
| 2. Recognize the | *oo* as in *food* | | | ● | | | | ● | | | | ● | | | | | ● | | | | | | | | | |
| vowel sound /oo/ | *u-e* as in *June* | | | | ● | | ● | ● | | | | ● | | | | | ● | | | | | | | | | |
| and its regular spellings: | *ue* as in *blue* | | | | ● | | ● | ● | | | | ● | | | | | ● | | | | | | | | | |
| | *ew* as in *chew* | | | | | ● | ● | ● | | | | ● | | | | | ● | | | | | | | | | |
| 3. Recognize vowel sound /uu/: | *oo* as in *book* | | | | | | | | ● | | | ● | | | | | ● | | | | | | | | | |
| 4. Recognize vowel sound /ou/ | *ou* as in *mouth* | | | | | | | | | ● | | ● | | | | | ● | | | | | | | | | |
| and its regular spellings: | *ow* as in *town* | | | | | | | | | | ● | ● | | | | | ● | | | | | | | | | |
| 5. Recognize the | *aw* as in *lawn* | | | | | | | | | | | | ● | | | | ● | | | | | | | | | |
| vowel sound /aw/ | *au* as in *Paul* | | | | | | | | | | | | ● | | | | ● | | | | | | | | | |
| and its regular spellings: | *a* + *ll* as in *ball* | | | | | | | | | | | | | ● | | | ● | | | | | | | | | |
| | *augh* + *t* as in *caught* | | | | | | | | | | | | | | ● | | ● | | | | | | | | | |
| | *ough* + *t* as in *bought* | | | | | | | | | | | | | | ● | | ● | | | | | | | | | |
| 6. Recognize vowel sound /oy/ | *oy* as in *boy* | | | | | | | | | | | | | | | ● | ● | | | | | | | | | |
| and its regular spellings: | *oi* as in *oil* | | | | | | | | | | | | | | | ● | ● | | | | | | | | | |
| 7. Recognize the sound for a vowel + *rr* | | | | | | | | | | | | | ● | | | | ● | | | | | | | | | |
| 8. Recognize the | *s* = /s/ as in *snake* | | | | | | | | | | | | | | | | | ● | | | | | | | | |
| four sounds for *s*: | *s* = /z/ as in *eggs* | | | | | | | | | | | | | | | | | ● | | | | | | | | |
| Note: the sound /zh/ | *s* = /sh/ as in *sure* | | | | | | | | | | | | | | | | | ● | | | | | | | | |
| is new in Lesson 17. | *s* = /zh/ as in *measure* | | | | | | | | | | | | | | | | | ● | | | | | | | | |
| 9. Recognize the | *ch* = /ch/ as in *child* | | | | | | | | | | | | | | | | | ● | | | | | | | | |
| three sounds for *ch*: | *ch* = /k/ as in *Chris* | | | | | | | | | | | | | | | | | ● | | | | | | | | |
| | *ch* = /sh/ as in *machine* | | | | | | | | | | | | | | | | | ● | | | | | | | | |
| 10. Recognize the | *c* = /k/ as in *cup* | | | | | | | | | | | | | | | | | | ● | | | | | | | |
| two sounds for *c*: | *c* = /s/ as in *city* | | | | | | | | | | | | | | | | | | ● | | | | | | | |
| 11. Recognize the | *g* = /g/ as in *go* | | | | | | | | | | | | | | | | | | ● | | | | | | | |
| two sounds for *g*: | *g* = /j/ as in *age* | | | | | | | | | | | | | | | | | | ● | | | | | | | |
| 12. Recognize these | *wr* = /r/ as in *write* | | | | | | | | | | | | | | | | | | | ● | | | | | | |
| spellings for | *kn* = /n/ as in *know* | | | | | | | | | | | | | | | | | | | ● | | | | | | |
| consonant sounds: | *mb* = /m/ as in *climb* | | | | | | | | | | | | | | | | | | | ● | | | | | | |
| | *ph* = /f/ as in *phone* | | | | | | | | | | | | | | | | | | | ● | | | | | | |
| | *gh* = /f/ as in *laugh* | | | | | | | | | | | | | | | | | | | ● | | | | | | |
| 13. Recognize the | *-tion* = /shun/ as in *direction* | | | | | | | | | | | | | | | | | | | | ● | | | | ● | |
| pronunciation of | *-ssion* = /shun/ as in *admission* | | | | | | | | | | | | | | | | | | | | ● | | | | | |
| these word endings: | *-sion* = /zhun/ as in *television* | | | | | | | | | | | | | | | | | | | | ● | | | | | |
| 14. Recognize these | *sw* as in *swim* | | | ● | | | | | | | | | | | | | | | | | | | | | | |
| new beginning | *scr* as in *scream* | | | | | | | | | | | | | | | | | | ● | | ● | | | | | |
| consonant blends: | *spr* as in *spring* | | | | | | | | | | | | | ● | | | | | ● | | | | | | | |
| | *squ* as in *square* | | | | | | | | | | | | | | | | | | | | ● | | | | | |
| 15. Recognize the new ending consonant blend *pt* as in *kept* | | | | | | | | | | | | | | ● | | | | | ● | | | | | | | |
| 16. Review other beginning or ending consonant blends | | | | ● | ● | ● | | | | | | | | ● | | | | | ● | | | | | | | |

Word recognition skills — Scope and Sequence Chart (by Lesson)

| Word recognition skills | 1 | 2 | 3 | 4 | 5 | 6 | 7 | 8 | 9 | 10 | 11 | 12 | 13 | 14 | 15 | 16 | 17 | 18 | 19 | 20 | 21 | 22A | 22B | 23A | 23B |
|---|---|---|---|---|---|---|---|---|---|---|---|---|---|---|---|---|---|---|---|---|---|---|---|---|---|
| 1. Recognize words by blending sounds | • | • | • | • | • | • | • | • | • | • | • | • | • |   | • | • |   | • | • | • | • | • |   | • | • |
| 2. Recognize same words by sight in context | • | • | • | • | • | • | • | • | • | • | • | • | • |   | • | • |   | • | • | • | • | • |   | • | • |
| 3. Recognize the number of syllables in a word | • | • | • | • |   | • | • |   |   | • | • | • |   |   | • |   |   | • |   |   | • |   |   |   |   |
| 4. Recognize which syllable is stressed | • | • |   | • | • | • | • |   |   |   | • |   |   |   |   |   |   | • |   |   | • |   |   |   |   |
| 5. Recognize contractions |   | • |   |   |   |   |   |   |   |   | • |   |   |   |   |   |   |   | • |   |   |   |   |   |   |
| 6. Recognize compound words | • | • | • |   |   | • |   | • |   | • |   | • |   |   | • | • |   |   |   |   |   |   |   | • |   |
| 7. Recognize words joined by a hyphen, as *all-around* |   |   |   |   |   | • |   |   |   | • |   |   |   |   | • |   |   |   | • |   |   |   |   |   |   |
| 8. Review endings, with -s or -es, -ing, -ed; recognizing variants of root words | • | • | • | • |   |   | • | • | • | • |   |   |   |   | • | • |   | • | • |   | • | • | • | • |   |
|    with -er, -est |   |   |   |   |   |   |   |   |   | • |   | • | • |   |   |   |   |   |   | • | • |   |   |   |   |
|    with -y |   |   | • |   | • |   |   |   |   |   |   |   | • |   | • |   |   |   |   |   |   |   |   |   |   |
|    with -ly |   |   |   |   |   |   |   |   | • |   | • |   |   |   |   | • |   |   |   | • |   | • | • |   | • |
|    with -ness |   |   |   |   |   |   |   |   |   |   |   |   |   | • |   | • |   |   |   |   |   | • |   |   |   |
| 9. Recognize variants of root words: with adjective ending -ful |   |   |   |   |   |   |   | • |   |   | • | • |   |   |   | • |   | • |   |   |   | • |   |   | • |
|    with adjective ending -less |   |   |   |   |   |   |   |   |   |   | • |   | • |   | • |   |   |   |   |   |   | • |   |   | • |
|    with adjective ending -al |   |   |   |   |   |   |   |   |   |   |   |   |   |   |   |   | • |   |   |   |   | • |   | • |   |
|    with adjective ending -ous |   |   |   |   |   |   | • |   | • |   |   |   |   |   |   |   |   |   |   |   |   |   |   | • | • |
|    with noun ending -hood |   |   |   |   |   |   |   |   | • |   | • | • |   |   |   |   |   |   |   |   |   |   |   |   |   |
|    with noun ending -ship |   |   |   |   |   |   |   |   |   |   |   |   |   |   |   |   |   | • |   |   |   |   |   |   | • |
|    with noun ending -ment |   |   |   |   |   |   |   |   |   |   |   |   |   |   | • |   |   |   |   |   |   | • | • |   | • |
|    with noun endings -ion, -tion, -ation, -sion |   |   |   |   |   |   |   |   |   |   |   |   |   |   |   |   |   |   |   |   |   |   | • |   |   |
|    with noun endings -or, -ist, -ian |   |   |   |   |   |   |   |   |   |   |   |   |   |   |   |   |   |   |   |   |   | • |   |   |   |
| 10. Recognize root words in words with endings |   |   | • |   | • | • |   | • |   |   |   |   |   |   |   |   |   |   | • |   |   |   |   |   |   |
| 11. Review prefixes *in-* and *non-* meaning *not* |   |   | • |   |   | • |   |   |   |   |   |   |   |   |   |   |   |   |   |   |   |   |   |   |   |
| 12. Recognize prefixes: *un-* meaning *not* |   |   |   |   |   |   |   |   |   | • |   |   |   |   |   | • |   | • |   |   | • |   |   |   | • |
|    *il-* meaning *not* |   |   |   |   |   |   |   |   |   |   |   |   |   |   |   |   |   |   |   |   |   |   |   |   |   |
|    *re-* meaning *back* or *again* |   |   |   |   |   |   |   |   |   |   |   |   |   |   |   |   |   |   |   |   | • |   |   |   |   |
|    *inter-* meaning *between* or *among* |   |   |   |   |   |   |   |   |   |   |   |   |   |   |   |   |   |   |   |   |   |   |   |   |   |
| 13. Recognize root words in words with prefixes |   |   | • |   |   |   |   |   |   | • |   | • |   |   |   | • |   |   | • |   |   |   |   |   | • |
| 14. Recognize regular noun plurals | • |   |   | • |   |   |   |   |   |   |   |   |   |   |   |   |   |   |   |   |   |   |   |   |   |
| 15. Recognize irregular noun plurals |   |   |   |   |   |   |   |   |   |   | • |   |   |   |   |   |   |   |   |   |   | • | • |   |   |
| 16. Recognize irregular verb forms |   |   |   |   |   |   |   |   | • |   |   |   |   |   |   |   |   |   |   |   |   |   |   |   |   |
| 17. Recognize words with same meaning (synonyms) |   |   |   |   | • |   | • |   | • | • |   |   |   |   | • |   |   |   |   | • |   |   |   |   |   |
| 18. Recognize words with opposite meanings (antonyms) |   |   |   |   |   |   |   |   |   |   |   | • |   |   |   | • |   |   |   | • |   |   | • | • |   |
| 19. Recognize words that sound alike (homonyms) |   |   |   |   |   |   |   |   |   | • |   |   |   |   |   |   |   | • | • |   | • | • |   |   | • |
| 20. Recognize multiple meanings of some words |   |   |   |   |   |   |   |   | • |   |   |   | • |   |   |   |   |   |   | • |   | • |   |   |   |
| 21. Recognize the symbols 1/4, 1/2, 3/4, 1/3, 2/3 |   |   |   |   |   |   |   |   |   |   |   |   |   |   |   |   | • |   |   | • |   |   |   |   |   |
| 22. Recognize Roman numerals I, II, III |   |   |   |   |   |   |   |   |   |   |   |   |   |   |   |   |   |   |   |   |   |   | • |   |   |
| 23. Recognize these abbreviations: *St.* (Street), *Ave.* (Avenue) |   |   |   |   |   |   |   |   |   |   |   |   |   |   |   |   |   |   |   | • |   |   |   |   |   |
|    *Mon., Fri., Aug., Sept., Dec.* |   |   |   |   |   |   |   |   |   |   |   |   |   |   |   |   |   |   |   |   |   |   | • |   |   |
|    *no.* (number) |   |   |   |   |   |   |   |   |   | • |   |   |   |   |   |   |   |   |   |   |   |   |   |   |   |
|    *St.* (Saint) |   |   |   |   |   |   |   |   |   |   |   |   |   |   |   |   |   |   |   |   |   | • |   |   |   |

Comprehension skills — correlation by Lesson

| Comprehension skills / Lesson | 1 | 2 | 3 | 4 | 5 | 6 | 7 | 8 | 9 | 10 | 11 | 12 | 13 | 14 | 15 | 16 | 17 | 18 | 19 | 20 | 21 | 22A | 22B | 23A | 23B |
|---|---|---|---|---|---|---|---|---|---|---|---|---|---|---|---|---|---|---|---|---|---|---|---|---|---|
| 1. Recognize the main idea of one or more paragraphs | • | • | • | • | • | • | • | • | • |  |  |  |  |  |  |  |  |  |  | • | • | • | • | • | • |
| 2. Summarize the main ideas of a story | • | • | • | • | • | • | • | • | • |  | • |  | • | • | • |  |  |  | • | • |  | • | • | • | • |
| 3. Read factual material to obtain information | • | • | • | • |  |  | • |  |  |  | • |  | • |  |  |  |  |  | • | • |  | • | • | • | • |
| 4. Scan story or paragraph to find specific information | • | • | • | • | • |  |  |  | • |  |  |  |  |  |  | • |  |  |  |  |  | • | • | • | • |
| 5. Recall important facts or details | • |  | • |  | • | • |  | • |  |  | • |  | • |  | • | • | • |  |  |  |  | • | • | • | • |
| 6. Read dialog and identify the speakers |  | • | • |  | • | • |  | • |  | • | • |  |  |  |  |  | • |  |  |  |  | • | • | • | • |
| 7. Identify the characters in the story |  | • | • |  | • | • |  | • | • | • |  |  | • | • |  |  |  | • |  |  |  | • | • | • | • |
| 8. Interpret the feelings of the characters |  | • | • |  | • |  | • | • | • | • |  |  | • | • | • |  |  | • |  | • |  | • | • | • | • |
| 9. Interpret facts and draw inferences |  | • | • |  | • |  |  | • | • | • | • |  | • | • |  |  |  | • |  | • |  | • | • | • | • |
| 10. Recall sequence of events |  | • |  |  |  |  |  |  | • | • |  |  |  |  |  |  |  |  |  |  |  | • | • | • | • |
| 11. Recognize cause and effect |  | • | • |  | • | • |  |  | • |  | • |  | • |  | • |  | • |  | • | • |  | • | • | • | • |
| 12. Predict outcomes | • |  |  |  |  |  |  |  |  |  |  | • |  |  |  |  |  |  |  | • |  | • | • | • | • |
| 13. Distinguish between fact and fiction | • | • |  |  |  |  | • |  |  |  |  |  | • | • |  |  |  |  | • |  |  | • | • | • | • |
| 14. Distinguish between fact and opinion | • |  |  |  |  |  | • |  |  |  |  |  |  |  |  | • |  |  |  |  |  | • | • | • | • |
| 15. Understand figurative language in a story |  | • |  |  | • |  |  |  |  |  |  |  |  |  |  |  | • | • |  |  |  | • | • | • | • |
| 16. Interpret the mood of a story |  |  |  |  |  |  | • |  |  |  |  |  |  |  | • |  | • | • |  | • |  | • | • | • | • |
| 17. Understand the story setting | • |  |  |  |  |  |  | • |  | • |  | • |  |  |  |  | • | • |  |  |  | • | • | • | • |
| 18. Recognize the author's purpose | • |  | • |  |  |  |  | • | • | • | • |  |  |  |  |  | • | • | • | • |  | • | • | • | • |
| 19. Relate the story to own experience, knowledge, values | • | • | • | • | • | • | • | • | • | • | • |  | • | • | • |  | • | • | • | • |  | • | • | • | • |
| 20. Read orally with expression | • | • | • | • | • | • | • | • | • | • | • |  |  |  |  |  | • | • | • | • |  | • | • | • | • |
| 21. Read and understand these practical everyday materials: |  |  |  |  |  |  |  |  |  |  |  |  |  |  |  |  |  |  |  |  |  |  |  |  |  |
| application with boxes | • |  |  |  |  |  |  |  |  |  |  |  |  |  |  |  |  |  |  |  |  |  |  |  |  |
| instructions in case of choking |  | • |  |  |  |  |  |  |  |  |  |  |  |  |  |  |  |  |  |  |  |  |  |  |  |
| want ads |  |  | • |  |  |  |  |  |  |  |  |  |  |  |  |  |  |  |  |  |  |  |  |  |  |
| community events news listings |  |  |  | • |  |  |  |  |  |  |  |  |  |  |  |  |  |  |  |  |  |  |  |  |  |
| phone listings for city offices |  |  |  |  | • |  |  |  |  |  |  |  |  |  |  |  |  |  |  |  |  |  |  |  |  |
| calendar for month |  |  |  |  |  | • |  |  |  |  |  |  |  |  |  |  |  |  |  |  |  |  |  |  |  |
| newspaper |  |  |  |  |  |  | • |  |  |  |  |  |  |  |  |  |  |  |  |  |  |  |  |  |  |
| table of contents |  |  |  |  |  |  |  | • |  |  |  |  |  |  |  |  |  |  |  |  |  |  |  |  |  |
| city map |  |  |  |  |  |  |  |  | • |  |  |  |  |  |  |  |  |  |  |  |  |  |  |  |  |
| large numbers |  |  |  |  |  |  |  |  |  | • |  |  |  |  |  |  |  |  |  |  |  |  |  |  |  |
| accident report form |  |  |  |  |  |  |  |  |  |  |  | • |  |  |  |  |  |  |  |  |  |  |  |  |  |
| calendar for year |  |  |  |  |  |  |  |  |  |  |  |  | • |  |  |  |  |  |  |  |  |  |  |  |  |
| letter in cursive writing |  |  |  |  |  |  |  |  |  |  |  |  |  | • |  |  |  |  |  |  |  |  |  |  |  |
| job application |  |  |  |  |  |  |  |  |  |  |  |  |  |  | • |  |  |  |  |  |  |  |  |  |  |
| recipe |  |  |  |  |  |  |  |  |  |  |  |  |  |  |  | • |  |  |  |  |  |  |  |  |  |
| voter registration form |  |  |  |  |  |  |  |  |  |  |  |  |  |  |  |  | • |  |  |  |  |  |  |  |  |
| medicine labels |  |  |  |  |  |  |  |  |  |  |  |  |  |  |  |  |  |  | • |  |  |  |  |  |  |
| adult education course schedule |  |  |  |  |  |  |  |  |  |  |  |  |  |  |  |  |  |  |  | • |  |  |  |  |  |
| dictionary |  |  |  |  |  |  |  |  |  |  |  |  |  |  |  |  |  |  |  |  | • | • | • | • | • |
| maps accompanying factual articles |  |  |  |  |  |  |  |  |  |  |  |  |  |  |  |  |  |  |  |  |  | • | • | • | • |

# Writing and spelling skills

| Lesson | 1 | 2 | 3 | 4 | 5 | 6 | 7 | 8 | 9 | 10 | 11 | 12 | 13 | 14 | 15 | 16 | 17 | 18 | 19 | 20 | 21 | 22 A | 22 B | 23 A | 23 B |
|---|---|---|---|---|---|---|---|---|---|---|---|---|---|---|---|---|---|---|---|---|---|---|---|---|---|
| 1. Write words and sentences from dictation | ● | ● | ● | ● | ● | ● | ● | ● | ● | ● | ● | ● | ● | ● | ● | ● | ● | ● | ● | ● | ● | ● | ● | ● | ● |
| 2. Write a paragraph from dictation | ● | ● | ● | ● | ● | ● | ● | ● | ● | ● | ● | ● | ● | ● | ● | ● | ● | ● |  |  |  | ● | ● | ● | ● |
| 3. Fill in missing words or numbers in sentences | ● |  | ● | ● | ● | ● | ● | ● | ● | ● | ● | ● | ● | ● |  |  |  |  |  |  | ● | ● | ● | ● |  |
| 4. Write short answers to questions |  | ● |  | ● | ● | ● |  | ● | ● |  |  |  |  | ● |  | ● |  |  | ● |  |  | ● | ● | ● |  |
| 5. Write sentence answers to questions |  |  | ● |  | ● |  |  | ● |  | ● |  |  | ● | ● |  |  |  |  |  |  |  |  |  |  |  |
| 6. Write questions based on reading material |  |  | ● |  |  | ● |  |  |  |  |  |  | ● |  |  |  |  |  |  |  |  |  |  |  |  |
| 7. Write original sentences |  |  |  | ● |  |  | ● |  | ● |  |  | ● | ● |  |  |  |  |  |  |  |  |  |  |  |  |
| 8. Write an original paragraph |  |  |  |  |  |  |  | ● |  |  |  |  |  |  |  |  |  |  |  | ● |  | ● |  |  |  |
| 9. Write a short summary of a story |  |  | ● |  |  | ● |  |  | ● |  |  |  |  |  |  |  |  |  |  |  |  | ● | ● | ● | ● |
| 10. List main events of story in sequence, with dates |  |  |  |  |  |  |  |  |  | ● |  |  |  |  |  |  |  |  |  |  |  |  | ● |  |  |
| 11. Write a notice or an ad |  |  |  | ● |  |  |  |  |  |  |  |  |  |  |  | ● |  |  |  |  |  |  |  |  |  |
| 12. Write a short personal letter from dictation |  |  |  |  |  |  | ● |  |  |  |  | ● |  |  |  |  |  |  |  |  |  |  |  |  |  |
| 13. Write an original letter to the editor |  |  |  |  |  |  |  |  |  |  |  |  | ● |  |  |  |  |  |  |  |  |  |  |  |  |
| 14. Write a business letter from dictation |  |  |  |  |  |  |  |  |  |  |  |  |  | ● |  |  |  |  |  | ● |  |  |  |  |  |
| 15. Address an envelope |  |  |  |  |  |  |  |  |  |  |  |  |  |  | ● | ● |  |  |  |  |  |  |  | ● |  |
| 16. Write an entry for a diary or journal |  |  |  |  |  |  |  |  |  |  |  |  |  |  |  | ● |  |  |  |  |  | ● | ● | ● | ● |
| 17. Fill in applications and forms | ● |  |  |  |  |  |  |  |  | ● |  |  |  |  |  |  | ● | ● |  |  |  |  |  |  |  |
| 18. Capitalize names of people, places, months, days |  |  | ● | ● | ● | ● | ● | ● | ● | ● | ● | ● | ● | ● | ● | ● | ● | ● |  |  | ● | ● | ● | ● | ● |
| 19. Write prices and money amounts, using $ and ¢ |  |  |  |  |  | ● |  |  |  | ● |  |  |  | ● |  |  |  |  |  |  | ● |  | ● |  |  |
| 20. Write large numbers and their number words |  |  |  |  |  |  |  |  |  | ● |  |  |  |  |  |  | ● | ● |  |  |  |  |  |  |  |
| 21. Write fractions $^1/_4$, $^1/_2$, $^3/_4$, $^1/_3$, $^2/_3$ |  |  |  |  |  |  |  |  |  |  |  |  |  |  |  | ● | ● |  |  |  |  |  |  |  |  |
| 22. Write Roman numerals I, II, III |  |  |  |  |  |  |  |  |  |  |  |  |  |  |  |  | ● | ● | ● | ● | ● |  |  |  |  |
| 23. Write abbreviations |  |  |  |  |  |  |  |  |  |  |  |  |  |  |  | ● |  |  |  |  |  |  |  |  |  |
| 24. Write times with numerals, colon, and *a.m.* or *p.m.* |  |  |  |  |  |  |  |  |  |  |  |  |  |  |  | ● |  |  |  |  |  |  |  |  |  |
| 25. Write contractions using an apostrophe |  |  |  |  |  | ● |  |  |  |  |  |  |  |  |  |  |  |  |  | ● | ● | ● | ● |  | ● |
| 26. Write dates, spelling out month and using comma |  |  |  |  |  | ● |  |  | ● | ● |  |  |  | ● |  |  |  |  |  | ● | ● | ● | ● |  |  |
| 27. Use comma and quotation marks for direct quotes |  |  |  |  |  |  |  |  |  |  |  |  |  |  | ● | ● |  |  |  |  |  | ● |  | ● |  |
| 28. Use comma after items in a series |  |  |  |  |  |  |  |  |  |  |  |  |  |  |  |  |  |  |  |  |  | ● |  |  |  |
| 29. Use comma after introductory clause |  |  |  |  |  |  |  |  |  |  |  |  |  |  |  |  |  |  | ● |  |  |  | ● | ● |  |
| 30. Write a list of words in alphabetical order |  |  |  |  |  |  |  |  |  |  |  |  |  |  |  |  |  |  |  |  | ● |  |  |  |  |
| 31. Write noun plurals | ● |  |  | ● |  |  |  |  | ● |  | ● | ● |  |  |  |  |  |  |  |  |  |  |  |  |  |
| 32. Form new words by adding these endings: *-ly* |  |  |  |  |  |  |  |  |  |  | ● | ● |  |  |  | ● |  |  |  |  |  | ● |  | ● |  |
| *-er* and *-est* |  |  |  |  |  |  | ● |  |  |  |  |  |  |  |  |  |  |  |  |  |  |  |  |  |  |
| *-ness* |  |  |  |  |  |  |  |  | ● |  |  |  |  |  |  |  |  |  |  |  |  |  |  |  |  |
| *-ful* |  |  |  |  |  |  |  |  |  |  |  |  |  | ● |  |  |  |  | ● | ● |  | ● | ● | ● |  |
| *-less* |  |  |  |  |  |  |  |  |  |  |  |  |  |  | ● | ● | ● |  | ● | ● |  | ● | ● | ● |  |
| *-ment* |  |  |  |  |  |  |  |  |  |  |  |  |  |  |  | ● | ● | ● | ● |  |  | ● | ● | ● |  |
| *-hood* |  |  |  |  |  |  |  |  |  | ● |  |  |  |  |  |  |  |  |  |  |  |  |  |  |  |
| *-ship* |  |  |  |  |  |  |  |  |  |  |  |  |  |  |  |  |  | ● | ● | ● |  |  |  |  |  |
| *-al* |  |  |  |  |  |  |  |  |  |  |  |  |  |  |  |  |  |  |  |  |  | ● | ● |  | ● |
| *-ous* |  |  |  |  |  |  |  |  |  |  |  |  |  |  |  |  | ● | ● |  |  |  |  |  |  | ● |

**Writing and spelling skills, cont.**

| Lesson | 1 | 2 | 3 | 4 | 5 | 6 | 7 | 8 | 9 | 10 | 11 | 12 | 13 | 14 | 15 | 16 | 17 | 18 | 19 | 20 | 21 | 22A | 22B | 23A | 23B |
|---|---|---|---|---|---|---|---|---|---|---|---|---|---|---|---|---|---|---|---|---|---|---|---|---|---|
| 33. Form new words by adding these prefixes: | | | | | | | | | | | | | | | | | | | | | | | | | |
|     un- | | | | | | ● | | | | | ● | | | | | | | | | | | ● | | | |
|     non- | | | ● | | | | | | | | | | | | | | | | | | ● | | | | |
|     in- | | | ● | | | | | | | | | | | | | ● | | | | | | | | | |
|     il- | | | | | | | | | | | | | | | | | ● | | | | | | | | ● |
|     re- | | | | | | | | | | | | | | | | | | ● | | | ● | | | | ● |
|     inter- | | | | | | | | | | | | | | | | | | | ● | ● | | | ● | | |
| 34. Know when to double the final consonant before endings | | | | | ● | | | ● | | ● | | ● | | | ● | ● | ● | | | ● | | | | | |
| 35. Know when to drop final silent e before endings | | ● | | | ● | | | ● | | ● | | | | | ● | ● | ● | | ● | | | | | | |
| 36. Know when to change final y to i before endings | | | | ● | | | | | | ● | | | | ● | | | | | | | | | | | |
| 37. Know how to spell /s/ at the end of a word | | | | | | | | | ● | | | | | | | | | ● | | | | | | | |
| 38. Know how to spell /j/ at the end of a word | | | | | | | | | ● | | | | | | | | ● | | | | | | | | |
| 39. Know that i usually comes before e | ● | | | | ● | | | | | | | | | | | | | | ● | | | | | ● | |

**Study skills**

| Lesson | 1 | 2 | 3 | 4 | 5 | 6 | 7 | 8 | 9 | 10 | 11 | 12 | 13 | 14 | 15 | 16 | 17 | 18 | 19 | 20 | 21 | 22A | 22B | 23A | 23B |
|---|---|---|---|---|---|---|---|---|---|---|---|---|---|---|---|---|---|---|---|---|---|---|---|---|---|
| 1. Follow written instructions | ● | ● | ● | | ● | ● | ● | ● | ● | ● | ● | ● | ● | ● | ● | ● | ● | ● | ● | ● | ● | ● | ● | ● | ● |
| 2. Keep a notebook for dictation and other writing | ● | ● | ● | | ● | ● | ● | ● | ● | ● | ● | ● | ● | ● | ● | ● | ● | ● | ● | ● | ● | ● | ● | ● | ● |
| 3. Organize notebook page following oral instructions | ● | ● | ● | | ● | ● | ● | ● | ● | ● | ● | ● | ● | ● | ● | ● | ● | ● | ● | ● | ● | ● | ● | ● | ● |
| 4. Take notes on a factual article | | | | ● | | | | | | | | | | | | | | | | | | | | | |
| 5. Classify words under topic headings | | | | | | | | ● | | | | | | | | | | | | | | | | | |
| 6. Write sentences under topic headings | | | | | | | | | ● | | | | | | | | | | | | | | | | |
| 7. Use a dictionary | | | | | | | | | | | | | | | | | | | | | ● | ● | ● | ● | |
| 8. Understand a map | | | | | | | | | | | | | | | | | | | | | ● | ● | ● | | |
| 9. Use a table of contents | | | | | | | | | | | | | | | | | | | | | ● | ● | ● | ● | |
| 10. Alphabetize words | | | | | | | | | | | | | | | | ● | | | | | | ● | | ● | |
| 11. Locate words in an alphabetical list | | | | | | | | | | | | | | | | | | | | | ● | ● | ● | ● | |
| 12. Observe simple footnotes | | | | | | | | | | | | | | | | | ● | ● | ● | | | | | ● | ● |
| 13. Adjust reading rate to type of material and purpose | | | | | | | | | | | | | | | | | | ● | ● | ● | ● | ● | ● | ● | ● |

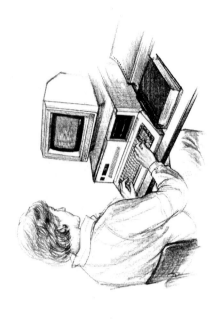

# Lesson 1

music
ū

cure
u_e = ū

human
u_e = ū

computer
u_e = ū

| | human | hū' mun | human |
|---|---|---|---|
| | computer | com pū' er | computer |
| | huge | hyje / hūj | huge |
| | use | uze / ūz | use |
| | amuse | u myze' / u mūz' | amuse |

## The Computer Age

| afraid | (u fraid') | airplane | (air' plane) | fact | | space | (spase) |
|---|---|---|---|---|---|---|---|
| become | (bē come') | business | (biz' ness) | game | | spaceship | (spase' ship) |
| machine | (mu shene') | record | (rec' ord) | | | everywhere | (ev' ery where) |

This is the age of the computer. A computer is a machine that works with facts like names and addresses. It works with facts like prices and lists of things in stores.

A computer can find answers to questions very quickly. This machine works much faster than a human. But a computer cannot think. A human must put facts into the machine. Then the human must tell the machine what to do with the facts.

Computers are used in business. Businesses use computers to keep records of sales. They use computers to write paychecks and to send bills. Banks use computers to keep records of money. Computers are used to help build huge buildings.

Computers run machines that make things. They run machines that make bread and cake. They help to make paper, cars, TVs, radios, and many other things.

Doctors use computers. Computers tell what sickness a person has. Then doctors know what cure is needed. Doctors do not have a cure for some sicknesses. Computers are helping doctors find cures.

Computers help you telephone to other places quickly. A computer can tell what repairs your car needs. Computers help to teach many kinds of things. You can learn with computers in class or at home.

form    print    social (sō′ shul)    security (se cŭr′ i ty)

Some applications and business forms can be read by computers. On these forms, you fill in boxes. You print one letter or number in each box.

Fill in the form below. Print your own name, address, and other facts. You can find your Social Security number on your Social Security card. You need this number to get a job or to save money in a bank. You use it when you pay some taxes. If you do not have a Social Security number yet, do not fill in that part. In the last three parts, put an X in the right box.

**PLEASE PRINT. USE CAPITAL LETTERS.**

NAME

☐☐☐☐☐☐☐☐☐☐☐☐    ☐☐☐☐☐☐☐☐
Last name                              First name

ADDRESS

☐☐☐☐☐☐☐☐☐☐☐☐
Number          Street

☐☐☐☐☐☐☐☐    ☐☐    ☐☐☐☐☐
City                    State    Zip Code

☐☐☐☐☐☐☐        ☐☐☐☐☐☐☐☐☐
Telephone number       Social Security number

Age ☐☐    Sex ☐ ☐    Married? ☐ ☐    Born in U.S.A.?
                M  F            Yes No            Yes No

---

Computers help to amuse humans. Some of them amuse you by making music or pictures. Some computer games can amuse you at home. You can play these games on your own TV. Other computer games are in shopping centers.

This is both the computer age and the space age. Computers are used to build airplanes and spaceships. People are trained to fly airplanes and spaceships with the help of computers. On space flights, computers help keep spaceships on the right path in space.

Some computers do just one job. Some do many jobs. A computer that does many jobs may be huge or little. It may be so huge that it fills a big office. Or the computer may be as little as a table radio.

The first computers cost a lot. But computers have become cheaper and cheaper. They have become so cheap that most businesses can afford them. People are even buying computers to use at home.

Computers help us in many ways. But they can be used to hurt us. Money can be stolen from banks and businesses by computer. Bombs can be made and dropped with the help of computers.

Some people say these machines are taking jobs away from humans. Computers *are* taking away some jobs and making others. But a person needs training for a computer job.

Some people are afraid of computers. They are afraid of machines with no feelings. They are afraid that humans will become cold and hard like these machines.

But we must not be afraid of computers. We live in a computer age. Computers are everywhere. We must learn to understand what they can do for us. And we must use them in the right ways.

## Story Checkup

**Answer each question with *yes* or *no*.**

1. Does a computer work faster than a human?    *yes*

2. Does a computer have to be huge?    *no*

3. Do some doctors use computers?    *yes*

4. Can computers be used to hurt us?    *yes*

5. Can a computer think?    *no*

6. Are some people afraid of computers?    *yes*

## Practice

example (eg zam′ pul), stress

**Say the words. Circle the words with the sound ū as in *music*.**

|   |       |       |          |
|---|-------|-------|----------|
| 1. | (huge) | (use) | us |
| 2. | (Cuba) | hurry | much | (music) |
| 3. | courage | business | (computer) | (cure) |
| 4. | church | (human) | Arthur | (amuse) |
| 5. | (future) | money | (security) | sentence |

**Say each word. Put the stress mark after the syllable that is stressed.**

Examples:

human          hu′man
application     ap pli ca′tion

1. machine      ma chine′
2. afraid       a fraid′
3. amuse        a muse′
4. music        mu′sic
5. security     se cur′i ty
6. computer     com put′er
7. radio        ra′di o
8. number       num′ber

**Read the word. Then write the two words that you see in it.**

1. paycheck      *pay*    *check*
2. airplane      *air*    *plane*
3. spaceship     *space*  *ship*
4. everywhere    *every*  *where*
5. understand    *under*  *stand*

---

## Homework

mean, blank

**Fill in each blank with the right word.**

1. Computers are helping doctors find _cures_.
2. A _human_ must put facts into the computer.
3. Some computer games can _amuse_ you at home.
4. We live in an age of _computers_.
5. Businesses use computers to keep _records_ of sales.

**Read each word. Then write each word in the form that means more than one.**

Example:    tax    _taxes_

1. business     _businesses_
2. sickness     _sicknesses_
3. address      _addresses_
4. box          _boxes_
5. airplane     _airplanes_
6. price        _prices_
7. class        _classes_
8. fact         _facts_
9. human        _humans_

**Write each of these words in the right blank.**

address, business, game, human, machine, sickness

1. A computer is a _machine_.
2. A store is a _business_.
3. A woman is a _human_.
4. 325 York Street is an _address_.
5. Hockey is a _game_.
6. A cold is a _sickness_.

## OBJECTIVES

To help your student:

- review the long sound for *u* as in *music*.
- recognize that *u* at the end of a syllable usually stands for the sound /ū/ as in *music*.
- recognize that the letters *u* and *e* separated by one consonant (*u-e*) usually stand for the sound /ū/ as in *cure*.
- read words in which the sound /ū/ is represented by *u* at the end of a syllable or by *u-e*.
- distinguish between the long and short sounds for *u*.
- determine the number of syllables in a word.
- understand the meaning of stress in a word.
- recognize which syllable in a word is stressed.
- recognize the use of the stress mark (') as an aid to pronunciation.
- recognize the new compound words *airplane*, *spaceship*, *everywhere*, and review other compound words.
- review adding the ending *-es* to words ending in *s, x, ch*, recognizing that the *-es* ending adds a syllable.
- read factual material to obtain information.
- recognize main ideas, key (topic) sentences, and supporting details.
- distinguish fact from opinion.
- recognize the author's purpose in a factual article.
- relate the story to own experience.
- fill in a form following written directions.
- write words and a paragraph from dictation.

## INTRODUCTION

T: In *Skill Book 3*, you learned the long sound for each vowel and the vowel sound /or/. In *Skill Book 4*, you will learn some other ways that the vowel sound /ū/ is written, and you will learn some new vowel sounds. You will also learn some more things about consonants. (On the title page, point to and read the full title, *Skill Book 4: Other Vowel Sounds and Consonant Spellings*.)

# I. Reading

## CHART: Page 2

**Title and key words.** Have S. read the title *Lesson 1*.

T: Please point to the vowel in the top right-hand corner. What is the name of this vowel? [S: *u*.] What is the long sound for *u*? [S: /ū/.]

T: (Point to the key word *music*.) What is the word? [S: music.] (Point to *ū* under *music*.) What is the vowel sound? [S: /ū/.] How is it written? [S: With *u*.] (In *music*,

draw a line between *mu* and *sic*.) *Music* is divided into two syllables like this. Notice that the sound /ū/ comes at the end of a syllable.

T: (Point to *u-e = ū* in the top right-hand corner.) Here is another way to write the sound /ū/. What are the letters? [S: *u* and *e*.] Notice that there is a dash between the *u* and *e*. The dash stands for a consonant. When *u* and *e* are separated by one consonant, they stand for what sound? [S: /ū/.]

T: (Point to *cure*.) Read this key word. [S: cure.] How is the sound /ū/ written in *cure*? [S: *u-e*.] (Point to *u-e = u* under *cure*.) The letters *u* and *e* separated by a consonant equal what sound? [S: /ū/.] What consonant separates *u* and *e* in *cure*? [S: *r*.]

## Line 1

T: Look at the first picture and the word next to it. (Point to them.) Read the word to yourself. Look at the third column if you need help in sounding out the word. What is the word? [S: human.]

T: (Point to column 3.) How many syllables are there in *human*? [S: Two.] Look at the little mark at the end of the first syllable. (Point to '.) This mark is called a stress mark. It shows which syllable is said with more force or stress. Listen to the word: *human*. Which syllable is said with more stress? [S: The first syllable.] In this book, where a new word is divided into syllables, you will see the stress mark after the stressed syllable. That will help you know which syllable to say with more force.

T: How is the sound /ū/ written in *human*? [S: With *u*.] Does the sound /ū/ come in the middle of a syllable or at the end of a syllable? [S: At the end of a syllable.] Is it the stressed syllable? [S: Yes.] (Point to the last column.) Read the word again. [S: human.]

## Line 2

T: Look at the next picture and word. If you need help in sounding out the word, look at the third column. What is the word? [S: computer.] How many syllables are there in *computer*? [S: Three.] Which syllable is stressed? [S: The second syllable.] Point to the stress mark. (If S. has difficulty telling which syllable is stressed, say the word and have him listen.) How is the sound /ū/ written in *computer*? [S: With *u*.] Look at the last column and read the word again. [S: computer.]

## Lines 3-6

T: Read the next word to yourself, and notice how the sound /ū/ is written. What is the word? [S: huge.] What letters stand for the sound /ū/? [S: *u* and *e*.] What consonant comes between *u* and *e*? [S: *g*.] What is the sound for *g* in *huge*? [S: /j/.]

T: How many syllables are there in *huge*? [S: One.] When a word has only one syllable, there is no need for a stress mark to help you pronounce it.

Have S. study the rest of the chart silently. Then have him read the words aloud. Have him tell how the sound /ū/ is written, the number of syllables in each word, and which syllable is stressed in *amuse*. Also, call attention to the sound /z/ for *s* in *use* and *amuse*.

**Review.** Have S. read each word aloud, including the key words. Go down the last column of the chart.

## STORY: Pages 3-4 (The Computer Age)

Have S. read the story title and new words. Call attention to the number of syllables in each word. If the word has more than one syllable, have S. tell which one is stressed.

T: The reading material in this lesson is a factual article. You may remember reading a factual article in *Skill Book 3* about getting a driver's license. Judging from the title, what would you say this article will give information about? [S: Computers.]

Have S. read the article to himself. Then have him number all the paragraphs in it before you continue.

**Paragraphs 1-2.** Have S. read paragraphs 1-2 aloud.

T: What do these first two paragraphs tell about? [S: What a computer is.] Right, that is the main idea of these two paragraphs. What are some of the facts about what a computer is that we learn from these two paragraphs? [S: It's a machine. It works with facts. It works faster than a human. It cannot think. A human has to tell it what to do.]

T: What do all of the paragraphs you just read tell about? [S: Some uses of computers.] What use of computers does paragraph 3 talk about? [S: In business.] Is there one key sentence in paragraph 3 that tells this? [S: Yes, *Computers are used in business.*] What examples of ways businesses use computers does this paragraph give? [S. gives examples.]

For paragraphs 4 and 5, follow the same procedure. Have S. tell what the paragraph is about, what the key sentence is, and what supporting details the paragraph gives.

T: Paragraph 6 tells about some personal uses of computers. What are some of these uses? [S. answers.]

For paragraph 7, have S. tell what the paragraph is about, what the key sentence is, and what supporting details are given. Follow the same procedure for paragraph 8.

**Paragraphs 9-13.** Have S. read paragraphs 9-13 aloud.

T: What paragraph talks about the size of computers and the number of jobs a computer can do? [S: 9.]

T: Are computers becoming cheaper or more expensive? [S: Cheaper.] What paragraph talks about this? [S: 10.]

For paragraphs 11-13, ask S. what each paragraph tells about, what the key sentence is, and what supporting details are given.

**Paragraph 14.** Have S. read the last paragraph aloud.

T: Up to this point, this article has given facts about computers. Look carefully at the last paragraph. It tells what we should do. Would you say that this paragraph is mostly fact or mostly the writers' opinions? [S: Opinions.] What ideas do the writers of this article have about what we should do? [S. answers.]

**Recognizing author's purpose.** Ask S. to tell which was the main purpose the writers of this article had:

1. To warn us that computers may take away our jobs.
2. To encourage us to learn to understand computers and use them wisely.
3. To keep us from becoming cold and unfeeling like machines.
4. To help us find a computer job.

**Relating the story to everyday life.** Discuss one or more of these questions briefly with S.

1. Have you ever used a computer? If so, in what ways? Did you enjoy it? If you haven't used one, would you like to? Why or why not?
2. What do *you* think is the main reason some people are afraid of computers? Do you agree with the reasons given in the article, or do you think there are other reasons?
3. Do you think that all young people in school should be taught to use computers? Why or why not?
4. What uses of computers do you know about that are not discussed in this article? What information given in the article is now somewhat out of date? Why is it hard to keep up to date with information about computers?

## STORY CHECKUP: Page 4

Have S. read the directions and write the answers. Check his answers. If any are wrong, have him scan the story to find the answers.

## READING FOR LIVING: Page 5

Have S. read the new words and introductory paragraphs first silently and then aloud. Have him read the directions at the top of the form and then fill in the form. If his street name or city name has more than one word, point out that he should leave an empty space between words. Give any other help needed.

# II. Skills Practice

Have S. close his book before doing these exercises.

## PRACTICE 1: Distinguishing the Long Sound for *u*

T: Which of these words has the long sound for *u*:

| | | |
|---|---|---|
| *hug, huge?* | *must, music?* | *human, hungry?* |
| *use, us?* | *cure, curl?* | *computer, complete?* |

## PRACTICE 2: Number of Syllables and Stress

T: Listen to each word I say. Tell how many syllables it has. Also, tell which syllable is stressed.

*afraid*   [2 syllables, second syllable is stressed]

*machine*  [2, second one is stressed]

*record*   [2, first one is stressed]

*security*  [4, second one is stressed]

*social*    [2, first one is stressed]

*become*  [2, second one is stressed]

**Note:** If S. loses his place counting the number of the stressed syllable in a longer word, write out the word divided into syllables, as *se cur i ty*, and have him point to the stressed syllable after you say the word.

## PRACTICE 3: Compound Words

Write these words in a column: *everywhere, paycheck, sometimes, understand, airplane, spaceship.* Ask S. to read each compound word and tell the two words that it is made from. As he answers, write the two words.

## PRACTICE 4: Adding the Ending -s or -es

Write these nouns in a column: *tax, fact, business, job, machine, address, watch, dish, bomb.*

Explain that these are all *singular* nouns. The singular form of a noun is the form that means one. It's easy to remember because *singular* sounds like *single.* The form of a noun that means more than one is called *plural.*

Ask S. to tell what ending to add to make the plural form of each noun. As he answers, write the plural forms in a second column.

Then have S. read the singular and plural form of each noun and tell what ending was added. Also, have him tell whether the ending adds a syllable.

# III. Writing

## CHECK HOMEWORK

Check any homework assignments from previous lessons that have not been checked in the student's notebook or in the *Laubach Way to Cursive Writing* workbook.

## WRITING LESSON (In Notebook)

**Note:** S. should have a new wide-ruled notebook with at least 50 pages to go along with *Skill Book 4.* More writing will be expected at this level. Before starting *Skill Book 4,* S. should have completed the *Laubach Way to Cursive Writing* workbook if he did not already know cursive writing. Most students should be encouraged to use cursive writing for most exercises and Writing Lessons in *Skill Book 4.* Some exercises and forms that require manuscript writing (printing) are included so that this skill is not forgotten. (Some individuals, however, prefer to print for all their handwriting. If your student has such a preference, allow him to print. From time to time, give him samples of cursive writing for practice in reading it.) Encourage your student to keep a neat notebook and to write legibly.

Have S. print his name and address on the cover of his notebook. Also, have him write the title *Skill Book 4.* Tell him that from now on he will use cursive writing in the notebook unless directed otherwise. He can refer to his *Cursive Writing* workbook as an aid in how to make any letters he is not sure of.

**Page arrangement.** In the upper left-hand corner of the page, have S. write *Lesson 1.* Under it, have him write the heading *Words* and then the numbers from 1 through 20 in two columns. (At this level, S. should be able to write on consecutive lines rather than skipping lines.)

**Words.** Dictate these words for S. to write. Encourage him to use cursive writing. Tell him that this dictation is to see which words he needs to study. He is not expected to get them all right.

| | | | |
|---|---|---|---|
| 1. music | 6. human | 11. afraid | 16. computer |
| 2. cure | 7. become | 12. form | 17. everywhere |
| 3. huge | 8. fact | 13. print | 18. business |
| 4. use | 9. game | 14. mean | 19. machine |
| 5. amuse | 10. record | 15. space | 20. airplane |

Check the words for correct spelling. Circle the number of any word S. misspelled. Have him compare the misspelled word with the correct spelling in the lesson to see which part is wrong. Have him spell the whole word correctly aloud. Then have him erase the word he wrote and write it again correctly.

**Sentences.** Have S. skip a space and then write the heading *Sentences.*

T: I will read a short paragraph from today's story. First, listen to the whole paragraph. Then, I will read each sentence for you to write. (Read the following paragraph.)

    This is the age of the computer. A computer is a machine that works with facts like names and addresses. It works with facts like prices and lists of things in stores.

T: I will read the paragraph again for you to write. Do not number the sentences. Indent the paragraph when you begin.

Read the paragraph again, sentence by sentence. Pause after each sentence for S. to write. But do not repeat the sentence.

Have S. check his own work by looking at paragraph 1 in the story. Have him circle any word he misspelled and put a check mark any place he omitted a word or a punctuation mark. Look over his work and the way he checked it. Underline any other corrections that are needed.

**Study.** Have S. skip a space or turn to the next page. Have him write the heading *Study.* Under it, have S. write the words he missed in the word dictation and any others he missed in the sentence dictation. Ask him to study these words at home.

## PRACTICE: Page 6

Have S. read the new words at the top of the page. Then have him read the directions for the first exercise and do it. Check his work. If he has any errors, have him read the words aloud and listen for the /ū/ sound.

Have S. read the directions for the second exercise. Go over the examples with him. Explain that in this exercise the words are not rewritten the way they sound because he has already learned to read these words in the lesson. But they are divided into syllables so that he will have room to put in the stress marks. If there is a word he can't read, refer him to the respelling of the word in the lesson. Have S. do number 1; then check it to make sure he knew what to do. If it isn't correct, say the word aloud and have him listen for the stressed syllable. Then have him complete the exercise. Check his work.

Have S. read the directions for the third exercise and do it. Check his work, and make any needed corrections.

## HOMEWORK: Page 7

Go over the new words and the directions for each exercise with S. Have him read the example for exercise 2 aloud. Ask him to complete this page at home. Also, encourage him to read the story again and study the words he listed in his notebook.

## CHECKING PROGRESS

The written practice exercises and those done orally in this lesson will give you some idea of your student's ability to recognize the /ū/ sound and his understanding of the concept of stressed syllables. He will have more practice of both of these skills in the next lesson, so don't plan extra practice now. But do note any difficulties he may have had in today's lesson.

Also, note your student's ability to read factual material. At this stage, he should be able to grasp the main facts in an article. If he had difficulty doing so in this lesson, plan extra practice for another session, following one of the suggestions given below.

## MEETING INDIVIDUAL NEEDS

Continue working on any skills from *Skill Book 3* that need reinforcing. Use some of the flashcards, slip strips, and other materials that you have made. Plan to use one or two reinforcement activities for the skills needed. But keep the practice short.

For extra practice in understanding factual material, you may want to use one of the following activities:

1. Write a short article of about three paragraphs on a topic S. is interested in. Try to use words he can read. Have S. read each paragraph and pick out the key sentence. Have him give the main fact and one supporting fact for each paragraph.

2. Go over some of the paragraphs in the stories "Helen Keller" and "Martin Luther King Jr." from *Changes*. Have S. tell the key sentence in each of several paragraphs.

3. Have S. list the facts that he learned from reading "Helen Keller" or "Martin Luther King."

4. Read a short factual article aloud to S. and have him pick out important facts. Articles from Book 2 or Book 3 of the In the Know series are ideal for this purpose.

**Using *Focus on Phonics*.** The workbook *Focus on Phonics-4: Other Vowel Sounds and Consonant Spellings* uses a word-family approach (rhyming words) to help students learn many new words with the vowel sounds and consonant spellings in *Skill Book 4*. It should be used only under your direction, with the help of the teacher's edition. This workbook is correlated to *Skill Book 4*. The numbered practices in the workbook may be used after the skill book lesson of the same number. For example, after Lesson 1, you may use Practices 1A-1B, which contrast the short and long sounds for *u* and cover the *u-e* word families.

**Using *More Stories 4*.** The reader *More Stories 4* contains extra stories correlated to the new words in each lesson of *Skill Book 4*. If S. needs extra reading practice, you may help him with these in class. If he can read independently, he may enjoy reading them at home.

**Using the *Workbook for Skill Book 4*.** Although this workbook was developed for ESOL students in the Laubach Way to English program, it can be helpful for native speakers of English, too. Many lessons contain a cloze exercise based on the story in the skill book lesson. In a cloze exercise, every 5th, 6th, 7th, 8th, or 9th word in the reading passage is left blank for the student to fill in. (The answer may be any appropriate word, not just the same word that was used in the story.) Cloze exercises integrate word recognition skills with the skills of using context and grammatical clues in the reading material. Among the writing skills developed in the *Workbook for Skill Book 4* are writing sentences and combining sentences.

**Using the *Crossword Puzzles for Skill Book 4*.** New words are reviewed in a puzzle for each lesson.

Choose supplements that will meet the student's needs, but don't overburden him with so much extra practice in skills that he loses a sense of progress.

On the other hand, as the student becomes a more independent reader, he will want to read more material for enjoyment. Consult the inside front cover of this manual or earlier manuals for suggested titles.

# Lesson 2

argue    ue = ū

ue = ū

ew = ū

few    ew = ū

ue = ū

ew = ū

| | | |
|---|---|---|
| rescue | res' cue | rescue |
| barbecue | bar' bu cue | barbecue |
| continue | con tin' ue | continue |
| view | vew | view |
| nephew | nef' ew | nephew |

---

| | | | |
|---|---|---|---|
| Hugh | (Hū) | hug | aunt (ant) | relative (rel' u tiv) |
| Huron | (Hūr' on) | rib | cousin (cuz' in) | grandfather (grand' father) |
| refuse | (rē fuze') | wave | niece (nēs) | grandmother (grand' mother) |
| reunion | (rē un'ion) | seen | piece (pēs) | haven't (hav' unt) |
| | | since (sins) | | aren't (arnt) |

## A Family Reunion

Last weekend, we had a family reunion. At first, I refused to go. I didn't think anyone my age was going. But my mother felt hurt when I refused. So I went.

The reunion was at the home of my Aunt Mary and Uncle John. Aunt Mary is my mother's sister. At 17, I am her youngest nephew. This was a reunion of my mother's family.

Aunt Mary and Uncle John have a big home on Lake Huron. Their home has a lovely view of Lake Huron. We live just a few miles from them. But we don't have a view of Lake Huron.

My aunt and uncle were planning a big barbecue for Saturday. More than thirty relatives were coming. My parents and I went on Friday to help my aunt and uncle get ready.

On Saturday, relatives came from far and near. My grandmother and grandfather came from Florida. They have lived there since my grandfather retired. Grandmother gave me a big hug and kiss. She said, "Hugh, I haven't seen you since you were a boy. You have become a man!"

My brother and his wife came from Texas with their little girl. I was glad to see my three-year-old niece for the first time. She gave me a big hug and said, "I like my Uncle Hugh."

A few of my cousins came from Canada. My mother was glad to see her nephews and nieces. These cousins are not much older than I am. So I was glad that someone my age was there.

At the barbecue, we had a lot to eat. I had some potato salad, a piece of ham, and some barbecued ribs. I liked the ribs best.

But my Aunt Ellen will never eat barbecued ribs again. While she was eating, she began to argue. She was arguing with my father. Then she got a funny look on her face, and she stopped arguing.

"What's the matter?" I asked. But she was not able to answer. "A piece of meat must be stuck in her throat," I said to Dad.

I acted fast to rescue Aunt Ellen. I got behind her and gave her a big hug. Up came the piece of meat!

Hugh's relatives in this story are his:

| grandfather | Aunt Mary | Aunt Ellen | father | brother | niece |
| grandmother | Uncle John | | mother | brother's wife | cousins |

**Write the answer. Which of Hugh's relatives—**

1. had the reunion at their home on Lake Huron? _Aunt Mary and Uncle John_
2. came from Florida? _grandfather and grandmother_
3. came from Texas? _brother and brother's wife_
4. came from Canada? _cousins_
5. said, "Hugh, I haven't seen you since you were a boy"? _grandmother_
6. choked on a piece of meat? _Aunt Ellen_
7. did Hugh see for the first time? _niece_
8. started telling family stories? _grandfather_
9. did Hugh rescue from the lake? _niece_
10. said, "You're glad you went to the reunion, aren't you?" _mother_

**In what order did these things happen?**
**Put a number by each sentence to show the right order.**

2 Relatives came from near and far.

5 Hugh acted fast to rescue his aunt.

1 Hugh and his parents went to Aunt Mary's home.

3 Aunt Ellen began to argue with Hugh's father.

8 Grandfather started telling family stories.

6 A big wave hit Hugh's niece.

4 Aunt Ellen choked on a piece of meat.

9 Hugh and some of his cousins went fishing.

7 Hugh rescued his niece from the lake.

That was my first rescue of the day. Later, I rescued my little niece. She was playing with a few other children on the shore. When the waves came in, the children ran away from them. But a big wave hit my niece. The wave carried her into water over her head. I got to her first. She was not hurt. But I became the big man of the day.

That evening, my grandfather started telling family stories. Then other relatives told more stories. We continued telling stories far into the night. I learned some things that I didn't know before.

The reunion continued the next day. I went fishing with a few of my cousins. When everyone was ready to leave, there were more kisses and hugs.

On the way home, my mother said to me, "I had a lot of fun this weekend. I haven't seen so many of my relatives since your brother's wedding. You're glad that you went to the reunion, aren't you, Hugh?"

"Yes, I am," I said. "I'm glad that I didn't refuse to go. In fact, I hope that we will continue to have family reunions."

**Say the words. Circle the words with the sound ū as in _few_ and _argue._**

1. (Hugh)   hug   (huge)   cousin   (nephew)
2. aunt   (view)   cousin   (continue)
3. (refuse)   (argue)   minute   (barbecue)

**Say each word. Put the stress mark after the syllable that is stressed.**

1. rescue       res´cue
2. barbecue     bar´be cue
3. relative      rel´a tive
4. nephew       neph´ew
5. continue      con tin´ue
6. refuse        re fuse´

**Read the word. Write the two words that it comes from.**

1. didn't    _did_  _not_     5. I'm      _I_  _am_
2. haven't   _have_  _not_    6. you're   _you_  _are_
3. what's    _what_  _is_     7. don't    _do_  _not_
4. aren't    _are_  _not_     8. can't    _can_  _not_

**These words are the names of some relatives. Write one word in each blank**

aunt   uncle   niece   nephew   cousin   grandmother   grandfather

1. Your mother's sister or your father's sister  _aunt_
2. Your aunt's child or your uncle's child  _cousin_
3. Your brother's son or your sister's son  _nephew_
4. Your mother's brother or your father's brother  _uncle_
5. Your mother's mother or your father's mother  _grandmother_

Lesson 2   **13**

---

choke       breathe
fist        minute (min´ut)
press       object (ob´ject)

### When a Person Chokes

Each year, many people die from choking. A person chokes when he is eating and something gets stuck in his throat. If you see this happen, you can save a life. But you have to act fast. A person will die in four to six minutes if he can't breathe.

### Signs of choking

— The person cannot breathe or speak.
— He may put his hands to his throat or look afraid.
— His face may turn a funny color.

If the person can breathe or speak a little, let him try to get the object up by himself. If he cannot get the object up after a few minutes, you can help.

If the person cannot breathe or speak, you must act quickly to help him.

### What to do

1. Stand behind the choking person.
2. Make a fist with one of your hands.
3. Put your fist just below the person's ribs, as the picture shows.
4. With your other hand, press your fist in and up quickly. Press hard enough so that air comes up. This will bring the object up from the person's throat.
5. The object may come up after you press the first time. But you may have to press again and again.

**12**   Lesson 2

Lesson 2   25

## OBJECTIVES

To help your student:

- recognize that the letters *ue* often stand for the sound /ū/, as in *argue*.
- recognize that the letters *ew* often stand for the sound /ū/, as in *few*.
- read words in which the sound /ū/ is represented by *ue* or *ew*.
- distinguish between the long and short sounds for *u*.
- determine the number of syllables in a word.
- recognize which syllable is stressed.
- recognize that some words that are spelled alike may have the stress on different syllables for different meanings, as in *an object* and *I object*.
- recognize the new compound words *grandfather, grandmother*, and review other compound words.
- recognize the new contractions *haven't, aren't*, and review other contractions.
- recognize that the prefix *re-* means back or again, as in *reunion*.
- add the endings *-s, -d, -ing* to words ending in *ue*.
- identify the characters in the story.
- recall the sequence of events in the story.
- scan the story to find specific details.
- recognize cause and effect.
- recognize figurative language in the story.
- read factual material to obtain information.
- read and understand directions.
- write words and a paragraph from dictation.

## INTRODUCTION

T: You have learned two ways that the sound /ū/ is written. How is the sound /ū/ written in the word *music*? [S: With *u*.] In the word *cure*? [S: *u-consonant-e*.] Today you will learn two other ways that the sound /ū/ is written.

# I. Reading

## CHART: Page 8

**Title and key words.** Have S. read the title *Lesson 2*.

T: Look at the first two letters in the top right-hand corner. What are they? [S: *ue*.] What sound do they equal? [S: /ū/.] Are they separated by a consonant? [S: No.]

T: (Point to *argue*.) Read the first key word. [S: argue.] What letters stand for the sound /ū/? [S: *ue*.]

T: (Point to *ew* = /u/.) What other two letters equal the sound /ū/? [S: *ew*.] Read the second key word. [S: few.] What letters stand for the sound /ū/? [S: *ew*.]

**Lines 1-3**

T: Look at the first picture and the word next to it. Read the word to yourself. Look at the next column if you need help in sounding it out. What is the word? [S: rescue.] How many syllables are there in *rescue*? [S: Two.] Which syllable is stressed? [S: The first.] How is the sound /ū/ written? [S: *ue*.]

Ask S. to study the next two lines (*barbecue, continue*) silently. Then have him read each word aloud, tell how many syllables are in each word, which syllable is stressed, and how the sound /ū/ is written.

**Lines 4-5.** Have S. study the next two lines and then read the words (*view, nephew*) aloud. Have him tell how the sound /ū/ is written in both words. Then ask him to tell which word has more than one syllable and which syllable is stressed. Also, call attention to the silent *i* in *view* and the sound /f/ for *ph* in *nephew*.

**Review.** Have S. read each word aloud, including the key words. Go down the last column of the chart.

## STORY: Pages 9-10 (A Family Reunion)

Have S. read the story title and new words. Have him tell the number of syllables in each word and which syllable is stressed if the word has more than one. Call attention to the compound words *grandfather, grandmother*. Point out that the compound word is rewritten to show the two words that it is made from, not the number of syllables. Call attention to the contractions *haven't, aren't*. Ask S. to tell the two words each is made from.

For *reunion*, point out that *union* is a word S. has learned before. The beginning part, *re-*, is called a prefix. A prefix is a part that is added to the beginning of a word to change the meaning. The prefix *re-* often means *back* or *again*. When the prefix *re-* is added to *union*, the word *reunion* means people coming back together again after they have been apart. Ask S. what other kinds of reunions people have besides family reunions. He may mention class reunions, reunions of army buddies or of childhood friends.

### Directed silent reading

T: Read the whole story to yourself. Find out who is telling the story and the main things that happened. Tell whether you think it is a true story or a madeup one and why you think so.

After S. reads the story silently, have him answer the questions you asked. Then have him give a summary of the story. When he gives the summary, have him tell it in the third person (*He*) instead of the first person (*I*). His summary might be similar to the following:

[Hugh was 17 years old. He went to a reunion of his mother's family at the home of his Aunt Mary and Uncle

John on Lake Huron. Many relatives came to the reunion. At the barbecue on Saturday, Hugh's Aunt Ellen choked on a piece of meat. Hugh rescued her. Later that day, Hugh rescued his little niece. She had been playing on the shore of the lake when a wave carried her into the deep water. On Saturday night, Hugh's grandfather told family stories. On Sunday, Hugh went fishing with some cousins. At first, Hugh had not wanted to go to the reunion. But he enjoyed it and hoped they would have other reunions.]

**Reading between the lines.** Discuss these questions briefly with S. Skip the last two numbered items here if you think they would make him uncomfortable.

1. Why do you think Hugh refused to go to the reunion at first? Why did he decide to go anyway?
2. Discuss the location of Lake Huron and the other Great Lakes. Have a map of the United States and Canada in class for S. to look at.
3. Does this story take place in the United States or Canada? What clue in the story tells you this? [Hugh says that some of his cousins came to the reunion from Canada, so it must take place in the U.S.]
4. Why did Hugh think that his Aunt Ellen wouldn't eat barbecued ribs again?
5. What does the word *funny* mean in the sentence. "She got a funny look on her face"?
6. What is meant by the expression "the big man of the day"?
7. Have you ever attended a family reunion? Was it anything like the one in the story? Did you enjoy it? Why or why not?
8. If you haven't been to a family reunion, would you like to? Do you think other members of your family would be interested? Why or why not?

## STORY CHECKUP: Page 11

Have S. read the title, the information before the first exercise about people in the story, and the directions for the first exercise. Then have him write the answers. Tell him he may look back at the story if he doesn't know an answer. Check his work. Have him scan the story to find the paragraph that gives the correct answer for any item he has wrong. Have him read that paragraph aloud.

Have S. read the directions for the second exercise, in which he is to number sentences in the order in which they happened in the story. Let him refer back to the story. Check his work, and help him correct any errors.

**Note:** If S. has difficulty with exercises of this type, write the sentences on separate index cards. Have him place the cards in the correct order and then number them. Then have him transfer the numbers to the sentences in the exercise.

## READING FOR LIVING: Page 12

Have S. read the title and new words first silently and then aloud. Ask him to tell the number of syllables and which syllable is stressed in *minute* and *object*.

Ask S. to read the first paragraph silently and tell what choking is and why it is important to act fast when someone is choking.

Ask S. to read the section under the subhead *Signs of choking* first silently and then aloud. Discuss how you might tell if a person can't breathe or speak.

Have S. study the section *What to do*. Ask him to read it two or three times to himself and then tell the steps in order without looking at the book. If he has difficulty remembering, have him read each item aloud and tell the key words.

Discuss briefly with S. any instances either of you know about in which a person has been saved by this method. Also, if you have two or more students, you may want to have them practice this rescue method on each other.

# II. Skills Practice

Have S. close his book before doing these exercises.

## PRACTICE 1: Distinguishing the Long Sound for *u*

T: I will say three words. Listen and tell which one has the long sound for *u* as in *music*:

| | |
|---|---|
| *cute, cut, coat* | *mew, mug, mercy* |
| *hug, hurt, Hugh* | *burden, buckle, bugle* |

Write the following pairs of words. Have S. read each pair and tell which word has the short sound for *u* and which has the long sound.

| | | |
|---|---|---|
| *us, use* | *mute, mutt* | *fuss, fuse* |
| *cute, cut* | *cub, cube* | *huge, hug* |

## PRACTICE 2: Number of Syllables and Stress

T: Listen to each word I say. Tell how many syllables are in the word and which syllable is stressed.

| | |
|---|---|
| *argue* | [2 syllables, first is stressed] |
| *barbecue* | [3 syllables, first is stressed] |
| *cousin* | [2 syllables, first is stressed] |
| *machine* | [2 syllables, second is stressed] |
| *behind* | [2 syllables, second is stressed] |
| *relative* | [3 syllables, first is stressed] |

## PRACTICE 3: Same Spelling, Different Stress

Write these sentences, underlining the words shown in italic here:

1. He must have an *object* stuck in his throat.
2. I *object* to paying higher taxes.

T: In English, there are some words that look alike. But the stress is on a different syllable in each word. Changing the stress to a different syllable changes the sound and meaning of a word.

T: Look at these two sentences. The underlined words look alike. But the words do not sound the same or have the same meaning. The underlined word in the first sentence is the same as the one you had in today's lesson. Please read the sentence.

After S. reads the sentence, have him read the underlined word and tell which syllable is stressed. After the first sentence, write *ob'ject*. Have S. tell the meaning of the word *object* as used in the sentence [a thing, something]. Point out that *an object* is a noun, or a word that names a person, place, or thing.

T: The underlined word in a second sentence is pronounced in a different way and has a different meaning. (Point to *object* in the second sentence.) Listen as I read the sentence. Then tell which syllable is stressed in this word.

Read the second sentence and have S. tell which syllable is stressed in the underlined word. Then write *ob ject'* after the sentence. Have S. read the word and tell the meaning [am against, am opposed to]. Point out that in *I object*, the word *object* is a verb, an action word that tells what someone does.

Follow the same procedure with the noun *record* and the verb *record* in these sentences:

1. The computer keeps a *record* of sales.
2. The teacher will *record* the student's marks.

If you think the vocabulary level would not be too difficult for S., continue with the verb *refuse* and the noun *refuse*. Use the sentences below, and explain that the noun *refuse* means trash.

1. Hugh did not *refuse* to go to the reunion.
2. We will help pick up the *refuse* in the park.

## PRACTICE 4: Compound Words

Write these words: *grandfather, grandmother, weekend, someone, everyone, something*. Ask S. to read each compound word and tell the two words that it is made from. As he answers, write the two words next to the compound word.

Write *grandchild, grandchildren, grandson, grandniece, grandnephew*. Tell S. these are some compound words he has not had yet, but he can read them because he knows both parts of each one. Have him read the new compound words and tell the meaning of *grandniece* and *grandnephew*.

## PRACTICE 5: Contractions

Write the contractions *haven't, aren't, didn't, don't, what's, you're, I'm* in a column. Have S. read each contraction and tell the two words it is made from. Write the two words by each contraction. Ask S. to read the contractions made from the word *not*.

## PRACTICE 6: Adding *-s, -d, -ing* to Words Ending in *ue*

Write *argue, rescue, continue* in a column. Next to *argue*, write *argues, argued, arguing*. Explain that, when a root word ends with *ue*, we add *-s* and *-d*, but we drop the final *e* before adding *-ing*.

Ask S. how to spell *rescues, rescued, rescuing* and *continues, continued, continuing*. As he answers, write the words in the appropriate columns. Finally, have S. read all four forms of each word.

# III. Writing

## CHECK HOMEWORK: Page 7

Check this page with S. Have him correct any errors.

## WRITING LESSON (In Notebook)

Have S. write the titles *Lesson 2* and *Words* and then number from 1 to 20 in two columns.

**Words.** In *view, niece, piece*, point out the silent *i* before *e*. Give the rule that *i* usually comes before *e* when these two letters are together in a syllable. (Exceptions will be taught later.) Also, point out silent letters in *breathe, minute, aunt, cousin*, and the *s* for /z/ in *cousin*.

Dictate the following words for S. to write. Then correct them, following the procedure described in Lesson 1.

| | | | |
|---|---|---|---|
| 1. few | 6. continue | 11. cousin | 16. grandfather |
| 2. view | 7. barbecue | 12. niece | 17. grandmother |
| 3. nephew | 8. refuse | 13. piece | 18. breathe |
| 4. argue | 9. reunion | 14. seen | 19. minute |
| 5. rescue | 10. aunt | 15. wave | 20. object |

**Sentences.** Have S. write the title *Sentences*. Dictate this paragraph from the lesson:

Each year, many people die from choking. A person chokes when he is eating and something gets stuck in his throat. If you see that happen, you can save a life. But you have to act fast. A person will die in four to six minutes if he can't breathe.

Have S. check his work against the first paragraph on page 12 and mark his corrections. Go over what he has done and mark any additional corrections needed.

Then have S. write the title *Study* and any words that he missed in the word and sentence dictation. Ask him to study these words at home.

## PRACTICE: Page 13

Have S. read the directions for the first exercise and do it. Check his work. If he has any errors, have him read the words aloud and listen for the /ū/ sound.

Have S. read the directions for the second exercise. Have him read aloud the first word in column 1. Have him read it aloud again in column 2 and then put in the stress mark. If he does this correctly, let him do the rest of the exercise by himself. If he didn't mark the first word correctly, say the word aloud and have S. listen for the stressed syllable. Give help such as this where needed, but encourage S. to do some of the exercise independently. Check his work.

## HOMEWORK: Page 13

Go over the directions for each exercise with S. You may want to have him do the first item in the second exercise in class to be sure he understands the exercise. Ask him to complete this page at home.

## CHECKING PROGRESS

Note your student's progress on the word recognition and comprehension skills emphasized in this lesson, such as:

— summarizing a story
— identifying characters
— scanning to find details
— understanding compound words and contractions
— recognizing syllables
— sounding out words for himself.

These skills were developed in earlier lessons. By now, S. should be able to apply them easily. If he is having difficulty with any of these skills, use some of the suggestions given in the next section.

## MEETING INDIVIDUAL NEEDS

**Summarizing a story.** Ask S. to tell you about some event in his own life. It might be about a holiday, a vacation, finding a job, some place he has visited, or anything of special interest to him. Give him a few minutes to think it through. Then have him tell you the most important things that you can write in one paragraph. Write down what he tells. Then read it back to him—or let him read it if it isn't too difficult, and ask if the paragraph gives the main ideas of his story.

Read a short story to S., and ask him to summarize it orally in a few sentences.

**Scanning.** Use *Changes* or some other book that S. can read easily (select from titles suggested on the inside front cover of this manual or the *Teacher's Manual for Skill Book 3*.) Ask a question, and have S. scan the page to find the answer. Increase the amount of material he needs to scan to find the answer. The first time, it might be just a paragraph, then half a page, then a page. Gradually, this can be increased to two or three pages. You may also use the incentive of time to make sure he scans instead of reading word for word. Ask him to see if he can find the answer in a minute, 30 seconds, or some other time limit, according to his ability.

**Identifying characters and relationships.** Put the name of each character in the story on a flash card. (Use the names given in the Story Checkup on page 11.) Ask questions about the story, and have S. find the name or names that answer the questions.

**Word recognition skills.** Use flash cards for the compound words and contractions introduced and reviewed in today's lesson. Have S. put together the two words that make a compound. Do the same thing for contractions.

In *Focus on Phonics-4,* you may use Practice 2, which gives practice with words in which *ue* or *ew* = /ū/.

oo

food
oo

| | | | |
|---|---|---|---|
| | room | room | room |
| | pool | pool | pool |
| | school | skool | school |
| | noon | noon | noon |
| | soon | soon | soon |
| | too | too | too |

---

## A First Apartment

| move (moov) | afternoon (af ter noon') | safe | mind (mīnd) | together (too geth' er) |
|---|---|---|---|---|
| Hoover (Hoov' er) | bedroom (bed' room) | swim | quiet (qui'-et) | forever (for ev'er) |
| O'Toole (Ō Tool') | roommate (room' mate) | | those (thoze) | landlord (land' lord) |
| | | | isn't (iz unt) | Sunday (Sun' day) |

Kitty O'Toole had her first job. She had just finished business school. The school had helped her get the job.

Kitty was living with her parents. She wanted an apartment of her own. She told her parents, "I have finished school, and I have a job. I want to be on my own. I have made up my mind. I am going to move into an apartment soon."

Her father said, "You can't afford an apartment. You don't make enough money to pay for food and rent. Here at home you don't pay any rent for your room. You just pay for food."

"We think you're too young to live by yourself," said Kitty's mother. "It isn't safe these days. We want you to live at home. You are safer here."

But Kitty O'Toole had made up her mind. "I'm 19 years old," she told them. "It's time for me to be on my own. You can't keep me here at home forever. On Sunday, I'm going to look for an apartment."

Kitty looked at the ads for apartments in the Sunday paper. Kitty liked to swim. She hoped to find an apartment in a building with a swimming pool. But she soon gave up that idea. The rent for those apartments was too much for her. There were only a few places that she was able to afford. And those were not in a very safe part of the city.

Kitty went to look at those places anyway. She left home before noon. She spent Sunday afternoon looking at apartments. But she didn't find one she liked.

"What shall I do?" Kitty asked herself. "I don't like the apartments I can afford, and I can't afford the ones I like. I need a roommate to share the rent."

"My parents said the same thing," said Jane. "Parents want to keep you at home forever, don't they?"

"Yes, they do," said Kitty. "Let's ask them to dinner soon. We'll show them that we were right."

Kitty started looking for a roommate. In the next few weeks, she spoke to people at work and at church. She spoke to friends from school. "Do you know anyone who needs a roommate?" she asked. But no one did.

At last, a friend told Kitty that Jane Hoover was looking for a roommate. Kitty had met Jane at a school party. But she didn't know her very well. Kitty O'Toole phoned Jane Hoover at work the next morning. They agreed to have lunch together that noon.

Kitty and Jane liked each other right away. They learned that they liked many of the same things. They liked the same kind of music. And they both liked to swim.

Jane said that she liked peace and quiet. "Me too!" Kitty said. "Sometimes I stay up late at night, but I play my radio quietly. And I don't give wild parties."

Kitty added, "I like to spend some time by myself. I want a roommate who will understand that." Jane said she felt the same way.

Kitty and Jane agreed to look for an apartment together. They spent three weekends looking. They looked at 22 apartments. Some cost too much. Some didn't look very safe or clean.

Late one Sunday afternoon, Jane said, "I'm tired. Let's quit for today."

"Oh, come on!" Kitty said. "Let's try one more."

The next apartment they looked at was just right. It had two bedrooms. From the living room, there was a view of a park. The kitchen needed paint. But the building was clean and quiet. And the rent was not too high.

Kitty and Jane asked the landlord a lot of questions. "Is there a bus stop near here? Are there any stores? Is the building safe at night?" The landlord answered yes to those questions. Then Kitty asked, "There isn't a swimming pool in the building, is there?"

"No," the landlord said. "But there is a pool in the park."

The two young women made up their minds in a hurry. "We'll take it!" they said. They paid the rent and got the key.

Kitty and Jane moved into the apartment together. They shared the cost of the rent, telephone, lights, and food. Each of them got a bed from home for her bedroom. Kitty's parents let her take some dishes and pans. The Hoovers let Jane take a rug and an old toaster. Jane had her own record player, and Kitty had a radio. They shopped for a used sofa, a table, and some chairs. They made end tables from boxes. Jane made curtains, and Kitty painted the kitchen.

After they had worked hard for two months, the apartment looked nice. Kitty and Jane were pleased. "My parents said I was too young to be on my own," said Kitty.

## Story Checkup

**Write one or two sentences to answer each question.**

1. Why did Kitty want an apartment of her own?

2. Why did her parents want her to live at home?

3. Why did Kitty look for a roommate?

4. What kinds of things did Kitty and Jane both like?

5. What kind of apartment did they rent?

6. What costs did Kitty and Jane share?

7. In what ways did they get the things they needed for their apartment?

---

heat  furnished (fur′ nisht)  utilities (ū til′ i tēz)
unfurnished (un fur′ nisht)  deposit (dē poz′ it)

Ads can help you find apartments for rent. The furnished ones have beds, tables, chairs, and other things. The unfurnished ones do not.

Utilities are lights, heat, and water.

A security deposit is money you pay when you move in. You get it back when you move away if you have not broken anything.

Read these ads, and write short answers to the questions.

| APARTMENTS—FURNISHED | Hill Top Apartments. |
|---|---|
| **2080 Baker Street.** 2-bedroom apartment on second floor of quiet family home. Security deposit. Utilities paid. $500. 424-1960. | Country living 20 minutes from city. Swimming pool & game room. 1- and 2-bedroom apartments, $625 and up. Business office open 9-5. 699-4051. |
| **Court Street Arms.** 3 rooms. Clean. No pets. Heat paid. $90 a week. 434-1083. | **North Side.** Woman needs roommate to share rent & utilities. Own bedroom. No smokers. $280. 426-3530 after 6 p.m. |
| APARTMENTS—UNFURNISHED | |
| **1216 Circle Drive.** 4 rooms, just painted. 5 minutes from university. Landlord pays everything. $475. Hurry. 427-8060. | **765 Oak Street.** 2 bedrooms, eat-in kitchen. Near bus stop, stores. $425, pay own utilities. Security deposit. 424-6734. |
| **223 First Street.** 3 bedrooms. On bus line. 424-1492. | **26 Union Place.** 2 bedrooms, large living room. Children OK. Parking. $535. Heat, hot water. 424-1489. |

1. Is the apartment on Circle Drive furnished or unfurnished? *Unfurnished*
2. Where is the furnished apartment in a family home? *At 2080 Baker Street*
3. Who pays the utilities at 765 Oak Street, the landlord or the renter? *The renter*
   Does the renter have to pay a security deposit at this place? *Yes*
4. Where is the rent paid weekly? *At Court Street Arms*
5. Which apartments have a pool? *The Hill Top Apartments*
6. What fact comes last in each of these ads? *The telephone number*
7. What time can you phone the woman who wants a roommate? *After 6 p.m.*
8. What utilities does the landlord pay for at 26 Union Place? *Heat and hot water*
9. Where does an apartment cost the most? *At Hill Top Apartments*

Homework | Practice (two-page spread)

## Practice

begin (bē gin′)

**Say the words. Circle the words with the sound *oo* as in *food***

1. (soon) spoke (noon) north
2. (food) future for (school)
3. phone (pool) too tore
4. more (move) (room) music
5. (Hoover) Hugo (O'Toole) United

**Put *un-* at the beginning of each word to make another word. Write the word.**

Example: furnished _unfurnished_

1. finished _unfinished_     5. loved _unloved_
2. married _unmarried_     6. used _unused_
3. painted _unpainted_     7. locked _unlocked_
4. answered _unanswered_     8. paid _unpaid_

**Fill in each blank with one of the words that begins with *un-*. (You may use the example word in your answers.)**

1. The child felt _unloved_ .
2. The rent is cheaper for an _unfurnished_ apartment.
3. The work I started last week is still _unfinished_ .
4. The back door was _unlocked_ when I came home.
5. Two _unmarried_ girls shared the apartment.
6. John has a lot of _unpaid_ bills.
7. Jane got some _unpainted_ chairs and painted them herself.
8. The question is _unanswered_ .
9. If I take the _unused_ can of paint back to the store, can I get my money back?

**20** Lesson 3

## Homework

root

**Drop the ending from each word. Write the root word.**

1. swimming _Swim_     8. choking _choke_
2. renter _rent_     9. toaster _toast_
3. quietly _quiet_     10. cities _city_
4. dishes _dish_     11. shopped _shop_
5. agreed _agree_     12. smoker _smoke_
6. shared _share_     13. youngest _young_
7. weekly _week_     14. parties _party_

**Read the word. Then write the two words you see in it.**

1. everywhere _every_ _where_
2. spaceship _space_ _ship_
3. bedroom _bed_ _room_
4. afternoon _after_ _noon_
5. landlord _land_ _lord_
6. roommate _room_ _mate_
7. grandmother _grand_ _mother_
8. airplane _air_ _plane_
9. Sunday _sun_ _day_
10. forever _for_ _ever_

**Write two questions that Kitty and Jane asked the landlord.**

1. _____
2. _____

Lesson 3   **21**

Lesson 3   33

## OBJECTIVES

To help your student:

- recognize the vowel sound /oo/, as in *food*.
- recognize that the letters *oo* often stand for the sound /oo/.
- read words in which the sound /oo/ is written *oo*.
- recognize words that sound alike except for the initial consonant (rhyming words).
- recognize the number of syllables in a word and which syllable is stressed.
- recognize the new beginning consonant blend *sw* and review *sk, st, sp, sl*.
- recognize the new compound words *afternoon, bedroom, roommate, forever, landlord, Sunday*.
- recognize the new prefix *un-* and review the prefixes *non-* and *in-*, which also mean *not*.
- review ways the *-ed* ending is pronounced.
- review adding *-ly* to words.
- understand cause and effect in the story.
- relate the story to own experience and values.
- read and understand information given in rental ads in newspapers.
- scan want ads to find information.
- write words, prices, and sentences from dictation.
- write a short summary of a story.

## INTRODUCTION

T: You have learned the short and long sounds for the vowels. Today you will learn a new vowel sound.

# I. Reading

## CHART: Page 14

**Title and key word.** Have S. read the title *Lesson 3*.

T: Look at the two letters in the top right-hand corner. What are they? [S: *oo*.] You have learned the short sound for *o*. What is it? [S: /o/.] And you have learned the long sound for *o*. What is it? [S: /ō/.] But two *o*'s together stand for a different sound.

T: (Point to the picture of *food* and the word.) Look at this picture and the key word. What is the word? [S: food.] Say the word again, and listen to the vowel sound. What is it? [S: /oo/] The sound /oo/ is very much like the long sound for *u*. If you leave off the /y/ sound at the beginning of the sound /ū/, you have the sound /oo/.

**Note:** The long sound /ū/ is really a blend of the sounds /y/ and /oo/, that is, /yoo/.

T: There are many words in which two *o*'s together stand for the sound /oo/. Look at the words in the chart.

**Line 1**

T: Look at the first picture and the word next to it. What is the word? [S: room.] How many sounds do you hear in *room*? [S: Three.] What is the vowel sound? [S: /oo/.] Read the word again. [S: room.]

**Lines 2-6**

T: Now look at the other words in the chart. In each of these words, the letters *oo* stand for the sound /oo/. Read the words to yourself.

After S. has studied the chart silently, have him read the words aloud, going down the last column of the chart. Also, explain that *too*, spelled in this way, means *also* or *more than enough*, as in *I want some, too* and *It's too hot*. Then ask these questions:

1. What is the vowel sound in all of these words? [S: /oo/.] What letters stand for the sound? [S: *oo*.]
2. Which word *ends* with the vowel sound /oo/? [S: too.]
3. Which word rhymes with *pool*? [S: school.]
4. Which word rhymes with *noon*? [S: soon.]
5. What is the sound for *ch* in *school*? [S: /k/.]
6. How many syllables are in each of these words? [S: One.]

**Review.** Have S. read each word again, including the key word. Cover the pictures, and have him read the words going down the last column of the chart.

## STORY: Pages 15-17 (A First Apartment)

Have S. read the story title and new words. Call attention to the *sw* blend in *swim*. Have S. tell which words are compound words. Have him tell how many syllables are in each compound word. Be sure he understands that the compound words in the respellings are divided into their word parts and not necessarily into syllables. He should note that *afternoon* and *forever* have three syllables.

Have S. tell how many syllables are in each of the other words and which syllable is stressed. Then have him read all of the words with the vowel sound /oo/.

**Directed silent reading.** Have S. mark the end of paragraph 7. Then ask him to read the first seven paragraphs to himself, and find out who Kitty O'Toole was, what she wanted to do, and what problems she faced.

After S. has read paragraphs 1-7, ask what facts we know about Kitty. He should be able to tell the following information. Ask questions to elicit any items he does not mention.

[Kitty was 19 years old. She had just finished business school. She had her first job. She was living at home with her parents. She wanted an apartment of her own.]

Ask S. to identify Kitty's problem. [The places Kitty could afford were not in a safe part of the city.] Have S. tell how he thinks Kitty could solve her problem. Some possible solutions might be to stay at home and save some money, to take an apartment she can afford even if it isn't in a safe part of the city, or to find a roommate.

Ask S. to read the rest of the story to himself and find out what Kitty's solution was.

After S. has finished reading, have him tell how Kitty solved her problem and whether or not he thinks this was a good solution. Have him give reasons for his opinion.

**Reading between the lines.** Discuss these questions.

1. Once Kitty had decided she needed a roommate, how did she go about finding one? Notice that she spoke to people she knew fairly well. Do you think that was a better idea than putting an ad in the paper or putting a notice on a bulletin board? Why or why not?
2. What kinds of things did Kitty and Jane talk about to find out if they could get along together as roommates? Are there any other important questions you think people should ask before becoming roommates?
3. What questions did Kitty and Jane ask the landlord? Are there any other important questions a person should ask before renting an apartment?
4. Judging from Kitty's actions, do you think she is a responsible young woman? Why or why not?
5. What objections did Kitty's parents have to her getting an apartment? Do you think they were all strong reasons or were some just excuses to keep her at home?
6. How would you describe the way Kitty acted toward her parents? Was she rude to them, did she assert herself, or did she obey their wishes?
7. At the end of the story, are Kitty and Jane hoping for their parents' approval, or don't they care? What shows this?
8. How can a parent and child recognize when the time is right for the child to leave home and be on his own?
9. What are some reasons that some young people who work continue to live at home with their parents? Do you think there are any good reasons for doing so?

If S. seems willing, let him discuss his own experiences either as a young person leaving home for the first time or as a parent whose child left home. But be very careful about probing into what might be a sensitive area.

## STORY CHECKUP: Page 18

Have S. read the title and directions. Then have him write sentence answers to the questions. Tell him to write the answers without looking back at the story. If there are any questions he can't answer, he should skip them. Most of the questions are about main points related to cause and effect.

After S. has finished, have him read each question and his answer. For any answer he has wrong or has omitted, have him look back at the story and find the correct answer.

## READING FOR LIVING: Page 19

Have S. read the title and new words first silently and then aloud. Ask him to tell the number of syllables in each word and which syllable is stressed.

Have S. read paragraphs 1-3 silently. Then ask him what *furnished, unfurnished, utilities,* and *security deposit* mean in apartment ads. Have him read aloud the last paragraph that gives directions for the exercise.

Before S. begins reading the ads, point out that the ads are divided into two sections: Apartments—Furnished, and Apartments—Unfurnished. In each section, the ads are listed in alphabetical order by place name.

Let S. read the ads and answer the questions. When he has finished, have him read aloud the questions and his answers. If any items are wrong, have him skim the ads for the key words that will help him find the answer.

# II. Skills Practice

Have S. close his book before doing these exercises.

## PRACTICE 1: Distinguishing the Sound /oo/

T: I will say three words. Listen and tell which one has the sound /oo/ as in *food*:

| | |
|---|---|
| *cool, cold, cost* | *music, must, moon* |
| *soap, soup, sock* | *few, fool, phone* |
| *boat, box, boot* | *who, Hugh, hug* |
| *stop, stoop, stone* | *mute, more, move* |

## PRACTICE 2: Substituting an Initial Consonant

List these words as headings over three columns: *pool, room, noon.* Ask S. to read the first word, *pool.* Then write *cool* under *pool.* Point out that it is just like *pool* except for the first letter, and ask S. to read it. Write these words in the same column, and have S. read them: *fool, tool, spool.*

Follow the same procedure for the other headings:

*room:*   *boom, bloom, broom, groom, zoom*
*noon:*   *moon, soon, spoon*

## PRACTICE 3: *sw* and Other *s* Blends

T: (Write *swim*, and have S. read it.) What consonant sounds do you hear before the vowel sound in *swim*? [S: /s/ and /w/.] This is a new consonant blend. (Underline *sw*.) What do you call this blend? [S: *sw*.]

T: Which word begins with the consonant blend *sw*:

| | | |
|---|---|---|
| *sing, swing?* | *sift, swift?* | *sweep, sleep?* |
| *wet, sweat?* | *switch, which?* | *slim, swim?* |

T: (Write the blends *sk, sl, sp, st, sw.*) This time, I will say two words that both begin with the same blend. Tell me which of these blends it is.

| | | |
|---|---|---|
| *skirt, skill* | *stop, start* | *sleep, sleeve* |
| *sweet, swap* | *speak, spell* | *swing, swamp* |

## PRACTICE 4: Prefixes *non-, in-, un-*

T: (Write *non-violent* and *injustice*.) Here are two words that you had in the book *Changes*. Read the first word. [S: non-violent.] (Point to *non-*.) Read this part of the word. [S: non.] What does it mean? [S: Not.] What does *non-violent* mean? [S: Not violent.]

Follow the same procedure with *injustice*.

T: The word parts *non-* and *in-* are called prefixes. They can be put in front of certain root words to make new words. Usually, a prefix changes the meaning of the word. I'm going to say some sentences that have words with the prefixes *in-* and *non-*. Tell me what the word with the prefix is and what it means.

1. That answer is *incorrect*.
2. I sat in the *non-smoking* section of the plane.
3. Jack has a *non-union* job.
4. It's hard to get a job if you are *inexperienced*.
5. I drink *non-fat* milk.
6. We use contractions when we're speaking *informally*.

T: You had a word with another prefix in today's lesson. (Write *unfurnished*.) Please read it. [S: unfurnished.] What is the root word? [S: furnished.] What is the prefix? [S: un-.] What does the prefix *un-* mean? [S: Not.] Yes, this is another prefix that means *not*.

Write these words: *clean, finished, opened, kind*. Have S. read each word and then tell what it would be with the prefix *un-*. Write *un-* in front of the word. Have him read the word with the prefix and tell the meaning.

## PRACTICE 5: Pronouncing the *-ed* Ending

T: You had several words in this lesson that end with *-ed*. You will recall that the ending *-ed* is not pronounced the same in all words. Let's look at some words with *-ed* from today's lesson.

Write *agreed, hoped, started* at the top of three columns. Have S. read each word and tell how the ending is pronounced and whether it adds an extra syllable. Under each word, write the way the ending is pronounced: *d, t, ed*. Say each word below, and have S. tell the sound for the *-ed* ending. As he answers, write the word in the correct column.

| | | | | |
|---|---|---|---|---|
| *painted* | *added* | *pleased* | *shared* | *needed* |
| *looked* | *moved* | *finished* | *liked* | *helped* |

Have S. read aloud all of the words in each column. Point out that, when the root word ends in *d* or *t*, the *-ed* ending is pronounced /ed/ and adds a syllable.

## PRACTICE 6: Ending *-ly*

Write these words in a column: *safely, quietly, cheaply, kindly*. Have S. read each word and tell what the root word is. As he answers, write the root word. Then have him read both forms of each word.

# III. Writing

## CHECK HOMEWORK: Page 13

Check the Homework with S., and help him correct any errors.

## WRITING LESSON (In Notebook)

**Words.** Have S. write the titles *Lesson 3* and *Words* and number from 1 to 20 in two columns. After he has finished the dictation, have him check his work by looking at the chart and story words.

| | | | |
|---|---|---|---|
| 1. too | 6. pool | 11. those | 16. bedroom |
| 2. food | 7. school | 12. swim | 17. roommate |
| 3. room | 8. move | 13. mind | 18. afternoon |
| 4. noon | 9. safe | 14. quiet | 19. together |
| 5. soon | 10. same | 15. Sunday | 20. forever |

**Prices.** Ask S. to write the title *Prices*. Demonstrate writing the prices *$250* and *$16.10*. Review putting the period (decimal point) between the dollars and cents. Then dictate these prices for S. to write. When he has finished, check his work. Have him correct any errors.

| | | |
|---|---|---|
| $125 | $563 | $55.25 |
| $75 | $17.50 | $8.05 |

**Sentences.** Have S. write the title *Sentences*. Have him number each sentence as you dictate it.

1. Ads can help you find apartments for rent.
2. Utilities are lights, heat, and water.
3. Kitty looked at an unfurnished apartment at 765 Oak Street.
4. Is the building safe at night?
5. Is there a swimming pool?
6. The apartment rents for $185 a month.

Check what S. has written, and have him correct any errors, including those in punctuation and capitalization. Have S. write the title *Study* and any words that he missed in the word and sentence dictation.

**Story summary.** Have S. write a short summary of the story. He should be able to write the main points in five or six sentences. Check his work, and have him correct any errors. Praise him for the thought content even if there are other kinds of errors.

## PRACTICE: Page 20

Have S. read the directions for the first exercise and then do it. Check his answers. If he has any wrong, have him read the words in the line aloud.

Go over the directions and example for the second exercise with S. Have him add the prefix *un-* to each of the words. Then have him read the directions for the third exercise and fill in the correct words with *un-* in the sentences. Have him read the completed sentences aloud and correct any errors.

## HOMEWORK: Page 21

Go over the directions and the new word *root* with S. Encourage him to read the story and apartment ads again at home and to practice writing any words he missed.

## CHECKING PROGRESS

Your student's answers in the exercises in Lessons 2-3 will help you check his progress. Check his ability to answer *why* questions by noting his responses in the Story Checkup for this lesson.

S. is now expected to read longer words. Check his progress in recognizing root words, endings, prefixes, and syllables.

If S. had difficulty with the sequence of events exercise in Lesson 2, plan a reinforcement exercise as suggested in the next section.

## MEETING INDIVIDUAL NEEDS

**Word endings.** Use these suggestions if S. needs additional practice with word endings.

1. Make flash cards of the following words with the *-ed* ending. Mix them up, and have S. sort them according to the way the ending is pronounced: /d/, /t/, or /ed/.

| | | |
|---|---|---|
| used | stressed | printed |
| continued | choked | wanted |
| waved | pressed | needed |
| breathed | furnished | added |

2. Make a list of the following words. Have S. write them with the *-ing* ending. Review doubling the final consonant after a short vowel and dropping the final silent *e*.

| | | | |
|---|---|---|---|
| use | argue | hug | mean |
| amuse | choke | print | swim |

**Prefix *un-*.** Make a slip strip or word wheel (described on pages 35 and 110 of the *Teacher's Manual for Skill Book 3*) for the prefix *un-*. Use any of the root words listed below as well as those in the Practice on page 20.

| | | | | |
|---|---|---|---|---|
| able | clean | kind | dressed | opened |
| afraid | happy | safe | heated | wanted |

**Substituting initial consonants.** Make slip strips for these word families:

*-ool* family:   c, f, p, t, sp, st, sch
*-oon* family:   m, n, s, sp
*-oom* family:   b, r, bl, br, gr

**Sequence of events.** If S. had difficulty with the exercise on sequence of events in Lesson 2, give a similar exercise on today's story. Write the sentences below (without numbers) on separate cards or strips of paper. Mix them up, and have S. arrange them in order. Then have him read the sentences aloud in order.

1. Kitty told her parents that she wanted to move out.
2. Kitty started looking at apartments, but they cost too much for her.
3. Kitty made up her mind that she needed a roommate.
4. Kitty asked friends to help her find a roommate.
5. Someone told Kitty that Jane Hoover needed a roommate.
6. Kitty and Jane had lunch together and got to know each other.
7. Kitty and Jane looked at 22 apartments that were not right for them.
8. The two young women rented a safe, clean apartment that didn't cost too much.
9. Kitty and Jane spent two months fixing up their apartment.
10. Kitty and Jane were ready to ask their parents to dinner.

**Sounds.** In *Focus on Phonics-4*, you may use Practices 3A-3D. They cover word families in which the sound /oo/ is spelled *oo*.

# Lesson 4

u‿e = oo
ue = oo

June
u‿e = oo

blue
ue = oo

| June |
|---|
| S M T W T F S |
| 1 2 |
| 3 4 5 6 7 8 9 |
| 10 11 12 13 14 15 16 |
| 17 18 19 20 21 22 23 |
| 24 25 26 27 28 29 30 |

| | | | |
|---|---|---|---|
|  | flute | flute / floot | flute |
| | salute | su lute / su loot' | salute |
| | rule | rule / rool | rule |
|  | rude | rude / rood | rude |
| | true | true / true | true |

---

## The Flag

| flag | July | (Joo lȳ') | honor | (on' er) | goes | (gōz) |
|---|---|---|---|---|---|---|
| drum | parade | (pu rade') | bugle | (būˉ' gul) | heart | (hart) |
| star | remove | (rē move') | maple | (māˉ' pul) | holiday | (hol' i day) |
| stripe | | | leaf | | daytime | (day' time) |

People show their love for their country when they honor their flag. The bright colors of the flag stand for the country, its people, and its ideas.

The flag of the United States is red, white, and blue. Red stands for courage. White stands for honor. And blue stands for justice. The flag has 13 stripes of red and white. These stripes stand for the first 13 states. The top left corner of the flag is blue with 50 white stars. The stars stand for the 50 states in the United States today. We sometimes give the U.S. flag a name. One name we use is the Stars and Stripes.

Some people say that a leader of the country made the first U.S. flag. That may be true. Other people say that a woman made the first flag in her home. That may be true. We may never know the true story.

In the United States, people honor their flag on June 14. June 14 is Flag Day. On June 14, people fly the flag on their homes, businesses, and city buildings.

The flag of Canada is white with a red maple leaf on it. On each side of the maple leaf is a red stripe. The red maple leaf stands for the country of Canada.

In both Canada and the United States, people fly the flag on holidays. In the United States, one big holiday is the Fourth of July. The Fourth of July honors the day the country was born. That day was July 4, 1776.

A big holiday in Canada is Canada Day on July 1. This holiday honors the day that the country was united. That day was July 1, 1867.

| club | meet | picnic (pic´ nic) | concert (con´ sert) | language (lang´ gwij) |
|------|------|-------------------|---------------------|------------------------|
| main | per  | zoo               | fireworks (fire´ works) | Thursday (Thurz´ day) |

Your paper can help you find things to do in your free time. Read this part of the Center City paper. Then fill in the blanks.

## Center City Weekly Bugle

**THINGS TO DO THIS WEEK**

**Sunday, July 3**

**Children's Petting Zoo** opens today. Zoo will be open every Sunday 1-5 p.m. Maple Road near Oak Hill. 25¢ per person.

**Dinner** at First Union Church, 121 Main Street. After-dinner speaker: Dr. Hugo Black, "Honoring God and Country." 6:30 p.m. $3.50.

**Monday, July 4**

**Fourth of July parade,** six marching bands, starts at 10 a.m. Marchers meet at high school at 9 a.m. Watch the parade as it goes up Main Street to Jones Park. Bring your flags!

**Picnic** at Jones Park following the parade. Bicycle races, games and prizes, singing. Bring your own food. Hot & cold drinks on sale at picnic.

**Fireworks and band concert** at Lake Shore Park, 9 p.m. $1 per car.

**Thursday, July 7**

**Free swimming lessons** at Jones Park pool on Thursday afternoons and evenings. Phone park office to sign up. 806-3811.

**Evening classes** at King's College: English as a second language, 7-9 in Building 3. Sign language, 7-10 at the Learning Center for the Deaf.

**Club meeting.** Blue Lake Fishing & Hunting Club meets at 8 p.m. in the Hoover Building, Room 16.

**Friday, July 8**

**Bake sale** put on by Parents of the Handicapped. North Way Shopping Center, noon to 6 p.m.

**Barbecue** at Valley Fire Department to raise money for rescue truck. 5:30-8:30 p.m. $8 per person.

**Saturday, July 9**

**Morning-to-night band concert,** 15 bands & 32 singers. Rock, blues, & country music. Lake Shore Park, 10 a.m. to 10 p.m. $10 per person.

**Camp** for boys and girls ages 6-18 July 9-July 23, at Maple Leaf State Park. Run by Camp Fire of Center City, 813-6080.

**Garden Club** weekly meeting at Porter Rose Garden, 2 p.m.

1. The Children's Petting Zoo opens on July ___3___.

2. The Fourth of July ___parade___ goes up Main Street.

3. At the picnic, you can buy drinks, but you must bring your own ___food___.

4. If six people go to the fireworks in the same car, they must pay ___$1___.

5. You can get free swimming lessons on ___Thursday___ afternoons and evenings.

6. The sign language class meets at the Learning Center for the ___Deaf___.

7. The hunting and fishing club meets at ___8 p.m.___ on Thursday.

8. The fire department is having a barbecue to raise money for a ___rescue___ truck.

9. The concert on July 9 lasts from ___10 a.m.___ to ___10 p.m.___.

---

There are many parades on Canada Day and the Fourth of July. Many bands march in the parades. The bands have drums, bugles, and flutes. The bands march to the drums. The bugles and flutes play march music. You can hear the drums, bugles, and flutes from far away.

A person carrying the flag marches at the head of the parade. When your country's flag goes by, you stand up and salute. A man removes his hat. He salutes by placing his hand over his heart. A woman does not remove her hat. She salutes by placing her hand over her heart, too.

It is rude not to stand when the flag of any country goes by. It is rude not to salute the flag of your own country. It is rude for a man not to remove his hat for his country's flag.

Most countries have rules for honoring the flag. Here are a few rules that many countries follow:

1. You may fly the flag in the daytime. If there is a light on the flag, you may fly it at night, too.
2. Do not fly the flag in the rain.
3. Do not let the flag touch the floor.
4. Do not throw away an old flag. Burn it with care.

These rules will help you honor the flag and show love for your country.

## Story Checkup

**Fill in each blank with the right word or number from the story.**

1. In the U.S. flag, there are ___fifty___ stars.

   Each star stands for a ___state___.

   The ___stripes___ stand for the first 13 states.

   Flag Day in the United States is on ___June 14___.

2. The flag of Canada is ___white___ with a ___red___ maple leaf.

   On each side of the maple leaf is a red ___stripe___.

   Canada Day is on ___July 1___.

**Write yes if the sentence is true. Write no if the sentence is not true.**

_yes_  1. On the U.S. flag, white stands for honor.

_No_  2. The stars on the U.S. flag are blue.

_No_  3. Helen Keller made the first U.S. flag.

_No_  4. Stars and Stripes is a name used for the flag of Canada.

_yes_  5. The red maple leaf stands for the country of Canada.

_yes_  6. By honoring the flag, you show love for your country.

**Read each word. Then write each word in the form that means more than one.**

1. country  _countries_

2. holiday  _holidays_

3. parade  _parades_

4. city  _cities_

5. story  _stories_

6. bugle  _bugles_

7. family  _families_

8. flute  _flutes_

**Write two rules for honoring your country's flag.**

1. _____

2. _____

---

**Say the words. Circle the words with the sound oo as in _blue_ and _food_.**

1. (rule)  drum  (room)  hurt

2. tree  (too)  (true)  club

3. (June)  Jane  noon  bugle

4. (pool)  school  (July)  few

5. (flute)  salute  amuse  Thursday

**Say each word. Put the stress mark after the syllable that is stressed.**

1. parade  pa rade´

2. remove  re move´

3. bugle  bu´gle

4. holiday  hol´ i day

5. July  Ju ly´

6. Thursday  Thurs´ day

7. picnic  pic´ nic

8. maple  ma´ ple

9. concert  con´ cert

**Write each of these words after its meaning.**

barbecue, concert, holiday, parade, reunion

1. Bands and people marching in a line  _parade_

2. A picnic at which meat is roasted over an open fire  _barbecue_

3. A day when businesses are closed and most people do not work  _holiday_

4. A show in which people sing or play music  _concert_

5. A time when people who have been away from each other come together again  _reunion_

## OBJECTIVES

To help your student:

- recognize that the letters *ue* and *u-e* stand for the sound /oo/ when preceded by *j*, *l*, or *r*, as in *June, blue, rule.*
- read words in which the sound /oo/ is written *ue* or *u-e*.
- distinguish between the long sound /ū/ as in *music* and the sound /oo/ as in *food.*
- recognize the number of syllables in a word and which syllable is stressed.
- recognize the new compound words *daytime, fireworks*, and review other compound words.
- review the beginning consonant blends *cl, fl, dr, tr, st, str*.
- review changing the singular form to plural by adding *-s* or *-es* or by changing final *y* to *i* and adding *-es*.
- read factual material to obtain information.
- identify the main topics in a factual article.
- recall important details.
- scan a reading selection to locate a specific detail.
- read and understand a newspaper listing of community events.
- relate reading material to own experience and values.
- write words and sentences from dictation.
- write a short description of a coming event, giving date, time, place, and cost.

## INTRODUCTION

T: You have learned that the letters *ue* and *u*-consonant-*e* stand for the sound /ū/ as in *cure* and *argue*. In today's lesson, you will find that *ue* and *u*-consonant-*e* also stand for the sound /oo/.

# I. Reading

## CHART: Page 22

**Title and key words.** Have S. read the title *Lesson 4*.

T: Look at the letters in the top right-hand corner. What are they and what sound do they equal? [S: *u*-consonant-*e* equals /oo/, *ue* equals /oo/.]

T: Read the first key word. [S: June.] What is the vowel sound? [S: /oo/.] What letters equal /oo/ in *June*? [S: *u*-consonant-*e*.] What consonant comes before the vowel sound? [S: *J*.]

T: Read the next key word. [S: blue.] What is the vowel sound? [S: /oo/.] What letters equal /oo/ in *blue*? [S: *ue*.] What letter comes before the vowel sound? [S: *l*.]

### Lines 1-5

T: Read the other words in the chart. Notice what letters stand for the sound /oo/ in each word. Also, notice what consonant comes before the sound /oo/.

After S. has studied the chart silently, have him read the words aloud, going down the last column. Then ask these questions:

1. What is the vowel sound in each of these words? [S: /oo/.]
2. How is the sound /oo/ written in the first four words? [S: *u*-consonant-*e*.]
3. How is the sound /oo/ written in the last word? [S: *ue*.]
4. What consonant comes before the sound /oo/ in *blue, flute, salute*? [S: *l*.]
5. What consonant comes before the sound /oo/ in *rule, rude, true*? [S: *r*.]
6. What consonant comes before the sound /oo/ in *June*? [S: *J*.]

T: Usually, the letters *ue* or *u*-consonant-*e* stand for the sound /oo/ when they come after *j*, *l*, or *r*.

**Review.** Have S. read each word aloud again, including the key words. Cover the pictures, and go down the last column of the chart. Ask S. to tell which word has more than one syllable [*salute*] and which syllable is stressed.

## STORY: Pages 23-24 (The Flag)

Have S. read the story title and new words. Have him tell the number of syllables in each word and which syllable is stressed. Ask him which words have the vowel sound /oo/ [*July, remove*] and which word has the vowel sound /ū/ [*bugle*]. Call attention to the way *le* sounds like /ul/ in *maple* and *bugle*. Ask S. to tell the two words from which the compound word *daytime* is made.

Mention that this is another factual article. Ask S. to read the whole article to himself and notice what some of the main topics are. [S. reads silently.]

T: Do you remember the short article about choking that you read? In that article, there were some subheads: *Signs of choking* and *What to do*. The subheads helped you recognize the main topics in the article.

T: If we wanted to put some subheads in this article to show what the main topics are, where would we put them and what would they say? Let's look at the article. Read the first paragraph aloud, please. [S. reads.] This paragraph is just an introduction to the rest of the article, so it doesn't need a subhead.

### The flag of the United States (paragraphs 2-4)

T: Now look at paragraphs 2, 3, and 4. (Let S. number the paragraphs as you go along if this is helpful.) What are these paragraphs about? [S: The flag of the United States.] Right, that's the first main topic. We could write that as a subhead over paragraph 2.

**Note**: Write the main topics on the board as you go along. Have S. write them in his notebook, also. Or, you may prefer to have him write them in his book as subheads in the story.

T: Now look over these three paragraphs again and tell some of the details that are given about the main topic.

Let S. tell the details he can recall about the U.S. flag. Ask questions from the list below to help him fill in any details he has omitted.

1. What colors are in the U.S. flag?
2. What do the colors stand for?
3. What does the design of the flag look like?
4. What do the stars and stripes stand for?
5. What name is sometimes given to the U.S. flag?
6. What is the name of the day and the date when people in the United States honor their flag?

### The flag of Canada (paragraph 5)

T: Look at paragraph 5. What is it about? [S: The flag of Canada.] Good. That's the second main topic. We could write it as the subhead over paragraph 5.

Have S. study paragraph 5 and tell the details about the main topic. Ask the following questions, if needed, to help him recall details.

1. What colors are in the flag of Canada?
2. What does the design look like?
3. What does the red maple leaf stand for?

### Flying the flag on holidays (paragraphs 6-8). Follow the same general procedure. The words S. gives for the main topic should include the words *holidays* and *flag*, such as "Flying the flag on holidays" or "Holidays when we fly the flag." Ask these questions to help S. recall the supporting details:

1. What does the Fourth of July honor?
2. What does Canada Day honor? What date is it?

### Saluting the flag (paragraphs 9-10). Follow the same general procedure. Ask these questions:

1. In what part of the parade does the flag come?
2. How does a man salute his own country's flag?
3. How does a woman salute her own country's flag?
4. What should we do when the flag of another country goes by?

### Rules for honoring the flag (remainder of article).
Follow the same general procedure. Ask S. to tell as many of the rules for honoring the flag as he can remember.

**Discussion.** Discuss one or more of these items briefly with S.

1. Besides the Fourth of July or Canada Day, depending on which country you are in, what are some other occasions when the flag is flown? What is often sung at these times?
2. You may want to discuss briefly the historical background of the Fourth of July or Canada Day.
3. If S. is from another country, he may like to describe that country's flag, ways of honoring it there, and some occasions when the flag is flown.

4. Ask S. how he likes to celebrate holidays like the Fourth of July or Canada Day. Does he usually watch the parades?
5. Ask S. to tell about some parade that he has seen or marched in.
6. Ask S. to tell why he thinks people have very deep feelings about their country's flag. When are people likely to be disrespectful toward the flag? When are they likely to be most respectful? What are some other ways to show honor to the flag besides following the rules given in the article?

### STORY CHECKUP: Page 24

Have S. read the title and directions. Then have him fill in the blanks without looking back at the story. Check his work. Have him find the correct answer for any items he has wrong or has omitted.

### READING FOR LIVING: Page 25

Have S. read the title and new words first silently and then aloud. Call attention to the word *per*, and have S. tell what it means [for each] in an example, such as: "The admission is $1.00 per person." When S. reads words with more than one syllable, have him tell the number of syllables in the word and which syllable is stressed. Have him tell the two words that make up the compound word *fireworks*. Ask which word has the vowel sound /oo/.

Ask S. to read the directions first silently and then aloud. Have him read aloud the name of the newspaper [*Center City Weekly Bugle*] and tell what *weekly* means. Explain that this selection from the newspaper is written in three columns. Have S. find the title *Things to Do This Week* and read the things listed for Sunday, first silently and then aloud. Then ask him to read silently what is listed for Monday, July 4. Have him tell the main events.

Ask S. to tell on what other days events are listed, and then have him read the information about those events to himself. (If this selection seems difficult for S., have him read all of it aloud.)

When he has finished reading, have him fill in the blanks in the sentences below. Check his work, and help him locate the correct answers for any items that he has wrong or omitted.

# II. Skills Practice

Have S. close his book before doing these exercises.

### PRACTICE 1: Distinguishing the Sound /oo/

T: Which of these words has the vowel sound /oo/:

*huge, who?*   *boot, bugle?*   *mule, rule?*
*true, use?*   *argue, glue?*   *loot, cute?*

## PRACTICE 2: Number of Syllables and Stress

T: Listen to each word. Tell how many syllables it has and which syllable is stressed.

| | |
|---|---|
| *parade* | [2 syllables, second syllable is stressed] |
| *bugle* | [2, first one is stressed] |
| *salute* | [2, second one is stressed] |
| *concert* | [2, first one is stressed] |
| *picnic* | [2, first one is stressed] |
| *country* | [2, first one is stressed] |
| *computer* | [3, second one is stressed] |
| *Canada* | [3, first one is stressed] |

## PRACTICE 3: Compound Words

Write these words in a column: *fireworks, afternoon, daytime, landlord, roommate.* Ask S. to read each compound word and tell the two words it is made from. As he answers, write the two words next to the compound word.

## PRACTICE 4: Review of Beginning Blends

Write the blends *cl, fl, dr, tr, st, str,* and ask S. to read them. Then say each word below, and ask S. to tell which consonant blend it begins with.

| | | | |
|---|---|---|---|
| *star* | *true* | *club* | *stripe* |
| *flute* | *drum* | *state* | *flag* |

## PRACTICE 5: Changing *y* to *i* before *-es*

Write *family, country, utility, key, boy, holiday* in a column. Have S. read each word and tell what it would be with the ending *-s* or *-es.* Have him spell the word with the ending as you write it next to the root word. Review the rule that after a consonant, final *y* is changed to *i* before adding *-es.* But, *y* is not changed when it comes after a vowel.

# III. Writing

## CHECK HOMEWORK: Page 21

Check this page with S. Have him correct any errors. Note the type of errors, and plan reinforcement exercises for the next session.

## WRITING LESSON (In Notebook)

Have S. write the titles *Lesson 4* and *Words* and then number from 1 to 20 in two columns. After S. has finished the dictation, have him check his work by looking at the chart and story words.

**Words.** Help S. study these words: *goes, heart, honor, parade, salute.*

| | | | |
|---|---|---|---|
| 1. June | 6. salute | 11. July | 16. stripes |
| 2. blue | 7. true | 12. bugle | 17. parade |
| 3. flute | 8. flag | 13. maple | 18. honor |
| 4. rule | 9. drum | 14. lead | 19. heart |
| 5. rude | 10. stars | 15. goes | 20. holiday |

**Sentences.** Have S. write the title *Sentences.* Have him number each sentence as you dictate it.

1. You may fly the flag in the daytime.
2. A man removes his hat when the flag goes by.
3. Burn an old flag with care.
4. Most countries have rules for honoring the flag.
5. You can watch the fireworks at Lake Shore Park.

Have S. write the title *Study* and any words he missed in the word and sentence dictation.

**Writing a notice about a coming event.** Have S. choose a coming event, real or imaginary, that he might write about. Have him give the following information before he writes about it: name of event, date, place, time, price of admission (if any), any special information needed. List the items as S. gives them. Give S. a choice of the form his notice will take:

1. A community events listing like the ones in the Reading for Living on page 25. (Let him look these over to see the form to use.) Have him notice that these do not always use complete sentences.
2. A poster that could be put up on a bulletin board.
3. A news story written in complete sentences.

When S. has finished, check his work for content, correct spelling, and punctuation.

## PRACTICE: Page 26

Have S. read the directions for the first exercise and then do it. Check his answers. If he has any wrong, have him read the words in the line aloud.

Go over the directions for the second exercise with S. Marking stressed syllables was covered in Lessons 1 and 2, but in case S. doesn't remember what to do, check his work on the first item before he completes the others. When he has finished, check his work. If he marked any words incorrectly, have him read them aloud and listen for the stressed syllable.

In the third exercise, have S. read aloud the directions and the list of words. Tell S. to check off each word in the list as soon as he has written it after its meaning. When he has finished, check his work and have him correct any errors.

## HOMEWORK: Page 27

Go over the directions with S. Encourage him to read the story and newspaper section again at home and to practice writing any words he missed.

## CHECKING PROGRESS

This lesson will help you check your student's progress in hearing the new vowel sound /oo/ and his ability to distinguish it from the long sound /ū/ which is similar. If S. has difficulty in doing this, plan a reinforcement exercise as given in the next section.

S. should be developing an understanding of the meaning of stress in a word. If he is having a problem identifying the stressed syllable in a word, plan further practice. But, notice whether he has more difficulty in oral or written exercises. If he can do the written exercises fairly well, but has trouble with the oral ones in the Skills Practice section, it may simply be that it is hard for him to identify the stressed syllable by *number* when he can't see the word. If so, write out the Skill Practice exercises on stress for him in the same form as the written exercises in the skill book. On the other hand, if S. has trouble with the written exercises, it may help him to say the words aloud as he does the exercises, or to have you say the words, emphasizing the stressed syllable.

S. should understand what is meant by main topics and should be able to select the important facts related to a specific topic. He may have trouble remembering facts because he doesn't know how to relate them to a main idea. You can plan to use some supplementary material to help him develop that skill.

## MEETING INDIVIDUAL NEEDS

**Vowel sound /oo/.** Read the following sentences, and have S. tell which words have the sound /oo/.

1. It is not *cool* in *June* and *July*.
2. Use that *broom* to sweep the leaves by the swimming *pool*.
3. The little boy is eating his *food* with a *spoon*.
4. Will the roses *bloom soon*?
5. He will play his *flute* in the concert at *school*.

Read the following pairs of sentences, emphasizing the words in italics. Have S. tell which word has the sound /oo/ and which has the sound /ū/.

1. I heard the cat *mew*. I heard the cow *moo*.
2. The mud *oozed* between his toes.
   The boy *used* the mud to make a fort.
3. Listen to the pigeon *coo*.
   The actor heard his *cue*, so he went on the stage.
4. The baby kicked off his *bootie*.
   That horse is a real *beauty*!
5. *Who* is coming? *Hugh* is coming.

In *Focus on Phonics-4*, you may use Practices 4A-4B. They cover words having the sound /oo/ written with *u-e* and *ue*.

**Listening for the stressed syllable.** Say the following words. You and S. should tap out the stressed and unstressed syllables together. You may need to exaggerate the stressed syllable. It may help if you mark the pattern of the stressed and unstressed syllables, as below. Help S. to see that in two-syllable words with an ending, the stress is on the root word.

| spéakĕr | swímmĭng | wántĕd |
|---------|----------|--------|
| marcher | reading  | weekly |

Say each group of words below. Mark the pattern of the stressed and unstressed syllables first. You and S. should tap out the stressed and unstressed syllables as you say the words. Help S. to see that in three-syllable words, the stress is usually on the first or second syllable; only a few words have the stress on the third syllable.

| présidĕnt | Octŏbĕr    | seventéen |
|-----------|------------|-----------|
| Canada    | reunion    | overcome  |
| relative  | continue   | cigarette |
| yesterday | computer   |           |
| syllable  | together   |           |
| Mexico    | remember   |           |
| handicap  | example    |           |
| minister  | apartment  |           |
| possible  | department |           |
| officer   | injustice  |           |

**Remembering details.** Select a short article that you can read aloud to S. on a topic that he is interested in. Tell him to listen for the main idea and the important facts about the topic. Note how many of the truly important facts he is able to recall, but don't insist that he remember every minor detail. Do this from time to time with other short selections.

Good sources of short, easy articles are the inside pages of the easy newspaper *News for You*, or its monthly supplement *Addition*, and Books 2 and 3 of the In the Know series.

ew = oo

chew
ew = oo

| | | |
|---|---|---|
| | grew | grew | grew |
| | crew | crew | crew |
| | threw | threw | threw |
| | Lewis | Lew′is | Lewis |
| | jewels | jew′ulz | jewels |
| | sewer | sew′er | sewer |

## The Family Jewels

| rich | cool | dirt | grow (grōw) | until (un til′) |
|---|---|---|---|---|
| poor | Luke | step | leaves (leavz) | leftover (left′ over) |
| | Judy (Joo′ dy) | | | |

Lewis Burns came from a poor family. He grew up with very little money. As a child, Lewis said to himself, "When I grow up, I will not be poor. When I grow up, I will have a fine car. My wife will wear jewels. We will have a fine home."

Lewis had this dream as he grew up. He went to school until his father died. Then Lewis had to grow up in a hurry. He quit school and went to work.

Lewis worked for the city on the sewers. He was on a work crew. The crew of workers cleaned the sewers. Dirt and leaves got into the sewers. The work crew used a machine to remove the dirt and leaves. The machine threw the dirt and leaves into a truck.

It was a dirty job. But Lewis went to work every day in clean clothes. The crew laughed at him. "Look at Lewis," they said. "He looks like a cool cat in the morning. But by evening he looks like a sewer rat!"

"That's OK," said Lewis. "I won't be a sewer rat forever."

When Lewis was 20, he met Judy. Judy's family wasn't rich. But they had more money than Lewis's family. Judy grew up with nice clothes and other things she wanted.

"I love Judy," Lewis said to himself. "But she won't want to marry a sewer rat. I must stop seeing Judy."

Judy had another view. She told her parents, "Lewis may be poor, but he is a fine man. He loves me, and I love him. If we both work hard, we will have enough money to marry."

Judy and Lewis got married. Judy worked until Lewis Jr. was born. Then two years later, baby Luke was born.

A few years passed. Lewis still worked on the city crew. The children grew bigger. Judy stayed at home with them.

Judy looked for ways to save money. She never threw anything away. She never threw food away. She used leftovers for another meal. She never threw old clothes away. She used them to make clothes for Lewis Jr. and Luke.

The Burns family was getting by. They had enough money to live on, but they didn't own their home. They didn't have a car. They had enough food to eat, but Judy didn't wear fine jewels. Sometimes Lewis remembered his old dream.

One hot day, as Lewis came up the steps, he heard Luke crying. Judy was giving dinner to the children. "Chew your meat well," she said to Luke. "Chew your meat, or you will choke on it."

"I don't like this meat," said the boy.

"I worked hard to buy that meat, so eat it!" Lewis yelled. "And do what your mother says! Chew it well!" After he yelled at his son, Lewis felt bad. But he didn't say anything until dinner was over.

After dinner, the family sat on the steps. It was cooler there. They sat on the steps and had a cool drink. They watched the traffic go by.

"You don't have much of a life in this hot city," Lewis said to Judy. "I wanted to give you a fine home and jewels. But I haven't. We are nearly as poor as my parents were. And we will never be rich."

Judy hugged her husband and kissed him. Then she hugged her two boys. "These are my jewels, Lewis," she said. "You and the boys are my jewels. I am a happy wife and mother. We are rich, not poor."

## Story Checkup

**Answer each question with one or two sentences.**

1. What was Lewis's dream? _____

2. In what ways did Judy save money? _____

3. Do you agree with Judy that she and Lewis are rich? _____

---

trash
pickup (pick′ up)
public (pub′ lic)
report (rē port′)
emergency (ē mer′ jen sy)
information (in for mā′ shun)

Lewis Burns worked for the public works department in his city. A city has many offices and departments. They give services to people who live in the city.

Sometimes you need to phone one of these offices for help or information. You can look up the number in the telephone directory. Look under the name of your city.

Here is the listing for some of the city offices where Lewis lived. Read the questions below, and look up the telephone numbers in the listing.

### OAK PARK—CITY OF
**EMERGENCY NUMBERS**

| | |
|---|---|
| Fire | 911 |
| Police | 911 |

CITY MUSIC CENTER
  220 Main Street
  Box Office ........ 363-7800
COURTS—Public Office Building
  Information ........ 342-4641
  Traffic Court ........ 342-4655
FIRE DEPARTMENT
  To Report a Fire ........ 911
HUMAN RIGHTS OFFICE
  Public Office Building ........ 342-6072
JAIL—595 Oak Street ........ 325-6112
PARKS DEPARTMENT
  319 Hoover Street
  Information ........ 342-4051
  Sullivan Zoo
    2763 Maple Drive ........ 342-7447
POLICE DEPARTMENT
  595 Oak Street
  Emergency ........ 911
  Other Police Business
    Bicycle Licenses ........ 325-6151
    Missing Persons ........ 325-7087
PUBLIC WORKS DEPARTMENT
  2861 Mason Street
  Ice & Snow ........ 342-6650
  Sewers & Street Cleaning ........ 342-6651
  Street Repair ........ 342-6652
  Trash Pickup ........ 342-6653
SCHOOLS
  Oak Park Public Schools,
  Main Office
    426 Freedom Circle ........ 342-6014

**What number do you phone—**

| | | |
|---|---|---|
| 911 | 1. to report a fire? | |
| 911 | 2. to get the police in an emergency? | |
| 342-4051 | 3. to ask when the public swimming pools are open? | |
| 342-6653 | 4. to ask when the trash is picked up? | |
| 325-7087 | 5. to report a missing person? | |
| 363-7800 | 6. to ask what time a concert starts? | |
| 342-6014 | 7. to get information on night classes? | |
| 342-6651 | 8. to get someone to clean your sewers? | |
| 342-4641 | 9. to get information on the city courts? | |
| 342-6653 | 10. to report that your trash was not picked up? | |

## Practice

opposite (op' u zit)

above (u buv')

**Say the words. Circle the words with the sound _oo_ as in _chew_, _food_, and _June_.**

1. (grew)   grow   (crew)   cure
2. (Lewis)   lunch   (June)   lake
3. throw   (true)   third   (threw)
4. (Judy)   music   (rude)   study
5. (jewel)   union   (Luke)   until

**In each line, circle the word that means the opposite of the first word.**

Example:

| fast | quick | (slow) | first |
|---|---|---|---|
| 1. poor | sad | happy | (rich) |
| 2. dirty | funny | (clean) | pretty |
| 3. hot | (cold) | high | sick |
| 4. big | huge | (little) | short |
| 5. young | nice | rude | (old) |
| 6. continue | say | (stop) | question |

**Say each word. Put the stress mark after the syllable that is stressed.**

1. public — pub' lic
2. report — re port'
3. emergency — e mer' gen cy
4. dirty — dirt' y
5. sewers — sew' ers
6. information — in for ma' tion
7. until — un til'
8. jewels — jew' els

**Drop the ending from each word. Write the root word.**

1. dirty — _dirt_
2. meeting — _meet_
3. speaker — _speak_
4. cooler — _cool_
5. bigger — _big_
6. nearly — _near_
7. remembered — _remember_
8. died — _die_
9. married — _marry_
10. hugged — _hug_
11. kissed — _kiss_
12. getting — _get_
13. giving — _give_
14. missing — _miss_

**Fill in each blank with one of the words in the list above.**

1. Lewis stayed in school _until_ his father died.
2. Then Lewis got a job with the _public_ works department.
3. Dirt and leaves got in the _sewers_.
4. Cleaning the sewers was a _dirty_ job.
5. To Judy, her husband and children are her _jewels_.
6. What number do you phone to get the police in an _emergency_?
7. Do you phone the same number to _report_ a fire?
8. Where can you get _information_ on night classes in the city?

**Answer each question below with the name of a city department.**

Where do you phone—

1. to report that a building is burning? _The fire department_
2. to report that something was stolen from you? _The police department_
3. to find out when city swimming pools will open? _The parks department_

## OBJECTIVES

To help your student:

- recognize that in some words *ew* stands for the sound /oo/, as in *chew*.
- recognize that *ew* usually stands for /oo/ when preceded by *j, ch, l,* or *r*, as in *jewel, chew, Lewis,* and *grew*.
- read words in which *ew* stands for the sound /oo/.
- distinguish between the long sound /ū/ as in *music* and the sound /oo/ as in *food*.
- recognize the number of syllables in a word and which syllable is stressed.
- review the beginning consonant blends *cr, gr, thr*.
- review the ending *-y*.
- recognize word opposites.
- review alphabetizing words to the third letter.
- understand figurative language in the story.
- understand the characters in the story.
- relate the story to own experiences and values.
- locate phone numbers in a listing of city offices, determining the appropriate city department for a particular problem and finding it in an alphabetical list.
- write telephone numbers.
- write words and sentences from dictation, using commas and quotation marks correctly in sentences that give direct quotes.

## INTRODUCTION

T: You have learned that the letters *ew* stand for the sound /ū/, as in *few*. In today's lesson, you will find that *ew* also stands for the sound /oo/.

# I. Reading

## CHART: Page 28

**Title and key words.** Have S. read the title *Lesson 5*.

T: Look at the letters in the top right-hand corner. What are they? [S: *ew.*] What sound do they equal? [S: /oo/.]

T: Read the key word. [S: chew.] What letters equal the sound /oo/ in *chew*? [S: *ew.*] What consonant sound do you hear before the vowel sound? [S: /ch/.] What letters stand for the sound /ch/? [S: *ch.*]

## Lines 1-6

T: Read the other words in the chart. In all of these words, the letters *ew* stand for the sound /oo/. Notice what consonant comes before the sound /oo/.

After S. has studied the chart silently, have him read the words aloud, going down the last column of the chart. Then ask these questions:

1. What is the vowel sound in each of these words? [S: /oo/.] How is it written? [S: *ew.*]
2. What consonant comes before the sound /oo/ in *grew, crew, threw*? [S: *r.*] What consonant comes before /oo/ in *jewel*? [S: *j.*] In *Lewis*? [S: *l.*] In *sewer*? [S: *s.*]

T: Usually, the letters *ew* stand for /oo/ when they come after the letters *ch, j, l,* or *r*. The letters *l* and *r* are often in a consonant blend like the *gr* before *ew* in *grew*.

**Note:** If S. happens to know the word *sew* and asks about it, you can explain that it is an exception. Otherwise, don't bring it up at this point; it will be introduced later in the book. There are few other words with *s + ew*.

**Review.** Have S. read each word aloud again, including the key word. Cover the pictures, and go down the last column of the chart. Ask S. to tell which words have more than one syllable and which syllable is stressed.

## STORY: Pages 29-30 (The Family Jewels)

Have S. read the story title and new words. Have him tell which words have the sound /oo/ and how it is written. Call attention to the compound word *leftover* and how many syllables it has. Note that in the respelling, it is divided between the two words instead of between syllables. Also, call attention to the number of syllables in *until* and which one is stressed.

**Directed silent reading**

T: Read the whole story to yourself. Find out what is meant in this story by *the family jewels* and the main things that happened in the story. Tell whether you think it is a true story or a made-up one.

After S. has read the story silently, have him answer the questions you asked. Ask him if he liked the story and his reasons for liking or not liking it.

**Reading between the lines.** Discuss these questions.

1. What is meant by the expressions *cool cat* and *sewer rat*? (See paragraph 4.)
2. What was Lewis's idea of being rich?
3. Why did Lewis think he should stop seeing Judy?
4. What is meant by the expression *view* in the sentence "Judy had another view"? What was Judy's other view and why did she have it?
5. What did Judy mean when she said, "We are rich, not poor"?
6. From what is told in the story, how would you describe the kind of person Lewis was? How would you describe Judy?
7. Even though this is a made-up story, does it seem true-to-life? Have you ever known a family like this one?

## STORY CHECKUP: Page 30

Have S. read the title and directions. Then have him write the answers. Emphasize that he should write complete sentences. When he has finished, have him read aloud each question and his answer. If the answers to the first two questions are incorrect or incomplete, have him scan the story to find the paragraph that gives the correct answer. The answer to the last question will be his own opinion, but he should give reasons for his answer.

## READING FOR LIVING: Page 31

Have S. read the title and new words first silently and then aloud. Have him tell the number of syllables in each word and which syllable is stressed.

Ask S. to read the three paragraphs to find out what kind of listing is given in the block on the right. Then have S. look over the listings of phone numbers as you discuss these points:

1. What is the name of the city?
2. What is the name of the department where Lewis worked? Have S. find the heading *Public Works Department*. Then have him scan the listings under this heading to find where Lewis worked [Sewers & Street Cleaning].
3. What kinds of numbers are given at the top of the listings? [Emergency numbers for fire and police.] Why do you think they are put there?
4. Have S. identify and read aloud the names of the main city departments that are shown as main headings. [They are the ones in all capital letters.] Explain the meaning of any he doesn't understand.
5. Have S. notice that the main headings are in alphabetical order. Then read aloud a heading and have S. point to it. Note whether or not he makes use of the alphabetical arrangement in locating the heading. Read another heading, and have him tell the first two letters it begins with before he tries to locate it in the listings. Do this for a few more headings.

Have S. read the line *What number do you phone* above the questions. Then have him answer the questions. For the first four, have him tell the name of the city department he thinks he should look under *before* he tries to find it in the listings. If you think he is ready, let him complete the exercise by himself. If not, continue in the same way.

When S. has finished, check his work, and help him find the correct answer for any items he has wrong. Also, help him figure out if he selected the wrong city office for a particular problem or if he copied the phone number incorrectly.

**Note:** S. may find it helpful to use a slip of colored paper or other marker to keep his place as he copies the phone numbers in this exercise.

You may want to show S. a similar listing for city offices in your local telephone directory.

## II. Skills Practice

Have S. close his book before doing these exercises.

### PRACTICE 1: Distinguishing the Sound /oo/

T: Which of these words has the vowel sound /oo/:

| | | |
|---|---|---|
| *Hugh, chew?* | *Lewis, Huron?* | *view, grew?* |
| *cube, crew?* | *Judy, beauty?* | *mule, jewel?* |

### PRACTICE 2: Beginning Blends *cr, gr, thr*

Write *crew, grew, threw*. Have S. read each word and tell what consonant blend it begins with. As he answers, underline *cr, gr, thr*.

T: I will say two words that both begin with the same blend. Tell me which of these blends it is.

| | | |
|---|---|---|
| *green, grow* | *crop, cry* | *grass, great* |
| *throw, three* | *throat, thread* | *cry, crow* |

### PRACTICE 3: Adjective Ending *-y*

Write *dirty, wavy, starry*. Have S. read each word, tell what the root word is, and tell how to spell the root word. As he answers, write *dirt, wave, star*. Review dropping final silent *e* before *-y*. Explain that when a one-syllable word ends in *ar* pronounced /ar/, the letter *r* is doubled before an ending that begins with a vowel.

Write the sentences below. Have S. fill in one of the words ending with *-y* in each blank and then read the sentences aloud.

1. It was a _____ night.
2. The child's hands were _____.
3. She has _____ hair.

### PRACTICE 4: Recognizing Opposites

Write the words *old* and *young*, and have S. read them. Explain that these words are opposite in meaning. Then say each word below, and ask S. to tell a word that means the opposite.

| | | |
|---|---|---|
| *first* [last] | *slow* [fast] | *yes* [no] |
| *dark* [light] | *hot* [cold] | *sick* [well] |

### PRACTICE 5: Alphabetical Order

Write each of these names on a separate card. Mix up the cards, and give them to S. Tell him that these are the names of people, with the last name first and then the first name, the same way names are listed in the phone book. Ask him to arrange the last names in alphabetical order.

| | |
|---|---|
| *Arthur, Carl* | *Jones, Bob* |
| *Black, Hugo* | *Keller, Judy* |
| *Burns, Lewis* | *Little, Rich* |
| *Fisher, Jimmy* | *Luther, David* |
| *Hoover, Jane* | *Martin, Mary* |
| *Hunter, Kim* | *Mason, Pam* |

Tell S. to say each letter of the alphabet and look to see if there is one or more names beginning with that letter. If there is one name or none, he should go on to the next letter. If there are two or more names that start with the same letter, he should look at the second letter. If the second letter is the same, he should look at the third letter. Let S. work on his own as much as possible, but give help when necessary.

## III. Writing

### CHECK HOMEWORK: Page 27

Check this page with S. If he has any incorrect answers in the first exercise, have him find the correct answer in the story. In the second exercise, have him write the word correctly for any answer that is not correct. In the third exercise, check the rules for honoring the flag that S. wrote for correct spelling, capitalization, and punctuation.

### WRITING LESSON (In Notebook)

Have S. write the titles *Lesson 5* and *Words* and then number from 1 to 20 in two columns. After he has finished the dictation, have him check his work by looking at the chart and story words.

**Words.** Have S. study *poor, cool, Judy, leaves, Luke.*

| | | | |
|---|---|---|---|
| 1. chew | 6. Lewis | 11. poor | 16. leaves |
| 2. grew | 7. sewer | 12. rich | 17. until |
| 3. threw | 8. Judy | 13. step | 18. leftover |
| 4. crew | 9. Luke | 14. grow | 19. trash |
| 5. jewel | 10. cool | 15. dirt | 20. pickup |

**Sentences.** Have S. write the title *Sentences.* Have him number each sentence as you dictate it. Before dictating the sentences, review writing direct quotations. Write these sentences, leaving out the commas and quotation marks. Have S. tell where to put them. Leave the sentences on the board as an example for S. to follow.

> *Lewis said, "I won't be a sewer rat forever."*
> *"I love Judy," Lewis said.*

1. "Look at Lewis," they said.
2. Luke said, "I don't like this meat."
3. The family sat on the steps and had a cool drink.
4. "We will never be rich," said Lewis.
5. "You and the boys are my jewels," said Judy.

Check what S. has written, and have him correct any errors, including those in punctuation and capitalization. Have S. write the title *Study* and any words he missed in the word and sentence dictation.

### PRACTICE: Page 32

Have S. read the directions for the first exercise and then do it. Check his answers. If he has any wrong, ask him to read the words in the line aloud and tell the vowel sound in each word.

Go over the directions and example for the second exercise with S. Then have him do the exercise. Check his work. Have him read the words aloud in any line where he has an error.

Have S. read the directions for the last exercise and then do it. Check his answers, and have him correct any errors. Have S. tell which root words were changed before the ending was added. Point out that a consonant following the vowel sound /oo/ as in *cool* is not doubled before an ending is added.

### HOMEWORK: Page 33

Go over the directions with S. Encourage him to read the story and Reading for Living section again at home and to practice writing any words he missed in the dictation.

### CHECKING PROGRESS

This lesson will help you check your student's progress in distinguishing the vowel sound /oo/. If he is having difficulty doing this, plan a reinforcement exercise as given in the next section. Continue to note progress in recognizing syllables and stress, consonant blends, and word endings.

### MEETING INDIVIDUAL NEEDS

**Vowel sound /oo/, written *ew*.** Make two slip strips for the word family *-ew*. Write *ew* on the folded card. On the narrow card that passes through the "window" in the folded card, write *ch, bl, fl, br, cr, dr, gr, thr, scr*. Have S. read the words formed by moving the strip up and down so that one blend appears in the "window" in front of *ew*.

In *Focus on Phonics-4*, you may use Practice 5. It covers words in which the sound /oo/ is written *ew*.

**Figurative language.** Read each of the following phrases, and have S. supply a word to complete it. Any word that makes a good comparison is acceptable.

| | |
|---|---|
| *as fast as . . .* | *as big as . . .* |
| *as dark as . . .* | *as old as . . .* |
| *as slow as . . .* | *as deep as . . .* |
| *as pretty as . . .* | *as sweet as . . .* |

**Alphabetical order.** Write the following names on separate cards. Use them in the same way as in Skills Practice 5 in this lesson.

| | |
|---|---|
| *North, Ed* | *Roberts, Ellen* |
| *Oliver, Ted* | *Romano, Tony* |
| *O'Toole, Kitty* | *Smith, John* |
| *Parks, Rosa* | *Turner, Fred* |
| *Porter, Steve* | *York, Carla* |
| *Price, Ray* | *Young, Kay* |

# Lesson 6

## ū or oo

## In some words, both ways are right.

| | | |
|---|---|---|
| | news | nūz<br>or<br>nooz |
| | Duke | Dūk<br>or<br>Dook |
| | student | stū′ dent<br>or<br>stoo′ dent |
| | tutor | tū′ ter<br>or<br>too′ ter |
| | Tuesday | Tūz′ day<br>or<br>Tooz′ day |
| | avenue | av′ e nū<br>or<br>av′ e noo |

34  Lesson 6

---

| math | knew (new) | newspaper (news′ paper) | believe (bē leve′ |
|---|---|---|---|
| coach | stupid (stū′ pid) | Newman (New′ mun) | interest (in′ ter est) |

## A New Start

Duke Miller was a student at Lake Avenue High School. When he got his report card on Tuesday, he felt very blue. "Another *F* in math!" he said to himself. "It's no use! I will never pass this stupid class! I'm going to quit school and get a job!"

Duke needed math to finish high school. He did well enough in his other classes. But math didn't interest him. He didn't understand it. And that made him feel stupid.

After school that day, Duke went to the office of the *Oak Park News*. He hoped to find a job in the press room. That was where the newspaper was printed. Duke asked to speak to Jack Newman, who ran the press room. Duke knew Mr. Newman from church camp. Mr. Newman was the sports coach there.

Duke told Mr. Newman that he was looking for a job. "But you're still a student, aren't you?" asked Mr. Newman.

"Yes, I'm a student. But I'm thinking of quitting school," Duke answered. "I'll be 16 next Tuesday. I'll be old enough to quit then."

"What's the matter with school?" asked Mr. Newman.

"It's the stupid math class!" Duke said. "I can't pass it no matter what I do. But I don't need math to run a printing press, do I?"

"Yes, Duke, I'm afraid you do," said Mr. Newman. "Anyway, 16 is too young to work on newspaper presses. You had better finish school first."

"I can't stand it any more," Duke said. "Math makes me feel stupid."

As the sports coach at church camp, Mr. Newman had spent a lot of time with Duke. He knew that Duke was not stupid. He believed that Duke just needed some help. "What you need is a tutor in math," he told Duke.

**35**

---

## Reading for Living

calendar (cal′ en der)
January (Jan′ ū ār y)
Wednesday (Wenz′ day)
birthday (birth′ day)

### JANUARY, 1997

| Sunday | Monday | Tuesday | Wednesday | Thursday | Friday | Saturday |
|---|---|---|---|---|---|---|
| | | | 1 New Year's Day | 2 | 3 | 4 |
| 5 | 6 | 7 | 8 | 9 | 10 | 11 |
| 12 | 13 | 14 | 15 | 16 | 17 | 18 |
| 19 | 20 Birthday of Martin Luther King Jr. | 21 | 22 | 23 | 24 | 25 |
| 26 | 27 | 28 | 29 | 30 | 31 | |

**Look at this calendar for January, 1997, and answer these questions.**

1. What holiday is on the first Wednesday of January, 1997?
   New Year's Day

2. Is New Year's Day on Wednesday every year?   No

3. Martin Luther King Jr. was born on January 15. But the holiday that honors his birthday comes on the third Monday in January. What is the date in 1997? January 20

4. Mr. Newman started tutoring Duke the second week in January.
   Duke was tutored every Tuesday and Thursday. Find the dates on the calendar.

   January 7          January 21
   January 9          January 23
   January 14         January 28
   January 16         January 30

5. Duke baby-sat for the Newmans every Saturday morning in January.
   On what dates in January did he work for them? Find the dates on the calendar.

   January 4          January 18
   January 11         January 25

---

"My family can't afford a tutor," said Duke.

Mr. Newman said, "I'll be your tutor. You can pay me by babysitting with my five-year-old son on Saturday mornings. My wife and I both work then."

Duke began going to Mr. Newman's home on Tuesday and Thursday evenings for his math lessons. The Newmans lived on Second Avenue, not far from Duke's home on Fourth Avenue.

Mr. Newman never made Duke feel stupid. He knew that Duke was interested in sports. So he asked Duke many questions on sports. Duke had to use math to find the answers. At last, Duke began to think that math was interesting. And he began to understand it.

Duke started doing his math lessons at school, too. By the end of the year, he was passing math. He went to his tutor with his report card. "I have some great news for you, Coach!" said Duke. "I passed! I got a C in math! See what you did for me!"

"You did most of it yourself," Mr. Newman said. "I just believed in you."

Duke smiled. "And thanks to you, I believe in myself, too."

### Story Checkup

**Write the story in a few sentences. Tell the main ideas.**

_____

_____

_____

_____

_____

_____

_____

_____

_____

_____

**Put *un-* at the beginning of each word to make another word. Write the word you make.**

**Example:** furnished ___unfurnished___

1. happy ___unhappy___
2. interesting ___uninteresting___
3. safe ___unsafe___
4. true ___untrue___
5. afraid ___unafraid___

**Fill in each blank with one of the words that starts with *un-*.**

1. Math was ___uninteresting___ to Duke.
2. Duke was ___unhappy___ in school.
3. That is an interesting story, but it is ___untrue___.
4. My nephew is ___unafraid___ of the big waves.
5. It is ___unsafe___ to be in the park at night.

**Drop the ending from each word. Write the root word.**

1. quitting ___quit___
2. needed ___need___
3. dirty ___dirt___
4. classes ___class___
5. passing ___pass___
6. countries ___country___
7. interested ___interest___
8. placing ___place___
9. believed ___believe___
10. studies ___study___

---

**Practice**

contraction (con trac' shun)

**Put together a word from List 1 and a word from List 2 to make a new word. Write the new word.**

| List 1 | List 2 | New Word |
|--------|--------|----------|
| 1. news | works | newspaper |
| 2. left | father | leftover |
| 3. fire | paper | fireworks |
| 4. after | over | afternoon |
| 5. air | ship | airplane |
| 6. room | noon | roommate |
| 7. grand | ever | grandfather |
| 8. every | plane | everywhere |
| 9. space | where | spaceship |
| 10. for | mate | forever |

**Underline the contraction in each sentence. Write the two words from which the contraction is made.**

**Example:** Math <u>didn't</u> interest Duke.   did   not

1. Aren't you still a student?   are   not
2. What's the matter with school?   what   is
3. I haven't passed a math test yet.   have   not
4. I don't need math to run a press.   do   not
5. I'll be your tutor.   I   will
6. My family can't afford a tutor.   can   not

## OBJECTIVES

To help your student:

- recognize that in some words, the vowel sound (spelled *u*, *u-e*, *ue*, *ew*) may be pronounced either /oo/ or /ū/, as in *news* and *student*.
- read words in which the vowel sound may be pronounced either /oo/ or /ū/, giving his own pronunciation.
- recognize that there is more than one correct way to pronounce some words.
- recognize the new compound words *newspaper*, *birthday*, and review other compound words.
- review contractions.
- add the prefix *un-* to root words to make new words.
- recognize cause and effect.
- recognize figurative language in the story.
- understand the feelings of the characters.
- relate the story to own experience and values.
- read a calendar for one month.
- recognize all the names of the days of the week.
- write a short summary of a story.
- write dates and the names of the days of the week.
- write words and sentences from dictation.

## INTRODUCTION

T: You have been studying the two vowel sounds /ū/ and /oo/. You have found that these sounds are much alike and that sometimes the same letters are used to stand for both sounds. In today's lesson, you will read some words in which it is correct to say either /oo/ or /ū/. The way you pronounce the vowel sound will probably depend on what part of the country you come from. For some words, the dictionary says either way is right.

# I. Reading

## CHART: Page 34

**Title and headings.** Have S. read *Lesson 6*. Then have him read the headings at the top of the chart, first silently and then aloud.

### Lines 1-6

T: Here are six words in which the vowel sound may be pronounced either /ū/ or /oo/. Read each word first to yourself and then aloud. Pronounce the word the way you usually say it. Then see if you can tell whether you are saying /ū/ or /oo/ in the word.

Have S. read each word aloud and listen for the vowel sound, /ū/ or /oo/. If he can't tell which way he is saying the vowel sound, tell him the way you think he is saying it. Have

S. circle his own pronunciation in the third column of the chart, where each word is respelled two ways.

**Note:** If your pronunciation is different from your student's, you may want to mention it, but be sure to emphasize that both ways are correct, and he should not change his pronunciation to match yours.

Have S. read the words again, going down the last column. Call attention to the way the vowel sound /oo/ or /ū/ is written in each word, the number of syllables, and which syllable is stressed.

**Review.** Have S. read the heading and read the words aloud a third time, going down the last column.

**Note:** After *d*, *t*, or *n*, the letters *u*, *u-e*, *ue*, *ew* may usually be pronounced either /ū/ or /oo/. There are some exceptions, like *continue*, that may be pronounced only one way. Do not explain any of this to S., however.

## STORY: Pages 35-36 (A New Start)

Have S. read the story title and new words. Call attention to the sound /ū/ or /oo/ and how it is written in *knew*, *stupid*, *newspaper*, *Newman*. The sound has not been respelled both ways. S. should pronounce it in the way that is natural for him. Also, call attention to the compound word *newspaper*. Mention that *interest* may be pronounced with either three syllables or two.

**Directed silent reading.** Ask S. to read the whole story to himself to find out what problem Duke had and how it was solved. After S. has finished reading, have him give a short summary.

Discuss the summary with S. If he didn't include the main points, ask questions to elicit them, as below:

1. Why did Duke want to quit school?
2. Where did he go to look for a job?
3. Why didn't Mr. Newman give him a job on the newspaper?
4. What suggestion did Mr. Newman make to help Duke?
5. In what ways did Mr. Newman help Duke?
6. How did Duke repay Mr. Newman for his help?
7. Was Mr. Newman's plan successful? Why?

**Reading between the lines.** Discuss these questions.

1. Do you think "A New Start" is a good title for this story? Why or why not? What other title can you think of for the story?
2. Do you think that quitting school would have been the right answer to Duke's problem? Why or why not?
3. Why do you think Mr. Newman was able to help Duke?
4. What does the expression *felt blue* mean?
5. What do you think Duke really meant when he referred to his math class as "that stupid math class"?
6. How would you describe Duke? Tell the reasons you would describe him that way.
7. Tell how you would describe Mr. Newman and why.

**Oral reading.** Have S. read the part of one character while you read the other. Encourage him to read with expression in the way he thinks the person would speak. Discuss the punctuation, and help S. observe it as an aid to reading clearly and with expression. Then reverse roles and read the story again.

### STORY CHECKUP: Page 36

Have S. read the directions and then write the short summary. He can look back at the story to find out how to spell words. Check what he has written for content, spelling, and punctuation.

### READING FOR LIVING: Page 37

**Note:** You may skip any of the discussion below that would be too simple for your student.

Have S. read the title and new words. Explain that this is a calendar for a certain month. Ask him to look at the heading of the calendar and tell what month and year it is for.

Call attention to the columns headed by the names of the days of the week. Have S. read the days of the week aloud. Ask how many days are in a week.

Call attention to the rows going down the calendar, and explain that they show the number of weeks in the month. Ask how many are shown for this month [five]. Explain that, when we refer to a certain week in the month, we usually refer to it as the *first week, second week*, and so on. Have S. point to each week and tell which week it is.

Call attention to the holidays marked on the calendar, and have S. read their names aloud.

T: How many days are in the month shown here? [S: 31.] Does every month have 31 days? [S: No.] So the calendar for every month does not look the same. On what day of the week does the month shown here start? [S: Wednesday.] On what day of the week does it end? [S: Friday.] On what day of the week will February, 1986, start? [S: Saturday.]

**Note:** You may want to show S. a calendar for January and February in a year other than 1986 to show that these months do not have the same number of days and that a month does not start on the same day of the week every year. But do not go into a lengthy discussion. There will be more about a full year's calendar in Lesson 13.

Ask S. to read the directions, and have him answer as many of the questions as he can by himself. Check his work. Discuss any items he omitted or answered incorrectly. Have him write the correct answers.

| | | |
|---|---|---|
| blue, chew | June, rule | beauty, pupil |
| true, glue | music, bugle | *new, stew |
| view, nephew | room, noon | *due, duty |
| cūte, use ○◌ | fuel, argue | *tutor, tune |

### PRACTICE 2: Prefix *un-*

Write *unfurnished*. Have S. read it and tell what the root word, ending, and prefix are.

T: What does the prefix *un-* usually mean? [S: Not.] We can put the prefix *un-* in front of many root words. Usually, *un-* will give the word an opposite meaning.

Write these words in a column: *able, hurt, broken, eaten, tied, covered, finished, named.* Have S. read each word and then tell what it would be with the prefix *un-*. Write the new word with *un-* next to the root word. Have S. use a few of the words in oral sentences.

### PRACTICE 3: Contractions of *not* and *will*

Write these contractions: *didn't, aren't, haven't, don't, can't.* Point out that they are all contractions of the word *not.* Have S. read each contraction and tell the two words it is made from.

T: Here are three contractions that you have not had, but I am sure you can read them because you know the two words from which each one is made.

Write *isn't, hasn't, doesn't.* Have S. read each one and tell the two words it is made from.

Follow the same procedure for contractions made with *will.* Have S. read those he knows: *I'll* and *we'll.* Then write these new ones: *she'll, he'll, you'll, they'll.* Have S. read each one and tell the two words it is made from.

### PRACTICE 4: Number of Syllables and Stress

Read each word below. Have S. tell how many syllables it has and which syllable is stressed. (All have the stress on the first syllable except *begin, believe,* and *contraction.*)

| | | | | | |
|---|---|---|---|---|---|
| begin | [2] | birthday | [2] | contraction | [3] |
| avenue | [3] | calendar | [3] | Saturday | [3] |
| January | [4] | Tuesday | [2] | newspaper | [3] |
| believe | [2] | question | [2] | Wednesday | [2] |

**Note:** Have S. give the number of syllables the way the word is pronounced, not the way it is written. For example, only two syllables are pronounced in *Wednesday.*

## II. Skills Practice

### PRACTICE 1: Distinguishing Sounds /oo/ and /ū/

Read each pair of words below, and have S. tell whether both of them have the vowel sound /oo/ or /ū/. Omit the starred (*) items in the last column if you and S. did not pronounce today's chart words the same way.

## III. Writing

### CHECK HOMEWORK: Page 33

Check this page with S. Have him correct any errors. In correcting the second exercise, have S. look back at the story to find correct answers if he had any wrong.

## WRITING LESSON (In Notebook)

Have S. write the titles *Lesson 6* and *Words* and number from 1 to 20 in two columns. After the dictation, have him check his work against the new words in the lesson.

**Words.** Help S. study *knew, January, Wednesday, calendar, believe.* In *believe,* review the rule that *i* comes before *e* when the two letters are together in a syllable. When you dictate *knew,* give a sentence.

| | | |
|---|---|---|
| 1. news | 8. stupid | 15. Wednesday |
| 2. newspaper | 9. Tuesday | 16. calendar |
| 3. Newman | 10. avenue | 17. math |
| 4. knew | 11. believe | 18. coach |
| 5. Duke | 12. interest | 19. begin |
| 6. tutor | 13. birthday | 20. Thursday |
| 7. student | 14. January | |

**Sentences.** Have S. write the title *Sentences.* Have him number each sentence as you dictate it.

1. Duke Miller was a student at Lake Avenue High School.
2. Mr. Newman ran the press room of the newspaper.
3. Duke went to Mr. Newman's home on Tuesday and Thursday evenings.
4. "I have some great news!" said Duke.
5. Mr. Newman said, "I just believed in you."

Check what S. has written. Have him correct any errors, including those in punctuation and capitalization. (In sentence 4, a comma would be acceptable after *news* instead of an exclamation point.)

**Days of the week.** Have S. write the days of the week in order. Check his work. If he has any wrong, have him look back at the calendar and write them correctly.

**Dates.** Dictate the following dates for S. to write. Check his work, and have him correct any errors.

| | |
|---|---|
| January 15, 1986 | May 31, 1979 |
| January 1, 1987 | June 14, 1980 |
| March 30, 1985 | July 4, 1776 |
| April 3, 1988 | October 12, 1492 |

## PRACTICE: Page 38

Have S. read the directions for the first exercise and then do it. Be sure he understands that the second compound word should begin with *left,* the third should begin with *fire,* and so on. When S. has finished, have him read aloud the compound words he has written. If he has an error, help him correct it.

Go over the directions and example for the second exercise with S. Then have him do it. Have him read aloud each contraction and the two words it is made from. Have him correct any errors.

## HOMEWORK: Page 39

Go over the directions with S. Encourage him to read the charts and stories in the first six lessons again at home. Tell him that the next lesson will be a review of the sounds he has had so far in this book.

## CHECKING PROGRESS

The skills practices and written exercises in this lesson will help you check your student's progress in recognizing and understanding contractions, compound words, syllables, stress, and words with the prefix *un-.* These skills will help S. become more independent in word recognition, but it is important for him to have opportunities to apply these skills by reading new material.

You can write some sentences or a paragraph using words with sounds he has learned, but with a few new words that he can sound out. You may include a few new compound words and contractions that contain word parts he has already learned. Or, you can use a selection from a supplementary book on this level, provided it does not have too many words with sounds he has not learned. (The number of such words that is "too many" or "just right" depends on how much sight vocabulary S. has learned from sources other than his study of this series.) You can also choose ads and headlines in newspapers; circle items you think S. should be able to read.

## MEETING INDIVIDUAL NEEDS

**Vowel sounds /ū/ and /oo/.** Make flash cards for the chart words in Lessons 1-6, plus any other new words with the sounds /ū/ and /oo/. Make separate flash cards for /ū/ and /oo/, and put these on the table. Have S. read each word card and put it under the right vowel card. (S. should classify words that may be pronounced with either /ū/ or /oo/ according to his own pronunciation.)

In *Focus on Phonics-4,* you may use Practices 6A-6C. They cover two-syllable words with /ū/ or /oo/ spelled *u,* as well as the irregular spellings *o, ou, oe, u, ui* for the sound /oo/.

**Contractions.** Make flash cards for these contractions: *didn't, haven't, aren't, don't, can't, won't, you're, we're, we'll, I'll, it's, that's, what's, I'm, let's.* On the back of each card, write the two words the contraction is made from. On separate flash cards, write *not, are, will, is, am, us.*

Mix up the contraction cards. First, have S. read each contraction and tell the two words it is made from. Then, turn the cards over. Have S. read the two words and tell what contraction can be made from them. Next, lay the other word cards (*not, are,* etc.) across the table. Have S. put all of the contractions that contain part of one of the words under that word.

**Syllables and stress.** Use any of the suggestions given for earlier lessons in this manual.

# More Reading with ū and oo

| music<br>ū | cure<br>u–e | argue<br>ue | few<br>ew |
|---|---|---|---|
| food<br>oo | June<br>u–e | blue<br>ue | chew<br>ew |
| student<br>ū or oo | Duke<br>u–e | Tuesday<br>ue | news<br>ew |

---

| page (pāje) | wish | cancer (can´ ser) | headline (head´ line) |
|---|---|---|---|
| daily (dāi´ ly) | rate | winter (win´ ter) | president (prez´ i dent) |
| climb (clīm) | board | given (giv´ en) | company (cum´ pu ny) |
| group (groop) | rope | lion (lī´ un) | animal (an´ i mul) |

## Reading a Newspaper Story

A daily newspaper in a city has many pages. Most people do not have time to read every story. Here are some ideas for reading your daily newspaper quickly.

Look at the first page of the paper. It has the main news stories of the day. Each story has a headline. The headline is in large print. The bigger the headline, the bigger the news story. The headlines can help you find the stories that you want to read.

Each news story tells five things. They are the Five *W*'s. They are *who*, *what*, *where*, *when*, and *why*. Look at the news story on this page. You can see where each of the Five *W*'s is.

**Who**

**Why**

### Boy gets wish before he dies

**Dallas, June 22**—Pablo Lopez, a six-year-old boy, died today of cancer.

A few weeks before he died, he got his wish. His wish was to meet the President of the United States.

"My little boy had great courage," his father, Carlos Lopez, said. "He knew he had cancer. He wanted to live, but he was not afraid to die."

Last year, the little boy's right leg was removed to try to stop the cancer. But there was no cure for the kind of cancer he had.

Pablo told his father that he wanted to meet the President. His father made the boy's wish come true. The two of them went to Washington, D.C. There they met the President.

The President told Pablo, "Young man, you have great courage."

**Where**

**When**

**What**

Use these ideas to read the newspaper on the next two pages. First, look at the headlines quickly. Then, as you read each news story, keep the Five *W*'s in mind.

# Huron City Daily News

**HURON CITY, NEW YORK**

## Hearings open on utility rates

The Valley Utility Company is asking the State Board of Public Utilities to let it raise its rates. If the state board agrees, the price of heat and lights will go up 15 per cent in October. Public hearings on this question began at 2:30 yesterday afternoon at the State Office Building.

At the hearing, Arthur Newman, president of the utility company, spoke first. He said, "The costs of running a utility company are going up. We have to pay more to workers. We need to make costly repairs and to buy new computers and other machines. We cannot continue to give today's services at today's rates."

More than 20 men and women from Huron United Citizens came to protest. The leader of that group, June Lewis, said, "The cost of heating homes must not go up this winter. The state must protect poor people. It must protect older people who are living on Social Security. If utility rates go up, they will not be able to afford both heat and food this winter."

Mike Romano spoke for a group of business leaders. He said, "High utility rates may make some businesses leave Huron City. New businesses will not come here when they can get cheaper rates in other cities."

The hearings will continue Thursday afternoon at 2:30 and will be open to the public.

## Human fly rescued

**Hoover City**—The fire department rescued Mike O'Toole from high on the Union Building this morning. O'Toole, who says he is a human fly, was trying to climb the side of the building. The Union Building, with 40 floors, is the highest building in this city. O'Toole had tried to climb it a few months ago. At that time, police told him not to try again. But O'Toole refused to listen.

O'Toole began his climb today at 7 a.m., before offices in the building were open. By 9:45, O'Toole was near the thirty-third floor, where he got stuck. He was not able to go up any higher, and he refused to go back below.

Traffic was tied up on the avenue below as people stopped to watch. When O'Toole got stuck, the people were amused. "Is he a human fly, or is he just stupid?" they asked.

O'Toole had been stuck for 20 minutes when the fire department came to his rescue. Fire fighters got a heavy rope from their fire truck. They carried the rope up to the thirty-fourth floor. There, they opened a window above O'Toole and threw the rope to him. O'Toole was able to climb the rope and go in the window.

After the fire fighters rescued O'Toole, police arrested him. "You can't stop me forever," O'Toole argued. "I haven't given up. I'll be back soon."

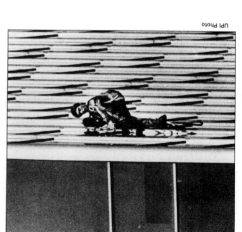

UPI Photo

## Will of music star made public today

The will of the late country music star Jimmy Lewis was made public today in Birmingham, Alabama.

Lewis left his shares in the Blue Star record company to his aunt Judy Jones, who raised him after his parents died. He left his home in Florida to his grandfather and grandmother, Mr. and Mrs. P.J. Lewis. He left $10,000 to each of his four nephews and nieces. To his cousin Luke Jones, who led Lewis's band, the young singer left his three sports cars.

Lewis died last year at the age of 27. A truck hit his car while he was driving to a Fourth of July concert in this city. Lewis grew up as a poor boy in Alabama. His music told of the hard life in the hills of Alabama and won him four gold records.

## Lions will help zoo

"This city needs a better zoo," said Hugh Baker at the noon meeting of the Lions Club yesterday. Baker is the public information officer for the Huron City Zoo.

Baker said that the zoo is too cool for the animals in the winter. And the big animals don't have enough room to move freely. Too many lions have to live together.

"The lions don't look happy," Baker said. That got a big laugh from the Lions Club.

Baker said that the water animals need a bigger pool, and the birds need more room to fly.

Every week, more than 5,000 people go to the zoo, Baker reported. "On Sundays," he said, "there are so many people at the zoo that it's hard to see the animals."

Baker added, "The children keep telling me that they like the zoo a lot. Both the children and their parents learn a lot from the animals."

Baker ended by saying, "We need to think of the future for both the children and the animals. We need a better zoo."

The Lions Club agreed to raise $1,000 to help the lions in the zoo.

## Tutors honored

Parents and teachers of Valley View High School had a dinner Tuesday evening to honor a group of 20 tutors. These men and women have given much of their time this past year to help students in math and reading.

Dr. Mary Luther, president of the school board, was the main speaker of the evening. She thanked the tutors for their service.

"You have each helped a student in reading or math," she told the tutors. "But better than that, you have helped a student believe in himself."

Dr. Luther said that many high school students did better on state math and reading tests this year. She added that fewer students quit school.

Tutors will be needed for the next school year in math, reading, and English as a second language. Those who want to become tutors may get application forms from the school board office at 1385 Main Street.

## Jewels stolen

The apartment of Mr. and Mrs. John Hoover of 1445 University Avenue was broken into late yesterday afternoon. Mrs. Hoover told police that a gold ring and her family jewels were missing from the bedroom. The Hoovers were not home at the time. But other people in the building remember seeing a man leaving the Hoovers' apartment. Police are looking for a young white man with red hair.

## Story Checkup

**After you have read "Human fly rescued," answer these questions. Write short answers.**

1. Who was rescued? _____

2. Where was he rescued? _____

3. When was he rescued? _____

4. What was he trying to do? _____

5. Why did he need to be rescued? _____

6. Who rescued him? _____

**After you have read "Tutors honored," answer these questions.**

1. Who was honored? _____

2. Who honored them? _____

3. When were they honored? _____

4. What was given to honor them? _____

## Practice

**Say each word. Put the stress mark after the syllable that is stressed.**

1. president    pres´ i dent
2. company    com´pa ny
3. daily    dai´ly
4. winter    win´ter
5. avenue    av´e nue
6. animal    an´i mal
7. believe    be lieve´

---

**Make up three questions that ask *who, what, where, when,* or *why* for each of these stories:**

**Jewels stolen**

1. _____

2. _____

3. _____

**Lions will help zoo**

1. _____

2. _____

3. _____

**Add *-er* and *-est* to each word to make new words. Write the new words.**

| | | |
|---|---|---|
| **Example:** poor | _poorer_ | _poorest_ |
| 1. rich | _richer_ | _richest_ |
| 2. cool | _cooler_ | _coolest_ |
| 3. dirty | _dirtier_ | _dirtiest_ |
| 4. safe | _safer_ | _safest_ |
| 5. few | _fewer_ | _fewest_ |
| 6. new | _newer_ | _newest_ |
| 7. young | _younger_ | _youngest_ |
| 8. funny | _funnier_ | _funniest_ |

## OBJECTIVES

To help your student:

- review the vowel sound /ū/ as in *music* and its most regular spellings: *u, u-e, ue, ew*.
- review the vowel sound /oo/ as in *food* and its most regular spellings: *oo, u-e, ue, ew*.
- review words in which the vowel sound may be pronounced either /ū/ or /oo/.
- apply phonics skills in reading new words with familiar sound-letter relationships.
- read short selections that review words introduced in Lessons 1-6, especially words with the sounds /ū/ and /oo/.
- read newspaper headlines and news stories to find out *who, what, where, when,* and *why*.
- develop further skill in alphabetizing words and in finding words in an alphabetical list.
- determine the number of syllables in a word and which syllable is stressed.
- review the endings *-er* and *-est*.
- recognize word opposites.
- recognize the new compound word *headline*.
- write words and sentences from dictation.

## INTRODUCTION

T: In today's lesson, you will review the sounds /ū/ and /oo/ and the main ways they are written. You will read some short newspaper stories. We'll also review some other things you studied in the first six lessons.

# I. Reading

## CHART: Page 40

Have S. read the titles *Lesson 7* and *More Reading with ū and oo*.

T: (Point to *music*.) Read this word. [S: music.] How many syllables are in *music*? [S: Two.] What is the vowel sound in the first syllable? [S: /ū/.] How is it written? [S: *u*.] Good. (Point to *ū*.) Say the sound again. [S: /ū/.]

Have S. read the other words in the first row and tell how the sound /ū/ is written in each of them.

T: (Point to *food*.) Read this word. [S: food.] What is the vowel sound? [S: /oo/.] How is it written? [S: *oo*.] Good. (Point to *oo*.) Say the sound again. [S: /oo/.]

Have S. read the other key words in the second row and tell how the sound /oo/ is written in each of them. Also, have him tell what letter comes before the sound /oo/. Remind

him of the rule that when *j, l, ch,* or *r* comes before one of these spellings, the sound is usually /oo/. Write *rule* as an example of *u-e*.

T: (Point to *student*.) Read this word. [S: student.] What is written below *student*? [S: /ū/ or *oo*.] Read the word again, and tell which way you pronounce the first vowel sound. (Have S. tell the way he pronounces the sound and which letters written under the word stand for the sound he says.)

Have S. read the other key words in the last row and tell how the sound /ū/ or /oo/ is written in each one.

## STORIES and STORY CHECKUP: Pages 41-44

T: The stories in this lesson are called news stories. They are like the ones you may read in your local newspaper. The first page is an introduction to reading the newspaper. It tells what to look for when you read news stories.

Have S. read the new words at the top of the page. Ask him to tell the number of syllables in each word and which syllable is stressed. Call attention to the compound word *headline*.

### Reading a Newspaper Story: Page 41

Have S. read the title and the first two paragraphs to himself. Then ask these questions:

1. What is usually on the first page of a newspaper?
2. Are the headlines all the same size? Which headlines are usually bigger in size?
3. How can the headlines help you?

Have S. read the third paragraph to find out the five things that a news story usually tells. Have him read the Five *W*'s aloud.

T: Look at the sample news story given here. What is the headline? [S: Boy gets wish before he dies.] This is a true story that was printed in many newspapers across the country. You will notice that the Five *W*'s are written in the margin with lines going to words in the story. That is to help you find the Five *W*'s in the story. First, read the whole story to yourself. Then see if you can tell the Five *W*'s.

After S. has read the story silently, have him tell *where, when, who, what happened,* and *why*—in that order. Point out that, in this story, the five *W*'s are all given in the first sentence. Discuss the purpose of the rest of the story. Have S. tell the other facts that are given in the story and why people might be interested in reading this particular story. Have S. read the whole news story aloud.

Ask S. to read the last paragraph on the page first silently and then aloud. (It introduces the mock newspaper on the next two pages.)

### Huron City Daily News: Pages 42-43

T: These two pages look like the front page of a newspaper. A newspaper page is printed in columns. There is white space to separate the columns. Look across the two pages of your book, and find out how many columns there are. [S: Four.]

T: Look at the top of these pages, and read the name of the newspaper. What is it? [S: Huron City Daily News.] Look under the name and read the line in smaller type. It tells where and when this newspaper was printed.

Have S. read the name of the city and state and the date of the newspaper. Point out to S. that this is not a real newspaper, and the stories in it are not true. They have been written and printed in the same way as a newspaper to give him practice in reading news stories. Then discuss the arrangement of the page. Here are some suggested questions:

1. How many news stories are on this newspaper page? Look across both pages of your book to find out. [S: Six.] How can you tell? [S: By the headlines.]
2. Which headline is in the largest print? Which headline is in the smallest print?
3. From reading the headlines, which story do you think would interest you the most? Why?
4. Which news story is the longest? [First one.] Which is next to the longest? [Second one.] Which is the shortest? [Last one.]
5. How many news stories are in the first two columns of this newspaper page? [Two.] Look at the first news story and read the headline to yourself.

**Story 1: Hearings open on utility rates.** Ask S. to read the first headline aloud. Have him point to the beginning and end of the news story. Ask S. to read the first paragraph to himself and find out which of the Five *W*'s are answered. Then have S. read the paragraph aloud, and discuss these points:

1. *What* issue is being discussed? [Whether the utility company can raise its rates.]
2. *Who* wants the rate increase? [The Valley Utility Company.]
3. *Who* will make the decision? [The State Board of Public Utilities.]
4. *What* began? [Public hearings on this question.]
5. *When* did the hearings begin? [Yesterday afternoon at 2:30.]
6. *Where* did the hearings take place? [At the State Office Building.]

**Note**: You may need to discuss what public hearings are and what *per cent* means. You can explain that public hearings give people a chance to express their views about some decision that a government agency is getting ready to make. *Per cent* means *for every one hundred.* Fifteen per cent means 15 out of every 100. The utility company wants to raise its rates 15 per cent. That means if your bill used to be $100, it will be $115 if the rates go up.

Ask S. to read the rest of this news story to himself and find out *who* spoke at the hearings and *what* they said. Then discuss these other points:

1. *Who* spoke in favor of the raise in utility rates? *Why* did he think the raise was necessary?
2. *Who* spoke against the raise? *Why* were they opposed?
3. Did the writer of this news story give his or her own opinion?
4. *What* will happen next and *when*?

**Story 2: Human fly rescued.** Have S. read this news story to himself to find the Five *W*'s. Then, without any discussion of the story, have him do the Story Checkup for this story on page 44.

**Story Checkup for "Human fly rescued": page 44**

T: This checkup is not part of the newspaper. But it will show you how carefully you read the news story. If you don't remember some of the facts, you may look back at the story.

Have S. read the directions for the first exercise and write the answers. Check his work, and have him correct any errors by looking back at the story.

**Story 3: Will of music star made public today.** Have S. look at the third column of the newspaper and read the first headline, silently and then aloud. Point to the figure $10,000 in the story, and explain that it is read as *ten thousand dollars.* Ask S. to read the story to himself and look for the Five *W*'s. When S. has finished reading, discuss these points:

1. Who is the main person the story is about? [Jimmy Lewis.] Who was Jimmy Lewis? [A country music star.] Was he living at the time of this news story? [No.]
2. What main event does this news story tell about? [Lewis's will was made public.] What main things does the story tell about the will? (Have S. look at the second paragraph and read what Jimmy Lewis left and to whom.)
3. When was the will made public? [Today.] What does the newspaper mean by *today*? [June 7, 1995.]
4. Does the news story tell *where* the will was made public? [Yes, in Birmingham, Alabama.]
5. What does the story tell that shows why a reader of this newspaper might be interested in reading about Jimmy Lewis's will? (Bring out these points: Jimmy Lewis was famous for his music. He had gone from poverty to riches. He had been killed in an accident on his way to Huron City.)

**Story 4: Lions will help zoo.** Ask S. to read the headline aloud. Have him point to the beginning and end of the news story. Point out the figures 5,000 and $1,000, and explain how these are read. Then ask S. to read the story to himself and look for the Five *W*'s. When S. has finished reading, discuss the Five *W*'s, and in this order:

1. Who is this news story mostly about? [Hugh Baker.] Who is he? [Public information officer for the Huron City Zoo.]
2. What did he do that was reported in this story? [He spoke to the Lions Club.] (You may need to explain that the Lions Club is a club for business and professional men; its purpose is to provide community services.)

3. Where did Baker speak? [At the noon meeting of the Lions Club. The story doesn't say where the meeting was.]
4. When did he speak? [Tuesday, June 3.]
5. Why did he speak? [To tell why the city needs a better zoo.]
6. What happened as a result of his speech? [The Lions Club agreed to raise $1,000 to help the zoo.]

Then, discuss these other points with S.:

1. Can a reader understand the headline without reading the story? What might a reader think the headline means? Why do you think the newspaper used a headline like this? (Explain that newspapers often use headlines that will catch the readers' attention.)
2. How does the news story show the exact words that Mr. Baker actually said? [There are quotation marks around them.] (Have S. find the quotes and read them aloud. Explain that these are called direct quotes and that a news writer has to be very careful that they are accurate.)
3. Does the news story tell anything else that Mr. Baker said that is not in direct quotes? Find those parts in the story, and read them aloud. (Explain that these sentences summarize some of the statements Mr. Baker made but are not in the exact words he said.)
4. Why do you think Baker's quote in paragraph 3 got a big laugh? (Have S. read this paragraph aloud.)
5. Does the writer of this news story give his or her own opinion?

**Story 5: Tutors honored.** Have S. read the news story to himself to find the Five *W*'s. Then, without any discussion of the story, have him do the Story Checkup for this story on page 44.

**Story Checkup for "Tutors honored": page 44.** Have S. read the directions for the second exercise and write the answers. Check his work, and have him correct any errors by looking back at the story.

**Story 6: Jewels stolen.** Have S. read this story to himself to find the Five *W*'s. After he has finished reading, have him tell *who* the story is about, *where* they live, *what* happened, *when*, and whether or not the story tells *why* it happened. Note that news stories don't always tell why something happened.

**Oral reading.** Have S. read aloud the story that he liked best. Note the following about his reading: fluency, expression, observation of punctuation marks, and recognition of words.

## READING FOR LIVING (Optional)

Reading the mock newspaper in this lesson serves as the Reading for Living, also. If time allows, you may want to review some of the Reading for Living selections in Lessons 1-6, asking questions that S. can answer orally that are different from those in the exercises. Or, you may want to give some practice in using the phone listings for your city government. If so, do not try to go over every city department. Select a few of the major ones that S. might have some reason to call.

You may want to leave these activities until the end of your lesson period. That will allow you to judge the time available. It will also give S. a change of pace if you now go directly to the Skills Practice exercises.

# II. Skills Practice

## PRACTICE 1: Distinguishing Sounds /ū/ and /oo/

Write *few* and *food*. Have S. read them and tell the vowel sound in each. Write $\bar{u}$ below *few* and *oo* below *food*.

T: I will say two words that have the same vowel sound. Tell me whether the vowel sound is /ū/ as in *few* or /oo/ as in *food*.

| | | |
|---|---|---|
| *tool, soon* | *cruel, jewel* | *argue, nephew* |
| *chew, shoe* | *blue, true* | *remove, salute* |
| *cube, use* | *union, united* | *menu, rescue* |

## PRACTICE 2: Recognizing Opposites

Write these words, and have S. read them: *new, poor, hard, winter, low, public, stupid.*

Say each of these words, and have S. read the word from your written list that means the opposite.

| | | | |
|---|---|---|---|
| *smart* | *easy* | *private* | *old* |
| *rich* | *high* | *summer* | |

## PRACTICE 3: Endings *-er* and *-est*

Write *rich, cool, safe, late, big, hot, happy, windy* in a column. Ask S. to tell what each word would be with the endings *-er* and *-est* and how to spell these forms. Write the *-er* and *-est* forms next to the root word. As needed, review the rules for:

- adding just *-r* when the root word ends in *e*.
- doubling the final consonant after a short vowel.
- changing *y* to *i* before adding *-er* and *-est*.

Finally, have S. read all three forms of each word.

## PRACTICE 4: Alphabetical Order

T: Sometimes you need to find a name in the phone book or a word in the dictionary. The names and words are listed alphabetically so that you can find the word you want quickly. For practice, please look at the word list at the back of your skill book. Turn to the beginning of the list on page 142.

T: I will say a word. Please see how quickly you can find it in the list. Point to the word, and tell me the lesson where it was new.

| | | | | |
|---|---|---|---|---|
| *amuse* | *wave* | *fact* | *Judy* | *pool* |
| *zoo* | *bugle* | *holiday* | *July* | *rule* |

Write these names from today's lesson on separate cards. Explain that these are more names of people, with the last names given first. Mix up the cards, and have S. arrange the names in alphabetical order. (Explain that, when the *last* names are the same—as with the two here named Jones, then they are listed in alphabetical order by *first* names.)

| | |
|---|---|
| *Baker, Hugh* | *Lopez, Carlos* |
| *Hoover, John* | *Luther, Mary* |
| *Jones, Judy* | *Newman, Arthur* |
| *Jones, Luke* | *O'Toole, Mike* |
| *Lewis, Jimmy* | *Romano, Mike* |

# III. Writing

## CHECK HOMEWORK: Page 39

Check this page with S. Have him correct any errors. Note the type of error, and plan an exercise to give extra practice on that skill.

## WRITING LESSON (In Notebook)

**Words.** Have S. write the titles *Lesson 7* and *Words* and number from 1 to 28 in two columns. Give S. a chance to study the new words in this lesson. Help him especially to study *animal, cancer, climb, group, lion, page, president.* Then dictate the words below for him to write. (For numbers 1-12, you may substitute words from his "Study" list in the last few lessons.) Check his work, and have him correct any errors.

| | | |
|---|---|---|
| 1. music | 11. chew | 21. daily |
| 2. food | 12. news | 22. climb |
| 3. student | 13. wish | 23. given |
| 4. cure | 14. rate | 24. group |
| 5. June | 15. board | 25. animal |
| 6. Duke | 16. lion | 26. president |
| 7. argue | 17. winter | 27. company |
| 8. blue | 18. cancer | 28. headline |
| 9. Tuesday | 19. rope | |
| 10. few | 20. page | |

**Sentences.** Have S. write the title *Sentences.* Have him number each sentence as you dictate it. Before dictating, review writing direct quotations. Write these sentences as examples, leaving out the commas and quotation marks. Have S. tell where to put them.

*"My little boy had great courage," his father said.*
*The President told Pablo, "You have great courage."*

1. The hearings will continue Thursday afternoon at 2:30.
2. Mr. Newman said, "We need to buy new computers."
3. "You can't stop me forever," O'Toole argued.
4. "The lions don't look happy," said Hugh Baker.
5. Dr. Mary Luther thanked the tutors for helping the students.
6. Mr. and Mrs. John Hoover live at 1445 University Avenue.

Check what S. has written, and have him correct any errors, including those in punctuation and capitalization. Have S. write the title *Study* and any words that he missed in the word and sentence dictation.

## PRACTICE: Page 44

Have S. read the directions for the exercise and do it. Check his work. If he marked any word incorrectly, have him read it aloud. If he can't identify the stressed syllable, read the word to him and have him listen.

## HOMEWORK: Page 45

Go over the directions for the first exercise with S. Have him give one or two questions orally to make sure he knows what to do. Go over the directions and example for the second exercise with S. Encourage him to read the chart and reading section again at home and to study any words he missed in the dictation.

## CHECKING PROGRESS

**Comprehension.** Through the oral and written checkups on today's stories, you can tell how well S. can read factual material. Check his progress in these areas:

1. Identification of the people in the story. Was S. able to tell *who* for each story?
2. Understanding of the main event. Was S. able to tell what happened?
3. Recognition of specific details such as *when* and *where* something happened.
4. Recognition of cause and effect, as indicated by his answers to any *why* questions about the stories.

**Word recognition.** Check your student's progress in terms of the following points:

1. Recognition of new words in the lesson by applying phonics skills and knowledge of syllables and root words.
2. Recall of most of the words previously taught as evidenced in reading the news stories.
3. Recognition of words with different endings.
4. Recognition of word relationships, as evidenced in Skills Practice 2 on word opposites.

**General achievement.** Check your student's progress in terms of these points:

1. Does he generally read the lessons with reasonable ease? Or, does he seem somewhat frustrated with the difficulty of the material or the amount he is expected to cover?
2. Does he generally complete the homework assignment before class? Is most of it accurate?
3. Does he seem to feel that his purpose in learning to read is being met? (Discuss this with him.)
4. Is there a balance in his progress in reading and writing?
5. Are personal problems interfering with his progress in his lessons? Discussion of his goals and objectives may help to bring out some of these problems. You may be able to refer him to other sources for help.

## MEETING INDIVIDUAL NEEDS

If S. did fairly well in this lesson, let him go on to Lesson 8. If he needs help in several areas, plan another review lesson. Use supplementary materials on this level or create your own, but do not repeat skill book lessons. If any of the Story Checkups, Practice exercises, or Homework pages have not been completed, however, you may have S. do these in class.

Encourage S. by having him read some supplementary material that he can read easily. Or, you might select some high-interest material that is somewhat "too difficult" for him and use it in duet reading. (This material could include some sight words with sounds he has not yet studied or with irregular spellings.) In duet reading, you sit next to S. and read aloud with him. Read at a fairly natural pace and with normal intonation, moving your finger beneath the line being read. At times, S. may skip a word or lag behind a bit, but you should keep reading, letting him join in as much as he can. If the material is interesting to him, S. will be motivated to try to keep up with you and to look ahead to anticipate words that are coming up. Do *not* ask comprehension questions about material read in this way. The purpose is to give S. practice in fluent reading and to give him an opportunity to stretch himself beyond what he thinks his limits are.

Suitable material for duet reading can be selected from suggested titles on the inside front cover of this manual or earlier LWR manuals. The material may be an article that you can complete in one sitting, such as those from the In the Know series and Remembering series. Or you may want to complete a longer story or a short, easy novel in this way, spending a few minutes at the end of each lesson period.

If S. is having a great deal of difficulty with fluent oral reading of stories in the lessons, you might also use a similar technique, called repeated reading, with any of the news stories in Lesson 7 that he has not yet read orally. Read the story aloud with S. But, in this case, repeat the story in this way until S. is thoroughly familiar with it. Then let him read it by himself. This technique is useful for students whose phrasing is poor and those who, because of timidity and overanalyzing, hesitate frequently on words they actually can read.

Another way to review stories in the skill book without actually repeating them is to turn them into cloze exercises. A cloze exercise is a reading passage in which every 5th, 6th, 7th, 8th, or 9th word is left blank for the student to fill in. Cloze exercises integrate word recognition skills with the skills of using context clues and grammatical clues in the reading material.

To create a cloze exercise from a skill book story, follow these steps:

1. If the story is fairly short, you may want to use all of it. If it's fairly long, select a portion that has a beginning and end.

2. Leave one or two full sentences at the beginning to establish the context. Start your count at the beginning of the next sentence.

3. Leave every 5th, 6th, 7th, 8th, or 9th word blank. Generally, the longer intervals (every 8th or 9th word) are somewhat easier, and the shorter intervals are harder. But you may want to experiment a bit before you choose the interval you want to use for a particular reading passage. For example, you may find that with every 8th word, the blanks consistently fall in awkward places, but every 7th word works just fine.

4. If a blank should fall on a proper name or number that can't be figured out from the context, simply move the blank over to the next word. From there, continue your count as before.

5. Leave one or two full sentences at the end of the exercise to provide a conclusion.

6. Tell S. to fill in *one* word in each blank. Encourage him to look for context clues that will help him figure out the word to write. Point out that he may need both to look back and to read ahead to find clues.

7. When checking the student's work, accept any *appropriate* word as an answer, even if it is not the same as the word used in the original reading passage. A word is appropriate if it is both grammatically correct and logical in the context and does not conflict with information given elsewhere in the reading passage.

In *Focus on Phonics-4*, you may want to use Practices 7A-7F. They provide a review of spellings for the sounds /ū/ and /oo/, plus a review of some word endings.

# Harris County Public Library
## ESL/Literacy

# Class Attendance Sheet

Please drop off at your branch library (or mail to Steve Zach at Harris County Public Library, 8080 El Rio Street, Houston 77054), **by the last day of the month.**

Tutor Name: _MaggieBaker_    Can you accept new students?   Yes/No

Library Branch _OF_    Month _Oct._

Meeting time _Varies_    Room No./Location _____

| Day of Week (Su, M, T, W, Th, F, S) | 10-10 | | | | | | | | | | | | | |
|---|---|---|---|---|---|---|---|---|---|---|---|---|---|---|
| Date | Th. | | | | | | | | | | | | | |
| Student Name | Write the length of class in hrs below. | | | | | | | | | | | | | Total Hrs |
| Sophie Saade | | | | | | | | | | | | | | |
| | | | | | | | | | | | | | | |
| | | | | | | | | | | | | | | |
| | | | | | | | | | | | | | | |
| | | | | | | | | | | | | | | |
| | | | | | | | | | | | | | | |
| | | | | | | | | | | | | | | |
| | | | | | | | | | | | | | | |
| | | | | | | | | | | | | | | |
| | | | | | | | | | | | | | | |
| | | | | | | | | | | | | | | |

Please note any students who were dropped this month_____

Book series_____ Level_____ Check if students completed a level this month_____
Other comments – any goals or accomplishments the student mentioned, your observations regarding progress in speaking, reading and writing, student outlook on his or her progress, or any assistance you would like.

book = buuk
oo = uu

uu

| | cook | cook | cook |
| | hook | hook | hook |
| | brook | brook | brook |
| | foot | foot | foot |
| | good | good | good |
| | woods | woodz | woods |

---

| Jake | Bush (Buush) | took (tuuk) | sugar (shuug' er) | notebook (note' buuk) |
| plant | push (puush) | could (cuud) | cabin (cab' in) | understood (under stuud') |
| catch | pull (puul) | would (wuud) | only (ōn' ly) | beautiful (bū' ti fuul) |
| note | full (fuul) | | | |
| stove | | | | |
| carve | | | | |

## The Good Life in the Woods

Sometimes a person knows a lot, but what he knows will die when he dies. With no relatives, friends, or students, he has no way of passing on what he knows to others.

The man in this story was that kind of person. Then someone wrote a book to share what that man knew. On the pages of a book, a person's ideas can live after him.

\* \* \*

No one understood Jake Bush. No one understood why he wanted to live alone in the woods. At 83, Jake Bush was living alone in the north woods of New York State. He had lived there for 30 years.

Jake didn't care if people understood him or not. To him, life in the woods was good.

Jake Bush lived in a one-room cabin near a beautiful brook. The brook was full of fish. Jake could catch fish nearly every time he threw his hook into the water. He took fish home to cook every day. He took his drinking water from the brook, too.

The woods were full of wild plants. Jake cooked many kinds of these plants for food. He knew which plants were good to eat and which ones were not safe.

Jake cooked and heated his cabin with a wood-burning stove. He cut wood for his stove from dead trees. He cut up the big trees. Then he pushed and pulled the heavy pieces back to his cabin. He cut them into little pieces for his stove.

Jake Bush took good care of the woods where he lived. He never took more from the woods than he needed. He never tried to catch more fish than he could eat. He never threw trash into the brook.

In 30 years, Jake had never needed a doctor. He was hardly ever sick. Sometimes, he would catch cold or not feel very well. Then he cured himself with leaves and roots. Jake picked leaves and pulled up roots from wild plants. He used them to cure himself.

Jake had no radio or TV. He had only the music of the brook and the singing of the birds.

This was the life that Jake Bush was living when Sam Cook met him. Sam Cook was a writer who came to the north country to camp. Sam met Jake at the store.

Jake went to the store only a few times a year. He went there to buy coffee, sugar, fish hooks, and a few other things. There was only one way from Jake's home in the hills to the store. And that way was 15 miles each way on foot.

One day in June, Jake was in the store. He had some baskets and some animals carved from wood. The owner of the store would sell these things for him.

While the store owner was getting Jake's sugar and fish hooks, Sam Cook came up to Jake. "You're Mr. Bush, aren't you? I'm Sam Cook. I have been looking at the animals you carved. They're beautiful."

Jake looked up, but he didn't say anything.

"I would like to watch you carve something," Sam Cook said. "Would you let me watch?"

Jake said, "I live 15 miles from here. And you would have to go on foot."

"That's OK," Sam Cook said. "I'm camping on Stony Brook near Miller Hill. That's near your place, isn't it?"

"It's not too far," Jake said.

The two men left the store together. Sam carried a heavy bag of sugar for Jake. On the way, Sam told Jake that he was a writer. He said he would like to write a book on living in the woods.

"You had better live in the woods before you try to write a book," said Jake.

"I would like to," Sam said. "Would you let me camp near you for the next few months? I could learn some things by watching you."

"I can't stop you," Jake said. "I don't own the woods. But don't get in my way."

So Sam Cook moved his tent and sleeping bag to the woods near Jake's cabin. The first week, Jake hardly said anything in answer to Sam's questions. But, little by little, Jake grew to like the younger man. He let Sam help him cut trees and pull them back to his cabin. Jake pulled the heavy pieces of wood and Sam pushed. By pushing and pulling, they got the wood to the cabin.

Sam watched Jake do many things. As he watched, he took pictures, and he took notes in his notebook. Soon Sam's notebook was full of notes. Every night, Sam used his notes to work on his book.

One night, Sam read the first part of his book to Jake. "That's beautiful," Jake said. "I didn't think you understood why I love woods. But from your book, I can tell that you love wild places and animals as much as I do."

"I have learned lots of things from you," said Sam. "And I hope to learn more. This book will pass on to others many of the things you know. But more than that, I hope the book will make people want to protect wild places like this."

"That idea is the main thing I want to pass on," said Jake.

**Write *yes* if the sentence is true. Write *no* if it is not true.**

Yes    1. Jake Bush had lived in the north woods for 30 years.

Yes    2. To Jake, life in the woods was good.

Yes    3. Jake heated his cabin with a wood-burning stove.

No    4. In the evenings, Jake watched TV.

No    5. When Jake was sick, he went to see a doctor.

Yes    6. Jake made baskets and carved animals from wood to sell.

Yes    7. Jake went to the store to buy things he could not make for himself.

No    8. Jake went to the store on his bicycle.

Yes    9. Sam Cook was a writer.

No    10. Jake asked Sam to stay with him in his cabin.

Yes    11. Jake liked the part of the book that Sam read to him.

Yes    12. A person's ideas can live after him on the pages of a book.

**Write sentence answers to these questions.**

1. What kind of book did Sam Cook want to write? _____

_____

2. Why did Sam want to live near Jake for a few months? _____

_____

3. What was the main thing that Jake wanted to pass on to others? _____

_____

_____

---

chapter (chap **'** ter)    contents (con **'** tents)    title (tī **'** tul)

By Sam Cook

### Table of Contents

Here are the cover and the table of contents for the book that Sam Cook wrote. In the table of contents, you can find the title of each chapter in the book. You can find the page on which each chapter begins. The title of the book is on the cover.

Look at the table of contents and the book cover, and answer these questions. Write short answers.

1. What is the title of the book? _Life in the Woods_

2. Who wrote the book? _Sam Cook_

3. What is the title of the first chapter? _The Beauty of Life in the Woods_

4. If you wanted to make baskets, which chapter would you read? _Chapter 6_

    What page does it start on? _97_

5. Which two chapters would help you get your meals from the woods?

    _Chapter 4_ and _Chapter 5_

6. Which chapter tells ways to take care of the woods? _Chapter 9_

    What page does it start on? _168_

**Put together a word from List 1 and a word from List 2 to make a new word. Write the new word.**

| List 1 | List 2 | New Word |
|---|---|---|
| 1. under | book | *understood* |
| 2. home | stood | *homework* |
| 3. note | times | *notebook* |
| 4. some | up | *sometimes* |
| 5. head | mother | *headline* |
| 6. pick | work | *pickup* |
| 7. grand | line | *grandmother* |
| 8. him | one | *himself* |
| 9. any | self | *anyone* |

**Would you like to live in the woods? Why or why not?**

_____

_____

_____

_____

_____

_____

---

**Say the words. Circle the words with the sound _uu_ as in _book_.**

| | | |
|---|---|---|
| 1. (foot) | food | noon |
| 2. too | (took) | (book) |
| 3. (pull) | pool | phone |
| 4. soon | (look) | (brook) |
| 5. (cook) | cool | coat |
| 6. (wood) | (hook) | hold |
| 7. (push) | much | (bush) |

**Add the ending _-ful_ to each root word. Write the new word in the blank.**

**Example:** beauty  *beautiful*

1. hope  *hopeful*
2. peace  *peaceful*
3. thank  *thankful*
4. help  *helpful*
5. trust  *trustful*
6. care  *careful*

**Fill in each blank with one of the new words with _-ful_.**

1. Jake's life in the woods was *peaceful*.
2. Sam was *hopeful* that he could write a book on life in the woods.
3. Duke was *thankful* for Mr. Newman's help.
4. Be *careful* when you swim in the lake.
5. Sam learned ways that he could be *helpful* to Jake.
6. At first, Jake was not *trustful* of Sam.

**Skill Book 4**
Pages 46-53

## OBJECTIVES

To help your student:

- recognize the vowel sound /uu/ as in *book*.
- recognize that the letters *oo* sometimes stand for the sound /uu/.
- recognize that when the letters *oo* are followed by *k*, they almost always stand for the sound /uu/.
- read words with the sound /uu/.
- distinguish between the sound /uu/ as in *book* and the sound /oo/ as in *food*.
- recognize the suffix *-ful* and how to add it to some familiar root words.
- recognize the new compound words *notebook, understood,* and review other compound words.
- recognize words that are alike except for the initial consonant.
- review the ending *-ing*, recognizing that the final consonant is not doubled after *oo* in the root word, whether *oo* stands for /oo/ or /uu/, as in *cooling* and *looking*.
- distinguish between fact and fiction.
- interpret facts and draw inferences.
- interpret feelings of characters in the story.
- relate the story to own experiences and values.
- write words and a paragraph from dictation.

## INTRODUCTION

T: You have learned that two *o*'s together often stand for the sound /oo/ as in *food*. In today's lesson, you will learn that two *o*'s together sometimes stand for another vowel sound.

## I. Reading

## CHART: Page 46

**Title and key word.** Have S. read the title *Lesson 8*.

T: Look at the picture and key word at the top of the page. What is the word? [S: book.] Say the word again, and listen for the vowel sound. What is the sound? [S: /uu/.]

T: The sound /uu/ is a little different from the sound /oo/ in *food* and also a little different from the sound /u/ in *up*. You have had two words with the vowel sound /uu/: *look* and *put*. But you have not studied the sound /uu/ until now.

T: There is no letter or combination of letters that always stands for the sound /uu/. In this skill book, two *u*'s are put together to stand for the sound /uu/.

T: (Point to respelling *buuk.*) Notice how *book* is rewritten. What letters are used for the sound /uu/? [S: *uu.*] (Point to *oo = uu.*) What sound do the two *o*'s in *book* equal? [S: /uu/.] When you see a new word respelled with two *u*'s, you will know the vowel sound is /uu/ as in *book*.

T: Look at the letters in the top right-hand corner. What are they? [S: *uu.*] What sound do they stand for? [S: /uu/.]

**Lines 1-6**

T: All of the words in this chart have the vowel sound /uu/. The two *o*'s in each of these words stand for the sound /uu/. So the words are not respelled. But any other new words in which the letters *oo* stand for the sound /uu/ *will* be respelled with *uu*. The respelling will let you know that the sound is /uu/, not /oo/.

T: Read the words to yourself. Notice how many sounds are in each word and which words rhyme.

After S. has studied the chart silently, have him read the words aloud, going down the last column. Then ask these questions:

1. What is the vowel sound in each of these words? [S: /uu/.] How is it written? [S: *oo.*]
2. Which words rhyme with *book*? [S: cook, hook, brook.] What letter comes after *oo* in each of these words? [S: *k.*] Usually, when the letters *oo* are followed by *k*, they stand for the sound /uu/.
3. What word rhymes with *wood*? [S: good.] Can you think of another word that rhymes with *good* and *wood*? (Accept as correct any word that rhymes with *good*, even if the spelling for /uu/ is different. But if S. says *food*, have him listen for the difference in the vowel sounds.)
4. How many syllables are there in each of these words? [S: One.]
5. How many sounds are in the word *brook*? [S: Four.] In the word *woods*? [S: Four.] How many sounds are in each of the other words? [S: Three.]
6. Which word has an *s* on the end? [S: woods.] This *s* is not like the usual *-s* ending. It doesn't make the word mean more than one; instead, it changes the meaning of the word. *Woods* means a place with a lot of trees, or a forest. What is the word without the *s*? [S: wood.] *Wood* is the material that we get from trees and use to make things.

**Review.** Have S. read each word aloud again, including the key word. Cover the pictures, and have him go down the last column of the chart.

## STORY: Pages 47-49 (The Good Life in the Woods)

Have S. read the story title and new words. Call attention to the words with the sound /uu/ and which ones have that sound spelled *oo*. Have S. point out the compound words (*notebook, understood*) and the words from which they are made. Ask him to read each word with more than one syllable, tell how many syllables the word has, and tell which syllable is stressed. Point out that *Bush* is written with a capital *B* because it is used as a person's last name in this story; when it is used to mean a plant or small tree, it is written with small *b*.

**Directed silent reading.** Ask S. to read the first two paragraphs silently and find out what kind of person this story is about. When he has finished reading, have him answer the question and then read the two paragraphs aloud.

Point out that the first two paragraphs are an introduction to the story. They give the main idea that the writer wants to get across. The introduction is separated from the main story by the three stars and extra white space.

Ask S. to read the third paragraph to himself to find out some specific details about the man in the story. Then ask these questions:

1. Who is the story about?
2. Where did Jake Bush live?
3. What was hard for people to understand about Jake?

Ask S. to finish the story silently and then tell what he understands about Jake and his reasons for living alone in the woods. When he has finished reading, have him tell about these points.

**Reading between the lines.** Discuss these questions.

1. Why did Jake need to buy only a few things at the store?
2. What do you think was Jake's first reaction to Sam Cook?
3. How did Sam go about making friends with Jake? What was Jake's response?
4. What do you think Jake found good about his life in the woods?
5. Do you think you would like to live the way Jake did? Why or why not?

## STORY CHECKUP: Page 50

Have S. read the title and the directions for the first exercise. Have him do the Yes/No exercise without looking back at the story. Check his work. Have him scan the story to find the sentence that tells the correct statement for any items he has wrong.

Have S. read the directions for the second exercise and do it. When he finishes, have him read aloud each question and his answer. The exact answers are not in the story. If your student's answer shows that he has not understood what he read, discuss the question with him, and have him find the parts of the story that help to answer it. Check his work, first, for ideas that are expressed. Give any praise that is merited. Then check for correct sentence structure, spelling, and capitalization. Be sure to give constructive suggestions.

## READING FOR LIVING: Page 51

Have S. read the title and new words first silently and then aloud.

T: This Reading for Living section is about using a table of contents for a book. You have used one in books like *Changes* and *City Living*. At the top of this page, you'll see a sample table of contents and the picture of a book cover. Before you look at them closely, read the first paragraph just below the table of contents.

Have S. read the paragraph to himself. Then have him tell what book the table of contents is for. Also, have him tell what he can find out by looking at the table of contents.

Ask S. to read the second paragraph, which gives directions for the exercise, and then write the answers. Check his work. Discuss any questions that he didn't answer correctly, and help him find the right answer.

# II. Skills Practice

## PRACTICE 1: Distinguishing the Sound /uu/

T: I will say three words. Listen and tell which one has the sound /uu/ as in *book*.

| | |
|---|---|
| *took, block, boot* | *pool, push, computer* |
| *fool, food, full* | *could, cute, cut* |
| *luck, look, Luke* | *flute, food, foot* |
| *should, shut, shoot* | *bush, bus, beauty* |

## PRACTICE 2: Substituting Initial Consonants

Write *book*, and have S. read it. Ask him to give other words that rhyme with *book*, but start with a different consonant sound. Write the words under *book*. (Possible words are: *brook, cook, crook, hook, look, nook, rook, shook, took*.)

Have S. read the words you have written. Then point out that when *oo* is followed by *k*, the vowel sound is almost always /uu/.

**Note:** An exception is the word *spook*.

## PRACTICE 3: Suffix *-ful*

Write *beautiful*, and have S. read it. Ask him what the root word is. Write *beauty* in front of *beautiful*.

T: What ending has been added to *beauty* to make the word *beautiful*? [S: *-ful*.] What change was made in the root word before the ending was added? [S: The *y* was changed to *i*.] You can add *-ful* to other root words to make new words.

Write *peace, thank, hope, care, help, play, forget, wonder*. Have S. read each word and tell what it would be with the ending *-ful* added. As he answers, write the word next to the root word. When the list is complete, have S. read both forms of each word.

T: The words in the first column are nouns and verbs. When we add the ending *-ful*, we change a noun or a verb into an adjective. An adjective is a word that describes something. Give a sentence using the word *beauty*. [S. gives sentence.] Now give a sentence using the word *beautiful*. (Have S. tell what word in his sentence *beautiful* describes.)

Have S. give sentences for *peace* and *peaceful* and for *help* and *helpful* to make sure he understands how they are used.

## PRACTICE 4: Compound Words

Write the new compound words *notebook* and *understood*. Have S. read each and tell the two words it is made from. As he answers, write the two words by the compound word. Follow the same procedure to review these compound words: *headline, newspaper, anyone, forever, something*.

In one column, write *some, my, pay, week*. In a second column, write *self, end, thing, check*. Have S. put together each word in column 1 with a word in column 2 to make a compound word. Write each compound word in a third column. Have S. read the compound words.

## PRACTICE 5: Ending *-ing*

Write these words in a column: *heat, look, cook, cool, room, catch, plant, plan, swim, carve, argue*. Have S. read each word and tell what it would be with the ending *-ing* added. Have him spell the new word. Write the new word in a second column as he spells it. Have S. tell the reason for any change in the root word before *-ing* is added.

Point out that in words like *looking* and *cooling*, the final consonant is not doubled after *oo*, whether it stands for the sound /uu/ or /oo/.

# III. Writing

## CHECK HOMEWORK: Page 45

Check this page with S. Have him correct any errors. Note the type of error, and plan reinforcement exercises for the skill needed.

## WRITING LESSON (In Notebook)

Have S. write the titles *Lesson 8* and *Words* and number from 1 to 20 in two columns. After he has finished the dictation, have him check his work by looking at the chart and story words.

**Words.** Have S. study these words: *could, would, sugar, push, pull, full, Bush, only*. Remind S. that *Bush* is written with a capital *B* only when it is used as a name. When dictating, give a sentence using *Bush* as a name and give a sentence for *would*.

| | | | |
|---|---|---|---|
| 1. book | 6. foot | 11. pull | 16. Jake |
| 2. cook | 7. good | 12. full | 17. plant |
| 3. took | 8. woods | 13. could | 18. stove |
| 4. hook | 9. Bush | 14. would | 19. note |
| 5. brook | 10. push | 15. sugar | 20. only |

**Sentences.** Tell S. that you will dictate a paragraph from the story. He will not number the sentences. Remind him to indent the paragraph. Tell S. to listen to the whole paragraph as you read it. Then read it again, a sentence at a time, for him to write. Read each sentence one more time if needed. Don't read the sentence word by word. But, you may need to dictate the last sentence in two segments, the first ending after *to eat*.

> The woods were full of wild plants. Jake cooked many kinds of these plants for food. He knew which plants were good to eat and which ones were not safe.

Check what S. has written, and have him correct any errors, including those in punctuation and capitalization. Have him write the title *Study* and any words he misses in the word and sentence dictation.

## PRACTICE: Page 52

Have S. read the directions for the first exercise and then do it. Check his answers. If he has any wrong, have him read the words in the line aloud.

Go over the directions and example for the second exercise with S. Have him add the ending *-ful* to each of the words.

Then have S. read the directions for the last exercise, and fill in the blanks with the words ending in *-ful*. Have S. read the completed sentences aloud and correct any errors.

## HOMEWORK: Page 53

Go over the directions with S. Encourage him to read the story again at home and to study any words he missed in the dictation.

## CHECKING PROGRESS

**Comprehension.** Your student's responses in "Reading between the lines" and the Story Checkup will enable you to note his progress in understanding main ideas, interpreting facts and drawing inferences, understanding the feelings of characters in the story, and recalling details. Note which of these skills, if any, are difficult for him. Plan reinforcement activities as suggested in the next section.

**Application of phonics skills.** Note your student's ability to read new story words with sounds and spelling patterns previously taught. If he is having difficulty with short vowels, long vowels, or consonant blends (beginning or ending), plan appropriate review.

**Writing skills.** S. should be able to write at least 15 of the 20 words correctly in the word dictation for each lesson. If he usually has more than a fourth of the words spelled incorrectly, check to see if the problem is in spelling or in writing letters unclearly. If the problem is in spelling, note whether it is caused by lack of skill in relating sounds and letters, reversal of letters, omission of letters, or carelessness. After you identify the problem, you may find some of the suggestions in the next section helpful.

## MEETING INDIVIDUAL NEEDS

**Comprehension skills.** You may find one of these activities helpful to your student:

1. Read something from a newspaper or magazine to S. Discuss the material with him, and get his reactions. Do this in a conversational manner without asking direct questions. You can tell by the discussion whether or not he understands the main ideas.

2. Ask S. to tell about an interesting experience. (He might tell about something he has done, a place he has visited, a hobby, how he got his job, some funny incident, the best time of his life, or the worst time.) Or, in keeping with the story in Lesson 8, ask him to tell about an unforgettable character he has known. Set a time limit before he begins to tell his story. Jot down the main points he says, and note whether he tells the story in logical sequence. Tell him what you liked about the way he told the story. Ask him to clear up any points you didn't understand.

3. Keep a record of stories S. tells. You may make a tape recording or have S. dictate the story for you to write. Play the tape recording, or read the story back to him after you have written it. Let him tell you if it sounds the way he meant to say it. At a different session, work on skills that will help him organize his ideas better or express himself more clearly. Notice his progress after several recordings of this nature.

4. Encourage S. to write an original paragraph or story. Have him read it to you. Tell him what you think the main idea is and find out if that is what he intended. Consider the content and ideas in what he has written. Do not be too concerned with sentence structure and spelling.

For further suggestions on how to use language experience stories and writing to reinforce reading skills, you may find these references helpful:

*Guidelines to Teaching Remedial Reading*, Lillie Pope. Book-Lab, Inc.

*Using Language Experience with Adults*, Kennedy and Roeder. New Readers Press.

*I Wish I Could Write*, Joan Barasovska. New Readers Press.

All three books are available from New Readers Press, Box 131, Syracuse, N.Y. 13210.

**Spelling skills.** Your student may not be able to write 20 spelling words for each lesson. It is important for him to learn the spelling patterns in the chart words. If several words follow the same pattern, you may omit some. Choose only those story words that will be most functional for your student.

Or, if you find that you need to spend two sessions on each lesson, divide the Writing Lesson so that S. will have about 10 words and 2-3 sentences to write in each session.

Give S. more time to study the words before you dictate them. Review the main steps in studying a word:

1. Look at the word.
2. Say the word.
3. Note the part that is written the way it sounds.
4. Note any part that is *not* written the way it sounds.
5. Note any special points to remember.
6. Say the word again.
7. Say the letters in sequence. (If the word has two or more syllables, you may have S. say the letters for each part of the word at this point.)
8. Look at the word again.
9. Close your eyes, and see the word in your mind.
10. Spell the word aloud.
11. Write the word without looking at a model.
12. Check to see if you are right.

Find out what S. needs to write or is interested in writing. At times, you may be able to substitute dictation sentences that use the lesson words in contexts more useful to S. In each lesson, you may also have S. copy a few words that he would like to be able to study even though they are not in the lesson.

**Handwriting skills.** If S. is having trouble writing legibly, review in the *Laubach Way to Cursive Writing* workbook any letters which give him difficulty. Work on a few in each lesson.

If his short and tall letters are not proportionate, S. may benefit from continuing to use top and bottom guidelines with a dotted center line. Make copies of the guidelines in the *Cursive Writing Teacher's Guide*, and let him use these for dictation exercises for a while.

Your student's handwriting may also be unclear because he is rushing. During any written exercises, try not to show impatience. Before you check dictated words, give S. a chance to recopy any he doesn't think are neat enough. When dictating sentences, first read the whole sentence at a normal pace. Then dictate it in meaningful segments, reading each segment at least twice. If S. is having much difficulty, the segments may be very short, as: *He knew / which plants / were good to eat / and which ones / were not safe.* As S. becomes more proficient, you can dictate longer segments, as: *He knew which plants / were good to eat / and which ones were not safe* or even *He knew which plants were good to eat / and which ones were not safe.*

ou

mouth
ou

| | | | |
|---|---|---|---|
| | south | south | south |
| | house | hous | house |
| | shout | shout | shout |
| | ground | ground | ground |
| | mountain | moun'tin | mountain |
| 1,000 | thousand | thou'zand | thousand |

---

## Neighbors on the South Side

| | | |
|---|---|---|
| out | without (with out') | discuss (dis cus') |
| our | about (u bout') | problem (prob' lem) |
| found | around (u round') | neighbor (nā' ber) |
| proud | council (coun' sil) | neighborhood (nā' ber huud) |
| | | loan |
| | | low (lōw) |
| | | housing (houz' ing) |

Mountain City was a beautiful city. But every part of Mountain City was not beautiful. On the south side of the city, people had a lot of problems.

The south side was an old neighborhood. The houses there had been standing since about 1900. At one time, they had been fine houses. But as the city grew, people moved out of the south side. The people that stayed were mostly people without much money. Some were older people who had owned their homes for many years.

The neighborhood changed from a rich one to a poor one. But the taxes stayed high. Many owners of houses said they had no money for repairs after they paid taxes. Some owners even stopped paying taxes, and the city took over their houses. These empty houses had broken windows. Trash covered the ground around them, and the grass was not cut.

A hundred thousand people lived in Mountain City. About twenty thousand lived on the south side. The people on the south side did not like what was happening to their neighborhood. Some of them formed a group to do something about their problems. They named their group the South Side Neighbors.

The South Side Neighbors met every month to discuss their problems. They worked on one problem at a time. First, they found out the facts. Then, they discussed that problem with someone on the city council. One of the first problems they discussed was what to do about the empty houses.

A large group of South Side Neighbors went to a city council meeting. "When is the city going to do something about the empty houses next door to me?" asked one woman. "I have found some of our neighborhood children playing with matches there many times."

"There are a lot of houses like that around here," said the man next to her. "That's not safe for our neighborhood."

The city council said that it would board up the houses. But the south side people didn't want a lot of empty houses in their neighborhood, even if they were boarded up. "Don't board them up! Fix them up instead!" one man shouted. "It's not safe to go by an empty house on foot!"

Some people formed a Neighborhood Watch. They took turns riding around the neighborhood at night. If anything looked funny, they reported it to the police. Everyone in the neighborhood felt safer.

After a few years, the south side was a cleaner, safer neighborhood. The South Side Neighbors were proud of their work. They were proud of their beautiful homes. They were proud of their clean parks and streets.

## Story Checkup

**Write two or three sentences to give the main ideas for each heading.**

Problems of the south side of Mountain City

_____

_____

_____

What the city agreed to do to help the south side

_____

_____

_____

Ways the South Side Neighbors helped their neighborhood

_____

_____

_____

"That's right!" another man shouted. "Our old people are afraid to go out!"

"That's true," said a woman. "Last month, my aunt was nearly killed on Maple Street. Two young men pushed her to the ground and pulled her into an empty house. They stole her money and told her not to open her mouth. But she tried to shout for help anyway, so they hit her in the mouth. Two of her teeth were broken, and she had to have ten stitches in her mouth. You must do something about those empty houses!"

The city council agreed to work on the problem. The council found out that the state had thousands of dollars for housing loans. Mountain City got some of that money. Then the city let people buy its old houses at low cost. The city loaned money for repairs at low cost. Other low-cost loans helped people pay for things that would save heat in the winter.

After much pushing by the South Side Neighbors, the city agreed to let older people pay lower taxes on their homes. And the city agreed to put in new sewers on the south side.

But the South Side Neighbors did not wait for the city to do everything. They found things they could do without much money. The group had clean-up days every month. Some people cleaned up trash and broken glass around the park. Others visited home owners and landlords and asked them to clean up the ground around their houses.

**In each line, circle the word that means the opposite of the first word.**

1. in — (out) — an — on
2. low — big — (high) — little
3. south — cold — (north) — mouth
4. old — (new) — little — child
5. full — little — (empty) — broken
6. good — beautiful — rude — (bad)
7. west — (east) — eats — fifth
8. with — (without) — about — around
9. push — carry — drop — (pull)

**Add the ending -ly to each word. Write the new word in the blank.**

1. most — _mostly_
2. proud — _proudly_
3. rude — _rudely_
4. day — _daily_
5. month — _monthly_
6. safe — _safely_
7. near — _nearly_
8. happy — _happily_

**Fill in each blank with one of the new words with -ly.**

1. The South Side Neighbors held a meeting _monthly_.
2. I like to read a _daily_ newspaper.
3. We cannot go out _safely_ at night.
4. The child is playing _happily_ by himself.
5. The people at the meeting were _mostly_ from the south side.
6. After a few years, the people were able to speak _proudly_ about their neighborhood.

Lesson 9    **59**

---

# Reading for Living

east    fifth    St. (Street)    courthouse (court'house)
west    sixth    Ave. (Avenue)

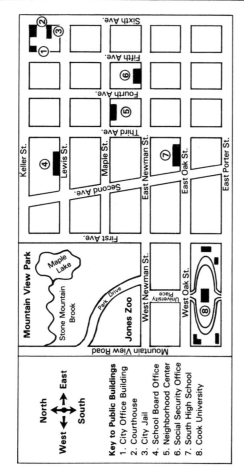

**North** / **East** / **West** / **South**

**Key to Public Buildings**
1. City Office Building
2. Courthouse
3. City Jail
4. School Board Office
5. Neighborhood Center
6. Social Security Office
7. South High School
8. Cook University

This is a map of the south side of Mountain City. Study the map and the key before answering the questions.

1. What does *St.* stand for? _Street_
2. What does *Ave.* stand for? _Avenue_
3. In this city, do the avenues run north and south or east and west? _North and South_
4. What school is on West Oak Street? _Cook University_
5. What school is on East Oak Street? _South High School_
6. At what avenue does West Oak Street become East Oak Street? _At First Avenue_
7. What public building is on Keller Street and Fifth Avenue? _City Office Building_
8. What public building is on Keller Street and Sixth Avenue? _The Courthouse_
9. What building on Sixth Avenue is south of the courthouse? _The City Jail_
10. What street is on the north side of Jones Zoo? _Park Drive_
11. To go from First Avenue to Sixth Avenue, do you go east or west? _east_
12. What street is the Neighborhood Center on? _Maple Street_

**58**  Lesson 9

## OBJECTIVES

To help your student:

- recognize the vowel sound /ou/ as in *mouth*.
- recognize that the letters *ou* usually stand for the sound /ou/.
- read words in which the sound /ou/ is written *ou*.
- distinguish the sound /ou/ from the sounds /oo/, /uu/, and /ō/.
- recognize word opposites.
- recognize the suffix *-hood* and its meanings, as in *neighborhood* and *childhood*.
- review adding *-ly* to root words, recognizing that final *y* in the root word is changed to *i* before *-ly,* as in *happily* and *daily.*
- review the ending *-ed,* recognizing that the final consonant is not doubled after *ou* in the root word, as in *shouted.*
- determine the meaning of a word by the use of context.
- understand cause and effect.
- organize the main ideas under topic headings.
- scan a story to find specific details.
- recognize the basic steps in problem solving as illustrated in the story.
- relate the story to own experience and values.
- read a simple city map.
- recognize the abbreviations *St. (Street)* and *Ave. (Avenue).*
- write words and a paragraph from dictation.

## INTRODUCTION

T: So far, you have studied three vowel sounds in this book. What is the vowel sound in *few*? [S: /ū/.] In *food*? [S: /oo/.] In *foot*? [S: /uu/.] In today's lesson, you will learn another new vowel sound.

# I. Reading

## CHART: Page 54

**Title and key word.** Have S. read the title *Lesson 9.*

T: Look at the picture and key word at the top of the page. What is the word? [S: mouth.] Say the word again, and listen for the vowel sound. What is the sound? [S: /ou/.] What letters stand for the sound /ou/? (Point to *ou* under *mouth*.) [S: *ou*.] Good.

T: (Point to *ou* in the top right-hand corner.) Read them again. [S: *ou*.] What sound do these two letters together stand for? [S: /ou/.]

**Lines 1-6.** Ask S. to read the other words in the chart to himself and notice how many sounds are in each word and which words have more than one syllable.

After S. has studied the chart silently, have him read the words aloud, going down the last column. Then call attention to the following points:

1. The words with three sounds (*south, house, shout*).
2. The word that begins with a blend (*ground*).
3. The words with more than one syllable (*mountain, thousand*) and which syllable is stressed (first).
4. The word that rhymes with mouth (*south*).

On a piece of paper, write *house* and *houses.* Have S. read them. Point out that when it is *one* house, the *s* in the root word is pronounced /s/, but in the plural form *houses* the *s* in the root word is pronounced /z/.

**Review.** Have S. read each word aloud again, including the key word. Cover the pictures, and have him read the words going down the last column.

## STORY: Pages 55-57 (Neighbors on the South Side)

Have S. read the story title and new words. Call attention to the words with the sound /ou/. Have S. read the words with one syllable aloud and tell which syllable is stressed. Point out that *without* is a compound word. For *housing,* point out that when we add an ending to *house,* the sound /s/ changes to the sound /z/.

### Directed silent reading

T: Read the first paragraph to yourself, and then tell what you think the main subject of this story will be. [S: The problems of the south side of Mountain City.]

T: Read the next two paragraphs, and find out what some of the problems were.

After S. reads the two paragraphs silently, have him list the problems and what the causes were. Then have him read the rest of the story silently to find out how the people on the south side went about solving their problems and if they were successful.

**Identifying steps.** After S. finishes the story, have him tell the steps that people on the south side took to solve their problems. (Refer to paragraphs 4 and 5.) List the steps as S. tells them. (You may need to help with one or two to get him started.)

1. Formed a group
2. Identified their problems
3. Worked on one problem at a time
4. Found out the facts
5. Discussed the problem with someone on city council
6. Got what help they could from city council
7. Worked on things they could do themselves

Then have S. summarize how the problem of the empty houses was solved. Also, have him tell what some of the other problems were and how they were solved.

**Scanning.** Ask S. to scan the story to find the paragraph that tells each of the following. (It may help to have him number the paragraphs first. There are 15.)

- the population of Mountain City and the number of people who lived on the south side [par. 4].
- how old the houses were on the south side [par. 2].
- how often the South Side Neighbors met [par. 5].
- where the homeowners on the south side were able to get loans to make repairs [par. 11].
- what people on the south side did to prevent crime in their neighborhood [par. 14].

### Word meanings

T: Some words have more than one meaning. It is necessary to read the sentence to find out what meaning is intended. In this story, the word *push* is used in two ways. Find paragraph 10, and then read the sentence with *pushed* in it aloud. [S: Two young men pushed her to the ground and pulled her into an empty house.] What does *pushed* mean in that sentence? [S: Used force to make her fall.] Now find paragraph 12, and read the sentence with *pushing*. [S: After much pushing by the South Side Neighbors, the city agreed to let older people pay lower taxes on their homes.] What does *pushing* mean here? [Possible answers might be *urging, persuading, nagging.* etc.]

T: Another example in this story is the word *funny.* What does *funny* usually mean? [S: Something to laugh at.] Look at paragraph 14, the second to last paragraph. Read the sentence with *funny* aloud. [S: If anything looked funny, they reported it to the police.] What does *funny* mean here? [S: Strange.]

### Reading between the lines. Discuss these questions.

1. What were some of the reasons the south side changed from a rich neighborhood to a poor one?
2. Why did the city take over some of the houses on the south side?
3. What was the opinion of the South Side Neighbors about the empty houses? On what facts was their opinion based?
4. Why didn't the South Side Neighbors want the City Council to board up the houses?
5. How would it help the neighborhood for the city to let older people pay lower taxes on their homes?
6. What did the South Side Neighbors do themselves to make their neighborhood safer and cleaner?
7. Do you think having a Neighborhood Watch was a good idea? Why or why not? Do you know any neighborhoods that have tried a similar plan? Has it worked?
8. Do you think the steps the South Side Neighbors took to solve their problems were good ones? Why or why not?
9. What suggestions can you make of other ways that they might have solved their problems?

### Oral reading. If time allows, have S. read aloud paragraphs 6-10 (the five paragraphs in which people spoke at the city council meeting). Encourage him to read with expression in

the way he thinks the people spoke. Review the use of the exclamation point.

## STORY CHECKUP: Page 57

Have S. read the title and directions. Have him read the first heading and tell the main ideas that might go under it. Then ask him to write the sentences. Have him read the other headings to himself and write the sentences that give the main ideas. Check his work. If he has not included the main ideas under the right heading, have him find the section in the story that is related to the main idea and have him read it over. Discuss the main points with him, and then have him put them into his own written sentences.

## READING FOR LIVING: Page 58

Have S. read the title and new words first silently and then aloud. Explain that *St.* and *Ave.* are written abbreviations, but we read them by saying the whole word. Have S. tell what each stands for. Point out that *St.* and *Ave.* are followed by a period. Also, point out that these abbreviations are used only as part of the name of a street or avenue, and that's why they are written with a capital letter. Call attention to the compound word *courthouse.*

Have S. read the paragraph under the map, first silently and then aloud.

T: Look at the direction marker on the map. Please read the words on the marker. [S: North, East, South, West.] Where is north on this map? [S: At the top.] Where is south? [S: At the bottom.] What direction is at the right of the map? [S: East.] What direction is at the left? [S: West.]

T: The direction marker shows that if you move from the top to the bottom of the map, you are going from north to south. (Trace the direction on the map as you say this.) If you go the other way, from the bottom to the top, you are going from south to north. (Trace the direction as you say this.)

Ask S. to look at the map and read the names of the streets that run north and south. Then follow the same procedure to explain the streets that run east and west, and have S. read their names.

Have S. look at the shaded areas in the top left corner of the map (park and zoo), read all of the place names, and read the name of the street that runs between the park and the zoo.

T: Look at what is written at the side of the map, under the direction marker. What is the title? [S: Key to Public Buildings.] What is the first building? [S: City Office Building.] Look for the number 1 on the map, and find this building.

Have S. read the names of several of the buildings and find them on the map. Then have him write the answers to the questions. If S. doesn't understand a question, give help in explaining the meaning, but let him answer it for himself. Check his work, and help him find the correct answer for any items he omitted or has wrong.

# II. Skills Practice

Have S. close his book before doing these exercises.

## PRACTICE 1: Distinguishing the Sound /ou/

T: I will say two words. Listen, and tell which one has the sound /ou/ as in *mouth*.

| | | |
|---|---|---|
| room, round | shoot, shout | hose, house |
| noon, noun | sound, soon | proud, prove |
| found, foot | poor, sour | loud, loan |

## PRACTICE 2: Suffix *-hood*

Write *neighborhood*, and have S. read it. Ask him what the root word is. Draw a line under *neighbor*.

T: What does the word *neighbor* mean? [S: A person living near another.] What ending has been added to *neighbor* to make *neighborhood?* [S: -hood.] What is the meaning of *neighborhood?* [S: A small section of a town or city.]

T: The ending *-hood* can be added to other root words to make new words. (Write *child, mother, father, sister, brother, parent.*) The ending *-hood* can be added to each of these words to make a new word. Read the root word, and tell what it would be with the ending *-hood* added.

Write the new word by the root word as S. says it. When the list is complete, have S. read both columns of words.

T: The ending *-hood* has a somewhat different meaning in these words than in *neighborhood.* In *neighborhood,* it meant a place. What meaning does *-hood* give to the word *child* in this sentence: "I had a happy childhood"? [S: The time of being a child.] In most of these words, *-hood* means the *time of being* or the *condition of being. Brotherhood* and *sisterhood* can also mean a group of people.

## PRACTICE 3: Ending *-ly*

Write *daily,* and have S. read it. Ask him what the root word is. Write *day* in front of *daily.*

T: What ending has been added to *day* to make *daily?* [S: -ly.] What change was made in the root word? [S: The *y* was changed to *i.*]

T: What does the word *daily* mean in this sentence: "The newspaper is published daily"? [S: Every day.] In some words, the ending *-ly* means *happening at regular times—* in this case, every day. Here are some other words to which you can add *-ly* to mean happening at regular times.

Write *week, month, year.* Have S. read each word and tell what it would be with the ending *-ly.* Write the new word by the root word.

Then write *loud, happy, angry.* Have S. read each word and tell what the word would be with *-ly* added. Also, have him tell what change, if any, needs to be made in the root word before *-ly* is added. If necessary, explain that final *y* is changed to *i.* Write the new word by the root word.

T: In the words *loudly, happily,* and *angrily,* the *-ly* ending means the way something is said or done. Please give a sentence using one of these words. (If S. cannot think of a sentence, give one for him to fill in the word, such as: "*He was angry when he spoke to me. He spoke to me _____ .*")

## PRACTICE 4: Ending *-ed*

In one column, write *owned, changed, formed, named, discussed, boarded, agreed, reported, stopped, pulled, shouted.* Have S. read each word, tell what the root word is, and tell how to spell the root word. As he answers, write the root word in a second column. Point out that a final consonant is not doubled after *ou,* as in *shouted.* Finally, have S. read both forms of each word.

# III. Writing

## CHECK HOMEWORK: Page 53

Check the first exercise with S. and have him correct any errors. Have him read what he has written for the second exercise. If he hasn't written anything, have him answer orally. Encourage the expression of his ideas. Then have him write the sentences. Emphasize that the important part of this exercise is to put his thoughts on paper. He can make any needed corrections in spelling and punctuation later.

## WRITING LESSON (In Notebook)

Have S. write the titles *Lesson 9* and *Words* and then number from 1 to 20 in two columns. After he has finished the dictation, have him check his work by looking at the chart and story words.

**Words.** Help S. study these words: *house, mountain, thousand, loan, council, neighbor.* Explain that *neighbor* is an exception to the rule of *i* before *e.* Give a sentence when dictating *our.*

| | | |
|---|---|---|
| 1. mouth | 8. out | 15. discuss |
| 2. south | 9. our | 16. without |
| 3. shout | 10. found | 17. problem |
| 4. ground | 11. about | 18. loan |
| 5. mountain | 12. around | 19. low |
| 6. house | 13. council | 20. proud |
| 7. thousand | 14. neighbor | |

**Sentences.** Tell S. that you will dictate a paragraph from the story. He will not number the sentences. Remind him to indent the paragraph. Read each sentence once. Repeat one more time if needed.

> After a few years, the south side was a cleaner and safer neighborhood. The South Side Neighbors were proud of their work. They were proud of their beautiful houses. They were proud of their clean parks and streets.

Check what S. has written, and have him correct any errors, including those in punctuation and capitalization. Have him write the title *Study* and any words he missed in the word and paragraph dictation.

## PRACTICE: Page 59

Have S. read the directions for the exercise and do it. Check his answers. If he has any wrong, have him read the words in the line aloud.

## HOMEWORK: Page 59

Go over the directions with S. Encourage him to read the story again at home and to study any words he missed in the dictation.

## CHECKING PROGRESS

Write the words below, and ask S. to read them. (In each group of words, the first is known and the others are new.) Note how many of the new words S. is able to figure out by comparing them with known words.

| | | | |
|---|---|---|---|
| *proud* | *house* | *shout* | *found* |
| *cloud* | *mouse* | *pout* | *round* |
| *loud* | *blouse* | *spout* | *pound* |
| | | | |
| *our* | *mount* | *west* | *east* |
| *sour* | *count* | *best* | *least* |
| *scour* | *amount* | *rest* | *yeast* |

Also, note your student's progress in understanding the main ideas of what he reads, in seeing cause and effect relationships, and in his ability to scan a page to find a specific detail.

Have S. evaluate his own progress in spelling and writing. Have him note the types of errors he had in the dictation in this lesson. Help him to analyze the cause of the errors and let him suggest what he can do to improve his spelling skills if needed.

## MEETING INDIVIDUAL NEEDS

Use flash cards of the chart words for the vowel sounds /oo/, /uu/, and /ou/, plus any story words having these sounds. Place the cards for the key words *food, book, mouth* in a row on the table. Mix up the other cards. Have S. sort the cards and place them under the right key word. Have him read the cards in each group aloud. If he has placed a card under the wrong key word, go over the word with him and help him to distinguish the vowel sound. Have him place it under the right key word.

Use suggestions given in the last lesson for help on comprehension skills.

In *Focus on Phonics-4*, you may use Practices 9A-9C. They cover *ou* word families.

# Lesson 10

ow = ou

town
ow = ou

| | | |
|---|---|---|
| | cow | cow | cow |
| | crowd | crowd | crowd |
| | down | down | down |
| | clown | clown | clown |
| | frown | frown | frown |
| | flower | flow' er | flower |

---

| drove | contest | (con'test) | horse | (hors) |
| fair | county | (coun'ty) | sure | (shuur) |
| feet | easy | (eaz'y) | against | (u genst') |
| held | ribbon | (rib'un) | excite | (ex site') |
| pie | summer | (sum'er) | unhappy | (un hap'py) |
| win | tractor | (trac'ter) | | |
| how | | | | |
| now | | | | |
| Brown | (How'erd) | | | |
| Howard | (Johns'town) | | | |
| Johnstown | | | | |
| Sue | | | | |

## At the Howard County Fair

Mr. and Mrs. Ed Brown and their two teenagers were in town for the county fair. The Howard County Fair was held in Johnstown at the end of the summer. Every summer, crowds of people came to town for the fair. The week of the fair was the most exciting week of the year in Johnstown.

The Browns lived on a farm in Howard County. They had worked hard to get ready for the fair.

The Browns' son Tom hoped to win a blue ribbon for his cow Beauty. He had raised this cow from birth. Beauty gave more milk than any other cow on their farm. Tom was sure that she would win first prize.

Tom's sister Sue was excited about the horse show. Last year, she and her horse Sugar won a red ribbon for second prize. "I'm sure that Sugar is ready for a blue ribbon now," Sue told her brother.

Tom answered, "Yes, and Beauty is ready now, too."

At the fair, Sue found a place for Sugar in the horse barn. And Tom put Beauty in the cow barn.

alike (u līk')

**In what order did these things happen?**
**Put a number by each sentence to show the right order.**

_7_  After their contests, Sue and Tom went on rides and watched the clowns.

_3_  Mr. Brown was the winner of the tractor-pulling contest.

_6_  Mr. Brown told Tom that he was proud of him.

_1_  When the Browns got to the fair, Sue and Tom put their animals in the barns.

_4_  Later that afternoon, Sue and Sugar won a blue ribbon at the horse show.

_8_  The Brown family watched the fireworks light up the dark night.

_2_  Mrs. Brown won a blue ribbon at the flower show that morning.

_5_  When Beauty won third prize, Tom was unhappy. He was the only one in his family who didn't win a blue ribbon.

---

**Practice**

**Some words sound alike. But they are not written the same way, and they do not have the same meaning. Read the words that sound alike. Then write the right word in the blank.**

**Example:**
(wood, would)  Sam ___would___ like to watch Jake carve some animals from ___wood___.

(won, one)  1. Sue ___won___ a blue ribbon at the fair, but her brother did not win ___one___.

(eight, ate)  2. Last night, I ___ate___ my dinner at ___eight___ o'clock.

(to, too, two)  3. ___Two___ sandwiches are ___too___ much for me ___to___ eat.

(new, knew)  4. Sam ___knew___ that he would learn many ___new___ things from Jake.

---

Mrs. Brown took her flowers to the flower show. It was held in the morning. There were many kinds of flowers in the show. Mary Brown got a blue ribbon for her yellow roses. But the apple pie she took to the pie contest didn't win any prize.

In the afternoon, the family watched while Mr. Brown drove in the tractor-pulling contest. One by one, 20 farmers drove their big farm tractors. Each tractor was hooked up to the pulling contest machine. It was easy for the tractor to pull against the machine for the first few feet. Then, with each foot, it became harder and harder for the tractor to pull against the machine.

One farmer went 80 feet while his tractor was pulling against the machine. Another went 86 feet. Ed Brown went 92 feet with his tractor. He was the winner of the contest.

"Dad sure knows how to drive that tractor!" Tom shouted as his father got the blue ribbon.

The horse show was held later that afternoon, at 4:30. In one contest, the riders showed how well their horses followed orders. Sue was riding Sugar. Sugar stepped high. He turned and did other things that Sue ordered him to do. Some of the things that Sue and Sugar did were hard. But they did them so well that everything looked easy. When Sue got down from her horse's back, she was happy. Sugar had followed every one of her orders very well. She and Sugar won first prize.

When Tom showed his cow, Beauty won only third prize. Tom was unhappy that his cow didn't win first prize. He was frowning when his parents came up to him.

"You look unhappy, Son," his mother said. "Why are you frowning? Your prize is something to be proud of."

"That's easy for you to say!" Tom answered. "You won a blue ribbon. Now I'm the only person in the family who didn't win one."

"Don't speak to your mother like that," said Tom's father. "And don't be unhappy, Son. We are proud of you. You have made Beauty the best cow on our farm."

After their contests were over, Sue and Tom went on some exciting rides. One of the rides went up and down and around so fast that it made them yell.

Then they watched the clowns. One clown had a smile painted on his face. Another clown had a frown, and the corners of his mouth turned down. The clowns made the crowd laugh. Tom laughed, too. He was feeling happier.

That evening, a crowd of ten thousand people listened to the band. The Browns were in the crowd. Later, they watched the fireworks light up the dark night. "This is the best fair that Howard County has ever had, isn't it?" asked Mrs. Brown. Her family agreed that it was.

## Reading for Living

million (mil′ yun)

### Reading Large Numbers

| | | | |
|---|---|---|---|
| 100 | one hundred | 250 | two hundred fifty |
| 1,000 | one thousand | 2,500 | two thousand five hundred |
| 10,000 | ten thousand | 25,000 | twenty-five thousand |
| 100,000 | one hundred thousand | 250,000 | two hundred fifty thousand |
| 1,000,000 | one million | 2,500,000 | two million five hundred thousand |

**Write the numbers for these words.**

a. two hundred          200

b. two thousand         2,000

c. twenty thousand      20,000

d. two hundred thousand   200,000

e. two million          2,000,000

**Write the words for these numbers.**

a. 750        seven hundred fifty

b. 7,500      seven thousand five hundred

c. 75,000     seventy-five thousand

d. 750,000    seven hundred fifty thousand

e. 7,500,000  seven million five hundred thousand

---

**Say the words. Circle the words with the sound *ou* as in *south* and *town*.**

| 1. | slow | (down) | (clown) | throw | low |
| 2. | (how) | (now) | know | show | |
| 3. | blow | (sound) | (proud) | yellow | (flower) |
| 4. | (cow) | snow | (crowd) | below | (around) |
| 5. | foot | (frown) | follow | (county) | (council) |
| 6. | (found) | (house) | young | touch | (shout) |

**Here are some more words that sound alike, but do not have the same meaning.
Read the words that sound alike. Then write the right word in each blank.**

(I, eye)      1. _I_ have something in my _eye_ .

(no, know)    2. _No_ , I do not _know_ the answer.

(hear, here)  3. Come _here_ so that I can _hear_ what you are saying.

(clothes, close)  4. Please _close_ the door when you change your _clothes_ .

(right, write)  5. Did I _write_ the _right_ answer to the question?

(their, there)  6. Sue and Tom are over _there_ with _their_ parents.

**Read the two words, and then write the contraction for them.
The first contraction is filled in for you.**

1. I am       _I'm_           5. do not    _don't_

2. we are     _we're_         6. did not   _didn't_

3. is not     _isn't_         7. have not  _haven't_

4. are not    _aren't_        8. that is   _that's_

## OBJECTIVES

To help your student:

- recognize that the letters *ow* sometimes stand for the sound /ou/, as in *town*.
- read words in which the sound /ou/ is written *ow*.
- recognize that the sound /ou/ is usually written *ow*, rather than *ou*, at the end of a word or syllable or when the word or syllable ends with *n*.
- distinguish the vowel sound /ou/.
- recognize that the letters *ow* may stand for the sound /ou/ or the sound /ō/ and determine which sound they stand for in certain words.
- distinguish between words that sound alike but are written differently (homonyms), as *one* and *won*.
- recall the sequence of events in a story.
- interpret the feelings of the characters in the story.
- interpret the mood of the story.
- read orally with expression.
- recognize the number of syllables in a word and which syllable is stressed.
- review the endings *-ing, -ed, -er*.
- review the prefix *un-* as in *unhappy*.
- read and write numbers of three to seven digits (hundreds to millions).
- read and write number words containing the words *hundred, thousand,* and *million*.
- write words, sentences, and numbers from dictation.

## INTRODUCTION

T: You have learned one combination of letters that stands for the sound /ou/ as in *mouth*. What are the letters? [S: *ou*.] In this lesson, you will learn another way that the sound /ou/ is written.

## I. Reading

### CHART: Page 60

**Title and key word.** Have S. read *Lesson 10* and then look at the letters in the top right-hand corner.

T: What two letters together equal the sound /ou/? [S: *ow*.] Read the key word. [S: town.] What is the vowel sound in *town*? [S: /ou/.] What letters stand for the sound /ou/ in *town*? (Point to *ow = ou*.) [S: *ow*.]

**Lines 1-6.** Tell S. that the other words in the chart have the sound /ou/ written with *ow* and that all of the words are

written the way they sound. Ask him to read the words to himself and notice where the sound /ou/ comes in each word. Also, he should notice which words rhyme.

After S. has studied the chart, have him read each word aloud. Have him tell which word has more than one syllable and which syllable is stressed. Also, have him tell which words rhyme. Point out that when a word ends with *n*, the sound /ou/ is usually written with *ow* instead of *ou*. Ask S. to read each word that begins with a blend and to tell what the blend is.

**Review.** Have S. read the words aloud again, including the key word. Go down the last column of the chart.

## STORY: Pages 61-62 (At the Howard County Fair)

Have S. read the story title and new words. Call attention to words with the sound /ou/ and how it is written. In words of more than one syllable, have S. tell the number of syllables and which syllable is stressed.

**Directed silent reading.** Ask S. to read the first two paragraphs to himself and find out who the story is about and where they are going. When he has finished reading, have him answer these questions.

Ask S. to finish the story and find out which contests each person in the Brown family entered and what prizes they won, if any. Note how long it takes S. to finish the story. Then, write the headings *Person, Contest,* and *Prize*. Have S. tell the name of each person in the order in which they went to their contests, the name of the contest, and what prize the person won, if any. Write the answers as S. gives them. When completed, your chart should look similar to this.

| Person | Contest | Prize |
|---|---|---|
| Mrs. Brown | Flower show | First |
| Mrs. Brown | Pie contest | None |
| Mr. Brown | Tractor-pulling contest | First |
| Sue Brown | Horse show | First |
| Tom Brown | Cow show | Third |

**Reading between the lines.** Discuss these questions.

1. What do you think made the fair exciting to the people who attended?
2. What color ribbon is given for first prize? [Blue.] For second prize? [Red.] Does the story tell what color ribbon is given for third prize? [No.] Do you happen to know? (If S. doesn't know, explain that it is white.)
3. Why was Tom sure that Beauty would win first prize?
4. The story says that Tom was unhappy when his cow didn't win first prize. How else might you describe how he felt? Give reasons for your description. (The answer should express that Tom felt jealous of others in his family. Ask questions to elicit this idea if necessary.)
5. How did Tom's parents react to him when he was upset about not winning first prize? Do you think they said the right thing? Why or why not?

6. From this story, how would you describe the Brown family? Give reasons for your description.
7. Have you ever been to a county or state fair? If so, what did you like about it? Did you enter any of the contests? If so, tell about your entry.

## STORY CHECKUP: Page 63

Have S. read the directions and do the sequence-of-events exercise at the top of the page. Remind him to read all of the sentences before he writes any numbers. If he has the order wrong, refer him to the story, and have him correct the errors. Also, help him understand how to use clues in the sentences themselves to put them in the right order. For example, the item telling that Tom was the only one in his family who didn't win a blue ribbon should come after the items telling that the others did win first place in their contests.

**Oral reading.** Have S. read aloud the last eight paragraphs of the story (beginning with the paragraph that starts "The horse show was held . . ."). Note whether he reads fluently and with expression.

**Note:** For now, skip the Practice exercise at the bottom of page 63, and go directly to the Reading for Living on page 64. The Practice exercise will be done later in the lesson, after the Writing Lesson.

## READING FOR LIVING: Page 64

Have S. read the title and the new word *million*. Then have him read the chart, *Reading Large Numbers,* first silently and then aloud. Point out that we use a comma after the number in the thousands' place, as in 1,000, and a comma after the number in the millions' place, as in 1,000,000. The commas make large numbers easier to read.

For further practice, ask S. to cover the number words and read only the numerals. Then have him cover the numerals and read only the number words.

Have S. read the directions for the first exercise and do it. Check his work, and have him make any needed corrections. Then have him read the directions for the second exercise. After he writes the words for 750, check to be sure he understands what to do. Then have him complete the exercise. Check his work, and have him correct any errors.

# II. Skills Practice

Have S. close his book before doing these exercises.

## PRACTICE 1: Distinguishing the Sound /ou/

T: I will say three words. Listen and tell which one has the sound /ou/ as in *mouth* and *town*.

| | |
|---|---|
| owl, old, rule | trout, throat, took |
| brook, brow, broke | grow, grew, growl |
| crow, cook, crown | noon, now, no |

## PRACTICE 2: The Two Sounds for *ow*

T: In this lesson, you had words in which the letters *ow* stand for the sound /ou/. In an earlier lesson, you had some words in which the letters *ow* stand for a different sound.

T: (Write *blow*.) Read this word. [S: blow.] What sound do the letters *ow* stand for in *blow*? [S: /ō/.] When you first learned the word *blow*, there was a line over the *o* to tell you that the sound is /ō/. (Put the line over the *o* in *blow*.) In this skill book, any new word in which *ow* stands for the sound /ō/ will have a line over the *o*. If there is no line over the *o*, you will know that *ow* stands for the sound /ou/.

Write these words (marking the *o*'s as shown here), and have S. read them: *now, cow, lōw, follōw, allow, crōw, crowd, clown.*

T: Other books will not have the long mark over the *o* to help you. But usually you can tell which way to say a word with *ow* by trying both sounds to see which makes a word.

Write these words: *owl, glow, gown, shown.* Ask S. to read each word silently by trying both sounds for *ow* to tell which is right. Then have him read the words aloud.

T: Often, when a word with *ow* is in a sentence, other words in the sentence will give you clues that will help you know what the word with *ow* is.

Write these sentences, underlining the words in italics here. Have S. read each sentence silently and then aloud. Ask him to tell which words in the sentences helped him know what the word with *ow* was.

1. The wind has *blown* for two days.
2. The king wore a *crown* on his head.
3. The angry dog began to *growl*.
4. He sleeps with his head on a *pillow*.
5. He dried his hands on a *towel*.
6. If you park there, the cops will *tow* your car away.
7. Which do you like better, a bath or a *shower*?
8. Mrs. Jones works in the garden while her husband *mows* the grass.

## PRACTICE 3: Number of Syllables and Stress

Write *again, alone, about, against, amuse, around.* Have S. read each word and tell how many syllables it has and which syllable is stressed.

T: What letter makes up the first syllable in each of these words? [S: *a.*] Is it stressed in any of these words? [S: No.] How is it pronounced? [S: /u/.] Usually, when *a* is a syllable by itself at the beginning of a word, it is not stressed, and it is pronounced /u/.

Say each word below. Have S. tell the number of syllables and which syllable is stressed.

| | |
|---|---|
| *neighbor* | (neigh' bor) |
| *neighborhood* | (neigh' bor hood) |
| *monthly* | (month' ly) |
| *ribbon* | (rib' bon) |

| | |
|---|---|
| *unhappy* | (un hap′ py) |
| *million* | (mil′ lion) |
| *discuss* | (dis cuss′) |
| *contest* | (con′ test) |
| *content* | (con′ tent) |

## PRACTICE 4: Endings *-ing, -ed, -er*

Write the words listed below in a column. Ask S. to read each word. Have him tell what the root word is, how to spell it, and what change—if any—was made in the root word before the ending was added. As he answers, write the root word in a second column.

| | | | |
|---|---|---|---|
| *exciting* | *pulling* | *later* | *stepped* |
| *raised* | *winner* | *riding* | *frowning* |
| *hooked* | *shouted* | *showed* | *happier* |

Point out that a final consonant is not doubled after *oo, ou,* or *ow.*

## PRACTICE 5: Prefix *un-*

Write *unhappy*, and have S. read it. Ask him to tell the root word and then the prefix. Review the meaning of the prefix *un-* (*not*).

Write *excited, sure, cooked, heated, written*. Have S. read each word and tell what it would be with the prefix *un-*. Write the new word by the root word. Have S. read both forms of each word.


# III. Writing

## CHECK HOMEWORK: Page 59

Check this exercise with S. Have him correct any errors.

### WRITING LESSON (In Notebook)

Have S. write the titles *Lesson 10* and *Words* and number from 1 to 24 in two columns. After he has finished the dictation, have him check his work by looking at the chart and story words.

**Words.** Have S. look at the story words on page 61. Ask him to read the words in which the sound /ou/ is written *ow*. Ask him to read the word in which /ou/ is written *ou*. Help him study the words *horse, ribbon, excite, against*. Have him notice what part of the word is written differently from how it sounds. Have him spell each of these words to himself and then practice the words. Also, have him practice writing *tractor* and *summer*. Then dictate these words:

| | | | |
|---|---|---|---|
| 1. cow | 7. Brown | 13. win | 19. county |
| 2. now | 8. frown | 14. feet | 20. against |
| 3. how | 9. crowd | 15. drove | 21. contest |
| 4. town | 10. flower | 16. fair | 22. summer |
| 5. down | 11. Howard | 17. held | 23. tractor |
| 6. clown | 12. Johnstown | 18. pie | 24. unhappy |

**Sentences.** Tell S. that you will dictate a paragraph from the story. Read the whole paragraph first. Then dictate it one sentence at a time, repeating the sentence once if needed. When S. has finished writing, ask him to listen to the whole paragraph again and note whether he has put in the correct punctuation.

> Tom's sister Sue was excited about the horse show. Last year, she and her horse Sugar had won a red ribbon for second prize. "I'm sure that Sugar is ready for a blue ribbon now," Sue told her brother.

Check what S. has written, and have him correct any errors, including those in punctuation and capitalization. Have him write the title *Study* and any words he missed in the word and paragraph dictation.

**Numbers.** Ask S. to write the heading *Numbers*. Tell him that you will dictate some numbers similar to those in today's lesson. He should write them in numerals, not number words. Have him write them in two columns, as given here. Then check what he has written.

| | |
|---|---|
| 300 | 650 |
| 3,000 | 6,500 |
| 30,000 | 65,000 |
| 300,000 | 650,000 |
| 3,000,000 | 6,500,000 |

**Note:** If this dictation seems too difficult for S., write some numbers with their number words for him to read and copy.

## PRACTICE: Page 63

Have S. read the directions and the example. Go over the meaning of the homonyms in the example, *wood* and *would*, asking S. to give a sentence for each. Then have him fill in these words in the example sentence.

Go over the homonyms given for each of the other four items, having S. give either an indication of the meaning or a sentence for each word. For example, for *won* and *one*, he might say—pointing to each word: "*Won* is like *We won the game; one* is a number." Then have S. fill in the homonyms in the blanks in the sentences. When he has completed the exercise, check his work, and help him correct any errors.

## HOMEWORK: Page 65

Have S. read the directions for each exercise. In the second exercise on more homonyms, go over the word meanings with S. as you did for the Practice exercise. Also, have him do the first sentence as an example of what to do. Encourage S. to read the story again at home and to study any words he missed in the dictation.

## CHECKING PROGRESS

Note your student's rate of silent reading in relation to his comprehension. The story in this lesson has about 700 words, and the content is simple—of the pleasure-reading type. S. was probably able to read it in five minutes or less. If he took longer, try some of the suggestions given in the next section to speed up his reading. If he read quickly but forgot or confused the main points, he needs a different type of reinforcement exercise.

At the *Skill Book 4* level, more emphasis is given to silent reading than to oral reading. But periodically you should make an opportunity for S. to read aloud a whole story or a section of it. His oral reading will enable you to check on his accuracy of word recognition and his ability to interpret meaning through phrasing, expression, and intonation.

Have S. evaluate his own progress. Ask him to tell which skills he feels confident in and which ones he needs to work on more. Find out what he is reading outside of class. Write a few long words, such as those given below, and see if he can read them. Note how he uses his phonics and word analysis skills.

| | | |
|---|---|---|
| *unhappiness* | *mouthful* | *neighborly* |
| *summertime* | *northerner* | *unfriendly* |
| *horseback* | *fountain* | *millionaire* |

## MEETING INDIVIDUAL NEEDS

**Speed of reading.** Find supplementary material that is easy for S. to read. (Consult the inside front cover of this manual and the manuals for earlier skill books for suggested titles.) Use a selection of about 600 words to be read in three minutes, or adjust the time limit proportionately to the length of an appropriate reading selection.

Tell S. to read as much of the passage as he can in three minutes. You will time him and ask a few questions about the passage. Ask him to mark the place he has reached when the three minutes are up. Ask five questions that have definite answers in the passage but are not too detailed. Keep a record of the number of words he read and the number of questions he answers correctly. Tell him that every few lesson periods, he will read a selection like this to see how his rate of reading improves.

Use slip strips to increase speed in reading phrases and sentences. Leave enough space between phrases or sentences so that when you pull the strip after he reads the line, a blank space will show through the "window." Use sentences or phrases about which you can ask a question to check his comprehension after he reads silently. Some examples are given below.

1. Jake had a big pan of water on his stove.
   (What did Jake have on his stove?)

2. five hundred thousand people
   (How many people?)

3. on the west side of town
   (Which side of town?)

For the first exercise of this nature, try exposing a sentence for about two seconds and a shorter phrase for about a second. Adjust the time so that it is a challenge to S. but not frustrating.

**Oral reading.** After the slip strip is used for silent reading, it can also be used for oral reading. Encourage S. to read in phrases and not word by word.

Use duet reading, as described in Lesson 7, as it will give S. a model of reading fluently and with expression. Also, if S. has small children at home, encourage him to read stories to them. Have some books for this purpose available for him to use.

**Phonics.** In *Focus on Phonics-4*, you may use Practices 10A-10B. They cover *ow* word families with the sound /ou/.

# Lesson 11

## More Reading
## with ū, oo, uu, and ou

| music ū | cure u–e | argue ue | few ew |
|---|---|---|---|
| food oo | June u–e | blue ue | chew ew |
| student ū or oo | Duke u–e | Tuesday ue | news ew |
| book uu | | | |
| mouth ou | town ow | | |

---

## 1. Will Jake Have to Leave the Woods?

horseback (horse′ back)    land    allow (u low′)

When Sam Cook's book came out, the state found out that Jake Bush was living on state land. Jake lived on White Mountain in a huge state park.

Officers of the state parks department discussed what to do about Jake. "People are not allowed to live on state land," they said. "Mr. Bush will have to move."

One of the officers went on horseback to Jake's cabin in the woods. He told Jake what the parks department had said.

Jake frowned and said, "I have been living here for 30 years. Why are you telling me about this now?"

The officer answered, "A lot of people know about you now. If we allow you to stay here, everyone will want to live on free land."

Jake got angry. "I'm not moving!" he shouted. "If you want me out, you'll have to carry me out!"

After the officer left, Jake went to the store on foot. There he phoned Sam Cook and told him the bad news. "I'll do my best to help you," Sam said. "I'll tell the newspapers."

Soon the newspapers were full of stories about Jake's problem. People who had read the book about Jake came to his rescue. They understood why Jake loved the woods. They didn't want the state to push him out. Thousands of people wrote letters to protest. Crowds marched in the state capital.

The parks department held another meeting. When it was over, one of the officers spoke to news reporters. He said, "We understand that Mr. Bush knows a lot about the woods and wild animals. If he will take good care of them for us, we will allow him to stay in his home. He can get a permit to live on state land in the park."

Sam Cook took the news to Jake. "Will you agree to this plan?" he asked the old man.

"I sure will!" said Jake. "It's just what I wanted."

## 2. Running for Office

Gladys (Glad' us)    should (shuud)

Gladys Brooks lived on the south side of Mountain City. She was raising her five children alone, and she didn't have much money. But she found time to work with the South Side Neighbors on housing problems. Gladys became a leader in that group. She got people to work together. And she learned how to speak in public.

Her friends told her, "No one on the city council knows what our life is like. They have never been poor. They have never been out of work for months and months. You should run for city council. You could speak for us."

"I'll have to think about it," Gladys said. She discussed the idea with many people. Everyone told her, "You should run for office."

Gladys made up her mind. "I'll run," she told the South Side Neighbors. "But I can't win without your help."

The South Side Neighbors went from house to house in their neighborhood. They told everyone what a good leader Gladys Brooks was. "You should vote for her," they said.

Gladys Brooks spoke to many groups on the south side. She told them what she would do on the city council. "We need more jobs and child care centers for working parents. We need low-cost housing and better schools. We need to make our streets safe. I will work hard to make the south side a better place to live."

When the people of Mountain City voted, Gladys Brooks won a place on the city council. The South Side Neighbors were proud of her. They gave her a party.

"Thank you for helping me to win," Gladys told them. "But our work has just started. We must work together for a better south side and for a better city."

## 3. Changes on the Farm

Brunoski (Broo nos' kē)    electric (e lec' tric)    power (pow' er)    plow

The Browns' farm had been in the family for 80 years. Ed Brown's grandfather, Joe Brunoski, came to America when he was 18 years old. When Joe came into the country, his name was changed from Brunoski to Brown. At first, Joe Brown worked on another man's farm. In time, he was able to get married and buy a farm in Howard County.

The farm land was good, but the house was old. Mrs. Brown was unhappy until she planted flowers around the house to make it more beautiful.

For many years, Joe and his wife Molly had to do everything by hand. There was no electric power. They had no electric lights or electric stove. Molly cooked on a wood-burning stove. Joe and Molly had to milk their cows by hand. Joe plowed the hard ground with a team of horses. The horses pulled the plow. On Saturdays, Joe and Molly drove the horses into town.

The Browns got a telephone and a radio sometime in the 1920s. The family was even more excited when they got their first car in the 1930s. With the car, they could go into Johnstown quickly.

When the Browns' oldest son, Jim, started to run the farm in the 1940s, he got a bank loan. With the loan, he got a tractor to pull the plow. About the same time, the county put in electric power. At last, the Browns had electric power for lights, heat, and cooking. With the electric power, they could use milking machines to milk the cows. By the 1950s, the Browns had running water in their house.

Jim Brown let his youngest son, Ed, take over the farm in the 1970s. Ed got bank loans to build a new house and buy more farm machines. Ed Brown is thinking of changing the family name back to Brunoski. He is proud of the farm that his grandfather started.

The Brown farm is like many family farms in America. Over the years, many changes have come to America's farms. Farmers now have machines, electric power, and even computers to help them. But they still work hard from the time the sun comes up until the sun goes down.

Write two questions about each story. Use the question words *why*, *how*, and *when*.

Story 1: Will Jake Have to Leave the Woods?

1. _____

2. _____

Story 2: Running for Office

1. _____

2. _____

Story 3: Changes on the Farm

1. _____

2. _____

In each line, circle the word that means the opposite of the first word.

1. up        out      (down)      about
2. winter    cold     hot         (summer)
3. happy     angry    (unhappy)   glad
4. beginning (end)    first       third
5. first     best     blue        (last)
6. easy      sure     (hard)      proud
7. leave     catch    discuss     (stay)
8. head      (foot)   hand        mouth

---

plural (pluʹr ul), loaves (loavz), tooth, vowel (vowʹ ul)

Read each word. Then write the word in its plural form.

Example:  loaf    _loaves_

1. foot   _feet_      5. child   _children_
2. tooth  _teeth_     6. wife    _wives_
3. man    _men_       7. leaf    _leaves_
4. woman  _women_     8. loaf    _loaves_

Fill in each blank with one of the words in the plural form.
(You may use the example word in your answers.)

1. A maple tree has pretty _leaves_.

2. It is not safe for _children_ to play with matches.

3. Workers may bring their husbands and _wives_ to the company picnic.

4. Two men and three _women_ are on the city council.

5. I had two _teeth_ pulled last week.

6. Get two _loaves_ of bread when you go to the store.

7. That mountain is about twenty thousand _feet_ high.

8. There are more women than _men_ over the age of 75.

In each line, circle the word with the same vowel sound as the first word.

1. book    too     (cook)    town
2. south   tooth   (shout)   soon
3. chew    snow    foot      (threw)
4. blue    (true)  blow      brook
5. town    took    (clown)   June
6. pool    pull    stole     (school)
7. music   (argue) mouth     woods

## OBJECTIVES

To help your student:

- review the sound /ou/ as in *south* and its most regular spellings: *ou* and *ow*.
- review the sound /uu/ as in *book*.
- review the sounds /ū/ and /oo/ in their most regular spellings: *u, u-e, ue, ew*.
- apply phonics skills in reading new words with familiar sound-letter relationships.
- read short stories that review words introduced in Lessons 8-10, especially words with the sounds /uu/ and /ou/.
- recognize word opposites.
- recognize the new compound word *horseback* and review other compound words.
- recognize irregular noun plurals.
- recognize the number of syllables in a word and which syllable is stressed.
- review the endings *-ful, -hood,* and *-ly*.
- review the prefix *un-*.
- interpret the feelings of characters in the stories.
- recognize main ideas and supporting details.
- make inferences from clues in the stories.
- develop further skill in writing words, sentences, questions, and dates.
- recognize where to use commas in a series of words.

## INTRODUCTION

T: In today's lesson, you will review the vowel sounds that you have had so far in this book and the main ways that they are written. You will read three short stories that have many words with these sounds. We'll also go over some of the other things that you have studied in the last three lessons.

## I. Reading

### CHART: Page 66

Have S. read the titles *Lesson 11* and *More Reading with ū, oo, uu, and ou*.

Have S. read each key word in the chart and tell what the vowel sound is and how it is written.

Ask S. to give a word that rhymes with *book*. Remind S. that when the letters *oo* are followed by *k*, they almost always stand for the sound /uu/. Then, write these words, and have S. read them:

| | | | | |
|---|---|---|---|---|
| *push* | *pull* | *put* | *sugar* | *could* |
| *bush* | *full* | | | *would* |

Point out that these are a few very common words with the sound /uu/ written in a way different from *oo*.

Ask S. to give a word that rhymes with *mouth* and with *town*. Ask S. what sound besides /ou/ the letters *ow* sometimes stand for [/ō/].

## STORIES: Pages 67-69

**Story 1: Will Jake Have to Leave the Woods?** Have S. read the story title and new words. Call attention to the compound word *horseback*.

T: Remember the story you read about Jake Bush, the man who lived alone in the woods? How did he like living there? What was his visitor, Sam Cook, planning to do? This story will tell you what happened when Sam Cook's book came out. The title of the story is a question. Please read this one-page story, and find out the answer to the question.

Have S. read the whole story silently. Note the time it takes for him to read the story. Have him answer the title question. Then discuss these questions:

1. Who told Jake he would have to move?
2. Why did the officers of the parks department think that Jake should move?
3. What made them change their minds?
4. What offer did the parks department make to Jake so that he wouldn't have to move?
5. Do you think it was a fair offer? Why or why not?
6. What did Jake think of the offer?
7. How had so many people come to know about Jake?
8. In what ways can publicity be helpful to a person? In what ways can it be harmful?

**Oral reading.** Have S. find each of the direct quotations in the story. Ask him to identify the speaker and read aloud what was said. Encourage S. to read with expression.

**Story 2: Running for Office.** Have S. read the story title and the new words.

T: You read a story about the South Side Neighbors and some of the problems they worked out. In this story, you will read more about that group and one of its leaders.

Ask S. to read the story silently to find out who ran for office and whether or not that person was elected. Time how long it takes S. to read the story. There are about 300 words. He should be able to finish it in two or three minutes. Record the time, but don't comment on it. Then discuss these questions:

1. Why did the South Side Neighbors want Gladys Brooks to run for office on the city council?
2. How did the South Side Neighbors help Gladys win?
3. What did Gladys do herself that helped her win?
4. How would you describe Gladys Brooks? Do you think she was a good choice for city council? Why or why not?

**Oral reading.** If S. has difficulty answering a question, have him scan the story to find the paragraph that helps to answer the question. Have him read the paragraph aloud.

Also, have S. find each direct quotation that Gladys said. Have him tell the number of the paragraph and then read the quotation aloud.

**Story 3: Changes on the Farm.** Have S. read the story title and the new words.

T: You read a story about the Brown family who went to the Howard county fair. In this story, you will learn more about their family farm.

Ask S. to read the story to himself to find out how long the farm had been in the family and what major changes had taken place over the years.

When S. has finished reading, have him tell how long the farm had been in the Brown family and which member first owned the farm. Write the heading *Joe (Brunoski) Brown.* Have S. tell what farm life was like during the time Joe was running the farm. Discuss these questions:

1. Why do you think *Brunoski* was changed to *Brown?* (If S. is not aware, explain that, while some people who came to this country changed their own names to make them easier and more American-sounding, many years ago, people's names were often changed without their permission by immigration officers who had trouble spelling and pronouncing long foreign names. Since the story says that Joe Brunoski's name *was changed,* not that *he* changed it, this is what happened to him.)
2. What happened in the 1920s that changed life on the farm?
3. What happened in the 1930s that brought a change?

Have S. tell the name of the next family member to run the farm and when he began to run it. Write the heading *Jim Brown.* Have S. tell the major changes on the farm during the time Jim was running it. Do the same thing for *Ed Brown.* Then discuss these questions:

1. For how many generations has the farm been in the Brown family? (Refer to the headings, and discuss the relationship of the three Brown men.)
2. Do you think the farm will remain in the family? Why or why not?
3. Why is Ed Brown thinking of changing the family name back to Brunoski? If you were Ed, would you change the name? Why or why not?

**Oral reading.** Have S. read the last three paragraphs aloud. Note his competence in word recognition, phrasing, intonation, and observation of punctuation marks. Check any words that he miscalls or omits. Do not comment on errors at this time, but plan reinforcement exercises for any special needs.

## STORY CHECKUP: Page 70

Have S. read the title and directions. Tell him that he may scan the story before writing the questions if he wishes. After he has written the questions, have him read them aloud. Check his work for correct spelling, capitalization, and punctuation.

## READING FOR LIVING (Supplementary Materials)

Use whichever of the following activities will fit comfortably within your lesson period and seem most appropriate to your student's abilities and interests.

**Table of contents.** Have available a supplementary book on the reading level of your student. Choose a book that has a table of contents. Refer to the Reading for Living section in Lesson 8, and ask similar questions for S. to answer orally about the book you have chosen.

**Neighborhood map.** Bring to class a map of your community. Mark a section of the map for S. to study. Or, make a simple map of a neighborhood—your student's or the one where your lessons are held. Ask questions about the map, similar to those given in Lesson 9. Or, you may review the map in Lesson 9 by asking questions that are different from those in the exercise for S. to answer orally. Or, have S. describe the route from one place to another on the map.

**Reading large numbers.** If S. had some difficulty with the exercise on large numbers in Lesson 10, review the numbers and number words in the chart on page 64. Then write a similar set of number words, such as those from *five hundred* to *five million,* and have S. write the numerals. Give another set of numerals, such as those from 325 to 3,250,000, and have S. write the number words for them.

If S. needs more of a challenge, review by writing the first five numbers below and having S. read them. Then, add the other three numbers and their number words, and have S. read them. Explain that a billion is a thousand million.

|  |  |
|---|---|
| 100 | |
| 1,000 | |
| 10,000 | |
| 100,000 | |
| 1,000,000 | |
| 10,000,000 | ten million |
| 100,000,000 | one hundred million |
| 1,000,000,000 | one billion |

Write the names and population figures for the four countries with the largest population. Explain to S. what these are, and ask him to try to read them.

| China | 1,048,840,000 | Soviet Union | 270,279,000 |
|---|---|---|---|
| India | 696,986,000 | United States | 230,891,000 |

(You may want to add another country in which S. is interested or the population of your city and state. These figures are from the 1980 census.)

# II. Skills Practice

Have S. close his book before doing these exercises.

## PRACTICE 1: Distinguishing Sounds /oo/ and /ou/

Write *food* and *book,* and have S. read them. Have him tell the vowel sound in each. Write *oo* below *food* and *uu* below *book.*

T: I will say two words with the same vowel sound. Tell me whether the vowel sound is like the one in *food* or the one in *book*.

| | | |
|---|---|---|
| took, cook | stood, good | pool, school |
| look, shook | chew, blue | put, full |
| tool, soon | pull, push | sugar, woman |

## PRACTICE 2: Distinguishing the Sound /ou/

T: I will say three words with different vowel sounds. Tell me which one has the sound /ou/ as in *mouth*.

| | |
|---|---|
| plow, spoon, clue | shoot, sour, shut |
| noon, now, nook | brown, broom, brook |
| door, Duke, down | fowl, fool, full |

## PRACTICE 3: Number of Syllables and Stress

Read each word listed below. Have S. tell how many syllables it has and which syllable is stressed. (The words are divided into syllables here for your convenience.)

| | | |
|---|---|---|
| beau' ti ful | dis cuss' | mil' lion |
| con' tents | neigh' bor | pres' i dent |
| chap' ter | a gainst' | an' i mal |
| a bout' | ex cite' | e lec' tric |

**Note:** Have S. give the number of syllables according to the way the word is pronounced, not the way it is written. For example, only two syllables are pronounced in *million*.

## PRACTICE 4: Compound Words

Make one set of flash cards for these words: *air, after, day, fire, head, horse, room, space, under.* Write the number 1 in the top right corner of each card.

Make a second set of flash cards for these words: *back, line, mate, noon, plane, ship, stood, time, works.* Write the number 2 in the top left corner of each card.

Mix up the cards in set 1. Have S. put them in alphabetical order in a column. Ask him to read the words. Then give him the cards in set 2. Ask him to put each card in set 2 after a card in set 1 to make a compound word.

**Note:** If S. forms *airline,* accept it as correct, but ask him what other word can be added to *air.* After he forms *airplane,* tell him he can use *line* again. (He will need it for *headline.*)

## PRACTICE 5: Endings -ful, -hood, -ly

Write these columns of words, leaving space to write the words with the endings later.

| -ful | -hood | -ly |
|---|---|---|
| beauty | child | proud |
| care | woman | fair |
| power | man | sure |
| wish | girl | safe |
| peace | boy | happy |
| wonder | neighbor | easy |

Ask S. to tell what each word would be with the ending added. Have him tell any change that needs to be made before the ending is added. Write the new word by the root word. After each column is completed, have S. read the root word and the word with the ending.

## PRACTICE 6: Prefix *un-*

Write the prefix *un-.* Under it, write these words in a column: *sure, excited, afraid, safe, told, written, plowed.* Have S. tell what each word would be with the prefix *un-* added. Write the new word. Have S. read each word with the prefix *un-* and then use the word in a sentence.

# III. Writing

## CHECK HOMEWORK: Page 65

Check this page with S. Have him correct any errors. Note the type of error, and plan an exercise to give extra practice on that skill.

## WRITING LESSON (In Notebook)

Have S. write the titles *Lesson 11* and *Words* and then number from 1 to 20 in two columns.

**Words.** Dictate the 15 words given below, plus 5 other words that S. may need to review. After he has finished the dictation, check his work.

| | | |
|---|---|---|
| 1. land | 6. power | 11. mouth |
| 2. allow | 7. plow | 12. without |
| 3. horseback | 8. book | 13. town |
| 4. should | 9. pull | 14. crowd |
| 5. electric | 10. found | 15. million |

**Sentences.** Have S. write the title *Sentences.* Have him number the sentences as you dictate them.

Before dictating, write this example sentence: *We get milk, butter, and cheese from cows.* Have S. read it aloud. Underline *milk, butter, and cheese.* Explain that when we write a list of three or more things, we use a comma between items and before *and.* Point out the commas in the example sentence. Leave the example on the board for S. to follow as you dictate the sentences.

1. Jake got food, water, and wood from the woods.
2. He got coffee, sugar, and fish hooks from the store.
3. Gladys Brooks worked for jobs, housing, and schools.
4. Farmers now have machines, electric power, and computers.
5. The Browns had electric power for lights, heat, and cooking.
6. The Browns had cows, horses, hens, and other animals on their farm.

Check what S. has written, and have him correct any errors, including those in capitalization and punctuation. Have S. write the title *Study* and any words he missed in the dictation.

**Note:** In a series, the comma before *and* is optional. Some publishers use it; others do not. It is taught here to follow the policy used in the Laubach Way to Reading series and other New Readers Press publications.

**Writing dates.** Dictate these dates for S. to write:

| | | |
|---|---|---|
| January 1, 1930 | March 15, 1946 | May 21, 1963 |
| October 31, 1984 | April 30, 1958 | June 18, 1979 |

## PRACTICE: Page 70

Have S. read the directions and do the exercise. Have him read aloud each word and the opposite that he has circled. Have him correct any errors.

## HOMEWORK: Page 71

Have S. read the new words. Go over the directions and example for the first exercise. Have S. tell orally what the plural form is for each of these words. Tell him to write the plurals at home.

Have S. read the directions for the second exercise and tell what the answer is for the first sentence. The last exercise is a familiar one, so there is no need to go over it with S.

Encourage S. to read the stories in this lesson at home and to study any words he missed in the dictation.

## CHECKING PROGRESS

**Comprehension.** Note your student's progress in the following areas, as shown in the reading of the stories in this lesson. Plan reinforcement activities for the skills with which he needs the most help.

1. Understanding main ideas.
2. Interpreting the feelings of characters.
3. Making inferences from clues in the story.
4. Recalling important facts, as in the story "Changes on the Farm."
5. Recognizing the sequence of events, as in the same story.
6. Scanning a story to find certain information.

**Word recognition.** Check your student's progress in these areas:

1. Recognition of new words by applying phonics skills and knowledge of syllables, root words, endings, and prefixes.
2. Recall of words previously taught, as evidenced in oral reading.
3. Recognition of compound words.
4. Recognition of word relationships, as evidenced in the written exercise on word opposites and the answers given orally in the preparation for the Homework exercise on irregular noun plurals.

**Spelling and writing.** The Story Checkup and dictation exercises will enable you to evaluate your student's progress in spelling and writing. Note his ability to use correct punctuation, to write complete sentences or questions, and to write legibly. If he has many errors in spelling, note the type and plan to review spelling rules that may help him.

## MEETING INDIVIDUAL NEEDS

If S. did fairly well in this lesson, have him go on to Lesson 12. If an additional review lesson is needed, use supplementary material on this level, or create your own exercises. Have S. complete in class any written exercises that he has not done for Lessons 8-11. Use duet reading to help him increase his speed of reading. Also, use *Focus on Phonics* for review of needed phonics skills.

In *Focus on Phonics-4,* you may use Practices 11A-11B. They provide a review of words with the sounds /uu/ and /ou/, plus a review of some word endings.

# Lesson 12

aw

lawn
aw

| | saw | saw | saw |
|---|---|---|---|
| | law | law | law |
| | claw | claw | claw |
| | crawl | crawl | crawl |
| | awful | aw′fuul | awful |
| | Dawson | Daw′son | Dawson |

---

| Shaw | bark | fence (fens) |
|---|---|---|
| long | dig | Jerry (Jerr′y) |
| strong | hole | sorry (sorr′y) |

dog
watchdog (watch′dog)
across (u cross′)

## 1. The Neighbors' Dog

Jerry Dawson had a beautiful lawn. His neighbors, the Shaws, had a big, strong dog. Their dog liked to dig holes with his long claws.

One Saturday morning, Jerry Dawson was cutting his lawn. He saw a big hole in the lawn near the fence. Jerry Dawson shouted across the fence to Bob Shaw. "Your dog has made an awful hole in my lawn again. He crawled under the fence. I can see his claw marks."

Bob Shaw came to the fence. He saw why Jerry Dawson was so angry. "I'm awfully sorry," Bob said. "But what can I do? He's a strong dog. He can dig a hole under my fence with his long claws."

"Being sorry isn't good enough," said Jerry. "Tie him up. That's the law. You know the law of this town as well as I do. It's against the law to let a dog run free."

"I don't let my dog run free on the streets," said Bob. "The law says a dog doesn't have to be tied up if you have a fence around your land. I don't want to tie my dog up. I need him as a watchdog."

"I'm sorry, but this has been going on long enough," said Jerry. "You'll have to fix the fence so your dog can't crawl under it. He had better not dig any more holes in my lawn, or I'll report you to the police!" By that time, Bob was awfully angry, too. Both men were shouting across the fence.

A few nights later, the sound of a dog barking woke Jerry up. The Shaw's dog was barking and barking. Jerry crawled out of bed and looked out the window. Just then, the lights came on in Bob's house. Both men saw someone running across Jerry's lawn and down the street.

Bob helped Jerry check his house. In the kitchen, they found a broken window. "Your dog is a good watchdog. I'm glad to have him as a neighbor," Jerry said. "But I still don't want him digging holes in my lawn. I'll help you make the fence stronger."

au = aw

Paul
au

| | | | |
|---|---|---|---|
| | haul | haul | haul |
| | sauce | saus | sauce |
| | laundry | laun′ dry | laundry |
| | cause | cauz | cause |
| | because | bē cauz′ | because |
| | automobile | au′ tō mō bēl | automobile |

---

## 2. An Accident in the Fog

| | | | |
|---|---|---|---|
| fault | along (u long′) | accident (ac′ si dent) | couldn't (could′ unt) |
| fog | exit (ex′ it) | tomato (tu mā′ tō) | highway (high′ way) |
| off | front (frunt) | | |
| wet | | | |

When Paul Jones came in the door, his wife cried out, "What happened?" Her husband was covered with something red and wet.

"It's only tomato sauce," Paul said. Then he told her what had happened.

That morning, Paul was driving a laundry truck along the highway. He was hauling clean laundry into the city. Paul was not driving fast. He had never had an accident in 15 years of driving trucks. But he was afraid of having one now.

It had stopped raining, but the highway was still wet. Fog covered everything. Because of the heavy fog, Paul could hardly see the road in front of him. Behind him was a huge truck. It was hauling big cans of tomato sauce. Paul could see the lights of the truck. But because of the fog, he couldn't tell how big it was.

There was a light gray automobile moving along next to Paul. But Paul couldn't see it because of the fog. The automobile's lights were off.

Paul was nearly at the exit where he wanted to turn off the highway. He was watching for the exit sign. It was hard to see the exit sign in the fog. Just then, the gray car cut in front of Paul's truck and slowed down for the exit.

Paul didn't see the automobile. His truck ran into it. Because the road was wet, the huge truck behind Paul couldn't stop in time. When the driver tried to turn out of the way, his truck went off the highway and turned over. The tomato sauce he was hauling went everywhere.

When the police came, it looked like the three drivers were badly hurt. But they were just covered with tomato sauce.

The police tried to find out what caused the accident. They asked each driver how it happened. Paul and the other truck driver said that it was not their fault. The police agreed.

The police said that the fog and the wet road were two of the causes. But the main cause was the driver of the automobile. "This accident was your fault," they told him. "You should not have been driving in the fog with your lights off. And you should not have cut in front of the truck."

Paul finished his story. "I'm sorry I had my first accident," he told his wife. "But I'm glad no one was hurt, and I'm glad I wasn't at fault." As he pulled off his clothes, Paul added, "Now I have to do some laundry of my own."

## Getting Accident Information

auto    insurance (in shuur′ uns)    complete (com plete′)    no. (number)
Ford    rear    damage (dam′ ij)    Ohio (Ō hī′ ō)

If you have an auto accident, your insurance company will help you complete an accident report. But you will need to find out some information at the time of the accident. The form below will help you remember what to find out. Complete the form, using these facts.

At 7:30 this morning, your car was hit from the rear by a brown 1990 Ford car, with Ohio license plates, number XCL 140. Your car was damaged in the rear and has a broken rear window. Peter Smith, of 500 Center St., River Town, Ohio 44433, was driving the Ford. His insurance company is National Auto Insurance. His Ford was not damaged. Jim Parker, of 140 Main St. in your city, saw the accident, which took place at the corner of Oak St. and Second Ave. in your city. No one was hurt.

Other driver's name and address _____

Other driver's license plate no. _____ State _____

Other driver's automobile: Make _____ Year _____ Color _____

Other driver's insurance company _____

Place of accident: State _____ City _____
                Streets _____

Date of accident _____ Time of accident _____ a.m. _____ p.m.

Damage to other automobile _____

Damage to my automobile _____

Name and address of any person who saw the accident _____

---

## Story Checkup

**Finish each sentence.**

### Story 1: The Neighbor's Dog

1. Jerry Dawson was angry with Bob Shaw because _____

2. Bob Shaw was angry with Jerry Dawson because _____

3. Bob Shaw didn't want to tie up his dog because _____

4. One night, Jerry woke up because _____

5. After that, Jerry was glad to have the dog as a neighbor because _____

### Story 2: An Accident in the Fog

1. Paul Jones was driving a truck along the highway because _____

2. Paul could hardly see the road in front of him because _____

3. The driver of the big truck couldn't stop in time because _____

4. The police said the driver of the gray automobile was at fault because _____

5. Paul's wife cried out when she saw him because _____

## Practice

**Circle the words with the sound *aw* as in *lawn* and *Paul*.**

| 1. | (saw) | snow | (claw) | car |
|----|-------|------|--------|-----|
| 2. | low | (law) | look | new |
| 3. | pull | hurt | (haul) | (awful) |
| 4. | (crawl) | rule | (paw) | cook |
| 5. | (Shaw) | (fault) | smell | (sauce) |
| 6. | (cause) | laugh | (haul) | (auto) |

**Add *-er* and *-est* to each root word to make new words.**
**Write the new words by the root word.**
**Then fill in each blank in the sentences with the right word.**

1. wet    *wetter*    *wettest*

   Mr. Brown says that this summer is *wetter* than last summer.

   He says it is the *wettest* summer he remembers.

2. strong    *stronger*    *strongest*

   Jerry, Paul, and Lewis had a contest to see which one was *strongest*.

   Jerry was *stronger* than Paul.

   But Lewis was the *strongest* of the three men.

3. long    *longer*    *longest*

   Hugh's boat is 12 feet long. Ed's boat is 14 feet long. Bob's boat is 16 feet long.

   Ed's boat is *longer* than Hugh's.

   Bob's boat is *longer* than Ed's.

   Bob's boat is the *longest* of the three boats.

---

**In each line, circle the word that is the opposite of the first word.**

| 1. | wet | cold | hot | (dry) |
|----|-----|------|-----|-------|
| 2. | light | (dark) | bright | brown |
| 3. | front | top | (back) | before |
| 4. | long | little | (short) | high |
| 5. | over | (under) | before | into |
| 6. | off | in | out | (on) |
| 7. | sorry | angry | sad | (glad) |
| 8. | rear | next | (front) | side |
| 9. | before | (after) | soon | along |

**Say each word. Put the stress mark after the syllable that is stressed.**

1. because    be cause´
2. automobile    au´ to mo bile
3. accident    ac´ ci dent
4. laundry    laun´ dry
5. across    a cross´
6. damage    dam´ age
7. tomato    to ma´ to
8. sorry    sor´ ry
9. unhappy    un hap´ py
10. excite    ex cite´
11. insurance    in sur´ ance
12. complete    com plete´

# LESSON 12

**Skill Book 4**
Pages 72-79

## OBJECTIVES

To help your student:

- recognize the vowel sound /aw/ as in *law* and *Paul.*
- recognize that the sound /aw/ may be represented by *aw* or *au.*
- recognize that the sound /aw/ at the end of a word is usually written *aw.*
- read words in which the sound /aw/ is written with *aw* and *au.*
- distinguish the sound /aw/ from the sounds /ou/, /uu/, /oo/.
- recognize the compound words *watchdog* and *highway.*
- recognize *couldn't* and review other contractions.
- recognize that the letters *rr*, as in *Jerry* and *sorry*, do not usually change the sound for the vowel they follow.
- recognize word opposites.
- recognize the abbreviations *no.* for *number* and review some other abbreviations.
- review the endings *-er* and *-est.*
- recognize that the endings *-ful* and *-ly* together (*-fully*) can be added to root words, as in *carefully.*
- recognize cause and effect.
- predict the outcome of a story.
- interpret the feelings of characters in the story.
- relate the story to personal experience and values.
- read a story written in two columns.
- fill out a form giving accident information.
- write words, sentences, and addresses from dictation.

## INTRODUCTION

T: In Lesson 11, you reviewed the five vowel sounds you have studied in this book and the ways they are written. In today's lesson, you will learn a new vowel sound and two ways it is written.

# I. Reading

## CHART: Page 72

**Title and key word.** Have S. read the title *Lesson 12.*

T: Look at the letters in the top right-hand corner. What are they? [S: *aw.*] Look at the picture and key word. Listen while I say the word, and then tell what vowel sound you hear: *lawn.* What is the sound? [S: /aw/.] What letters stand for the sound /aw/ in *lawn?* [S: *aw.*]

**Lines 1-6.** Ask S. to read the other words in the chart to himself and notice how many sounds are in each word, which words rhyme, and which words have more than one syllable.

After S. has studied the chart silently, have him read the words aloud, going down the last column. Then call attention to these points:

1. The words that rhyme (*saw, law, claw*). Have S. tell where the sound /aw/ comes in these words—in the middle or at the end. Ask him to think of one or two other words that rhyme with these words.
2. The words that begin with a blend and what the blend is (*claw, crawl*).
3. The words with more than one syllable and which syllable is stressed. Point out that the sound /aw/ comes at the end of a syllable in these words. Also, point out that *Dawson* is a person's last name.

**Review.** Have S. read each word aloud again, including the key word. Cover the pictures, and go down the last column of the chart.

## STORY 1: Page 73 (The Neighbors' Dog)

Have S. read the story title and new words. Note that the words *dog, long, strong, across* have not been respelled. In some regions, these words are pronounced with a short *o* sound; in other regions, they are pronounced with an /aw/ sound. Most dictionaries give both pronunciations. Have S. say the words the way he normally says them. Point out the compound word *watchdog.*

Call attention to the two *r*'s in *Jerry* and *sorry* and the short sound of the vowel that precedes them. Explain that the letters *rr* usually do not change the sound of the vowel they follow. The two *r*'s are left in the respelling to show that the vowel remains short instead of changing as it usually does when followed by one *r.*

**Directed silent reading.** Have S. cover the last two paragraphs of the story. Ask him to read all of the story except those paragraphs to find out what problem the neighbors were having. After S. finishes reading silently, ask him to tell who the neighbors were and what their problem was.

Have S. tell how he thinks the neighbors might solve the problem. Then have him read the rest of the story to see what happened and how the problem might be solved.

**Reading between the lines.** Discuss these questions.

1. Do you think this was the first time that Jerry Dawson and Bob Shaw had argued about the dog? What are the reasons for your answer?
2. Which neighbor do sympathize with? Why?
3. What are some feelings other than anger that are shown by what the men said or did in the story?
4. Have you ever had a similar problem with neighbors? How was the problem resolved?

## STORY CHECKUP: Page 76 (Story 1)

**Note:** For now, skip over the second chart and story, and go to the Story Checkup for story 1 on page 76.

Have S. read the title and directions. Ask him to complete the sentences for story 1. Have him do as many as he can without looking back at the story. Check his work. Have him refer to the story for any answers he had wrong or omitted.

## CHART: Page 74

**Note:** Turn back to the second chart on page 74.

T: In this chart, you will find another way the sound /aw/ is written. Look at the letters in the top right-hand corner. What letters equal the sound /aw/? [S: *au*.]

Have S. read the key word, *Paul*. Have him tell the vowel sound and the letters that stand for that sound.

**Lines 1-6.** Ask S. to read the other words in the chart to himself and notice whether *au* is in the middle or at the end of the word or syllable.

After S. has studied the chart silently, have him read the words aloud, going down the last column. Then call attention to these points:

1. The words with more than one syllable and which syllable is stressed.
2. The one-syllable words in which /aw/ spelled *au* is in the middle.
3. The two-syllable words in which /aw/ spelled *au* is the middle sound of one of the syllables.
4. The sound /aw/ is written either *au* or *aw* when it comes at the beginning or in the middle of a word or syllable. It is usually written *aw* when it comes at the end.

**Review.** Have S. cover the pictures and read the words again, including the key word.

## STORY 2: Page 75 (An Accident in the Fog)

Have S. read the story title and the new words. Call attention to the contraction *couldn't* and the compound word *highway*.

Point out that this story is written in two columns, similar to the newspaper stories in Lesson 7. Have S. show where the first column is. Tell him to read the whole first column before beginning the second column.

Ask S. to read the whole story to himself to find out who had an accident and what caused it.

## STORY CHECKUP: Page 76 (Story 2)

As soon as S. finishes reading, have him do the Story Checkup for story 2 on page 76. Check his work, and note how many answers he has right. Then have him look back at the story to find the correct answers for any that he had wrong or omitted. Have him read the sentences with the correct answers aloud.

**Reading between the lines.** Discuss these questions.

1. Why do you think Paul was afraid that he might have an accident that morning?
2. Why did the three drivers look like they were badly hurt?
3. How do you think Paul's wife felt when she saw him come in the door? How do you think she felt after she heard his story?

**Note:** To be sure S. understood how the accident occurred, you may want to have him draw a simple sketch of it from a bird's-eye view. The sketch should show the highway, the exit, and the relative position of the three vehicles as the gray car cut in front of Paul's laundry truck. This is a useful skill, as accident reports often ask for a sketch of what happened.

## READING FOR LIVING: Page 77

Have S. read the title and new words first silently and then aloud. Call attention to the abbreviation *no.*, which is read as the full word *number*.

Ask S. to read the first paragraph silently to find out what kind of form is given here. After he has read the paragraph, have him tell what kind of form it is and the purpose in filling it out. Emphasize that this is not a complete accident report form. Also, point out that he should always fill in forms by printing, even if the form doesn't mention this.

Ask S. to read the second paragraph carefully to get the facts. Then have him fill in the information asked for in the form. Give help where S. needs it in understanding the form. Check his work, and help him find the correct answers for anything he had wrong or omitted.

# II. Skills Practice

Have S. close his book before doing these exercises.

## PRACTICE 1: Distinguishing the Sound /aw/

T: I will say three words. Tell me which one has the sound /aw/ as in *lawn* and *Paul*.

| | |
|---|---|
| *jaw, June, throw* | *pat, plow, paw* |
| *hole, haul, hook* | *bowl, bawl, book* |
| *cause, cook cool* | *frown, crawl, school* |

Write *book, food, mouth, lawn,* and have S. read them.

T: I will say a word. Tell me which of these key words has the same vowel sound even if it's not spelled the same way.

| | | | | |
|---|---|---|---|---|
| *shook* | *pound* | *crook* | *yawn* | *wool* |
| *wood* | *boot* | *pause* | *trout* | *shawl* |
| *raw* | *fault* | *booth* | *choose* | *stout* |

## PRACTICE 2: Contractions

Write the contraction *couldn't*. Have S. read it and tell the two words it stands for. Write *could not* by *couldn't*. Ask S. to give a sentence using *couldn't*.

Then read these sentences, and have S. tell what contraction he hears in each one and the two words it is made from. As he answers, write the contraction and the two words.

1. "I'm awfully sorry," said Bob.
2. He's a strong dog.
3. I don't want to tie my dog up.
4. You'll have to fix the fence.
5. The law says a dog doesn't have to be tied up.
6. I'll report you to the police.
7. It's only tomato sauce.
8. Paul didn't see the automobile.
9. I wasn't at fault.
10. Paul couldn't see the car because of the fog.

## PRACTICE 3: Vowels with *rr*

Write these pairs of words: *match, march; hen, her; big, bird; shot, short; hunt, hurt.* Have S. read each word and tell the vowel sound. As he does, underline the letter or letters that stand for the vowel sound. Review the rule that *r* usually changes the sound of the vowel it follows.

Then write these pairs of words, and have S. read them: *cat, carry; jet, Jerry; miss, mirror; sock, sorry.* Have S. tell the vowel sound in each word and the letter that stands for the sound. Underline *a,e,i,o* as he answers. (In order for S. to hear the short vowel sounds in the *rr* words clearly, you may need to pronounce them in a somewhat exaggerated way, dividing them into two syllables, like this: *ca/rry, Je/rry, mi/rror, so/rry.*) Point out that the letters *rr* do not usually change the sound for the vowel they follow.

Then call attention to these exceptions:

1. The letters *orr* may also be pronounced like the *or* in *short.* Say the word *sorry* both ways (that is, like *sah-ry* and *sore-y*). Then have S. tell which way he pronounces it.
2. In words like *hurry* (write it), the letters *urr* stand for the same sound as *ur* in *hurt.*

Write these words, and ask S. to try reading them. (Be sure to mark the second *o* in *borrow*.) If S. pronounces *orr* differently in the two words here, assure him that it's perfectly all right.

| | | | | |
|---|---|---|---|---|
| *marry* | *berry* | *irritate* | *borrōw* | furry |
| *Larry* | *cherry* | | Morris | purring |

Write *star, starry,* and have S. read them. Point out that when *r* is doubled before an ending, the pronunciation of the vowel sound in the root word does not change when the ending is added.

## PRACTICE 4: Endings *-er* and *-est*

Write these root words in a column: *old, young, new, rich, proud, poor, hot, wet, easy, angry, foggy.* Ask S. to add the ending *-er* and then the ending *-est* to each root word. Ask him to spell the new words. Write the *-er* and *-est* forms in columns 2 and 3. Have S. note which root words are changed before the ending is added and how they are changed. Finally, have S. read all three forms of each word.

## PRACTICE 5: Endings *-ful* + *-ly* (*-fully*)

Write *awfully,* and have S. read it. Underline *-fully* and explain that the endings *-ful* and *-ly* can both be added to a root word.

In a column, write *care, peace, hope, beauty.* Ask S. to add the ending *-ful* to the root word and then to add *-ly* to the new word. Write the forms with *-ful* and *-fully,* such as *careful* and *carefully,* in columns 2 and 3.

Read these sentences, and have S. tell which word that ends with *-fully* completes each sentence.

1. He is sleeping _____ .
2. The roads are icy, so drive _____ .
3. She sings _____ .
4. The letter hasn't come yet, but I am waiting _____ .

# III. Writing

## CHECK HOMEWORK: Page 71

Check this page with S. Have him correct any errors. Note the type of error, and plan an exercise to give extra practice on that skill.

## WRITING LESSON (In Notebook)

Have S. write the titles *Lesson 12* and *Words* and then number from 1 to 24 in two columns. After he has finished the dictation, have him check his work by looking at the chart and story words.

**Words.** Help S. study these words: *fence, sauce, cause, fault, front, couldn't, accident.* Give a sentence when dictating the word *hole.*

| | | |
|---|---|---|
| 1. saw | 9. strong | 17. auto |
| 2. law | 10. across | 18. off |
| 3. lawn | 11. hole | 19. tomato |
| 4. claw | 12. fence | 20. couldn't |
| 5. crawl | 13. sorry | 21. accident |
| 6. awful | 14. Paul | 22. fault |
| 7. dog | 15. haul | 23. highway |
| 8. long | 16. because | 24. exit |

**Sentences.** Have S. write the title *Sentences.* Have him number the sentences as you dictate them.

1. Our neighbors have a dog, a cat, and a horse.
2. I don't like to drive in rain, fog, or snow.
3. Jerry said, "Your dog crawled under the fence."
4. "I'm awfully sorry," Bob said.
5. Dogs, cats, birds, and other animals have claws.
6. Most accidents happen because the drivers do not look.

Check what S. has written, and have him correct any errors, including those in capitalization and punctuation. Have S. write the title *Study* and any words he missed in the dictation.

## PRACTICE: Page 78

Have S. read the directions for the first exercise and then do it. Check his answers. If he has any wrong, have him read the words in the line aloud.

Go over the directions for the second exercise with S. Check his answers for item 1 before he does the others. If he has errors, give any help needed, and then have him do the other items.

## HOMEWORK: Page 79

Go over the directions with S. Encourage him to read the stories in the lesson again at home and to study any words he missed in the dictation.

## CHECKING PROGRESS

**Comprehension.** Your student's responses in "Reading between the lines" and the Story Checkup will enable you to note his progress in recognizing cause and effect, predicting the outcome of a story, and interpreting the feelings of the characters. Note which of these skills, if any, are difficult for him. Plan reinforcement activities as suggested in the next section.

**Word recognition.** Note your student's progress in recognizing new words by applying phonics skills and his knowledge of syllables, root words, endings, and rhyming words. If he is having considerable difficulty in reading new words, use some of the helps suggested in the next section.

**Writing skills.** Evaluate your student's progress in writing according to the suggestions given in Lesson 8.

## MEETING INDIVIDUAL NEEDS

**Comprehension skills.** You may use activities suggested in Lesson 8 to reinforce some of the comprehension skills needed by your student. Other suggestions are given below.

**Recognizing cause and effect.** Make two sets of flash cards, one of sentence beginnings and one of sentence endings. (Number the sentence beginnings so that they don't get mixed up with the endings.) Mix up each set of cards, and have S. match them.

#### Sentence beginnings
1. I did not wake up on time because
2. The children cannot play outside because
3. Joe and Molly did their farm work by hand because
4. Tom was unhappy after the cow show because
5. That mountain is hard to climb because
6. Mike O'Toole calls himself a human fly because
7. I couldn't do the laundry because
8. The Parks Department didn't make Jake move because

#### Sentence endings
- the alarm didn't go off.
- it is raining very hard.
- they did not have electric power yet.
- his cow didn't win first prize.
- it is rocky and steep.
- he climbs up the side of tall buildings.
- thousands of people protested.
- the electric power went off.

After S. has matched the cards, ask him to tell which part of the sentence tells the cause and which tells the effect.

**Interpreting the feelings of characters.** Read a short story aloud to S. Discuss the feelings of the characters and how those feelings are shown. Does the author describe the feelings, or does the author show the feelings by something the character says or does?

Ask S. to give some words that describe how a person may feel such as *angry, unhappy, disappointed, excited, lonely.* Have S. select one of the words without telling you which one it is. Ask him to give three or four sentences about a character that will let you know how the person feels but will not actually use the word he has in mind. See if he can do this well enough so that you can interpret the right feeling.

Reverse roles. Give some sentences yourself about a character's feelings, and see if S. can interpret the feeling you want to portray.

**Word recognition.** For more practice in adding the adjective endings *-er* and *-est*, make a word wheel with the root words *safe, cool, poor, rich, low, fair, long, strong.*

Make a slip strip for the word family *aw*, with these beginning letters and blends: *j, l, p, r, s, th, cl, dr, fl, str.*

Make flash cards for rhyming words. Choose those that use the same spelling pattern, such as these: *lawn, dawn, yawn; Paul, haul, Saul; cause, pause, clause; draw, claw, thaw; long, strong, song; tomato, potato.*

Use suggestions given in Lesson 4 for help in recognizing stressed syllables.

In *Focus on Phonics-4,* you may use Practices 12A-12B, which cover words with *aw* and *au.*

all = awl

ball = bawl
all = awl

| | | | |
|---|---|---|---|
| | wall | wall | wall |
| | hall | hall | hall |
| | fall | fall | fall |
| | call | call | call |
| | small | small | small |
| | baseball | base' ball | baseball |

## Jackie Robinson

| Jackie (Jack' ē) | Rickey (Rick' ey) | crack | basketball (bas'ket ball) |
|---|---|---|---|
| Robinson (Rob' in son) | also (awl' sō) | track | football (foot' ball) |
| Brooklyn (Brook' lin) | chance (chans) | fame | California (Cal i forn' yu) |
| Dodgers (Doj' erz) | major (mā' jer) | fan | manager (man' ij er) |
| national (nash' un ul) | series (sēr' ēz) | kept | prejudice (prej' uu dis) |
| league (leeg) | talk (tawk) | Branch | |

National Baseball Hall of Fame & Museum, Cooperstown, N.Y.

Crack! At the crack of the bat, the ball went flying over the wall. A home run for Jackie Robinson! The crowd was excited. Fans yelled for Jackie and the Brooklyn Dodgers.

The year was 1947. That fall, the Brooklyn Dodgers were the top baseball team in the National League. Jackie Robinson was voted the best new player of the year. He was also the first black player in the major leagues.

Until 1947, all the baseball players in the major leagues were white. A wall of prejudice kept black players out. There were many good black players and some great ones. But they weren't allowed to play in the major leagues. Blacks had to play in smaller black leagues.

Branch Rickey, the president and manager of the Brooklyn Dodgers, had the courage to go against the all-white rule. He believed that any player, black or white, should have the chance to play in the major leagues.

Branch Rickey looked for a black player for his Brooklyn Dodgers. He knew that many fans would not like having a black player on the team. The fans would call him names. Some Dodger players would refuse to talk to him. Some teams would refuse to play the Dodgers. It would take a very strong man to stand up to this prejudice. He would also have to be a very good player.

Rickey picked Jackie Robinson. Jackie was born in the South in 1919. When he was small, his mother moved to California with her five children. Jackie went to high school and college in California.

Jackie became a sports star in high school. He played basketball, football, and baseball. He was also a track star. Then he went to a small two-year college, where he continued to be a sports star. His record in sports gave him a chance to go to the University of California. There, he was the first student to win a letter in all four sports—football, basketball, baseball, and track.

When Jackie's mother got sick, he dropped out of college and went to work. Then he went into the armed services. When he got out, he played ball for one of the black teams. That was where the manager of the Dodgers found him.

Branch Rickey talked with Jackie Robinson. The manager said it would be hard to play with the Dodgers. The first black player would have to stand up to prejudice without fighting back. "Do you think you can do that?" Rickey asked.

"I have been fighting prejudice all my life," said Jackie. "This is a chance to do it by playing ball."

That first year was hard. Fans called Robinson names. Players on other teams called him names. Some players threw the baseball to hit him. Jackie did not fight back. He just kept on playing the best he could.

Jackie played so well that the fans began to like him. The team liked him, too. The wall of prejudice began to fall. After three years, Rickey agreed that Robinson could talk back if anyone called him a name.

Jackie played with the Dodgers for 10 years. He played in six World Series. He led the Dodgers to win the Series in 1955. That was a great time in Jackie's life. Another came in 1962 when he was voted into the National Baseball Hall of Fame.

Jackie Robinson was the first black voted into baseball's Hall of Fame. He was voted into the Hall of Fame because he was a great all-around baseball player. He didn't get that honor because he was the first black player in the major leagues. But he is remembered mainly for that. Jackie Robinson opened the doors for other black players in major league baseball.

## Story Checkup

Write sentence answers to each of these questions.

1. What kind of black player did Branch Rickey want for the Brooklyn Dodgers?

2. Why was the first year as a player on the Brooklyn Dodgers hard for Jackie?

3. Why was Jackie Robinson voted in the National Baseball Hall of Fame?

---

# Reading for Living

| | | |
|---|---|---|
| spring | September (Sep tem' ber) | Thanksgiving (Thanks giv'ing) |
| February (Feb' roo ār y) | November (Nō vem' ber) | Christmas (Cris' mus) |
| August (Au' gust) | December (Dē sem' ber) | season (sēa' zun) |

## Calendar for the Year 2000

**Dates to remember**

| | |
|---|---|
| January 1 | New Year's Day |
| January 17 | Martin Luther King's birthday |
| February 22 | Washington's birthday |
| March 21 | First day of spring |
| June 14 | Flag Day |
| June 21 | First day of summer |
| July 1 | Canada Day |
| July 4 | Fourth of July |
| September 4 | Labor Day |
| September 21 | First day of fall |
| October 9 | Thanksgiving Day in Canada |
| November 23 | Thanksgiving Day in United States |
| December 21 | First day of winter |
| December 25 | Christmas |

**On the calendar, circle each date in the list. Then write short answers to these questions.**

1. On what day of the week does Christmas come in 2000? _Monday_
2. Which U.S. president was born on February 22? _George Washington_
3. Which country has its Thanksgiving Day in November? _The United States_
4. Are there any holidays in August? _No_
5. When does each season begin? Write the dates.

Spring: _March 21_    Summer: _June 21_

Fall: _September 21_    Winter: _December 21_

6. Which season does August come in, spring or summer? _Summer_
7. What holiday comes in September? _Labor Day_
8. Which month does Christmas come in, November or December? _December_

## Practice

false (fawls), compound (com' pound)

**Write the right word in the blank.**

(clowns, claws, clean)   1. The cat hurt the baby with its __claws__ .

(lawn, law, lake)   2. Jerry cut his __lawn__ every week.

(holes, hauls, halls)   3. Paul __hauls__ laundry in his truck.

(laws, low, paws)   4. We should know the __laws__ of our country.

(well, wall, fall)   5. The ball went flying over the __wall__ .

(smile, small, smell)   6. Jackie moved to California when he was __small__ .

**Each of these words has two or more meanings.**
**Write sentences to show two meanings for each word.**

Example:   right   1. I write with my right hand.
　　　　　　　　　 2. I wrote the right word in the blank.

fall   1. _____
　　　 2. _____

star   1. _____
　　　 2. _____

fair   1. _____
　　　 2. _____

left   1. _____
　　　 2. _____

**Write True if the sentence is true. Write False if the sentence is false.**

_False_   1. Jackie Robinson was born in California.

_True_   2. Jackie became a sports star in high school.

_False_   3. Until 1950, all the baseball players in the major leagues were white.

_False_   4. Branch Rickey believed that only white players should play in the major leagues.

_True_   5. In 1947, Jackie Robinson was voted the best new player of the year.

_False_   6. When fans called Jackie names, he refused to play.

_True_   7. Jackie Robinson played with the Dodgers for 10 years.

_False_   8. Jackie Robinson was voted into baseball's Hall of Fame because he was the first black player in the major leagues.

**Put together a word from List 1 and a word from List 2 to make a new word.**
**Write the compound word. (You may use words in List 2 more than one time.)**

| List 1 | List 2 | Compound word |
|--------|--------|---------------|
| 1. base | father | 1. _baseball_ |
| 2. foot | back | 2. _football_ |
| 3. high | ball | 3. _highway_ |
| 4. watch | way | 4. _watchdog_ |
| 5. basket | paper | 5. _basketball_ |
| 6. left | dog | 6. _leftover_ |
| 7. news | over | 7. _newspaper_ |
| 8. horse |  | 8. _horseback_ |
| 9. grand |  | 9. _grandfather_ |

## OBJECTIVES

To help your student:

- recognize that *all* equals /awl/ in *ball* and other one-syllable words, plus compound words formed from them, such as *baseball*.
- read words in which /awl/ is written *all*.
- distinguish the sound /aw/ from other vowel sounds.
- recognize the new compound words *baseball, football, basketball,* and review other compound words.
- recognize words joined by a hyphen, as *all-around, all-white, two-year*.
- recognize the beginning consonant blend *spr* as in *spring*.
- recognize the ending consonant blend *pt* as in kept and review other ending blends.
- recognize that some words that sound alike (homonyms) do not have the same meaning.
- distinguish between fact and fiction.
- recognize cause and effect.
- recall important facts.
- interpret the feelings of the characters.
- relate the story to personal values and experience.
- understand figurative language in the story.
- read a calendar for a full year.
- recognize all the names of the months.
- read and write dates.
- write words, sentences, and a paragraph from dictation.

## INTRODUCTION

T: You have learned two ways that the sound /aw/ is written. How is /aw/ written in the word *lawn?* [S: *aw.*] In the word *Paul?* [S: *au.*] Good. In today's lesson, you will learn another way the sound /aw/ is written.

## I. Reading

### CHART: Page 80

**Title and key words.** Have S. read the title *Lesson 13.*

T: Look at the letters in the top right-hand corner. What are the letters before the equal sign? [S: *all.*] How are they pronounced? [S: /awl/.]

T: Look at the picture and the key word. What is the word? [S: ball.] What vowel sound do you hear in *ball?* [S: /aw/.] What vowel letter do you see? [S: *a.*] What letters follow *a?* [S: *ll.*]

T: Look at this combination of letters under the word *ball.* (Point to *all.*) This is also a word. What is the word?

[S: all.] What sound do the letters *all* equal? [S: /awl/.] There are many words ending in *all*. You will read some of them in the chart.

**Lines 1-6.** Have S. study the chart silently. Then have him read the words aloud, going down the last column. Call attention to the following points:

1. The meaning of *hall*. Contrast it with *haul* in the previous lesson. Have S. use each in a sentence.
2. The word that begins with a blend (*small*).
3. The compound word *baseball*.
4. The number of syllables in each of the words besides *baseball* (one).

Explain that *all* stands for the sound /awl/ in one-syllable words and compound words made from them.

**Review.** Cover the pictures, and have S. read each word aloud, going down the last column. Also, have him read the key words *ball* and *all*.

### STORY: Pages 81-82 (Jackie Robinson)

Have S. read the story title and new words. Call attention to the words with the sound /aw/. Have S. tell which words are compound words.

**Directed silent reading.** Have S. look at the story and note that it covers nearly two pages and is written in two columns. Ask him to tell how many paragraphs are on the first page.

T: Read the first five paragraphs to yourself, and find out who Jackie Robinson was. Also, find out what important change came in major league baseball in 1947 and who brought about that change.

After S. reads the paragraphs, discuss the questions. If he is not familiar with major league baseball in the United States and Canada, explain what is meant by *major league, National League,* and *Brooklyn Dodgers*. Also, discuss what is meant by the figurative term *wall of prejudice,* as used in paragraph 3.

Ask S. to read the next three paragraphs (paragraphs 6-8) to find out some facts about Jackie Robinson's early life. When S. has finished, have him summarize the facts.

Have S. read the next two paragraphs (9-10) to find out what Rickey talked about to Jackie and what Jackie's reaction was. Discuss what S. thinks Jackie meant by "fighting prejudice." Ask S. to read the next paragraph (11) and tell what was hard about the first year.

Ask S. to finish the story to find out some other facts about Jackie's baseball career. Have him summarize these facts.

**Reading between the lines.** Discuss these questions.

1. Do you think this story is fact or fiction? How can you tell?
2. Do you like to read stories about real people? Why or why not? (Ask S. to consider also the true stories about Helen Keller and Martin Luther King that he read in *Changes*.)
3. In what ways do you think this story about Jackie Robinson might be of help to someone else?

4. What do you think might have happened if Branch Rickey had selected a different kind of person as the first black player on his team?
5. What do you think is meant by the expression "Jackie Robinson opened the doors for other black players"?

## STORY CHECKUP: Page 82

Have S. read the directions to himself and answer the questions. When he has finished, have him read aloud each question and his answer. If an answer is not correct, have him scan the story to find the paragraph in which the question is answered. Have him read the paragraph aloud. Then have him write a sentence that gives the correct answer. After he has read his answers orally, check his work for sentence structure, capitalization, punctuation, and spelling.

## READING FOR LIVING: Page 83

Have S. read the title and new words first silently and then aloud. Call attention to the word with the sound /aw/ (*August*) and how it is written.

Ask S. to read aloud the title of the calendar and the names of the months in order. Then have him read aloud the list of dates to remember.

Go over the directions for the exercise. First, have S. circle on the calendar the dates in the list. Check his work, and have him correct any errors. Then have S. answer the questions. Check his answer after item 1 to make sure he knows what to do. Then let him answer the other questions independently. Check his work, and help him find the correct answer for any items he had wrong or omitted.

# II. Skills Practice

Have S. close his book before doing these exercises.

## PRACTICE 1: Distinguishing the Sound /aw/

T: I will say two words. Tell me which one has the /aw/ as in *lawn* and *ball*.

| | | |
|---|---|---|
| *tall, tell* | *hawk, hook* | *crowd, crawl* |
| *full, fall* | *small, smell* | *cause, grows* |
| *wall, wood* | *could, call* | *look, lawn* |
| *pool, Paul* | *clown, claw* | *walk, well* |

## PRACTICE 2: Substituting an Initial Consonant

Write *saw, ball, talk* at the top of three columns. Have S. read the words.

T: I will say a word that is just like one of these words except for the beginning consonant. Listen to the word I say, and tell me which of these three words it is like. Then tell what consonant letter or blend it begins with. I will write the word under the word you say it is like.

Say each of these words: *stall, thaw, raw, balk, walk, mall, draw, chalk, tall, stalk, fall*. Write the word under the word

S. says it is like—*saw, ball, talk*. If he makes an error, let him compare the spellings and tell which word it should go under.

Have S. read all of the words ending with *all*. Remind him that *all* usually sounds like /awl/ in one-syllable words, either by themselves or when they become part of a compound word.

Explain that when *all* is in words of two or more syllables, *a* has the short vowel sound /a/. Write these words as examples, and have S. read them: *valley, alley, gallon, Sally, shallōw*. (Be sure to mark the *o* in *shallow*.)

Call attention to the exception *shall* (an old word), a one-syllable word in which *a* has the short vowel sound /a/.

## PRACTICE 3: Recognizing Hyphenated Words

Write these words, and have S. read them: *twenty-one, baby-sit, baby-sitter*.

T: You had these words in earlier books. The words are like compound words, but the two words that make up a word are joined together by a hyphen. It is easy to see the two words that make up the big word. We call these words *hyphenated words*. You had some in today's lesson. They were not listed as new because you could read them easily.

Write these words: *all-around, all-white, two-year*. Ask S. to read the words and use each in a sentence.

T: Here are some other hyphenated words that you can read easily because they are made up of two words you know.

Write these words, and have S. read them: *all-out, all-star, all-time, two-way, two-faced, T-shirt*.

## PRACTICE 4: Beginning Blends *spr, str, sp, sw, pr*

T: (Write *spring*, and have S. read it.) What consonant sounds do you hear before the vowel sound in *spring*? [S: /spr/.] This is a new consonant blend. (Underline *spr*.) How many letters are in this blend? [S: Three.]

Write *street, swim, space, print*. Have S. read each word and tell what blend it begins with. Underline the blend as S. says it.

T: I will say two words that both begin with one of these blends. Tell me which blend it is.

| | | |
|---|---|---|
| *string, stream* | *spell, speak* | *press, proud* |
| *spray, sprinkle* | *sweep, swift* | *sprain, spread* |

## PRACTICE 5: Ending Blends *pt, st, nt, nd*

T: (Write *kept*, and have S. read it.) What consonant sounds do you hear after the vowel sound? [S: /pt/.] This is a new ending blend. (Underline *pt*.)

Write *plant, fist, land*. Have S. read each word and tell the ending blend. Underline the blend as he says it. Then say each pair of words, and have S. tell which blend they end with.

| | | |
|---|---|---|
| *print, aunt* | *slept, wept* | *mind, found* |
| *mind, pound* | *east, west* | *crept, swept* |

Write *keep, kept* and *sleep, slept*. Have S. read each pair of words. Explain that a few words that end in *eep* change in this way instead of adding the *-ed* ending.

Write *stopped* and *stepped*, and have S. read them. Point out that the end of these words sounds like /pt/, but they are not written with the consonant blend *pt*.

# III. Writing

## CHECK HOMEWORK: Page 79

Check this page with S. Have him correct any errors he made in the first exercise. Make a note of the errors, and plan a reinforcement exercise on recognizing opposites.

In the second exercise, if S. marked the stressed syllable incorrectly for any word, have him say the word aloud. If he pronounces the word correctly, have him tap for the beats of the syllable and note which one is stressed. If he does not pronounce the word correctly, say the word yourself, and have him listen for the stressed syllable.

## WRITING LESSON (In Notebook)

Have S. write the titles *Lesson 13* and *Words* and then number from 1 to 30 in two columns. After the dictation, check his work, and have him correct any errors by writing the whole word correctly.

**Words.** Help S. study these words: *also, chance, February, December, Christmas, false.* Point out that *Branch* is written with a capital *B* in the book because it is part of the name *Branch Rickey.* When *branch* is used as a branch of a tree or a branch office of a bank, it is written with a small *b.* Give a sentence when dictating *branch*, such as: *The bird sat on the branch of a tree.*

|     |     |     |     |     |     |
| --- | --- | --- | --- | --- | --- |
| 1.  | all      | 11. | fame    | 21. | spring       |
| 2.  | ball     | 12. | fans    | 22. | season       |
| 3.  | call     | 13. | kept    | 23. | August       |
| 4.  | fall     | 14. | crack   | 24. | September    |
| 5.  | hall     | 15. | track   | 25. | November     |
| 6.  | wall     | 16. | branch  | 26. | December     |
| 7.  | small    | 17. | also    | 27. | Christmas    |
| 8.  | baseball | 18. | talk    | 28. | Thanksgiving |
| 9.  | basketball | 19. | chance | 29. | February    |
| 10. | football | 20. | Robinson | 30. | false       |

**Sentences.** Have S. write the title *Sentences.* Have him number each sentence as you dictate it.

1. Washington's birthday is on February 22.
2. March 21 is the first day of spring.
3. Jackie Robinson was born in 1919.
4. Are there any holidays in August?
5. The fall months are September, October, and November.

**Paragraph.** Tell S. you will dictate a short paragraph from the story. He will not number the sentences. Tell S. to listen to the whole paragraph as you read it. Then read it a sentence at a time for him to write. Read each sentence once. Read it one more time if needed.

Jackie Robinson was the first black voted into baseball's Hall of Fame. He was voted into the Hall of Fame because he was a great all-around baseball player. He didn't get that honor because he was the first black player in the major leagues. But he is remembered mainly for that.

Check what S. has written, and have him correct any errors, including those in punctuation and capitalization. Have him write the title *Study* and any words he missed in the dictation exercises.

## PRACTICE: Page 84

Have S. read the directions for the first exercise and then do it. When he has finished, have him read each sentence aloud with the word he filled in. If he has an error, have him read all three words that he was to choose from. Have him circle the one he should have selected.

Go over the directions for the second exercise with S. Have him read the example aloud. Have him write sentences for the two meanings of *fall.* Check what he has written to see if he understood what to do. Then have him complete the exercise.

When he has finished, have him read each pair of sentences aloud. Discuss the meaning of any of the words that he has not used correctly. Then check what he has written for sentence structure, spelling, punctuation, and capitalization. Note the type of errors, and plan reinforcement exercises.

## HOMEWORK: Page 85

Go over the new words (*false, compound*) and directions with S. Have him do number 1 in the first exercise to make sure he understands what to do. Tell him that when he does the exercise at home he should write the answers without looking back at the story. Then, he should check his work by referring to the story. Also, encourage him to study any words he missed.

## CHECKING PROGRESS

**Comprehension.** You student's responses in the Story Checkup and the discussion of the story will enable you to evaluate his progress in the comprehension skills emphasized in this lesson. Was he able to recognize the story as being factual? Was he able to recall the important facts? Has he mastered the skill of scanning a story to find a specific fact? Does he understand figurative language? Did his responses in the Story Checkup indicate that he can relate cause and effect?

**Word recognition.** There are many new words in this lesson, but they should not be difficult for your student to read. Note his ability to see similarities in word patterns, such as in *September, November, December.* Does he recognize compound words and rhyming words? Does he associate the vowel sounds with the spellings he has learned for them?

Use suggestions given in the next section or those given in the last lesson for reinforcement of needed word recognition skills.

**Spelling and writing.** The Story Checkup and dictation exercises will help you evaluate your student's progress. If he has many errors in spelling note the type, and plan a review of spelling rules that may help him.

## MEETING INDIVIDUAL NEEDS

**Comprehension skills.** You may use suggestions given in Lessons 1, 4, 8, and 12 to reinforce comprehension skills emphasized in this lesson.

Discuss some common expressions that are examples of figurative language, such as: *in hot water, heart stood still, get cold feet, have eyes in the back of one's head, start the ball rolling, small talk, heart leaped with joy, face fell, behind the Iron Curtain,* or others. (Do not bring up very many of these at one time if yours is an ESOL student.) Use the expression in a sentence, and have S. tell what it means.

**Reading for living.** If S. is an avid sports fan, you might want to take this opportunity to introduce a current almanac. Use the index to illustrate using an alphabetical listing. Under *Baseball,* look up *Rookie of the Year, Most Valuable Player,* and *Batting Champions,* and then find Jackie Robinson in these listings. Find the location of the Hall of Fame for baseball or for some other sport S. prefers.

**Word recognition.** Make a slip strip for the word family *-all,* using these beginning letters: *b, c, f, h, m, t, w, sm, st.*

Make flash cards for the compound words reviewed in the Homework for this lesson. Have S. match the words that make a compound word.

Make a flash card for each new word in this lesson that has more than one syllable. Have S. arrange the cards into groups according to the number of syllables. Have him read all of the two-syllable words and tell which syllable is stressed. Then have him do the same thing with the other groups of words.

Make flash cards for word opposites. Use those in the Homework of Lesson 12 and the Practice exercises in Lessons 5 and 11.

In *Focus on Phonics-4,* you may use 13A-13B, which cover words with *all* and *al* having the sound /awl/.

aught = aut
ought = aut

caught = caut
aught = aut

bought = baut
ought = aut

| | | |
|---|---|---|
| taught | taught | taught |
| daughter | daugh'ter | daughter |
| fought | fought | fought |
| thought | thought | thought |
| brought | brought | brought |

---

## Between Two Worlds

| | |
|---|---|
| American | (U mār' i can) |
| classroom | (class' room) |
| grandchildren | (grand' children) |
| Tran Ty Lan | (Tran Ty̅ Lan) |
| Viet Nam | (Vē et Nom') |
| desk | |
| walk | (wawk) |
| war | (wor) |
| Wong | |
| between | (bē tween') |
| often | (awf' en) |
| pencil | (pen' sil) |
| ticket | (tick' et) |
| trouble | (trub' ul) |

Tran Ty Lan found a desk in the classroom and sat down. She took out the new pencils she had bought. "It feels good to sit down," Lan thought as she put her pencils on her desk.

As Tran Ty Lan waited for her night class to begin, she thought about her job at the nursing home. She was tired from working there all day. But she liked taking food to the old people. She liked listening to them talk and doing things to make them feel better. "But I don't understand American ways," Lan thought. "In Viet Nam, old people are not put in nursing homes. Grandmothers and grandfathers live with their children and grandchildren. Children are taught to take care of their parents when their parents get old."

Lan thought about her own parents, her brother, her two daughters, and her cousin. They were all living together in a small apartment in New York.

Then Lan thought about Viet Nam. Her husband had fought in the war and died. Her father-in-law was dead, too, but he had not fought in the war. After the war, rats brought sickness to the city. Her father-in-law had caught the sickness and died. Now Lan was trying to help her mother-in-law in Viet Nam. Every month, she bought sugar, pencils, clothes, and other things to send to her mother-in-law.

The other students began to arrive for class. Molly Hall sat at the desk next to Lan's. Molly and Lan often sat together. Molly's husband had fought and died in the Viet Nam war, too. But Molly had married again. "My children needed a father," Molly often told Lan. "Your children need a father, too. And you, Lan, don't you want to marry again?"

When Molly spoke this way, Lan told her, "You are American. In Viet Nam, we are taught that a good daughter marries only one time." But Lan was beginning to think that Molly's idea was not so bad. On TV, Lan saw that many American women married a second time.

Just as Molly sat down, Tom Wong walked into the classroom. Tom taught the math class in night school. He had lived in America all his life; his grandfather had come to America from China. "Now there's the man for you," Molly told Lan. "He's handsome and kind. And I think he likes you. He looks at you often when he's teaching."

After class, Lan started walking to the bus stop. "Want a ride?" she heard. Lan jumped at the sound of Tom Wong's words. "It's too much trouble for you," she said.

"No trouble at all," Tom said. "Come on. It's late, and this neighborhood isn't very safe at night." Lan got into the car. She wondered what her mother and father would think.

Lan's father saw the car stop in front of the apartment. He saw Tom Wong get out and open the car door for his daughter. He saw the man walk her to the door, talk to her, and smile.

When Lan came in, her mother asked, "Daughter, who brought you home?"

"My teacher brought me," Lan said.

"I hope he is only your teacher and not also your boy friend," said her mother.

Two days later, Lan got a phone call from her aunt in Canada. "Your daughters need all of your love," she told Lan. "You ought to think of their needs and their future. If you have a boy friend, you will not give as much time to them. If you marry again, your new husband may not love your children. I see trouble for them."

Lan's brother told her, "Mother and Father have been calling and writing to our relatives. Mother and Father are afraid. If you marry again, our people will talk. They will say you do not care about your children and your family. You ought to think of us. You ought to think of our relatives in Viet Nam."

Then Lan got letters from Viet Nam. Her mother-in-law asked, "How are my grandchildren? Do they remember me? Do you tell them about their father? Remember what you were taught as a child, and teach them the ways of our country."

Lan's sister-in-law wrote from Viet Nam, "I hope you don't marry again. We love you. Don't forget us."

One day, Tom Wong stopped by the apartment. "Look what I caught!" he said. "I thought your family would like some fresh fish."

When Lan saw Tom, her heart jumped. She smiled. "Thank you," she said. "Come in."

Tom talked to Lan's father and mother. "You have a fine daughter," he said. "She's a good student." Lan's father and mother smiled and thanked Tom.

Two days later, Lan's father bought three bus tickets. He told his daughter, "These tickets are for you and your children. You are going to California to live with your cousin there." He went on, "I am thinking of your children and your husband's family. Give all of your love to them. It will be better that way."

Tran Ty Lan took the tickets. She took her daughters to California as her father told her to. On the bus, Lan had much time to think. She thought about her family and the old ways of Viet Nam. She thought about her new friends Molly and Tom and their American ways. "I feel caught between Viet Nam and America," she thought. "I feel caught between old ways and new."

---

## Story Checkup

**Answer each question in one or two sentences.**

1. Why did Lan question the idea of putting old people in nursing homes?

_____

2. Why didn't Lan's family want her to marry again?

_____

3. Why was Lan beginning to think that marrying again was not a bad idea?

_____

**Write *True* if the sentence is true. Write *False* if the sentence is false.**

*True*    1. Lan's husband had fought in the war in Viet Nam.

*False*   2. Lan's mother-in-law lived in Canada.

*False*   3. Lan's family wanted her to marry again.

*True*    4. Lan's friend Molly was an American.

*False*   5. Tom Wong was born in China.

*True*    6. Tom Wong brought Lan's family some fish.

*False*   7. Lan refused to go to California to live.

*True*    8. Lan felt caught between two worlds.

**Add the ending -ness to each root word. Write the new word in the blank.**

Examples: sick ___sickness___    lovely ___loveliness___

1. kind ___kindness___    3. quiet ___quietness___
2. sad ___sadness___      4. happy ___happiness___

**Fill in each blank with one of the new words with -ness.**

1. Lan's life was filled with ___sadness___ when her husband died.
2. Lan thanked Molly for her ___kindness___.
3. My friend's grandchildren are her greatest ___happiness___.
4. Jake likes the ___quietness___ of the woods.

**Circle the words with the sound aw as in law, Paul, ball, taught, bought.**

1. caught   could   cute   bought
2. night    thought   fall   throw
3. teach    right    small   taught
4. laugh    daughter   walk   trouble
5. false    fought   fight   football

**Answer with two or three sentences.**

Why did Tran Ty Lan feel caught between two worlds? _____

---

## Reading for Living

156 Park Street
Roberts, California 95102
June 15, 1995

Dear Molly,

Are you wondering what happened to me? My daughters and I moved to California to live with my cousin. My father thought it would be best for me to leave New York.

I'm sorry I could not talk with you before I left. You are a very good friend. I will never forget you.

You helped me understand this new land. I hope I helped you understand the ways of my people and why a daughter must follow her father's wishes.

I miss school and Tom Wong. I want to explain American ways and my feelings about Tom to my parents. I want to become more American, but I want to keep the ways of Viet Nam too. I want to change, but change is very hard.

I hope we will continue to be friends. Please write to me.

Your friend,
Lan

## OBJECTIVES

To help your student:

- recognize that *aught* as in *caught* equals /aut/.
- recognize that *ought* as in *bought* equals /aut/.
- read words in which /aut/ is written *aught* or *ought*.
- distinguish the sound /aw/ from other vowel sounds.
- recognize the suffix -*ness* and how to add it to some familiar root words.
- recognize the new compound words *classroom* and *grand-children* and review other compound words.
- recognize hyphenated words, such as *sister-in-law*.
- distinguish between fact and fiction.
- interpret facts and draw inferences.
- understand figurative language used in the story.
- understand the values of another culture and relate the story to personal values and experience.
- read a letter written in cursive writing.
- write a short personal letter in cursive writing.
- address an envelope in cursive writing.
- write words and sentences from dictation.

## INTRODUCTION

Write *lawn* and *Paul*. Have S. read each word and tell what the vowel sound is and how it is written. Write *ball*, and have S. read it. Ask him to tell what letters equal /awl/. Underline *all*.

T: In today's lesson, you will learn some other combinations of letters in which the vowel sound is /aw/.

# I. Reading

## CHART: Page 86

**Title and key words.** Have S. read the title *Lesson 14*.

T: Look at the letters in the top right-hand corner. In the first line, what are the letters before the equal sign? [S: *aught*.] How are they pronounced? [S: /aut/.] What vowel sound do you hear? [S: /aw/.]

T: (Point to *ought* under *aught*.) What other combination of letters equals /aut/? [S: *ought*.]

T: Look at the first picture and key word. What is the word? [S: caught.] What vowel sound do you hear in *caught?* [S: /aw/.] What vowel letters do you see? [S: *au*.] You have learned that the letters *au* stand for the sound /aw/. That is true in this word. But there is a special combination of consonants after the vowels *au* that is important. What are the consonants? [S: *ght*.] What consonant sound do you hear? [S: /t/.] The consonants *gh* are silent.

T: Look under the word *caught*. What combination of letters do you see? [S: *aught*.] How is it pronounced? [S: /aut/.] You will see this combination of letters in a number of words. Some of them are in this chart and story. When you see the letters *aught*, how will you pronounce them? [S: /aut/.]

T: Look at the next picture and key word. What is the word? [S: bought.] What vowel sound do you hear? [S: /aw/.] There are several letters in this word to stand for the sound /aw/. When the letters *ough* are followed by *t*, they usually stand for the sound /aw/. You will see this combination of letters under *bought*. What are the letters? [S: *ought*.] How are they pronounced? [S: /aut/.] This combination of letters is also a word. What it it? [S: ought.]

## Lines 1-2

T: All of the chart words have /aut/ in them. In some of the words /aut/ is written *aught*. In other words, /aut/ is written *ought*.

T: Look at the picture in the first line and the word by it. What is the word? [S: taught.] How many sounds does it have? [S: Three.] What is the vowel sound? [S: /aw/.] What consonants follow the vowel sound? [S: *ght*.] What consonant sound do you hear after the vowel sound? [S: /t/.] Which key word has /aut/ written the way it is in *taught?* [S: caught.]

T: Read the word in the next line. [S: daughter.] How many sounds does it have? [S: Four.] How many syllables? [S: Two.] How is /aut/ written in *daughter?* [S: *aught*.] Which key word is it like? [S: caught.]

## Lines 3-5

T: Read the words in the next three lines to yourself. Notice which key word they are like. Notice which way /aut/ is written.

**Review.** Cover the pictures, and have S. read each word aloud, going down the last column. Also, have him read the key words *caught, bought, ought*.

## STORY: Pages 87-88 (Between Two Worlds)

Have S. read the story title and new words. Have him tell which words are compound words and which words are names.

**Directed silent reading.** Have S. look at the story and note that it covers two pages and is written in two columns. Ask him to tell how many paragraphs are on the first page. Then have him read the first four paragraphs to himself to find out what country Tran Ty Lan was from and what she was thinking about.

After S. reads paragraphs 1-4, have him tell the country Tran Ty Lan was from and the country she was living in at the time of the story. Have him give the sentence that indicates she was living in the United States.

Explain that in Viet Nam and other countries in the Far East, the family name comes first and then the personal name. Have S. tell, judging from how she is referred to in the story, what part of the name *Tran Ty Lan* is her personal name [Lan].

Then discuss these questions:

1. At the beginning of the story, where was Lan?
2. What was she waiting for?
3. What was she thinking about?

List the main things Lan was thinking about as S. gives them, such as the following:

1. Her job at the nursing home.
2. American ways of taking care of old people.
3. Her family living with her in America.
4. Viet Nam.

Have S. read the next two paragraphs (paragraphs 5-6) to find out who Molly Hall was and what idea she often discussed with Tran Ty Lan. After S. reads the paragraphs, have him give some facts about Molly and tell the idea she discussed with Lan. Have S. tell Lan's reaction to Molly's idea.

Have S. read the next paragraph (paragraph 7) and then tell what he found out about Tom Wong.

Then ask S. to finish the story and find out the reaction of Lan's family to her friendship with Tom Wong. Have S. summarize what happened and why.

**Reading between the lines.** Discuss these questions.

1. When Tom Wong came to Lan's home the second time, is there any clue that she might have been starting to think of him as more than her teacher? (Discuss the meaning of the figurative language used in this sentence: *When Lan saw Tom, her heart jumped.*)
2. Do you think that when a person goes to a different country to live he should try to hold on to his own customs and beliefs? Why or why not? What customs and beliefs might be good to keep?
3. Have you ever lived for some time in a country different from the one you were brought up in? What did you find most different? Which of your own customs did you keep? Which did you change?
4. What are some things you think Lan may have found strange about American life?
5. Do you think "Between Two Worlds" is a good title for this story? Why or why not?
6. Do you think this is a factual story about a real person? Why or why not? (Note: Explain that this story is made up, but it is based on true incidents.)

## STORY CHECKUP: Page 89

Have S. read the directions for the first exercise to himself and write the answers to the questions. When he has finished, check his work by having him read each question and answer aloud. If an answer is not correct, discuss the question with S. The answers are not given directly in the story, but must be inferred. Have S. read aloud the paragraph giving the information that will help him answer the question. Discuss the main ideas, and then have S. answer the question orally.

If he can give a better answer than the one he wrote originally, then have him rewrite the answer. Then correct his work for sentence structure, capitalization, punctuation, and spelling.

Have S. read the directions for the True/False exercise and then do it. Check his answers. If any are wrong, refer him to the part of the story that gives the answer. When all of the answers are correct, have S. read aloud each "True" statement. Then have him change each "False" statement orally so that it is true. (For example, he should change number 2, "Lan's mother-in-law lived in Canada" to "Lan's mother-in-law lived in Viet Nam.")

## READING FOR LIVING: Page 90

T: In *Skill Book 3*, you read a thank you letter and learned how to write one. In the Reading for Living section of this lesson, you will read a longer personal letter, and in your Writing Lesson, you will practice writing one.

Ask S. to read the whole letter to himself. Then have him answer the following questions orally:

1. Who wrote the letter?
2. Where was Lan living when she wrote the letter?
3. What is her complete address as given in the letter?
4. On what date did Lan write the letter?
5. To whom did she write the letter?
6. What greeting did Lan use to begin the letter?
7. How many paragraphs are in the letter?
8. How did Lan end the letter?
9. What are the main things she told her friend?
10. How do you think Molly will feel when she reads the letter?
11. Do you think Molly will answer the letter? Why or why not?
12. Does the letter give Molly's address?

Help S. locate these places on a map or globe: Viet Nam, North America, United States, Canada, New York State, New York City, California. Explain that Roberts is not the name of an actual city in California, but the zip code indicates a place near San Jose. Point out San Jose. Discuss the distance from New York to California (about 3,000 miles) and how long it may have taken for the bus trip (three to four days). Also, mention how long it will probably take a letter to get to Molly. Point out that first class mail is usually sent by air from one big city to another. The letter will probably arrive in two or three days.

Have S. read the whole letter aloud.

# II. Skills Practice

## PRACTICE 1: Distinguishing the Sound /aw/

T: I will say two words. Tell me which one has the sound /aw/.

| | | |
|---|---|---|
| took, talk | could, caught | threw, thought |
| out, ought | foot, fought | brought, brown |
| walk, work | taught, took | daughter, trouble |

## PRACTICE 2: Suffix *-ness*

Write *sickness*, and have S. read it. Ask what the root word is. Write *sick* in front of *sickness*.

T: What ending has been added to *sick* to make *sickness*? [S: *-ness.*] You can add *-ness* to other root words to make new words.

Write *blind, good, happy, empty, great, kind* in a column under *sick*. Have S. read each root word and tell what it would be with the ending *-ness* added. Write the word with the ending in the second column. For *happiness* and *emptiness*, point out that when a root word ends with a consonant and *y*, the *y* is changed to *i* before *-ness*. When the list is complete, have S. read both forms of each word.

T: The words in the first column are adjectives. Remember, an adjective is a word that describes something. When we added the ending *-ness*, we changed the adjective into a noun. The words in the second column are nouns.

Have S. give a sentence for *blind* and *blindness*, *happy* and *happiness* to make sure he understands how they are used.

## PRACTICE 3: Compound Words

Write the new compound words *classroom, grandchildren.* Have S. read each one and tell the two words it is made from. As he answers, write the two words by the compound word. Ask S. to tell some other compound words that begin with *grand.* Some that he might give are: *grandmother, grandfather, grandparents, granddaughter, grandson, grandniece, grandnephew.*

Write these compound words ending with *room*, and have S. read them: *bedroom, lunchroom, schoolroom.* Also, write *roommate*, and have S. read it.

## PRACTICE 4: Recognizing Hyphenated Words

Write *father-in-law, mother-in-law, sister-in-law.* Have S. read the words and tell how the parts of each word are joined. Ask him to think of other hyphenated words that can be made with *in-law.* List the ones S. gives and add others to include *daughter-in-law, son-in-law, brother-in-law.*

# III. Writing

## CHECK HOMEWORK: Page 85

Check this page with S. Have him scan the story to find the correct answer for any he had wrong in the True/False exercise. Then have him read the list of compound words he wrote for the second exercise and make any needed corrections.

## WRITING LESSON (In Notebook)

Have S. write the titles *Lesson 14* and *Words* and then number from 1 to 20 in two columns. After the dictation,

check his work, and have him correct any errors by writing the whole word correctly.

**Words.** Help S. study these words: *often, pencil, trouble, war.* Give a sentence when dictating *war.*

| | | |
|---|---|---|
| 1. caught | 8. desk | 15. American |
| 2. taught | 9. walk | 16. classroom |
| 3. daughter | 10. war | 17. grandchildren |
| 4. ought | 11. often | 18. between |
| 5. bought | 12. pencil | 19. father-in-law |
| 6. brought | 13. trouble | 20. mother-in-law |
| 7. fought | 14. ticket | |

**Sentences.** Have S. write the title *Sentences.* Have him number each sentence as you dictate it.

1. Lan's husband had fought in the war.
2. Tom Wong was an American.
3. Tom taught the math class at night school.
4. Lan took her daughters to California.

**Form for letter.** Have S. look at the letter on page 90 in his skill book.

T: The form used for this letter is the one generally used in writing a personal letter. By a personal letter, we mean one written to a friend or relative, not one for business. Let's look at the main parts of this letter before you write one of your own.

Call attention to each part of the letter, as follows:

**Heading.** Written in top right-hand corner. Writer's full address is given. Date is written just below the address.

**Greeting.** Begins at the left margin. First word begins with a capital. *Dear* is often used for a greeting. This is followed by the name the writer usually calls the person to whom he is writing. The name is followed by a comma.

**Body of the letter.** May be one or two paragraphs or several pages. First word of each paragraph is indented.

**Closing.** Begins with a capital. Written on a new line, lined up with the heading. *Your friend* is the closing in this letter. Other closings for a personal letter might be *Love, Sincerely, As ever.* The closing is followed by a comma.

**Signature.** Written on a new line just below the closing. If writing to a close friend or relative, sign the name the person usually calls you. For other personal letters, sign your first and last names.

**Writing a letter.** Tell S. you will dictate part of a letter that Molly might write to answer the one from Lan. Have S. use a new page in his notebook for the letter. Ask him to show you where the heading will be written. Ask S. to listen to the whole address before he begins to write. Read this address:

> 1342 East 10th Street
> Apartment 8
> New York, NY 10009

Have S. listen again to the first line. Write *10th*, and explain that *tenth* may be written with the numeral followed by *th.* Have S. write the first line. Then under it, have him write *Apartment 8.* Explain that the first *New York* means the city and should be written in words. For the second *New York,* which means the state, he may use the abbreviation *NY.* Have S. write the rest of the address, giving whatever help is needed. Then read the date: *June 30, 1986.* (Or, have S. write today's date.) Ask S. to write the date under the address. Then dictate the rest of the letter, one sentence at a time.

> Dear Lan,
>
> I was happy to get your letter. I didn't know what had happened to you. Tom Wong and I went to your house, but no one came to the door. We thought all of your family had moved. We're glad to know your address, but we're sorry you are so far away. We miss you.
>
> > As ever,
> > Molly

Check what S. has written in both the dictation of the letter and dictation of sentences. Have him correct any errors, including those in punctuation and capitalization. Have him write the title *Study* and any words he missed.

**Note:** You may want to take this opportunity to point out that a comma is used when two shorter sentences are joined in one sentence by the word *but.* Do this without seeming to correct an error, however.

**Addressing an envelope.** Fold a sheet of paper into the shape of a large, business-size envelope. Review the placement of the address and return address. Have S. address the envelope to *Ms. Tran Ty Lan* at the address given in her letter on page 90 of the skill book. For the return address, have him use Molly Hall's name and her address from the letter he just wrote.

**Note:** If S. has already had adequate practice in addressing an envelope, you may omit this part.

## PRACTICE: Page 91

Go over the directions and examples with S., and then have him do the first part of the exercise. Have him read the words with the *-ness* ending. Then ask him to do the second part. Check his work by having him read each sentence aloud. Have him correct any errors.

## HOMEWORK: Page 91

Go over the directions with S. Encourage him to read the story again at home and to study any words he missed in the Writing Lesson.

## CHECKING PROGRESS

**Comprehension.** Ask S. to summarize the story "Between Two Worlds" in a few sentences. Note whether he includes the main points and gives them in logical order.

**Oral reading and word recognition.** Have S. read aloud paragraphs 8-13 of the story, in which Tom Wong gives Lan a ride home and her parents question her. As he reads, note any words he says incorrectly or omits. Note the types of errors—whether in consonant sounds or blends, vowel sounds, endings or in substituting a different word. If there are several errors, analyze the types, and plan reinforcement

exercises. Also, note your student's observation of punctuation marks and ability to read fluently and with expression.

**Spelling and writing.** The Story Checkup and dictation exercises will enable you to evaluate your student's progress. If he has many errors in spelling, punctuation, or capitalization, note the type of errors, and plan reinforcement exercises. If his handwriting was somewhat untidy in the personal letter, you might ask him to recopy it as neatly as he can at home.

## MEETING INDIVIDUAL NEEDS

**Comprehension.** On separate cards, write some sentences about characters in the story, such as: *He died from a sickness in Viet Nam* or *She worked in a nursing home.* Write the names of the characters on other cards. Have S. match them.

Make a cloze exercise, as described in Lesson 7, from a section of one of the stories in Lessons 12-14.

**Word recognition.** Make flash cards for words S. missed in the oral reading above. Help him divide long words into syllables. Also, you can put pairs of words like those below on flash cards for vowel discrimination.

| | | |
|---|---|---|
| *pal, Paul* | *down, dawn* | *hill, hall* |
| *fan, fawn* | *low, law* | *smell, small* |
| *bell, ball* | *show, Shaw* | *fight, fought* |
| *out, ought* | *hole, haul* | *bright, brought* |
| *tight, taught* | *take, talk* | *work, walk.* |

In *Focus on Phonics-4,* you may use Practices 14A-14C. They cover words with *aught* and *ought,* plus words in which *o* is often pronounced /aw/, such as *dog, long.*

oil
oi

| | | | |
|---|---|---|---|
| | coin | coin | coin |
| | join | join | join |
| | point | point | point |
| | noise | noiz | noise |
| | voice | vois | voice |
| | avoid | u void' | avoid |

---

oy

boy
oy

| | | | |
|---|---|---|---|
| | toy | toy | toy |
| | annoy | u noy' | annoy |
| | enjoy | en joy' | enjoy |
| | employ | em ploy' | employ |
| | employee | em ploy' ee | employee |
| | destroy | dē stroy' | destroy |

## The Year I Was Unemployed

| Roy | Joyce | (Joys) | almost | (awl′ mōst) | employment | (employ′ ment) |
| laid | shook | (shuuk) | always | (awl′ wayz) | unemployment | (un employ′ ment) |
| less | truth | (trooth) | worry | (wur′ y) | unemployed | (un employd′) |
| might | wrong | (rong) | support | (su port′) | disappoint | (dis u point′) |
| slept | I've | | downtown | (down′ town′) | | |
| | they'll | | hopeless | (hope′ less) | | |
| | | | Johnson | (John′ son) | | |

I'll never forget the year I was out of work. That year almost destroyed me. It almost destroyed my family, too.

My name is Roy Johnson. I was 36 that year. I had been employed at a small factory for almost 10 years. My job was to take care of the machines. I cleaned and oiled them. I often repaired them when they broke down. I enjoyed my job, and I liked my employer.

But that year, business started slowing down. The company had less work. At first, only the newest employees were laid off. I was one of the last employees that got laid off.

For three weeks, I avoided telling my wife Joyce the truth. Every morning, I left the house and went out to look for work. Then one day, Joyce tried to phone me at work. My older boy, Jimmy, had been hurt at school. My employer told Joyce that I had been laid off.

That news almost destroyed my wife. She was disappointed in me. She felt that I didn't trust her enough to tell her the truth. It wasn't that. I didn't want to worry her. I thought I might be able to find another job soon. I asked Joyce not to tell our boys. I didn't want them to worry.

I was reading the employment ads in the paper every day. There were not many ads for jobs I could do. I went to the state employment office. I thought I might get some help there. The employment office did send me to a lot of companies. But everywhere I went, I always got the same answer, "Leave an application." A lot of other people were unemployed that year. At some companies, they had boxes of applications that people had left.

I was able to get unemployment insurance. And my wife was working part time. With her pay and my unemployment insurance, we were able to get by. But it wasn't easy.

Weeks went by, and then months. It wasn't as easy to find another job as I had thought. After a while, I gave up trying so hard. I was sure that my wife was disappointed in me. So I began to avoid her and the boys. Many times, I didn't join them for meals. Often, I stayed out late drinking beer. Some days, I stayed in bed and slept all day.

Little things began to annoy me. My wife's voice annoyed me when she asked, "Where did you look today?" The noise she made cleaning house annoyed me. My children's voices annoyed me when they were playing in the next room. I often yelled, "Keep your voices down! I can't stand all this noise!"

My unemployment insurance ran out in November. I felt hopeless. I couldn't support my family. And Christmas was coming. My family had always enjoyed Christmas. But this year, I was worried. I didn't want to disappoint my family. But with less money, how would I buy toys for the boys?

One day, I was walking downtown with my little boy, Bobby. As we walked along the streets, Bobby pointed to the big, beautiful Christmas trees in the store windows. He pointed to the Christmas toys. At one store, Bobby stopped and pointed to an electric train. "That's what I want for Christmas, Daddy!" he said. "Can I have it?" I was so choked up that I couldn't answer. I just pulled him away from that window and kept walking.

I still had not told my children that I was unemployed. My boys had always looked up to me. I couldn't face them with the truth that I couldn't support them.

One morning, my wife sat down on the bed and took my face in her hands. I couldn't avoid her eyes. "Roy," she said, "the boys don't understand what's wrong. They think that you must be sick or that you don't love them any more. Don't be so proud, Roy. Tell the boys what's wrong. They'll still love you. I do."

That night after dinner, I joined my boys in the living room. I told them what had happened. "I'm still looking for a job," I said. "But it's not likely that I'll find one before Christmas. So we'll have less money to spend for gifts this year. You'll get fewer toys, and they won't cost very much. I'm sorry about that." My voice shook as I talked.

"Oh, Daddy," said my older son, Jimmy. "I'm glad to know what's wrong. I thought you were sick. You slept so much that I was afraid you were going to die. If we need money, I can help. The neighbors will pay me to clean the snow off their walks."

My younger son, Bobby, ran to his room and came back with his toy bank. He opened it up and shook out the coins. "Here, Daddy," he said. "You take the coins I've been saving." He hugged me as he put the coins in my hand.

I hugged the boys and thanked them. What great sons! That night I slept better than I had for months.

Just before Christmas, one of my friends told me about a job opening at the factory where he worked. They needed someone to oil and repair the machines. I was able to see the employment officer there the next day. I told him about the job I had had for almost 10 years. I said I was good at repairing, cleaning, and oiling machines.

1. the    5. the
2. a       6. the
3. a       7. the
4. a       8. an
           9. an

The employment officer said I would have to join the union. The job paid less than my last job. And this factory was noisier and dirtier. But I was glad when the employment officer shook my hand and told me to start work the following Monday.

I'll always remember that awful year. Now that it's past, I can talk about it. It was the lowest point in my life. If my wife and boys had not been so understanding, our family might not be together today.

---

## Story Checkup

during (duur´ ing)

**Answer each question with one or two sentences.**

1. What are some facts that Roy tells about himself? _____

_____

2. What were some of the feelings that Roy had during this year of unemployment?

_____

3. What do you think Roy learned during his year of unemployment?

_____

## Practice

**Add the ending -less to each root word. Write the new word in the blank.**

**Example:** hope _____hopeless_____

1. home _____hopeless_____    3. sleep _____sleepless_____

2. care _____careless_____    4. friend _____friendless_____

**Fill in each blank with one of the new words with -less. You may use the word in the example, also.**

1. The family was left ___hopeless___ after the fire.

2. The fire started because someone was ___careless___ with matches.

3. After many months without a job, I felt ___hopeless___.

4. I spent many ___sleepless___ nights during that year.

5. When Luke first moved to a big city, he felt ___friendless___.

**Add the ending -ment to each root word. Write the new word in the blank.**

**Example:** employ ___employment___

1. pay ___payment___          3. amuse ___amusement___

2. agree ___agreement___      4. state ___statement___

**Fill in each blank with one of the new words with -ment. You may use the word in the example, also.**

1. I make a ___payment___ on my car loan every month.

2. My landlady and I came to an ___agreement___ about the rent.

3. The children enjoyed the rides at the ___amusement___ park.

4. The state ___employment___ office sent me to many companies to look for a job.

5. The man made a false ___statement___ about the money he has.

**In each line, circle the word that has the same meaning as the first word.**

**Example:**

shout          talk          (yell)          speak

1. repair          broke          (fix)          sell

2. finish          fast          start          (end)

3. unhappy          happy          (sad)          sick

4. almost          (nearly)          all          quickly

5. quick          slow          quiet          (fast)

6. start          stop          (begin)          end

7. allow          show          alone          (permit)

8. small          huge          large          (little)

---

# Reading for Living

apply (u plÿ')          experience (ex pēr' ē ens)
grade          signature          (sig' nu chur)

To apply for most jobs, you must fill out a job application. Complete the job application below. Pick a job that you would like to apply for. Give your own school and work experience. Sign your own name on the signature line.

## Job Application

Please print.

Name _____          Telephone _____

Address _____          Social Security No. _____

          U.S. citizen _____

Job you are applying for _____          Date you can start _____

**Work experience:** Begin with your latest job.

| Name & address of employer | Kind of business | From: Month/year | To: Month/year | Work you did | Rate of pay | Why you left |
|---|---|---|---|---|---|---|
| 1. | | | | | | |
| 2. | | | | | | |
| 3. | | | | | | |

**Service experience:** Were you in the U.S. armed services? _____ Date you went in _____ Date you got out _____

Branch of service _____          Work you did in armed services _____

**School and other training:**

Circle highest grade completed.

|  | Grade school | High School | College |
|---|---|---|---|
|  | 1 2 3 4 5 6 7 8 | 1 2 3 4 | 1 2 3 4 |

| Name of school | Address of school | From: Month/year | To: Month/year |
|---|---|---|---|
| Grade school | | | |
| High school | | | |
| College | | | |
| Other training | | | |

Do you have a driver's license? _____ Do you own an automobile? _____ Are you willing to work nights? _____

List machines you know how to run. _____

Signature _____

## OBJECTIVES

To help your student:

- recognize the vowel sound /oy/ as in *boy* and *oil*.
- recognize that the sound /oy/ may be represented by *oy* or *oi*.
- read words in which the sound /oy/ is written with *oy* or *oi*.
- distinguish the sound /oy/ from other vowel sounds.
- recognize the suffixes *-less* and *-ment* and how to add them to some familiar root words.
- recognize the new compound word *downtown* and review other compound words.
- recognize the new contractions *I've* and *they'll* and review other contractions.
- recognize words with the same meaning (synonyms).
- recognize diminutives of names, such as *Bobby*.
- interpret the feelings of the characters in a story.
- recognize the mood of a story.
- recognize cause and effect.
- relate the story to personal experience and values.
- read a job application and fill it out.
- write words, sentences, and paragraphs from dictation.

## INTRODUCTION

T: In today's lesson, you will learn one more vowel sound. When you have learned this sound, you will know all of the vowel sounds.

# I. Reading

## CHART: Page 92

**Title and key word.** Have S. read the title *Lesson 15*.

T: In this lesson, you will study two charts before you read the story. Let's look at the first chart.

T: What are the letters in the top right-hand corner? [S: *oy*.] Look at the picture and key word. You have had this word. What is it? [S: boy.] What vowel sound do you hear in *boy*? [S: /oy/.] What letters stand for the sound /oy/ in *boy*? [S: *oy*.]

**Lines 1-6.** Ask S. to read the other words in the chart to himself and notice how many syllables each word has. Also, ask him to notice how many of the words end with the sound /oy/ written *oy*.

After S. has studied the chart silently, have him read the words aloud, going down the last column. Then call attention to these points:

1. The words with more than one syllable and which syllable is stressed.

2. The blends *pl* in *employ* and *str* in *destroy*. (Point these out in the third column of the chart, where the words are divided into syllables.)

3. The sound /oy/ written *oy* comes at the end of all of these words except *employee*, which is made from *employ*. The sound /oy/ is usually written *oy* at the end of a word, such as *employ*, and in words made from such words, such as *employee*.

**Review.** Have S. read each word aloud again, including the key word. Cover the pictures, and go down the last column. Ask what letters stand for the sound /oy/ in each of these words.

## CHART: Page 93

T: Look at the chart on the next page. What are the first two letters in the top right-hand corner? [S: *oi*.] What sound do they stand for? [S: /oy/.]

T: Look at the picture and key word. What is the word? [S: oil.] What vowel sound do you hear in *oil*? [S: /oy/.] What letters stand for the sound /oy/ in *oil*? [S: *oi*.]

**Lines 1-6.** Ask S. to read the other words in the chart to himself and notice whether *oi* comes in the middle or at the end of a word. Also, ask him to notice which words have more than one syllable.

After S. has studied the chart silently, have him read the words aloud, going down the last column. Then call attention to the following points:

1. The sound /oy/ comes between two consonants in these words.

2. When the sound /oy/ comes at the end of a word, it is usually written *oy*. When it comes between two consonants, the sound /oy/ is usually written *oi*.

3. The word with more than one syllable (*avoid*) and which syllable in it is stressed.

4. The rhyming words *coin* and *join*. Ask S. to give a word that rhymes with *oil* [possible answers are *boil, coil, foil, toil, soil, spoil*].

5. The ending consonant blend *nt* in *point*.

**Review.** Have S. read each word aloud, including the key word. Cover the pictures, and go down the last column. Ask what letters stand for the sound /oy/ in each of these words.

## STORY: Pages 94-96 (The Year I Was Unemployed)

Have S. read the story title. If he needs help in reading *unemployed*, refer him to the new story words.

Have S. read the first two columns of words. Call attention to the number of syllables, the contractions *I've* and *they'll* and what they stand for, the words with the sound /oy/ and how it is written, and the ending consonant blend *pt* in *slept*.

Have S. read the third column of words. Call attention to the words with the sound /aw/, the number of syllables in each word, and which syllable is stressed. Point out that both syllables in *downtown* are stressed equally. Ask S. to tell the words that make up *downtown* and *Johnson*.

Have S. read the last column of words. Ask him to tell the part that is the same in the first three words (*employ*). Call attention to the prefix *un-* and what it means. Ask S. to read the last word (*disappoint*) and tell the number of syllables and how the sound /oy/ is written.

**Directed silent reading.** Ask S. to read the first three paragraphs to himself to find out who is telling the story and what he tells about himself in these paragraphs. When S. has read the paragraphs, have him summarize the information. Explain that this part of the story is an introduction. Ask S. what he thinks the main part of the story will be about. Discuss what Roy may have meant by the terms "almost destroyed me" and "almost destroyed my family."

Ask S. to read the next three paragraphs (paragraphs 4-6) to find out what Roy did during his first weeks of unemployment. After S. finishes reading, have him tell what Roy did. Discuss the reason that Roy gave for not telling his wife he was unemployed. Ask S. if he thinks there might have been some other reason, too.

Ask S. to read to the end of paragraph 13 silently. (You might want to have him mark the place before he begins reading. Paragraph 13 begins: "One morning, my wife sat down on the bed . . .") When S. has finished reading, discuss the following questions:

1. At first, how did the family manage financially?
2. Why did Roy begin to avoid his family?
3. What things began to annoy him? Why do you think they annoyed him?
4. In November, why did Roy begin to feel hopeless?
5. What happened when Roy was walking downtown with his son Bobby?
6. Why hadn't Roy told his boys that he was unemployed?
7. What did Roy's wife want him to do?

Ask S. to finish reading the story to find out what happened. When he finishes, have him summarize the ending of the story.

**Reading between the lines.** Discuss these questions.

1. Do you think that Roy was right not to tell his wife that he had lost his job as soon as it happened? Why or why not? When do you think he should have told his sons? Why?
2. Why was it so hard for Roy to find another job?
3. How do you think Roy's wife felt during this year? What do you think was hardest for her? What do you think Roy might have done to make things easier for her?
4. Do you think Joyce should have told the boys herself that their father was out of work? Why or why not?
5. Does this story seem true to life? Why or why not? Have you had a similar experience?

## STORY CHECKUP: Page 97

Have S. read the title, new word, and directions. Have him write the answers to the questions. When he has finished, have him read aloud each question and his answer. Refer him to the story to make any corrections in content. Then check his work for sentence structure, capitalization, punctuation, and spelling.

**Note:** For now, skip the Practice exercise at the bottom of page 97, and go directly to the Reading for Living on page 98. The Practice exercise will be done later in the lesson, after the Writing Lesson.

## READING FOR LIVING: Page 98

Have S. read the title and new words first silently and then aloud. Call attention to the number of syllables in each word. Go over the directions with S. Call attention to the direction *Please print* on the job application form. Point out to S. that, since some of the spaces on the form are rather small, he will have to make his printing small enough to fit.

Have S. fill out as much of the application as he can by himself. Go over with him any parts that he doesn't understand. Give help with the spelling of his answers, such as names of past employers, as needed.

When S. has finished, check his work, and have him make any needed corrections. Tell S. that he may want to use this application as a sample for filling out other applications. Suggest that he may want to put some of the information on a card to carry with him. That way, he'll have the information at hand when he needs it. Help him to write such a card if he is interested.

# II. Skills Practice

Have S. close his book before doing these exercises.

## PRACTICE 1: Distinguishing the Sound /oy/

T: I will say three words. Tell me which one has the sound /oy/ as in *boy* or *oil*.

| | |
|---|---|
| *paint, joint, sent* | *soy, saw, so* |
| *sail, soon, soil* | *jaw, jar, joy* |
| *broil, crawl, brook* | *cow, coy, claw* |
| *most, must, moist* | *Jane, join, June* |

## PRACTICE 2: Substituting an Initial Consonant

Write *boy*, and have S. read it. Ask him to make new words by substituting another consonant for *b*. Write the words as he says them. (Possible answers are *joy, coy, Roy, toy, soy*.) Do the same thing for the word *boil* (*spoil, foil, coil, toil, broil*).

Then write these pairs of words, and ask S. to read them. (In each pair, the first is known and the second is new.)

| | | |
|---|---|---|
| *point* | *voice* | *coin* |
| *joint* | *choice* | *loin* |

## PRACTICE 3: Suffix -less

Write *hopeless,* and have S. read it. Ask what the root word is, and write *hope* in front of *hopeless.*

Ask S. what ending has been added to *hope,* what the ending -*less* means [without], and what *hopeless* means [without hope].

Under *hope,* write these words in a column: *life, noise, voice, help, law, fault.* Have S. read each root word and then give the word with the -*less* ending. Write the word with the ending in the second column. When the list is complete, have S. read both forms of each word.

T: The words in the first columns are nouns. We add the ending -*less* to change a noun into an adjective, a word that describes something. I will read a sentence using a noun from the first column. Then I will read a second sentence with one word missing. Choose an adjective ending with -*less* from the second column to complete the sentence.

Read the following sentences, and have S. supply the missing word.

1. At first, Roy had hope that he would find another job soon. But after some months, he felt _____. (Ask who the word *hopeless* describes.)
2. We may not like to obey some laws. But we would find it hard to live in a _____ country. (Ask what the word *lawless* describes.)
3. A few minutes ago, my puppy was full of life. But now he is lying in the road _____. (Ask what the word *lifeless* describes.)

## PRACTICE 4: Suffix -ment

Write *employment,* and have S. read it. Ask what the root word is. Write *employ* in front of *employment.*

T: What ending has been added to *employ* to make *employment?* [S: -*ment.*] The ending -*ment* can mean several things. In *employment,* the ending -*ment* means *the condition of being.* So, *employment* means the condition of being employed. *Employ* is an action word, or verb. *Employment* is a noun. We add the ending -*ment* to verbs to make nouns.

Under *employ,* write these words in a column: *move, excite, argue, disappoint.* Have S. read each word and then tell what it would be with the ending -*ment* added. Explain that a final silent *e* in the root word is not usually dropped before -*ment,* as in *movement* and *excitement.* But the final *e* in *argue* is dropped when the ending -*ment* is added to make *argument.*

When the list is complete, have S. read both forms of each word. Point out that the words in the first column are verbs and the words in the second column are nouns.

Read the following sentences, and have S. supply the missing word as in the previous exercise.

1. Hugh's aunt began to argue with his father. She choked on some food during the _____.

2. Roy did not want to disappoint his sons at Christmas. He thought that, for them, not getting a lot of toys would be a great _____.

## PRACTICE 5: Compound Words

Write the new compound word *downtown.* Have S. read it and tell the two words it is made from. As he answers, write the two words by the compound word. Continue in the same way with *downstairs* and *downhill* and then with *upstairs* and *uphill.*

Write the new name *Johnson,* and have S. read it. Have him tell the new words it is made from. As he answers, write the two words. Point out that several family names are made up of a man's first name and the word *son.* Then continue in the same way with *Jackson, Carlson, Robertson.*

## PRACTICE 6: Contractions

Write the new contraction *I've.* Have S. read it and tell the two words it is made from. Write *I have* by *I've.* Ask what letters are left out of *have* in the contraction [*ha*]. Under *I have,* write *we have, you have, they have.* Ask S. to read each of these, tell what the contraction would be, and tell how to write the contraction. Write the contractions under *I've.*

Write the new contraction *they'll.* Have S. read it and tell the two words it is made from. Write *they will* by *they'll.* Ask what letters are left out of *will* in the contraction [*wi*]. Under *they will,* write *I will, we will, she will, he will, you will.* Have S. read each of these, tell what the contraction would be, and tell how to write the contractions. Write the contractions under *they'll.*

Cover the column of words from which the contractions are made. Have S. read each contraction and tell the two words it is made from.

## PRACTICE 7: Diminutives of Names

Write *Bob* and *Bobby,* and have S. read them. Explain that these are different forms of the same name. Have S. tell what ending was added to make *Bobby* [-*y*], and review the rule for doubling the final consonant after a short vowel sound. Under *Bob,* write these names: *Jim, Tom, Bill, Ted, Pat, Dad.* Have S. read each name, tell what it would be with -*y* added, and tell how to spell it. Write the names with -*y*. Point out that *Dad* and *Daddy* are both affectionate names for *Father.*

Write the following names in two columns, and have S. read them.

*Ann, Annie*     *Jack, Jackie*
*Rose, Rosie*     *Will, Willie*
*Kate, Katie*

Point out that sometimes the ending is -*ie* instead of -*y*. Often, -*ie* is used for women's names, but it is used with some men's names too. Also, explain that, since people are free to choose the spelling for their own names and nicknames, people's names do not always follow rules in the way they are spelled.

# III. Writing

## CHECK HOMEWORK: Page 91

Check your student's responses in the first exercise. If he has an error, have him read the words in that line aloud and listen for the vowel sound. Have him tell the vowel sound in each word and then underline the ones with the /aw/ sound. This way, you can make a note of his errors and plan for extra practice.

Have S. read aloud the sentences that he wrote for the second exercise. Discuss his answer if it doesn't express the main idea of why Lan felt caught between two worlds. Have him read the last paragraph of the story again and also the last two paragraphs of Lan's letter. Check the sentences he has written for sentence structure and spelling.

## WRITING LESSON (In Notebook)

Have S. write the titles *Lesson 15* and *Words* and then number from 1 to 30 in two columns. After the dictation, check his work and have him correct any errors by writing the whole word correctly.

**Words.** Help S. study these words: *noise, voice, Joyce, laid, wrong, almost, always, truth.*

| | | |
|---|---|---|
| 1. boy | 11. avoid | 21. shook |
| 2. oil | 12. noise | 22. truth |
| 3. enjoy | 13. voice | 23. wrong |
| 4. employ | 14. Joyce | 24. almost |
| 5. coin | 15. Roy | 25. always |
| 6. join | 16. Johnson | 26. worry |
| 7. annoy | 17. laid | 27. support |
| 8. destroy | 18. less | 28. employment |
| 9. employee | 19. might | 29. disappoint |
| 10. point | 20. slept | 30. downtown |

**Sentences.** Have S. write the title *Sentences*. Have him number each sentence as you dictate it.

1. I'll never forget the year I was unemployed.
2. My unemployment insurance ran out in November.
3. Roy Johnson had been employed at a small factory for almost 10 years.

**Paragraph.** Tell S. you will dictate a short paragraph. He will not number the sentences. Ask S. to listen as you read the whole paragraph. Then read it a sentence at a time for him to write. Read each sentence once. Read it one more time if needed. After S. finishes writing the paragraph, ask him to read it back to you.

> My younger son ran to his room and came back with his toy bank. He opened it up and shook out the coins. "You take the coins I've been saving," he said. Bobby hugged me as he put the coins in my hand.

Check what S. has written, and have him correct any errors, including those in punctuation and capitalization. (In

sentence 3, it doesn't matter if S. wrote *10* or *ten*.) Have S. write the title *Study* and any words he missed in the dictation exercises.

## PRACTICE: Page 97

Go over the directions and example with S. Then have him do the exercises. Check his work by having him read aloud the words and sentences. Have him correct any errors.

## HOMEWORK: Page 99

Go over the directions and example with S. for the first two parts on the ending *-ment*. Go over the directions and example for the last exercise. Have S. do the first line to make sure he understands what to do. Encourage him to reread the story at home and to study any words he missed in the dictation.

## CHECKING PROGRESS

**Comprehension.** Your student's responses on the Story Checkup and the discussion questions will help you evaluate his progress in understanding main ideas, recalling important facts, drawing inferences, and interpreting the feelings of the characters. For a further check on his understanding of cause and effect, you may find the following exercise helpful.

Use two cards or strips of paper for each of these sentences. On one card, write the first part of the sentence through *because*. On the other card, write the rest of the sentence. Mix each set of cards, and have S. match them.

1. Roy lost his job because / business slowed down.
2. Joyce tried to phone Roy at work because / Jimmy had been hurt.
3. Roy didn't tell Joyce he had lost his job because / he didn't want her to worry.
4. Roy had a hard time finding a job because / many people were looking for work.
5. When Bobby asked for a train for Christmas, Roy couldn't answer because / he was so choked up.

**Word recognition.** The exercises in this lesson should help you evaluate your student's ability to apply word recognition skills. Is he able to distinguish vowel sounds? Does he recognize compound words, contractions, root words, and word endings? Was he able to read the longer words in this lesson, such as *unemployment* and *disappointment?*

Have S. read a paragraph orally from the story. Note his accuracy in word recognition. Analyze the types of errors as suggested in the last lesson. Use suggestions given in the last lesson or in the next section for reinforcement of needed word recognition skills.

## MEETING INDIVIDUAL NEEDS

**Comprehension.** If S. needs reinforcement of comprehension skills emphasized in this lesson, use some of the suggestions given in Lessons 7 and 8 of this manual. Continue to use supplementary reading material to reinforce comprehension skills.

**Word recognition.** For more practice on adding the suffixes *-ness*, *-ful*, *-less*, and *-ment*, use word wheels. Make a wheel for each suffix. Write the suffix on the pointer. Write the root words around the edge of the wheel. Root words you may use are suggested below.

For *-ful*, use: *hope, peace, thank, care, help, trust, rest, law, play, power, forget, wonder.*

For *-less*, use: *hope, home, care, sleep, name, friend, color, heart, sugar, power, law, thought, point, noise.*

For *-ment*, use: *pay, agree, amuse, state, move, excite, appoint, disappoint, employ, enjoy.*

For *-ness*, use: *sick, sad, dark, good, kind, blind, great.*

Use flash cards for the compound words and contractions that were introduced or reviewed in this lesson as suggested in Lesson 2.

In *Focus on Phonics-4*, you may use Practices 15A-15B. They cover words with *oy* and *oi*.

# More Reading
## with ū, oo, uu, ou, aw, and oy

| | | | |
|---|---|---|---|
| music<br>ū | cure<br>u-e | argue<br>ue | few<br>ew |
| food<br>oo | June<br>u-e | blue<br>ue | chew<br>ew |
| student<br>ū or oo | Duke<br>u-e | Tuesday<br>ue | news<br>ew |
| book<br>uu | | | |
| mouth<br>ou | town<br>ow | | |
| lawn<br>aw | Paul<br>au | ball<br>all | caught<br>aught   bought<br>ought |
| boy<br>oy | oil<br>oi | | |

---

## Finding What You Want in Your Newspaper

| | | |
|---|---|---|
| health | (helth) | advertise (ad' ver tize) | according (u cord' ing) |
| movie | (moo' ve) | classified (clas' i fīd) | belong (bē long') |
| section | (sec' shun) | different (dif' runt) | bottom (bot' um) |
| through | (throo) | editor (ed' i ter) | sharp |
| | | editorial (ed i tor' ē ul) | thankful (thank' ful) |

— What's happening in my city?
— What's on TV tonight?
— Are there any job openings I could apply for?

You can find the answers to these questions, and many others, in different parts of your newspaper.

News stories give the facts about things that have happened in your city, the country, and the world. The main news stories start on the front page of the first section.

One part of the newspaper is marked so that you can tell it is not news. This part is called the editorial page. In editorials, editors try to get readers to agree with their ideas. The editorial page also has letters from readers. Through letters to the editor, we can all have a voice in the newspaper.

The family life section has stories about food, clothes, health, and getting the most for your money.

This section may be called by different names in different newspapers.

Another section tells about TV shows, movies, and other things to see or do for fun.

People who get a newspaper mainly for sports turn to the sports section first. The sports section is found near the back of most newspapers.

Ads are found in all sections of the newspaper. Through advertising, companies can tell readers what they have to sell. And, through advertising, readers can find out about things they want to buy.

One section of the paper has only ads. That is the classified ad section. Both businesses and readers can advertise in this section. In the classified ads, small ads are grouped together under headings like Help Wanted or Autos for Sale.

This lesson has examples from different parts of the newspaper. This lesson will give you an idea of what you can find in your own newspaper.

---

*News story*

### Oil truck turns over, fire destroys two homes

Two houses near downtown were destroyed by fire this morning. The fire was caused by an 18-wheel truck hauling 10,000 gallons of oil.

John Howard of New York City was the driver of the truck. According to police, Howard was driving down Lewis Hill along Hill St. about 5 a.m. He could not make a sharp turn at the bottom of the hill, and the truck turned over. Howard was able to crawl from his truck and was not hurt.

Oil from the truck caught fire as it ran down the street. Two houses at the corner of Hill St. and Maple Ave. caught fire. By the time fire trucks arrived, the houses were almost destroyed.

The house at 101 Maple Ave., which belonged to Center City Land Company, was empty. The house at 100 Hill St. belonged to Mr. and Mrs. Paul Robinson. They were out of town.

Mary Garcia, of 105 Maple Ave., told reporters what she saw. According to Garcia, she was out walking her dog at the time of the accident.

"The truck couldn't make the sharp turn at the bottom of the hill," Garcia said. "The next thing I knew, the truck was over on its side. I saw the truck driver crawl out and run. Then I heard a big noise, and the oil caught fire. The burning oil was like a river of fire as it ran down to the houses."

Garcia ended by saying, "I'm glad no one was hurt. I'm sorry that the Robinsons' home was destroyed. But I'm thankful that the burning oil didn't get as far as my house."

mess
sidewalk (side'walk)
mental (men'tul)
depress (dē press')

aide (aid)
hour (our)
lost
wash (wosh)

grand
male
female (fē'male)
self

Mon. (Monday)
Fri. (Friday)
Aug. (August)
Sept. (September)

*Editorial*

**Get truck traffic off Lewis Hill**

It's time for our town to do something to stop accidents at the corner of Hill St. and Maple Ave.

The awful accident this morning at the bottom of Lewis Hill.

This is the sixth accident there in two years. Four of them were caused by big trucks that couldn't make the sharp turn on Hill St.

We can all be thankful that no one has been killed in these accidents. But unless we do something soon, someone will be killed.

For a long time, this newspaper has been saying that we need a new highway around our town. Then we could keep big trucks off Hill St.

We need state help to build that highway. Please call or write your council person. Tell him or her to ask the state for help NOW, before it's too late.

*Letters to the editor*

**Dogs have rights, too**

Dear Editor:

In Tuesday's paper, J.D. said that his neighbor's dog messed up his lawn. The lawns should be fenced in, not the dogs.

Pets have rights, too. And one of them is the right to run. It's not fair to keep a healthy dog tied up all the time. There ought to be a law against it.

—Carlos Smith

**Those dirty dogs!**

Dear Editor:

I agree with J.D. that the city should crack down on owners who let their dogs run free. Not only do they dig up the lawns, but they also mess up the sidewalks. There ought to be a law to make the dog owners clean up after their dogs. I'm tired of the mess dogs make.

—G.P.

*Family life*

**Being out of work can make you sick**

Unemployment and health problems go together. This was the finding of a new study by the Center for Work and Mental Health in Washington, D.C.

Doctors across the country took part in the study. Information from them showed more sickness in places where many people are out of work. The study found that unemployed people smoke and drink more. They hit their children more. And they have more family fights.

"People show they are under stress in different ways," says the study report. "Some get sick. Others become angry or depressed. They drink too much or become violent."

Two out of every four laid-off workers at one factory reported that they could not sleep. Others said they could not eat or got sick when they did. These are signs of mental stress.

According to the study, most people can stand a few weeks of unemployment without health problems. The hardest time comes after six months when unemployment insurance stops. After a year, unemployed workers often feel so hopeless that they stop looking for a job.

If you are unemployed, what can you do to avoid health problems? Doctors at the Center for Work and Mental Health give these answers.

You are almost sure to feel angry and depressed. But you should not keep these feelings to yourself. Bring them out in the open.

(continued on page 103)

**Unemployment and your health**

(continued from page 102)

Don't be angry with yourself. It's not your fault that business is bad. Many people are out of work. You are just one of many hurt by hard times.

Talk openly with your family about your feelings. Talk about the problems all of you will face. In this way, your family can feel that you are all helping each other in a time of trouble. And you will not feel alone.

Tell children the truth. They will know that something is wrong, anyway.

Try to make the most of your free time. Do some jobs at home that you have been putting off. Learn how to do something you have always wanted to learn. Spend time with your family and friends even if you don't have much money to spend.

Don't avoid telling people that you are out of work. The more people that know, the better chance you have to hear about job openings.

Above all, don't give up looking for a job. Going from place to place and hearing "no" is depressing. But if you stop looking, you have little chance of finding a job.

*Classified ads*

**HELP WANTED**

**Auto repairs**—Work on used cars, 3-5 years experience needed. Apply in person to City Auto Sales, 350 Dawson St. 2-5 p.m. Mon.-Fri.

**Baker**—24 hours a week. Experienced, all kinds of bread. The Bread Basket, 789 Fourth Ave., 7-9 p.m., Mon.-Fri.

**Car wash**—Full time. No experience needed. Fast worker, over 18 years old. Apply Cal's Car Wash, 218 Main.

**Cook**—Experienced and fast. Apply Terry's, 645 Maple St., 9-11 a.m.

**Home health aide**—Take care of sick people in their homes. Some cooking, cleaning, and child care. Apply to Lewis County Department of Health, 244 Main St., Mrs. Wong.

**Kitchen helper**—Oak Park Country Club, 2-4 p.m., Mon.-Fri.

**Laundry**—Person to run self-service coin laundry 8-12 nights. Lee's Wash & Dry, Grand Shopping Center.

**Nurse's aide**—Will train. Good pay & hours. Friendly person to work with older people. Shaw's Nursing Home, 351 Park Road. 479-7999.

**Teacher's aide**—Part time, mornings. Experience with small children. Oak Park School, 476-2131.

**Truck driver**—48-state carrier. Good driving record. Over 25 and belong to union. 451-2364.

**LOST AND FOUND**

**Cat**—Male, black, white on back and neck. Lost near Oak Park High School Aug. 29. Call 571-8907.

**Cat**—Female, gray. Found Sept. 1 near First Ave. and Lewis St. Call 572-9870 after 5.

**Dog**—Male, black and brown. White feet. Short hair. Lost Aug. 31 at Grand Shopping Center. 571-6344.

**Glasses**—Found Porters Department Store, Aug. 30. Call in person.

**Puppy**—Female, 10 months old. Light brown with white face. Lost Sept. 2 near Front St. 663-4053.

**Ring**—Gold wedding band found Sept. 1 in ladies' room Newman's. 481-9805.

**PETS FOR SALE**

**Birds**—Many kinds, some talkers. Bright colors. Easy to care for. Bird World. 6519 Main St.

**Cat**—Free to good home. 2-year-old female. All shots. 542-8765.

**Dog**—Short-haired pointer. Male, trained, 2 years old. Moving out of state. 447-9087 after 5.

## Tonight on TV

| | 6:00 | 6:30 | 7:00 | 7:30 | 8:00 | 8:30 | 9:00 | 9:30 |
|---|---|---|---|---|---|---|---|---|
| 3 | News | NBC News | Around Town | Roy Hall | Movie of the Week: "It Came out of the Fog" | | | |
| 5 | News | CBS News | Wild Country | Law & You | Voices of Thanksgiving | | | Mothers & Daughters |
| 9 | News | ABC News | True or False | Open Phone | Football: New York at Washington | | | |
| 24 | Health | Business | At the Movies | Meet Your City Council | | The New China | | Small Talk |

## Story Checkup

offer (off' er)

**Write a short answer to each question.**

1. What is the headline for the news story? _____

2. What are three important facts that are given in the news story?
_____
_____

3. In the editorial, what idea does the newspaper offer for stopping accidents on Hill Street?
_____

4. In the letters to the editor, which letter writer do you agree with? Why?
_____

5. Who did the study on unemployment and health problems?
_____

6. In the Help Wanted ads, which job offers training? _____

7. What is the TV Movie of the Week? _____

   What time does it start? _____

## Practice

**In each line, circle the words that have the same vowel sound as the first word.**

| 1. law | low | (haul) | (taught) | laid |
| 2. oil | (coin) | cool | (Joyce) | cook |
| 3. ought | out | voice | moon | (caught) |
| 4. boy | buy | (join) | book | (toy) |
| 5. cloud | (town) | (claw) | call | (plow) |
| 6. fault | (fall) | (Paul) | few | (false) |

---

**In each line, circle the word that means the opposite of the first word.**

| 1. lost | last | (found) | saw | (top) |
| 2. bottom | side | last | rear | human |
| 3. female | woman | manager | (male) | working |
| 4. employed | destroyed | (unemployed) | disappointed | write |
| 5. right | bad | good | (wrong) | right |
| 6. true | fair | (false) | fault | nearly |
| 7. same | alike | almost | (different) | (small) |
| 8. large | most | major | complete | sharp |
| 9. quiet | (noisy) | truth | depressed | all |
| 10. less | mess | (more) | often | (sick) |
| 11. healthy | well | worry | hopeless | might |
| 12. always | (never) | also | almost | |

**Write the missing ending in each blank.**

*-ful, -less, -ly, -ment, -ness, -y*

1. To stay health__y__, you should eat right and get enough sleep.

2. Roy read the employ_ment_ ads in the newspaper every day.

3. The news reporter thought that Mary Garcia's story sounded truth_ful_.

4. We can all be thank_ful_ that no one was hurt in the accident.

5. The word *ad* is a short form for the word *advertise_ment_*.

6. I'm sorry that my thought_less_ words hurt your feelings.

7. Everyone remembers Mrs. Brunoski's good_ness_ to those in trouble.

8. The new employee did the work quickly, but he was often care_less_.

9. Being unemployed can cause sick_ness_.

10. At first, Roy kept his disappoint_ment_ to himself.

11. The house was complete_ly_ destroyed by fire.

12. She washed her dirt__y__ hands.

## OBJECTIVES

To help your student:

- review the vowel sound /ū/, /oo/, /uu/, /ou/, /aw/, /oy/ and their most regular spellings.
- apply phonics skills in reading new words with familiar sound-letter relationships.
- read sample newspaper selections that review words introduced in Lessons 12-16, especially words with the sounds /aw/ and /oy/.
- recognize the abbreviations *Mon., Fri., Aug., Sept.* for *Monday, Friday, August, September.*
- recognize word opposites.
- recognize the new compound word *sidewalk* and review other compound words.
- review the endings *-ful, -less, -ly, -ment, -ness, -y* and how to add them to some known words.
- review the prefixes *un-, in-,* and *non-,* meaning not.
- recognize root words in words with prefixes and suffixes.
- review the sound for vowels followed by *r* and *rr.*
- recognize the number of syllables in a word and which syllable is stressed.
- understand where to look in the newspaper for certain information.
- read sample selections from main sections of a newspaper: news story, editorial, letters to the editor, health article, classified ads, TV listing.
- understand the facts in a news story.
- understand the opinions expressed in an editorial and in a letter to the editor.
- distinguish between fact and opinion.
- locate certain information in classified ads and in a TV listing.
- develop further skill in writing words, sentences, and questions.
- write a short letter to the editor, following the form for a business letter.
- address an envelope.

## INTRODUCTION

T: In today's lesson, you will review the vowel sounds that you have had so far in this book and the main ways they are written. You'll read some selections that have many words with these sounds. You'll learn more about reading a newspaper. We'll also review some of the other things you have studied in the last four lessons.

# I. Reading

## CHART: Page 100

Have S. read *Lesson 16* and the title *More Reading with ū, oo, uu, ou, aw, and oy.* Then have him read the key words for each vowel sound. For each word, have him tell what the vowel sound is and how it is written.

## STORIES: Pages 101-103

**Finding what you want in your newspaper.** Have S. read the story title and new words. Call attention to the difference in meaning between *through* and *threw.*

T: You have had one lesson about reading a newspaper. In that lesson, you had practice in reading newspaper headlines and news stories. In today's lesson, you will read another news story and some selections from other parts of the paper.

T: The first part of this page is an introduction to your lesson. Notice that there is a line near the middle of the page. The introduction is given in the two columns above the line. Read this part, and find out what the main sections of the newspaper are.

After S. reads silently, have him tell what the main sections of the newspaper are and what kind of information is found in each.

### News story

T: Look at the story below the line that divides the page. The first line tells what type of selection this is; the second line is the headline. What type of selection is this? [S: News story.] You have learned the five things a news story tells. We refer to them as the Five *W*'s. What are they? [S: Who, what, when, where, why.] (If S. doesn't remember, have him look back at page 41 in Lesson 7.)

Have S. read the news story silently to find out the Five *W*'s. When he has finished, have him read the headline aloud and answer these questions:

1. What happened?
2. Who was the driver?
3. Who saw the accident?
4. Where did the accident happen?
5. When did it happen?
6. Why did it happen?

**Editorial.** Have S. read the new words at the top of the page. Explain that the words in the last column are abbreviations. Call attention to the difference in meaning between *hour* and *our.*

T: Look at the heading at the top of the first column. What type of selection is given here? [S: Editorial.] What is the purpose of an editorial? [S: To get the reader to agree with the editor's idea.] Read this editorial, and find out what idea it presents.

After S. reads the editorial silently, have him tell the idea that the editorial presents [that a new highway should be built around the town to get truck traffic off Hill St. and prevent accidents]. Also, have S. tell what the editorial asks the reader to do [call or write council person to urge him or her to ask for state help in building the highway].

Discuss the difference between editorials and news stories about an important public issue. Bring out points like the following: Editorials try to persuade you to agree with their opinions. News stories try to give you information so that you can form your own opinion.

An editorial may show just one side of an issue. (This one does. Some people may have reasons for not wanting a highway around the town. Other people may have different ideas for preventing accidents on Hill St.)

News stories report on the different sides of an issue and give people with different views a chance to express them. (Recall the news report of the public hearings on the raise in utility rates in Lesson 7 as an example.)

A single news story might not tell us everything we need to know. So we would have to follow the news over a period of time before we got enough information to form our own opinon. We would not be fair to ourselves if we let a single editorial persuade us.

**Letters to the editor.** Have S. read the letters to the editor silently. Then discuss these questions:

1. Who wrote the letters?
2. Whose letter were they responding to? What opinion had J.D. given?
3. Did Carlos and G.P. agree with what J.D. had written?

**Family life.** Have S. read the first line and tell what section of the newspaper this article would be in [family life section]. Mention that this section might be called by different names in different papers.

Have S. read the headline, *Being out of work can make you sick,* and then look at the end of column 2 and read this line: *Continued on page 103.* Have S. find the rest of the article on page 103 and read the headline, *Unemployment and your health,* and the line that says: *Continued from page 102.* Explain that newspaper articles are often continued on another page. The continuation will have a headline that gives the topic of the article, but this headline might be worded differently from the headline at the beginning of the article.

Have S. read the article silently, and then discuss these questions:

1. What was the main finding of this study?
2. What kinds of health problems do unemployed people often have?
3. What is meant by the word *stress* as it is used in this article?
4. Why do unemployed workers often stop looking for a job?
5. What are five things an unemployed worker can do to avoid health problems?

**Classified ads**

T: What section of the newspaper is this next sample selection from? [S: Classified ads.] Look at the headings, and tell the three kinds of ads that are given here. [S: Help Wanted, Lost and Found, Pets for Sale.] Look at the first words in each ad, which are in darker type. How are the ads arranged in each group? [S: Alphabetically.]

Ask S. to read all of the Help Wanted ads to himself. Then discuss these questions:

1. What facts do most of the ads give?
2. Do any of the ads specify which sex the applicant must be?
3. Which ad says that the applicant must belong to a union?
4. Which of these jobs do you think would require little or no experience?

Have S. read the following ads aloud: Baker, Truck driver, Laundry, Home health aide, Auto repairs.

Ask S. to read the Lost and Found ads. Then ask him to tell which ad might help him if he had lost each of the following: gold wedding ring, male dog, gray cat. Have him locate the ad and read it aloud. Also, have S. read aloud the three ads for Pets for Sale. Ask him which pet actually does not cost anything.

**Tonight on TV.** Ask S. to look over the TV listings. Then discuss the following:

1. How many channels are listed, and what are their numbers? Which one is probably a public televison channel? What makes you think so?
2. On which channels are there news at 6:00 and 6:30? What is probably the difference between the kind of news given at 6:00 and that given at 6:30?
3. On which channel can you see a football game? What time does it start?
4. What are the names of the programs that begin at 7:30? If you watch all of the program about the city council, can you see the start of the movie?
5. Do you think the program listed for 7:00 on channel 24 is a movie? Why or why not?

## STORY CHECKUP: Page 104

Have S. read the title and directions. Tell him that he may look back at the newspaper section to find the answer if he needs to. After he has written the answers, check his work by having him read each question and his answer aloud. If he has an error, have him look back at the appropriate reading selection to find the answer. Have him write the correct answer. Then check his work for correct spelling.

## READING FOR LIVING (Supplementary Materials)

**Note:** You may want to do these activities in a separate class session.

**Job application forms.** S. may need more practice in filling out job applications. Obtain some application forms that are used locally, and help S. fill them out. If he is interested in applying for a job at a particular place, try to get an application form from that place. Go over the form with him, and help him fill it out.

**Local newspaper.** Have a local newspaper available. Before class, note which items may be easy enough for S. to read. If the news stories and editorials are too hard for him to read, mark some headlines, section headings, classified ads, or letters to the editor that he may be able to read. Try to find one article that is continued on a different page and has headlines S. can read. Do not have him read the whole article, but have him find where it is continued.

In class, have S. find the sections that he studied about in this lesson. If the paper has an index, you can point that out to him and show him how to use it. Also, point out sections that were not mentioned in the lesson, such as the weather report, cartoons, puzzles, obituaries, and business section. Have S. find the entertainment section and TV listing.

**Easy newspaper** *News for You.* You may be interested in subscribing to *News for You* for your student. This is a newspaper written at the 4th to 6th grade level especially for adults and older teenagers with limited reading skills. A monthly four-page supplement is published eight times during the school year. You may obtain samples of the newspaper by writing to New Readers Press, Box 131, Syracuse, NY 13210 or by phoning (800) 448-8878. If you will be tutoring your student beyond *Skill Book 4*, you may also be interested in obtaining the teacher's resource book *Making the Most of News for You.*

# II. Skills Practice

## PRACTICE 1: Distinguishing Vowel Sounds

Write these words at the top of six columns: *music, food, book, mouth, lawn, boy.* Have S. read each key word and tell the vowel sound (for the first syllable only in *music*). Under each word, write the letter or letters that stand for the vowel sound: *ū, oo, uu, ou, aw, oy.*

Say each word below, and have S. tell which key word has the same vowel sound, even if the vowel sound is written differently. Write the word under the key word.

| shook | foot | tooth | brought | taught |
| soon | pool | use | full | noon |
| loud | walk | enjoy | coin | sauce |
| huge | shout | town | cook | crowd |
| oil | view | room | few | hook |
| paw | push | union | school | toy |
| house | point | good | wall | could |

Have S. read the words in the list for each sound.

## PRACTICE 2: Compound Words

Write the new compound word *sidewalk.* Have S. read it and tell the two words it is made from.

In one column, write: *watch, foot, high, grand, class, down.* In a second column, write: *ball, town, children, way, dog, room.* Have S. put each word from column 1 together with a word from column 2 to make a compound word. Write the compound words in a third column.

Write these new compound words, and have S. read them: *sideways, granddaughter, grandson, footprint, classmate.*

## PRACTICE 3: Recognizing Root Words

In a column, write *messy, healthy, noisy, mainly, hourly, completely, enjoyment, disappointment, advertisement.* Have S. read each word and tell what the ending is and what the root word is. As he answers, write the root words in a column in front of the words with endings. Review dropping the final silent *e* in *noise* when *-y* is added. Then have S. read both forms of each word.

## PRACTICE 4: Endings *-ful, -ly, -less, -ness*

Write *thankful,* and have S. read it. Have him tell the root word and the ending that has been added.

Write *thankfully* and *thankfulness.* Point out that sometimes two endings can be added to a root word. Have S. read each word and tell what endings have been added.

Write the words below in two columns. Have S. read each word in the column and tell what the root word is and what ending or endings have been added.

| careful | thoughtful |
| carefully | thoughtfully |
| careless | thoughtless |
| carelessly | thoughtlessly |
| carelessness | thoughtlessness |

## PRACTICE 5: Prefixes *un-, in-, non-*

Write *unhappy, injustice, non-violent.* Have S. read each word and tell the prefix and the root word. As he does, underline each prefix. Point out that in these words all three prefixes mean the same thing. Ask S. to tell what they mean [not]. Then write the following prefixes and words in three columns, as shown here.

| un- | in- | non- |
|---|---|---|
| employed | complete | stop |
| healthy | human | payment |
| damaged | experienced | support |

Ask S. to put the prefix at the top of the column with each word in the column to make a new word. Have him say the root word and the new word. Then write the prefix in front of the root word so that he may see the new word.

Point out that the prefix *in-* does not always mean *not.* Sometimes, it means *in.* Write these words as examples, and have S. read them: *inside, indoors, income.*

**Note:** A hyphen is not necessary in words formed with *non-*, but *nonviolent* was introduced as *non-violent* in the correlated reader for *Skill Book 3* to make it easier for S. to see the two parts of the word. S. may be allowed to spell words that have the prefix *non-* either with or without the hyphen.

## PRACTICE 6: Vowels Followed by *r* or *rr*

Write the groups of words below.

*cat, car, carry*
*fed, fern, ferry*
*bit, bird, mirror*
*box, born, borrow*

In each group, have S. read the first and second words and tell the vowel sound in each. Underline the vowel and the vowel + *r*. Then have him read the third word and tell whether the vowel sound is like the first word or the second. Underline the first and third words if he answers correctly. If not, ask him to listen as you read the words, and then underline the correct words.

Review the rule that one *r* changes the short sound of the vowel it follows, but two *r*'s usually do not change it.

Write *sorry, Morris, horrible,* and have S. read them. (Give help with *horrible* if necessary.) If he pronounces any of the words with the /or/ sound, review the exception that the letters *orr* may also be pronounced the same as *or*.

Then review this exception: in words like *hurry*, the letters *urr* stand for the same sound as *ur* in *hurt*.

Write the following items, and have S. read them.

| | | |
|---|---|---|
| star | starred | *Who starred in that movie?* |
| stir | stirred | *She stirred the eggs and milk.* |

Review the rule that when a one-syllable word ends with one *r*, we double the *r* before adding an ending that begins with a vowel. The vowel sound in the root word does not change.

## PRACTICE 7: Number of Syllables and Stress

Say each word below, and have S. tell whether the stress is on the first or second syllable.

| | | | |
|---|---|---|---|
| *section* | *support* | *along* | *because* |
| *apply* | *bottom* | *laundry* | *depress* |

Write the words below. Have S. read each one and tell the number of syllables and which one is stressed.

| | | |
|---|---|---|
| *advertise* | *experience* | *disappoint* |
| *according* | *employment* | *unemployed* |
| *editorial* | *signature* | *accident* |

## III. Writing

## CHECK HOMEWORK: Page 99

Check this page with S. Have him correct any errors. Note the type of errors, and plan an exercise to give extra practice on that skill.

## WRITING LESSON (In Notebook)

Have S. write the titles *Lesson 16* and *Words,* and then number from 1 to 20 in two columns. Dictate the 15 words below and 5 other words that S. may need to review. After he has finished, check his work.

**Words.** Help S. study these words: *health, movie, wash, through, hour.* Review the meaning of *through* and *hour.* Give a sentence for *through* and *hour* when you dictate these words.

| | | |
|---|---|---|
| 1. health | 6. bottom | 11. lost |
| 2. most | 7. sharp | 12. wash |
| 3. movie | 8. thankful | 13. male |
| 4. through | 9. sidewalk | 14. female |
| 5. belong | 10. hour | 15. self |

**Sentences.** Have S. write the title *Sentences.* Have him number each sentence as you dictate it. Remind him to use the correct punctuation for questions, direct quotations, exclamations, and items in a series.

1. "It's only tomato sauce," Paul said to his wife.
2. "I can't stand all this noise!" yelled Roy.
3. The fire was caused by a truck hauling 10,000 gallons of oil.
4. What can you do to avoid health problems if you are unemployed?
5. Lan lived with her parents, her brother, her two daughters, and her cousin.

Check what S. has written, and have him correct any errors, including those in punctuation and capitalization. Have S. write the title *Study* and any words he missed in the word and sentence dictation.

**Abbreviations.** Dictate each of the following words and ask S. to write the abbreviations: *Street, Avenue, number, Monday, Friday, August, September.* Check what he has written.

**Note:** If time allows, you may want to take this opportunity to teach the abbreviations for all the days of the week (*Sun., Mon., Tues., Wed., Thurs., Fri., Sat.*) and for the months that are commonly abbreviated: (*Jan., Feb., Mar., Apr., Aug., Sept., Oct., Nov., Dec.*). Point out that *May, June,* and *July* are not abbreviated because the names are so short, and that *March* and *April* are usually written in full because they are also fairly short.

**Writing a letter.** Ask S. to write a short letter to the editor—on the same topic as the letters to the editor in this lesson or on another topic he is more interested in. Before he writes the letter, have him tell orally the ideas he wants to express.

Then have him write a few sentences on a piece of scratch paper as a first draft. Check what he has written, and give any needed help for sentence structure, spelling, and the like, but do not change his ideas.

If S. wants to send his letter to the local paper, give him a sheet of paper to write on. If he wants to write the letter just for practice, have him write it in his notebook. Have S. write his own address for the heading and then stop writing.

Explain that a letter to the editor is a business letter. The form for a business letter is somewhat different from the form for a personal letter.

Above the greeting, we write what is called the *inside address*. This is the address of the place we are writing *to*. It is the same as the address we put on the envelope. We use the person's title and name if we know the name. If we don't know the name, we can use the job title instead. In this case, we can use *Editor* as the first line of the inside address. Have S. write *Editor* plus the rest of the inside address. Have available the name and address of the local newspaper—complete with zip code—for him to copy. Or, if the letter is just for practice, you can have him use the address shown below.

Have S. look at the letters to the editor on page 102 of his book and note that, in a business letter, the greeting is followed by a colon (:) instead of a comma. Have S. leave a little space under the inside address and then write the greeting. The completed inside address and greeting should look like this:

Editor
Huron City Daily News
1421 Lake Ave.
Huron City, NY 13003

Dear Editor:

Have S. recopy the body of his letter from his corrected first draft. Then explain that the closing for a business letter is more formal than for a personal letter. Have S. use *Sincerely, Sincerely yours,* or *Yours truly* for the closing—followed by a comma.

Have S. sign the letter with his full name.

**Note:** If S. plans to send his letter, ask if he would want his full name to appear in the paper. If not, explain that he can ask the paper to use his initials or something like "Concerned Citizen" instead. Show him how to add a postscript at the bottom of the letter, such as: *P.S.: If my letter is printed, please use my initials instead of my full name.* Also, explain that a newspaper gets many letters to the editor and cannot print all of them so that he will not be unduly disappointed if his letter is not printed.

**Addressing an envelope.** Supply a business-size envelope if S. plans to send his letter. Otherwise, fold a piece of paper to the correct size. Review the form for addressing an envelope, and have S. address it.

## PRACTICE: Page 104

Have S. read the directions for the exercise and do it. Check his work. If he has an error, have him read each word in the line and tell its vowel sound. Then have him circle the words with the same vowel sound as the first word in the line.

## HOMEWORK: Page 105

Go over the directions with S. Have him do the first item in each exercise to make sure he understands what to do. Encourage him to read the lesson again at home and to study any words missed in the dictation.

## CHECKING PROGRESS

**Comprehension.** This lesson will help you evaluate your student's progress in reading factual material, such as the news story, article on health, and classified ads. Was he able to select the main facts given, find specific information, and answer questions as to who, what, when, where, and why? His answers on the Story Checkup will indicate his accuracy in reading factual material. Also, you can determine his ability to understand the author's viewpoint, as given in the editorial.

**Word recognition.** Check your student's progress in these areas:

1. Recognition of new words in the lesson by applying phonics skills and knowledge of syllables and root words.
2. Recall of most of the words previously taught, as evidenced in reading the newspaper selections.
3. Recognition of new compound words made from known word parts, as evidenced in Skills Practice 2.
4. Recognition of new words made by adding a prefix or an ending to a known root, as evidenced in Skills Practices 3-5.

**Spelling and writing.** You can evaluate your student's progress by comparing his performance in the writing exercises of this lesson and the last review lesson, Lesson 11. Note his ability to use correct punctuation, write complete sentences, and write legibly. Was he able to express his thoughts in writing the letter? Does he know the form to use in writing a letter and addressing an envelope? If he has many errors in spelling, note the type. Plan to review spelling rules that may help him.

## MEETING INDIVIDUAL NEEDS

If S. did fairly well in this lesson, have him go on to Lesson 17. But if he needs more help in distinguishing the vowel sounds taught in this book, plan a review lesson.

Note which vowel sound-letter relationships give S. the most difficulty. Plan reinforcement exercises using slip strips for word families, such as *-aw, -all, -aught, -ought.* See suggestions given in Lessons 12 and 13. Use word pairs as suggested in Lesson 14. Also, use *Focus on Phonics-4* for review of needed phonics skills.

For reinforcement of needed comprehension skills, use supplementary reading material on this level or create your own. Do not repeat skill book lessons. If any of the Story Checkups, Practice exercises, or Homework pages have not been completed, however, you may have S. do those in class during a review session. Also, you can make cloze exercises from skill book stories as described in Lesson 7. Some of the Reading for Living sections may be used again by asking different questions or substituting a similar form to fill out.

Encourage S. by having him read some supplementary material that he can read easily. Discuss his main purpose in learning to read and see if that purpose is being realized. Continue to use duet reading, as described in Lesson 7.

In *Focus on Phonics-4,* you may use Practices 16A-16F. They review spellings for the sounds /aw/ and /oy/, review some endings, and cover some irregular spellings for short vowel sounds, such as *o* for the sound /u/ as in *mother* and *a* for the sound /o/ as in *father.*

# Lesson 17    Four Sounds for s

consonant (con' su nunt)

| s = s as in snake | s = z as in eggs |
|---|---|
| **s = s at the beginning of most words**<br>see    said    step    smile    swim | **s = z at the end of these words**<br>has    his    was<br>as    is |
| **s = s at the end of these words**<br>*gas    yes    this    bus<br>us | **s = z in some words that end with a vowel and se**<br>raise    these    rose    noise    amuse |
| **s = s when a word ends with a consonant and se**<br>false    nurse    license | **s = z when s comes before other consonants or vowel sounds**<br>husband    easy    visit    thousand<br>Tuesday    cousin    music    president |
| **s = s in some words that end with a vowel and se**<br>base    house | **s = z when the -s or -es ending follows other consonants or vowel sounds**<br>jobs    plays    ties    faces<br>beds    trees    cries    pages<br>dogs    chews    babies    boxes<br>loves    laws    goes    dishes<br>calls    radios    tomatoes    watches |
| **s = s when s comes before the sound for the consonants p, t, k**<br>*aspirin    yesterday    basket<br>rescue | |
| **s = s when the -s ending follows the sound for the consonants p, t, k, f**<br>lips    hats    looks    *cuffs<br>helps    hunts    picks    laughs<br>hopes    gates    likes<br>            picnics | |
| **ss = s in most words**<br>miss    discuss    lesson    possible | |

| s = sh as in sure | s = zh as in measure |
|---|---|
| **s = sh in these words:**<br>sure    *issue    (ish' oo)<br>insurance    *pressure (presh' ur)<br>sugar | **s = zh in these words:**<br>*measure (mezh' ur)    *usual (ū' zhoo ul)<br>*pleasure (plezh' ur)    *usually |

*New words

## 1. The Moon Shines On

| | | |
|---|---|---|
| doesn't | seem | excuse (ex cuze')    pleasant    (plez' unt) |
| moon | shine | Kansas (Kan' zus)    unpleasant |
| rode | | remark (rē mark')    passenger (pas' en jer) |

In Kansas City, I met a man I will never forget. He was a bus driver in Kansas City. He usually drove at night, and I often rode home from work with him.

I used to watch him as the passengers got on the bus. He had a pleasant smile for each one. It was a pleasure to see how many passengers lost their frowns and smiled back.

There was one passenger who never smiled back. He usually pushed his way onto the bus and hurried to sit down. When he climbed over other passengers, he never excused himself. When he stepped on their feet, he never excused himself. He was rude, but that didn't stop the bus driver's smile. The driver gave the unpleasant man his usual bright smile.

The rude man never seemed to see that smile. He would blow his nose loudly and make unpleasant remarks about the way the bus driver was driving. He usually made one or two unpleasant remarks each night, and he made sure everyone heard them.

The rude man's remarks took the pleasure out of the ride for me. But the bus driver never seemed upset. He just went on smiling at the passengers as they got on and off the bus.

I wanted to get to know this friendly bus driver, so one night I rode the bus to the end of the line.

"Excuse me," I said. "I have wanted to tell you what a pleasure it is to have a driver like you. You're the friendliest bus driver in Kansas City. But why don't you throw that one rude man off the bus?"

The bus driver gave me one of his brightest smiles. "That man doesn't annoy me," he said. "Let me tell you about my neighbor's dog. The man next door to me has a dog. Every time the moon shines, the dog barks and barks."

"Well," I asked, "what about the dog and the moon?"

"Oh," he said, "the moon keeps on shining."

# Three Sounds for ch

## ch = ch as in child

**ch = ch in most words**

| | | | | | |
|---|---|---|---|---|---|
| child | *chip | each | lunch | catch | rich |
| choke | *choose (chooz) | peach | branch | match | which |
| chair | *chose (choze) | teach | march | watch | much |
| check | *Charles (Charlz) | *speech | church | stitch | *such |
| chart | *chocolate (choc′u lut) | | | kitchen | touch |
| | | | | *Mitchell | sandwich |

## ch = k as in Christmas

**ch = k in some words**

| | | | |
|---|---|---|---|
| Christmas | school | *chorus (kor′ us) | *Michael (Mi′ kul) |
| *Chris | *schedule (skej′ ule) | *chemistry (kem′ is try) | *mechanic (me kan′ ic) |

## ch = sh as in machine

**ch = sh in a few words**

| | | |
|---|---|---|
| machine | *Chicago (Shi cog′ ō) | *chef (shef) |
| | *Charlotte (Shar′ lot) | *Chevy (Shev′ y) |

*New words

---

## 2. Open House at Central High School

| | | | |
|---|---|---|---|
| I'd | homeroom | central (sen′ trul) | notice (nō′ tis) |
| here's | lunchroom | cookie (cook′ y) | program (prō′ gram) |
| wouldn't | welcome | gym (jim) | |

"Look, Mother! Here's a notice about the open house at my school." Chris handed her mother the notice.

> *Welcome to Open House*
> *Chicago Central High School*
> *Wednesday, October 17*
> *7:30 p.m.*
>
> *(Please bring a cake or cookies.)*

Charlotte Mitchell read the notice and thanked her daughter. "I wouldn't miss it," she said. "Your dad and I always welcome the chance to meet your teachers."

"Can you bake some chocolate chip cookies?" Chris wanted to know.

"You and your brother Michael can bake them," her mother answered.

Chris and her younger brother baked the cookies. Charlotte made sure that her husband Charles was free on Wednesday evening.

At dinner on Wednesday, Chris told her parents she wouldn't ride to school with them because she had chorus practice at 6:30. She would meet them at her homeroom.

By 7:30, Mr. and Mrs. Mitchell and Michael arrived at the school in their old Chevy. They took the cookies to the lunchroom and went to meet Chris.

Chris's homeroom teacher met them at the door and said, "Welcome to Chicago Central High. Here's your daughter's schedule of classes. You may choose the classes you wish to visit. The bell will ring when the program is ready to begin in the gym."

Charles Mitchell looked at the schedule and said, "I'll choose social studies, chemistry, and English."

His wife looked at the schedule and said, "I'll choose the machine shop and math." Then, both of them chose to go to the cooking class.

Chris chose to go along with her father. Michael chose to join his mother because he wanted to see the machine shop.

The chemistry teacher told Chris's father that she was a good student. Chris said, "Some girls don't like chemistry, but I do. We wouldn't have many of the good things in life without chemistry."

The Mitchells all met at the cooking class. Mr. Mitchell wanted to know if there were any male students. "Oh, sure," the teacher said. "Almost everyone will live alone at some time in his life. So everyone should know how to cook. And some of my students will

## Story 1: The Moon Shines On

**Answer each question in a few words.**

1. In what city did the story take place? _____

2. How did the bus driver try to make his passengers happy? _____

3. What showed that one passenger was rude? _____

4. What did the bus driver do when the rude man made unpleasant remarks? _____

5. Do you think the title of the story is a good one? Why or why not? _____

## Story 2: Open House at Central High School

**In what order did these things happen?**
**Put a number by each sentence to show the right order.**

_5_  Chris's homeroom teacher welcomed Mr. and Mrs. Mitchell.

_2_  Chris and Michael baked chocolate chip cookies for the open house.

_8_  The open house ended with snacks in the school lunchroom.

_3_  Chris went to chorus practice at 6:30 on Wednesday.

_7_  The Mitchells went to the gym for the program.

_6_  Chris's parents visited some of her classes.

_4_  Mr. and Mrs. Mitchell arrived at the school in their old Chevy.

_1_  Chris brought home a notice about an open house at her high school.

---

become chefs. Being a chef is a good job for both men and women."

"When I get to high school, I'd like to study auto mechanics," Michael told his parents. "Then, when you give your old Chevy to Chris and me, I can be the best mechanic in Chicago, and I'll keep that old Chevy running forever!"

Just then, the Mitchells heard the bell ring for the start of the program in the gym. Chris ran to take her place in the chorus. Everyone enjoyed the chorus and the speeches. They were glad that the speeches were short.

After the program in the gym, all the parents and their children went into the lunchroom. The Mitchells saw their chocolate chip cookies on the big table with lots of other cookies and cakes.

As they rode home that night, the Mitchells talked about the open house. "We had such a good time," Mrs. Mitchell said. "I enjoyed your teachers, the classes, the chorus, and even the speeches."

**In each line, circle the words in which *s* has the same sound as in the first word.**

**Example:** is     bus     (has)     (rose)     gas

1. seem          (yes)      step      base      (miss)
2. pleasant      (music)    (noise)   stops     (these)
3. pleasure      discuss    (usual)   (measure)
4. passenger     (class)    easy      boxes     (this)

**In each line, circle the words in which *ch* has the same sound as in the first word.**

1. child       (chip)       chorus     chef      (choose)
2. Christmas    machine     (mechanic)  (school)   Charles
3. Chicago      chose       speech     (Chevy)    (machine)
4. lunch        (watch)      Michael    (chocolate) Charlotte

**Read the two words, and then write the contraction for them.**

1. I have ____ I've____          4. does not ____doesn't____
2. here is ____here's____        5. they will ____they'll____
3. could not ____couldn't____    6. would not ____wouldn't____

**Put together a word from List 1 with a word from List 2 to make a compound word.**

| List 1 | List 2 | Compound word |
|--------|--------|---------------|
| 1. class | town | 1. classroom |
| 2. grand | spoon | 2. grandchildren |
| 3. down | room | 3. downtown |
| 4. side | children | 4. sidewalk |
| 5. tea | walk | 5. teaspoon |

Lesson 17     **113**

---

## Reading for Living

| flour | beat | sift | | measure | (mezh′ ur) | ½ | (one half) |
|-------|------|------|--|---------|------------|---|------------|
| mix | beaten | soft | | recipe | (res′ i pē) | ⅔ | (two thirds) |
| nut | spoon | salt | (sawlt) | shortening | (short′ ning) | ¾ | (three fourths) |
| stir | teaspoon | soda | (sō′ du) | vanilla | (vu nil′ u) | | |

**Chocolate Chip Cookies**

Mix by hand with a large spoon, or use electric mixer.
Use a measuring cup and measuring spoons.

1. Mix well. . . . . . . . . . . . . . . . . {⅔ cup soft shortening (part butter)
                                           {¾ cup white sugar
                                           {½ cup brown sugar (packed)
2. Add, and stir in. . . . . . . . . . . . {2 well-beaten eggs
                                           {1½ teaspoons vanilla
3. Sift together, and stir in. . . . . {2 cups sifted flour
                                           {1 teaspoon salt
                                           {1 teaspoon baking soda
4. Stir in . . . . . . . . . . . . . . . . . {1 large bag of chocolate chips
                                           {½ cup broken nuts
5. Drop from teaspoon onto cookie pan. Leave space between cookies.
6. Bake 8 to 10 minutes at 375. Cookies should still be soft.
   Cool for a few minutes before removing from pan.
                                    Makes about 50 cookies.

**Read this recipe,
and write short answers
to the questions below.**

1. What should be used for part of the shortening? ___Butter___

2. What do you do to the brown sugar as you measure it? ___Pack it___

3. In the first step of this recipe, what things do you mix together?
___Shortening, butter, white sugar, and brown sugar___

4. In the second step of this recipe, what things do you add and stir in?
___Eggs and vanilla___

5. Do you beat the eggs before you add them to the shortening and sugar? ___Yes___

6. Are the flour, salt, and baking soda added before or after the eggs? ___After___

7. Do you sift the sugar with the flour, salt, and baking soda? ___No___

8. How much vanilla is used in this recipe? ___1½ teaspoons___

9. What is stirred in at the same time as the nuts? ___Chocolate chips___

10. How long should you bake the cookies? ___8 to 10 minutes___

## OBJECTIVES

To help your student:

- recognize that *s* stands for four consonant sounds: /s/ as in *snake*, /z/ as in *eggs*, /sh/ as in *sure*, and /zh/ as in *measure*.
- understand that *s* most often stands for /s/ as in *snake*.
- recognize some ways to tell whether *s* stands for /s/ or /z/ in a word.
- recognize some of the words in which *s* stands for /sh/ and /zh/.
- distinguish the consonant sound /zh/ as in *measure*.
- recognize that *ch* stands for three consonant sounds: /ch/ as in *children*, /k/ as in *school*, /sh/ as in *machine*.
- understand that *ch* most often stands for /ch/ as in *children*.
- read a story containing words with each of the four sounds for *s*.
- read a story containing words with each of the three sounds for *ch*.
- recognize the new contractions *doesn't*, *I'd*, *here's*, *wouldn't*, and review other contractions.
- recognize the new compound words *lunchroom*, *homeroom*, *teaspoon*, and review other compound words.
- review adding *-ing* and recognize when to double the final consonant of a two-syllable root word.
- recall the sequence of events in a story.
- recognize the author's purpose.
- read dialog and indentify the speakers.
- interpret facts and draw inferences.
- relate the stories to personal experience and values.
- read a recipe.
- read the fractions ½, ⅔, ¾.
- write words, sentences, and numbers from dictation.
- write a notice or an ad.

## INTRODUCTION

T: You have studied all of the vowel sounds. In today's lesson, you will learn a new consonant sound. You will also study different sounds that *s* and *ch* can sometimes stand for.

# I. Reading

## CHART: Page 106

**Title and chart format.** Have S. read the titles *Lesson 17* and *Four Sounds for s*. Also, have him read the new word *consonant* in the top right-hand corner.

T: This lesson and the three lessons that follow are mostly about consonants. You will notice that this chart looks quite different from the ones in the previous lessons. There are four main sections. (Point these out.) Each section tells about one of the sounds for *s*. Notice that the heading for each section is printed in black on a colored background. Most of the words in the chart are old words.

## Section 1: *s = s* as in *snake*
## Section 2: *s = z* as in *eggs*

**Note:** These two sections of the chart are to be read at the same time. Read across each row, completing first the block of *s = s* material on the left and then the block of *s = z* material on the right. This will give S. a comparison of how *s* is pronounced in similar positions in words. When reading items like *s = s* and *s = z*, have S. give the name for the letter before the equal sign and the sound for the letter after the equal sign.

T: (Point to *s = s* as in *snake*.) The heading for section 1 tells the sound you have already learned for *s*. Read the heading. [S: *s* = /s/ as in *snake*.]

T: That is the most common sound for *s*. The second most common sound for *s* is given in section 2 at the right. Read the heading. [S: *s* = /z/ as in *eggs*.]

T: Before this lesson, any new word with an *s* for the sound /z/ was respelled for you. In this lesson, you will compare some words in which *s* equals /s/ with some words in which *s* equals /z/. This study will help you see which of the two sounds *s* is more likely to stand for in a particular word. After this lesson, *s* will not be respelled if it equals /z/.

### Row 1, left and right blocks

T: Look at the first block on the left, just under the large heading *s = s*. Read the material to yourself. [S. reads.] How is *s* pronounced at the beginning of most words? [S: /s/.]

Have S. look at the empty block on the right under the large heading *s = z*. Discuss why there are no words in this block. Point out that *s* never equals /z/ at the beginning of a word.

### Row 2, left and right blocks.
Have S. read the material in both blocks to himself. Call his attention to the asterisk (*) in front of *gas* and the note at the bottom of the page that tells what it means (new words).

Ask S. to read aloud the words in each block to note the difference in the sounds for *s* at the end of a word.

T: Most of these words are old words, so you know how to pronounce the *s* at the end of them. If you come to a new word that ends in *s*, first try the sound /s/. Most words that end in *s* have the sound /s/. If that doesn't sound right, then try /z/.

**Row 3, left and right blocks.** Have S. read the *s* = *s* material in the block on the left, first silently and then aloud. Ask S. to note what consonant comes before *se* at the end of each word (*false, nurse, license*).

Have S. look at the empty block on the right for *s* = *z*. Discuss why there are no words in that block. Point out that when a word ends with a consonant and *se*, the *se* always equals /s/ and never equals /z/.

**Row 4, left and right blocks.** Go over both blocks in this row in a similar manner. Explain that after a vowel sound, *se* at the end of a word is more likely to stand for /z/ than /s/, but there is no way to be sure.

**Row 5, left and right blocks.** Explain that, up to now, the chart has discussed the sound for *s* at the beginning or end of a root word. This row is about the sound for *s* in the middle of a root word.

Have S. read the heading for the *s* = *s* block on the left, first silently and then aloud. Then ask him to read the words to himself. Have him read each word aloud and tell the consonant sound that comes after *s*. Call attention to the different spellings for the sound /k/ in *basket* and *rescue*. Point out to S. that he is used to pronouncing *s* as /s/ before the sounds for *p*, *t*, *k* in the consonant blends *sp*, *st*, *sk*.

Have S. read the heading and words in the *s* = *z* block on the right, first silently and then aloud. In the first column of words, have him tell what consonant sound comes after *s*. In the other columns of words, have him note that *s* comes before a vowel sound; in fact, *s* comes between vowel sounds.

Point out that if he can remember that *s* = /s/ before the sounds /p/, /t/, and /k/, then he will know *s* usually equals /z/ before any other sound.

**Row 6, left and right blocks.** Ask S. to read the heading for the *s* = *s* block on the left, first silently and then aloud. Then have him read aloud the three words in the first column (*lips, helps, hopes*) and tell what consonant sound the -*s* ending follows in all three words. Point out that although -*s* follows the letter *e* in *hopes*, the sound it follows is /p/. Follow the same procedure for the other columns of words. Call attention to the various spellings for /k/ in the third column and the two spellings for /f/ in the last column.

Follow the same procedure for the *s* = *z* block on the right. Have S. tell the consonant sound that the -*s* ending follows in each word in the first column and the vowel sound that -*s* follows in each word in the second and third columns. In the last column, ask S. to tell what consonant sound comes before -*s* in each word (*faces, pages, boxes, dishes, watches*). Explain that it would be difficult to say either /s/ or /z/ directly after these consonant sounds. So, the *e* is pronounced, and the -*es* ending becomes a syllable. When the -*es* ending is a syllable, it is usually pronounced /ez/. Compare

the words *faces* and *pages*, in which the *e* is pronounced, with the words *hopes, gates, likes, loves*, in which the *e* is silent before the -*s* ending.

**Row 7, left and right blocks.** Have S. read the *s* = *s* material in the block on the left, first silently and then aloud. Point out that *ss* can come either at the end of a word or in the middle of a word.

Have S. look at the empty block on the right for *s* = *z*. Discuss why there are no words in that block. Point out that *ss* usually equals /s/ and almost never equals /z/.

**Note:** The letters *ss* stand for /z/ in only a very few words. The common ones are *dessert, dissolve, possess,* and *scissors*.

## Section 3: *s* = *sh* as in *sure*

T: (Point to *s* = *sh* as in *sure*.) This section is about another sound for *s*. Read the heading. [S: *s* = /sh/ as in *sure*.] There are not many words in which *s* stands for the sound /sh/. Here are a few of the most common ones. You have already had the first three words, and you can easily sound out the other two. Please read this section to yourself.

After S. has read the section silently, have him read it aloud. Point out that the two *s*'s together stand for the sound /sh/ in *issue* and *pressure*.

## Section 4: *s* = *zh* as in *measure*

T: The letter *s* can stand for one more consonant sound. It is a consonant sound that you have not had. The sound is like /sh/, but it is voiced not whispered. You can hear this new sound in the word *measure*. Say *measure*. [S: measure.] I will say the word again. Listen for the consonant sound at the end of the first syllable: *measure*. What is the sound? [S: /zh/.] Good.

T: Look at the heading for the last section of the chart. You will see the letters *zh* after the equal sign. These two letters are used to stand for the sound /zh/. Read the heading. [S: *s* = /zh/ as in *measure*.] You will not see the letters *zh* together in a word, but when you see them in a respelling, you will know that they stand for the sound /zh/. Read the rest of this section to yourself.

After S. has read silently, have him read the section aloud. Have him contrast the sound for *s* in *pleasure* with the sound for *s* in *pressure*. Point out that the letters *s* and *ss* usually have the sound /sh/ or /zh/ when followed by *ure*. Mention that in the skill book any new word that has the sound /sh/ or /zh/ for *s* will be respelled.

**Review.** Have S. read each section heading aloud. Then have him read aloud each new word marked with an asterisk (*gas, aspirin, cuffs, issue, pressure, measure, pleasure, usual, usually*).

## STORY 1: Page 107 (The Moon Shines On)

Have S. read the story title and new words. Have him tell the sound for *s* in each word that has an *s*, except for the digraph *sh*.

**Silent reading.** Have S. note that this story is written in two columns and is complete on one page. Ask S. to read the whole story quickly to himself. Time his reading. He should be able to complete it in two or three minutes. Make a note of the time it took. Then, without any discussion of the story or oral reading, have S. do the Story Checkup for story 1 on page 111.

## STORY CHECKUP: Page 111 (Story 1)

Ask S. to read the directions to himself and do the checkup for story 1. He may look back at the story to find an answer or the correct spelling for a word. Tell him you would like to see if he can finish the whole checkup in 10 minutes or less. If he finishes in less than 10 minutes, make a note of the time. If he doesn't finish in 10 minutes, have him circle the number of the last item he finished answering. Then let him complete the checkup.

Check your student's work by having him read each question and his answer. Make a note of the number of questions he answered correctly. Refer him to the story to find the correct answer for any he has wrong. Discuss the last question if he had difficulty in answering it.

**Reading between the lines.** Discuss these questions.

1. Did you like this story? Why or why not?
2. What do you think the author's purpose was in writing this story? In other words, what point was the author trying to make?
3. Can you picture this story in your mind? Can you picture the bus driver? Can you picture the rude man? What helps you get a mental picture of these characters?
4. Can you describe an interesting person you have met somewhere? What made you remember the person? Think about this person for a few minutes, and then tell something about the person, so that I can get a mental picture of what he or she is like.

**Note:** If S. doesn't know of anyone he can tell about, read a character sketch—or a portion of one—from another book or magazine. Or, you may want to tell S. about someone you know. Emphasize telling things that a person does that reveal a certain trait rather than describing the person's looks.

**Oral reading.** Have S. read the story aloud. Note his ability to interpret the story as shown by expressive reading. Give suggestions if he needs help in improving his oral reading.

## CHART: Page 108

Have S. read the title *Three Sounds for ch*. Have him note that there are three sections in this chart.

## Section 1: *ch* = *ch* as in *child*

T: The first heading tells the sound you have already learned for *ch*. Please read it. [S: *ch* = /ch/ as in *child*.] Read the smaller heading in dark type just above the list of words. [S: *ch* = /ch/ in most words.]

**First two columns.** Ask S. to read the first two columns of words to himself and notice where the sound /ch/ comes in each word.

After S. has read the words silently, have him read them aloud. Ask where the sound /ch/ comes in these words [at the beginning]. Call attention to the sound for *s* in *choose, chose, Charles*. Point out that *chocolate* may be pronounced with three syllables (*choc' u lut*) as shown in the book or with two syllables (*choc' lut*).

**Last four columns.** Ask S. to read the remaining four columns of words in section 1 and notice where the sound /ch/ comes in these words. After he has studied the chart silently, call attention to these points.

1. The letters *ch* come at the end of all the words except *kitchen* and *Mitchell*. In those words, *ch* comes at the end of a syllable.
2. In the first column, *ch* comes after a long vowel sound.
3. In the second column, *ch* comes after *r* or *n*.
4. In the third column, the sound /ch/ comes directly after a short vowel sound. When it comes after a short vowel sound, the sound /ch/ is often written *tch*. The *t* is silent.
5. The last column gives some words with short vowels that are followed by *ch* rather than *tch*.

## Section 2: *ch* = *k* as in *Christmas*

Have S. read the large section heading aloud. Then ask him to read the smaller heading and tell when *ch* = /k/. Have S. read the words first silently and then aloud. Call attention to these points:

1. The letters *ch* stand for the sound /k/ when they are part of a consonant blend, such as *chr* in *Christmas* and *Chris* and *sch* in *school* and *schedule*.
2. Other than this, there is no way to tell when *ch* stands for the sound /k/ in words. Most such words came from the Greek language. In the skill book, the word is respelled when *ch* = /k/.

## Section 3: *ch* = *sh* as in *machine*

Have S. read the large section heading aloud. Then ask him to study the section by himself. When he has studied it silently, have him read it aloud.

Explain that in the French language, *ch* is always pronounced /sh/. In words that we have taken from French, *ch* stands for the sound /sh/.

**Note:** You may also want to point out that *Chevy* in the list refers to *Chevrolet*, which comes from French. But in the place name *Chevy Chase*, Chevy is pronounced with /ch/.

**Review.** Have S. read each section heading aloud. Then have him read aloud each new word that has an asterisk in front of it.

## STORY 2: Pages 109-110
### (Open House at Central High School)

Have S. read the story title and new words. Call attention to the contractions and compound words, and have S. tell the two words each one is made from.

**Note:** The word *cookie* may be spelled either *cookie,* as in the book, or *cooky.*

**Silent reading.** Have S. note that this story is written in two columns and continues on a second page. Ask S. to read the whole story quickly to himself. Time his reading. He should be able to finish in five minutes or less. Make a note of the time it took. Then, without any discussion or oral reading, have S. do the Story Checkup for story 2 on page 111.

## STORY CHECKUP: Page 111 (Story 2)

Ask S. to read the directions to himself and do the checkup. Tell him he may refer back to the story if he needs to. Allow about five minutes for him to do the checkup. If he finishes in less time, make a note of the time it took. If he needs more time, let him finish the exercise, but make a note of how long it took. Check his work. Record the number he had right. Then have S. refer back to the story to make any needed corrections.

**Reading between the lines.** Discuss as many of these questions as apply to your student. If S. is a young person in school, you may want to omit the last three questions and discuss school open houses from a student's perspective instead. If S. is a young person out of school, you may want to find out if any adult education programs in your area have open houses and discuss them with S.

1. Why did the school have an open house? Do you think it is a good idea to have an open house?
2. What do you think Chris's parents learned from going to the open house? What do you think Michael learned?
3. Do you think it was a good idea for both of Chris's parents to go? Why or why not?
4. How do you think it made Chris feel to have her parents attend the open house?
5. Have you been to a school's open house? What did you learn from the experience?
6. If it isn't possible for a parent to attend open house, what are some other ways to find out more about his school?
7. If you don't have children in school, do you think you should visit schools in your community? Why or why not?

**Oral reading.** Have S. name the characters who speak in the story. Have him select one or two characters whose conversation he'd like to read aloud. Note his ability to interpret the character through his expression in reading. If you have several students, they may want to dramatize the story.

## READING FOR LIVING: Page 112

**Note 1:** S. probably knows how to cook but may not have used a recipe or standard measures. To help him understand the written recipe, have on hand these items:

1. One-cup glass measuring cup with clear fractional markings.
2. Set of measuring cups for $1/4$, $1/3$, $1/2$, and 1 cup.
3. Set of measuring spoons for $1/2$ teaspoon, 1 teaspoon, 1 tablespoon.
4. Any dry ingredient which can be measured for practice. This might be white sugar, flour, salt, uncooked rice, or even a nonfood item like clean sand.
5. Liquid for measuring practice. This can be water.
6. Table knife with one *straight* edge.
7. Brown sugar.
8. Flour sifter and bowl.
9. Stick of butter or margarine showing markings for tablespoons and fractions of a cup. (Make a drawing of one if it's too messy to bring.)

**Note 2:** You may want S. to make the cookie recipe in class if you have the time and facilities. If so, bring the ingredients and equipment needed for the recipe. Or, you may want to have S. study the recipe in this session and make it at another time.

**Introduction.** Have S. read the title and new words, first silently and then aloud. Call attention to the compound word *teaspoon* and the the the way the fractions $1/2$, $2/3$, $3/4$ are written. Use the term *fractions* when referring to them.

Have S. read the directions that are to the left of the recipe, first silently and then aloud.

T: A recipe is written in a certain form and uses special terms. (Point to the recipe.) This is one of the forms that is often used for recipes. On the left-hand side are step-by-step directions. On the right-hand side is a list of the things that go into the recipe. These are called the ingredients.

Have S. read the title and tell what the recipe is for. Then have him read the two sentences just below the title, first silently and then aloud.

**Demonstrate measures.** Show the one-cup glass measuring cup, and explain that it is used for measuring liquids like water or milk. Point out the markings for 1 cup, $1/4$ cup, $1/2$ cup, $3/4$ cup, $1/3$ cup, and $2/3$ cup, and be sure that S. understands what they mean.

Then show the set of measuring cups. Explain that they are used for dry ingredients such as flour and sugar. If the markings are clear, have S. read the size of each measure. Otherwise, write each fraction on a slip of paper, and have S. place the measuring cup by the right label.

Also, show the measuring spoons, and help S. identify the tablespoon, 1 teaspoon, and $^1/_2$ teaspoon.

**Skimming for ingredients.** Explain that when we read a recipe, usually the first thing we do is to skim through the list of ingredients on the right to be sure we have everything we need. If we are ready to make the recipe, we also get the ingredients out to have them ready.

Ask S. to skim the list of ingredients to find out what is needed. Tell him not to be concerned at this point about the exact measurements in cups and teaspoons. He should just find out what the ingredients are.

When he has finished skimming, have him tell what is needed. Let him refer to the recipe if he needs to. His list should include shortening, butter, white sugar, brown sugar, 2 eggs, vanilla, flour, salt, baking soda, chocolate chips, and nuts. (If you have the ingredients on hand, have him indicate each item as he names it.)

**Step 1.** Explain that when we are ready to make the recipe, we go back and read everything very carefully.

Point to number 1. Have S. read the directions, including the ingredients, first silently and then aloud. Have him find the "dry" measuring cup to be used for each of the ingredients. For the $^2/_3$ cup shortening (part butter), explain that he can use the $^1/_3$ cup to measure the shortening and can cut a $^1/_3$-cup piece off a stick of butter. Also, explain that to pack brown sugar means to press it down in the measuring cup until it sticks together and holds its shape.

You may want to have S. practice measuring the dry ingredient you have brought. Explain that you level it off with the straight edge of a knife. You should never tap or shake the cup to level off.

**Step 2.** Have S. read the directions and ingredients for step 2. Be sure he understands that the eggs are to be beaten before they are added to the sugar-shortening mixture. Have him measure $1^1/_2$ teaspoons of the liquid you brought.

**Steps 3-4.** Go through steps 3-4 of the recipe in the same manner. Be sure S. understands that the flour is sifted before it is measured (unless you happen to have a presifted flour). Then the flour, salt, and soda are sifted together.

**Step 5.** Have S. read step 5. Explain what it means if he doesn't understand.

**Step 6 to end.** Have S. read step 6 and the line at the bottom of the recipe, first silently and then aloud. Ask if there is any part of the recipe he doesn't understand. Go over it with him. If it seems helpful or necessary, have him look at the recipe and tell in his own words the steps he would follow to make the cookies.

**Exercise.** Have S. write the answers to the questions. Check his work, and help him correct any errors. Emphasize the importance of reading a recipe carefully.

Have S. follow the recipe to make the cookies if you have planned for this. Otherwise, give extra practice in measuring the ingredients you have brought.

## II. Skills Practice

### PRACTICE 1: Distinguishing the Sound /zh/

Write *measure*, and have S. read it. Ask him to tell the sound for *s* in *measure*. Write *zh*.

T: I will say two words. Tell me which one has the sound /zh/ as in *measure*. It may or may not be spelled with *s*. Listen for the sound /zh/.

| | | |
|---|---|---|
| *sure, usual* | *cause, casual* | *pleasure, pleasant* |
| *vision, visit* | *trees, treasure* | *occasion, discussion* |
| *easy, Asia* | *beige, batch* | *measles, measure* |

### PRACTICE 2: Distinguishing /sh/, /ch/, /zh/

Write *children, shop, measure*. Draw a line under *ch* in *children*, *sh* in *shop*, and *s* in *measure*. Have S. read each word and tell the sound for the letter or letters underlined.

T: I will say two words that both have one of these sounds. Tell me what the sound is and which of the words I wrote has the same sound. Listen: *chef, sure*. What is the sound? [S: /sh/.] Which word that I wrote has the same sound? [S: shop.]

Continue in the same way with these words:

| | |
|---|---|
| *chip, chocolate* | *such, speech* |
| *pleasure, treasure* | *tissue, issue* |
| *machine, Chicago* | *usually, confusion* |
| *vision, usual* | *shine, shortening* |
| *sugar, sure* | *choose, chance* |

### PRACTICE 3: Sound Substitution, /s/ and /z/

T: I will say a word that has the sound /s/ as in *snake*. Tell me what the word would be if you changed the sound /s/ to the sound /z/ as in *zipper*. Listen to this word: *sip*. [S: zip.]

Write the headings *s* and *z*. Under them, write *sip* and *zip*. Continue in the same way with each pair of words below. Say the first word with the sound /s/. Have S. substitute the sound /z/. Then write both words.

| | | |
|---|---|---|
| *seal, [zeal]* | *dose, [doze]* | *close, [close]* |
| *bus, [buzz]* | *loose, [lose]* | *use, [use]* |
| *fuss, [fuzz]* | | *excuse, [excuse]* |

After you have written all of the words, have S. read each pair of words. Have him tell what letter or letters stand for the sound /z/ in each word in the *z* column.

Point out that the last three words (*close, use, excuse*) are written the same way whether they are pronounced with /s/

or /z/. When we see these words in a sentence, the meaning tells us which way to pronounce them. Have S. pronounce *close* with the sound /z/ and give a sentence showing its meaning (such as: *Close the door*). Then have him pronounce *close* with the sound /s/ and give a sentence (such as: *I live close to my parents*). Do the same for *use* and *excuse*.

## PRACTICE 4: Sound Substitution, /sh/ and /ch/

Write the headings *sh* and *ch*, and do an exercise similar to the one above. In each pair of words below, say the first word with the sound /sh/. Have S. substitute the sound /ch/. Then write both words.

| | | |
|---|---|---|
| ship, [chip] | cash, [catch] | wish, [witch] |
| shin, [chin] | mash, [match] | mush, [much] |
| shop, [chop] | dish, [ditch] | |

Have S. read each pair of words. Have him tell which words end in *tch*.

## PRACTICE 5: Contractions

Write these words in a column: *does not, would not, could not, did not, cannot, has not, have not, is not, are not, do not, will not*. Have S. read each pair of words and tell what contraction can be made from them. Have him spell the contraction as you write it beside the pair of words. When the list is complete, have S. read the contractions. Have him note that all of the contractions except *won't* are made by substituting an apostrophe for the *o* in *not*. Call attention to the formation of the contraction for *will not*.

Follow the same procedure for these words: *I will, he will, she will, we will, you will, they will, I have, I am, I would, here is, it is, that is*.

## PRACTICE 6: Compound Words

Write these words: *lunchroom, homeroom, classroom, bedroom, roommate, teaspoon, tablespoon*. Have S. read each compound word and tell the two words it is made from. Write the two words as he says them.

## PRACTICE 7: Ending *-ing*

Write these words in a column: *ride, shine, measure, swim, choose, cook, run, smile, step*. Ask S. to add the ending *-ing* to each root word to make a new word. Ask him to spell the new word. Write the new word in another column as he spells it. Have S. tell the reason for any change made in the root word before *-ing* is added.

Point out that when a one-syllable word ends in a short vowel sound plus a consonant, the final consonant is doubled before *-ing*. Then write *mix, mixing*, and have S. read them. Explain that final *x* is an exception. The letter *x* is never doubled before an ending. Write *fix*, and have S. read it. Have him tell what the word would be with *-ing* and how to spell it. Write *fixing*.

At the head of two columns, write *forget, forgetting*. Have S. read them. Point out that *forget* ends with a short vowel plus a consonant. Have S. tell which syllable in *forget* is stressed [the last]. Explain that in words with more than one syllable, the final consonant is doubled before *-ing* if the last syllable is stressed.

Across from *forget, forgetting*, write *visit, visiting* at the head of another two columns. Have S. read them. Point out that *visit* also ends with a short vowel plus a consonant. Have S. tell which syllable in *visit* is stressed [the first]. Explain that when the last syllable is unstressed, the final consonant is not doubled before *-ing*.

Say each root word in the pairs below. Have S. tell whether it is like *forget* (with the last syllable stressed) or like *visit* (with the last syllable unstressed). Write the word in the appropriate column. Then have S. tell what the word would be with *-ing* and how to spell it. Write the word with *-ing* as he spells it.

| | |
|---|---|
| upset, upsetting | open, opening |
| begin, beginning | happen, happening |

# III. Writing

## CHECK HOMEWORK: Page 105

Check your student's answers in the first exercise. If he has an error, have him read the first word in the line to be sure he recognizes it. Then have him read each of the other words in the line. If he has difficulty recognizing the opposites, discuss the meaning of the words or use them in sentences.

Check his answers in the second exercise. If S. has an error, have him read the sentence aloud. He may note what the correct ending should be from the way the sentence sounds. If not, help him find the correct ending. Note the errors he made, if any, and then have him erase them and write the correct endings.

## WRITING LESSON (In Notebook)

Have S. write the titles *Lesson 17* and *Words* and number from 1 to 30 in two columns. After the dictation, check his work, and have him correct any errors by writing the whole word correctly.

**Words.** Help S. study these words: *usual, pleasant, mechanic, measure, welcome, notice, flour, salt, recipe*. When dictating, give a sentence for *flour* and for *excuse* with a /z/ sound, such as: *Please excuse me*.

| | | |
|---|---|---|
| 1. gas | 11. usual | 21. welcome |
| 2. doesn't | 12. chip | 22. notice |
| 3. moon | 13. choose | 23. program |
| 4. rode | 14. chose | 24. flour |
| 5. seem | 15. such | 25. excuse |
| 6. shine | 16. mechanic | 26. teaspoon |
| 7. measuring | 17. I'd | 27. soft |
| 8. pleasant | 18. here's | 28. salt |
| 9. passenger | 19. wouldn't | 29. speech |
| 10. remark | 20. lunchroom | 30. recipe |

**Sentences.** Have S. write the title *Sentences.* Have him number each sentence as you dictate it. Before dictating the sentences, write this example: *"Well," he asked, "what's the hurry?"* Explain that this is an example of a quoted sentence that is interrupted by words like *he asked* or *she said.* Point out that each part of the quoted sentence has quotation marks around it. The first part is set off with a comma inside the quotation marks. Another comma is used after words like *he asked.* The second part of the quoted sentence begins with a small letter rather than a capital. Leave the sentence on the board as an example for S. to follow.

1. The bus driver had a pleasant smile for each passenger.
2. "Well," I asked, "what about the dog and the moon?"
3. "Oh," he said, "the moon keeps on shining."
4. "When I get to high school," Michael told his parents, "I'd like to study auto mechanics."
5. "I enjoyed your teachers, the classes, the chorus, and even the speeches," said Mrs. Mitchell.

Give S. a little extra time to look over his punctuation. Then check his work, and have him correct any errors, including those in punctuation and capitalization. Give special attention to the use of quotation marks and commas. If S. needs help, plan some reinforcement exercises to be done later.

**Fractions.** Show S. how to write $1/2$, $1/3$, $3/4$, and $1 1/2$. Have him practice writing these. Then dictate the following for him to write in numerals:

| | | |
|---|---|---|
| one third | three fourths | two and a half |
| one half | two thirds | one and a fourth |

Have S. write the title *Study* and any words or fractions he missed in the dictation exercises.

**Writing a notice or ad.** Have S. write a notice such as would be put up on a bulletin board. It might be about a community event like a group picnic or sports events, a garage sale, an item he wants to sell, a service he wants to offer for hire, or something lost or found. Or, S. may prefer to write a classified ad instead of a notice. Let him refer to the Reading for Living section of Lesson 4 (community events), the classified ads in Lesson 16, or the notice in story 2 of Lesson 7 for ideas about information to include.

## PRACTICE: Page 113

Go over the directions and example with S., and have him do both exercises. Check his work. If he has an error in the first exercise, have him read the first word in the line aloud and tell the sound for *s.* Then have him read each word in the line aloud and tell the sound for *s.* Have him correct his errors. Go over the second exercise in the same way, noting the sound for *ch* in each word of any line where he has an error.

## HOMEWORK: Page 113

Go over the directions for both exercises with S. Have him write one contraction in the first exercise as an example of what to do. Encourage him to reread the two stories at home and to study any words he missed in the dictation.

## CHECKING PROGRESS

**Comprehension.** Your student's responses on the Story Checkup and discussion questions will help you evaluate his progress in understanding main ideas, recalling sequence of events, drawing inferences, and recognizing the author's purpose. Note which of these skills need reinforcement.

**Word recognition.** Note your student's ability to recall the familiar words on the charts in this lesson. Are they in his sight vocabulary, or did he have to apply word recognition skills in order to read them? Was he able to recognize the new words by applying his knowledge of letter-sound relationships, root words and endings, and syllables? How accurate was his word recognition in the oral reading passages? Note the types of errors. S. should be able to recognize by sight most of the words he has had so far in the skill books. If he has to analyze these words before he can read them or if he reads them inaccurately, plan short practices on the words he most needs.

**Rate of silent reading.** If your student's rate of reading was slower than that suggested in the lesson, try to analyze the reason. Is it because he doesn't recognize words? Does he read word by word rather than by phrases? Does he have difficulty in comprehension, so that he rereads a passage in an effort to understand it? Or, is the problem a lack of concentration? Have you discussed with S. the need for different rates of speed according to the nature of the material being read? The two short stories in the lesson should be read much faster than the recipe, for example.

## MEETING INDIVIDUAL NEEDS

**Comprehension.** Use short selections from supplementary reading materials to reinforce the skills emphasized in this lesson.

**Word recognition.** Make flash cards for some of the words on the first chart. Write the letters *s* and *z* on separate cards. Put the letter cards face up. Have S. put each flash card under *s* or *z* depending on which sound *s* stands for in the word. When he has finished, have him read both sets of words and make any needed corrections. You may give a similar practice exercise for the words in chart 2, using *ch, k,* and *s* as headings.

If S. had difficulty in recognizing any words in today's reading, put them on flash cards to use in another session.

In *Focus on Phonics-4,* you may use Practices 17A-17H, which cover the four sounds for *s* and the three sounds for *ch*.

**Rate of reading.** Use duet reading to increase speed of reading and fluency of oral reading. Also, a slip strip with phrases for S. to read silently may help to increase his rate of silent reading. Give him just a second or two to read the phrase, and then ask a question that will determine his comprehension. Some items you might use are:

| Phrases | Questions |
|---|---|
| in the gym | Where? |
| at 8:00 p.m. | When? |
| speeches and music | What? |
| by the high school chorus | Who? |
| a bus driver in Chicago | What city? |

Instead of asking questions, you might expose the phrase for a second, and then ask S. to repeat it without looking at it again. Selections of two or three sentences may also be used. Use familiar words but not the exact wording from the skill book lesson.

## Lesson 18    Two Sounds for c

| c = k as in cup | c = s as in city |
|---|---|
| **c = k before a consonant**<br>class   cry   *scream   act   back | |
| **c = k before e, i, or u**<br>ca     co     cu<br>cat    cop    cut | **c = s before e, i, or y**<br>ce     ci     cy<br>cent   city   icy |
| **cc = k before a, o, or u**<br>cca     cco     ccu<br>*occasion   according   *occupation<br>(o kā' zhun)      (ok ū pā' shun) | **cc = ks before e or i**<br>cce     cci<br>*accept   accident<br>(ak sept') |
| **c = k at the end of a word**<br>music   public   *medic | **ce = s at the end of a word**<br>face    service    *difference |

## Two Sounds for g

| g = g as in go | g = j as in age |
|---|---|
| **g = g before a consonant**<br>glass   glad   grow   grade   *Grace | |
| **g = g before a, o, or u**<br>ga     go     gu<br>game   got    gun | **g = j before e, i, or y**<br>ge       gi             gy<br>*gentle   *Ginger        *energy<br>(jen' tul)   (Jin' jer)   (en' er jy)<br>Note: In a few words, g = g before e or i.<br>Some examples are get, gift, girl, give. |
| **gg = g even before e, i, or y**<br>bigger   hugging   foggy | |
| **g = g at the end of a word**<br>leg   big   hug   fog<br>dig   rug   dog | **ge or dge = j at the end of a word**<br>age    courage   change   *edge<br>page   *bandage   *strange   *bridge |

*New words

---

| | | | |
|---|---|---|---|
| aid | danger (dān' jer) | graduate (graj' oo āte) | tale |
| army | enemy | lay | themselves |
| Chang | Gene | soldier (sōl' jer) | wound (woond) |
| | Gordon | shoot | |

## A Strange Tale of War

It was strange how much alike Gene Bridges and Gordon Chang were. When they were young, they both took care of hurt animals. They bandaged the animals and nursed them back to health. They enjoyed helping the animals get well.

Gene Bridges and Gordon Chang both longed to become doctors so they could help people get well. They both learned to give first aid. They read many books about doctors with great courage. In the books they read, doctors gave their lives and their energy to helping people in sickness and danger. Both Gene and Gordon longed to be doctors like that.

How much alike Gene and Gordon were! There seemed to be only one difference between them. They lived in different countries on opposite sides of the world.

When Gene graduated from high school, it was a proud occasion for the Bridges family. Gene was accepted by a college near his home. He hoped to work his way through college and become a doctor. Gordon Chang graduated from high school the same year Gene did. It was a proud occasion for the Chang family, too. Gordon was also accepted by a college and hoped to become a doctor.

But just after Gene and Gordon graduated from high school, their countries called them to war. Before he went off to war, Gene married his girl friend Ginger. Gordon married Grace, the girl he loved.

In the armed services, both Gene and Gordon became medics. Each was a medic in his own country's army. (Medics rescue soldiers who have been wounded in the fighting. They give first aid and other emergency care.)

All their lives, both Gene and Gordon had wanted to help other people. They were gentle men. It was hard for them to accept war and killing. Many times, their hearts grew heavy, and they felt very tired. But they found new energy to rescue and bandage wounded soldiers. They tried to forget the hurt in their gentle hearts.

The medics went where the fighting was going on. They carried out wounded soldiers. On those occasions, the medics carried guns to protect themselves. Gene and Gordon didn't like carrying guns, but they knew there was danger. They could get shot. Each of them hoped that he would never have to shoot another man.

Gene wrote to his wife Ginger. He said he didn't like being in this strange country. He wanted to be with Ginger and their baby girl who had been born while he was away.

Gordon didn't like war any more than Gene did. He read the letters from his wife Grace over and over. He, too, longed to go home and see their new baby boy.

It's true that Gene and Gordon were very much alike. But now there was a big difference between them. Because their countries were at war, they were enemies.

One long hot day, bombs were falling, and there was a lot of shooting. Gene was sick of bandaging arms and legs that were half shot off. He was sick of seeing young men with parts of their faces missing. By the time the sun began to go down, Gene had no energy left. Then he heard a scream from the edge of the river. Gene knew he would be walking into danger if he went there. It was an open place. But he heard the scream again. His heart jumped. He would have to go to the edge of the river to get that wounded soldier.

As he ran to the screaming soldier, Gene heard a sound from across the river. He looked up and saw an enemy standing over a wounded man. The enemy saw him at the same time.

Both of them went for their guns. It was shoot or be shot. They both shot.

Two medics lay dying on the edges of the river. Gene Bridges would never know that the man he shot was Gordon Chang. He would never know that the last thing he did in life was to kill a man who was as gentle and kind as he. Gordon Chang would never know the kind of man he killed.

So ends the strange tale of two gentle-hearted men.

**Write sentence answers.**

1. What were four ways in which Gene Bridges and Gordon Chang were alike?

_____

_____

_____

_____

2. What was one way in which the two men were different?

_____

3. Why were the two men enemies?

_____

4. What do you think is the main idea of this story?

_____

**In each line, circle the words that _begin_ with the same sound as the first word.**

1. cup (cat) cent city (class) (cry)
2. city (civil) cause (center) (citizen) cabin
3. game (good) Ginger (Grace) gentle (Gail)
4. jump gold (Gene) (gym) gun (Ginger)

**In each line, circle the words that _end_ with the same sound as the first word.**

1. miss music (house) price back (service)
2. bake (back) medic space ice (picnic)
3. leg page (fog) bridge (egg) (big)
4. age (edge) hug (huge) (strange) (large)

enroll (en rōl')
mail
middle
present (prez' unt)

register (rej' is ter)
registration (rej is trā' shun)
occupation (oc ū pā' shun)
election (ē lec' shun)
residence (rez' i dence)

citizenship (cit'izen ship)
political (pu lit' i cul)
Democratic (Dem u crat' ic)
Republican (Rē pub' lic un)

If you want to vote in elections, you must register to vote. Voter registration forms are different from state to state. But most registration forms ask for the same kinds of information.

Fill out this voter registration form for yourself. In the blank marked *Occupation*, print *Student* if you go to school full time.

### VOTER REGISTRATION FORM—PLEASE PRINT

| Last name | First name | Middle name | |
|---|---|---|---|
| Street no. | Street or road | ADDRESS OF RESIDENCE/City or town, zip code | Mailing address if different from residence |

| Date of birth | Sex | Color eyes | Color hair | Telephone no. (if listed) | If residence is apartment | | Time at this residence | | |
|---|---|---|---|---|---|---|---|---|---|
| | | | | | Floor no. | Apartment no. | Years | Months | Days |

| Occupation | Name & address of employer or school |
|---|---|

**Have you ever voted in an election before in this state?** ☐ Yes ☐ No  **If yes, complete the following line.**

| In what year did you last vote in an election in this state? | Did you register under your present name? ☐ Yes ☐ No | If not, under what name did you register? | Did you then live at your present address? ☐ Yes ☐ No  If no, give address then. Street ___ City or town ___ County ___ |
|---|---|---|---|

**Were you born in the U.S.A.?** ☐ Yes ☐ No  **If no, complete the following line.**

| Citizenship papers ☐ Own ☐ Husband or wife ☐ Mother ☐ Father | Number on citizenship papers | Date of citizenship papers | Court | City & state | Name of person citizenship papers were given to |
|---|---|---|---|---|---|

**TO ENROLL IN A POLITICAL PARTY:**
(Check only ONE)

If you wish to enroll in a political party, check the name of that party.
☐ Democratic  ☐ Republican  ☐ Other
☐ I do not wish to enroll in any political party.

I wish to change from:
☐ Democratic to Republican
☐ Republican to Democratic
☐ _____ to _____

I state that the information I have given here is true.

Signature _____  Date _____

**FOR OFFICE USE ONLY**  Voter registration no. _____

| Last name | First name | Middle name |
|---|---|---|
| Street address | | |

**Write *True* if the sentence is true. Write *False* if the sentence is false.**

| | |
|---|---|
| False | 1. Gene Bridges and Gordon Chang were from the same country. |
| False | 2. The Bridges family and the Chang family were good friends. |
| False | 3. Gene and Gordon became doctors before they went off to war. |
| True | 4. Gene and Gordon both became medics in the armed services. |
| False | 5. The war took place in Gene's country. |
| True | 6. Gordon's wife was named Grace. |
| True | 7. Gene went to the edge of the river to rescue a wounded soldier. |
| False | 8. The story tells which country won the war. |

**Write the missing ending in each blank.**

-al, -hood, -ment, -ship

1. I don't need citizen*ship* papers because I was born in this country.
2. The Fourth of July is a nation*al* holiday in the United States.
3. Martin Luther King's leader*ship* helped blacks get more civil rights.
4. Tran Ty Lan often thought of her child*hood* in Viet Nam.
5. The enroll*ment* in our English class is bigger than last year.
6. Chris will sing in a music*al* program at the high school tonight.
7. Baseball is a season*al* sport.
8. The neighbor*hood* changed from a rich one to a poor one.
9. Lan was thankful for Molly's friend*ship*.
10. Clocks give us a measure*ment* of time.
11. Molly writes a lot of person*al* letters to friends and relatives.
12. In most states, the law says that adult*hood* begins at the age of 18.

## OBJECTIVES

To help your student:

- recognize that *c* stands for two consonant sounds: /k/ as in *cup* and /s/ as in *city*.
- recognize that *c* = /k/ before a consonant, before *a, o, u,* and at the end of a word.
- recognize that *c* = /s/ before *e, i, y*.
- understand how to pronounce *cc*.
- recognize that *g* stands for two consonant sounds: /g/ as in *go* and /j/ as in *age*.
- recognize that *g* = /g/ before a consonant, before *a, o, u,* and at the end of a word.
- recognize that *g* usually = /j/ before *e, i, y*.
- recognize that *gg* = /g/ even before *e, i, y*.
- recognize that after a short vowel sound, /j/ is usually written *dge*.
- read a story containing words with the two sounds for *c* and the two sounds for *g*.
- recognize the suffixes *-al* as in *political* and *-ship* as in *citizenship* and how to add them to root words.
- recognize the beginning consonant blend *scr* and review the blends *spr* and *str*.
- review the ending consonant blends *pt, nt, ft, st*.
- recognize the number of syllables in a word and which syllable is stressed.
- interpret facts and draw inferences.
- interpret figures of speech in the story.
- understand the mood of a story.
- understand the author's purpose.
- relate the story to personal experience and values.
- read and fill out a voter registration form.
- write words and sentences from dictation.

## INTRODUCTION

T: In Lesson 17, you learned that *s* can stand for four sounds and that *ch* can stand for three sounds. In today's lesson, you will study two other consonants that can stand for more than one sound.

# I. Reading

## CHARTS: Page 114

**Note:** Each chart on this page is divided into two sections. Both sections of a chart are to be read at the same time. Read across each row, completing first the block of material on the left and then the block of material on the right. This will give S. a comparison of how *c* (and then *g*) is pronounced in similar positions in words. When reading items like *c* = *k* and *c* = *s*, have S. give the name for the letter before the equal sign and the sound for the letter after the equal sign.

## Chart 1: Two Sounds for *c*

Have S. read the title *Lesson 18*. Point out that there are two charts on this page. Have S. read the title for the first chart, *Two Sounds for c*.

T: The chart about *c* is divided into two sections. The section on the left tells about the sound you have already learned for *c*. Read the heading. [S: *c* = /k/ as in *cup*.] In most words, the letter *c* stands for the sound /k/. But in some words, *c* stands for another sound.

T: Look at the section on the right, and read the heading. [S: *c* = /s/ as in *city*.] In this section, you will find out when *c* = /s/ in a word.

**Row 1, left and right blocks.** Have S. read the *c* = *k* material in the first block on the left, silently and then aloud. Ask him to tell the name of the consonant that *c* comes before in each word.

Have S. look at the empty block on the right for *c* = *s*. Point out that there are no words in which *c* = /s/ before a consonant.

## Row 2, left and right blocks

T: Look at the second block on the left. Read the small heading in dark type. [S: *c* = /k/ before *a, o,* or *u*.] What kind of letters are *a, o,* and *u*? [S: Vowels.] Look at the examples. Say the names of the two letters and then read the word under them. [S: *ca*—cat, *co*—cop, *cu*—cut.]

T: Look at the block on the right. This tells before which vowels *c* = /s/. Study this block. Learn the rule, and read the examples.

After S. has studied this block, have him tell when *c* = /s/. Then have him read the examples aloud in the same way that he read the examples in the left block.

**Rows 3-4.** Follow the same procedure in teaching the other two rows. Have S. read material in the block on the left, first silently and then aloud. Then have him read the material in the block on the right.

Point out that an asterisk (*) marks new words and that the respelling is *under* each new word.

**Review.** Explain that the two most important things to remember from this chart are:

1. *c* = /s/ before *e, i,* or *y*
2. *cc* = /ks/ before *e* or *i*

Point out that if he remembers these two things, then he will know that *c* equals /k/ before all other letters and at the end of a word. (The combination *ch* is an exception.) Explain that after this lesson, a word in which *c* stands for the sound /s/ usually will not be respelled if *c* comes before *e, i,* or *y*.

Have S. read aloud the new words in this chart.

**Note:** The combination *ccy* is not in the rules because it does not occur in any English word.

## Chart 2: Two Sounds for *g*

Have S. read the title of the second chart, *Two Sounds for g*. Then have S. read the heading for the section on the left (*g* = *g* as in *go*). Point out that /g/ is the sound he has already learned for *g* and the one that it stands for in most words. Then have him read the heading for the section on the right (*g* = *j* as in *age*).

**Rows 1-4.** Follow the same procedure as used in teaching the chart about *c*. For each row, have S. read the *g* = *g* material in the block on the left and then study the corresponding *g* = *j* material in the block on the right. Where a block is empty, discuss the reason.

**Note:** In row 3, the word *suggest* is an exception to the rule that *gg* = /g/. You can mention this to S. if you wish. However, *suggest* is not used in *Skill Book 4* or its correlated reader.

**Review.** Point out that the one most important thing to remember from this chart is: *g* = /j/ before *e*, *i*, or *y*.

Point out that if he remembers this, then he will know that *g* = /g/ before all other letters and at the end of a word. Explain that after this lesson, a word in which *g* stands for /j/ usually will not be respelled if *g* comes before *e*, *i*, or *y*.

Have S. read aloud the new words in this chart.

## STORY: Pages 115-116 (A Strange Tale of War)

Have S. read the story title and new words. Have him tell the sound for *g* in each word that has a *g*.

**Note:** Beginning in this lesson, *g* and *c* are not respelled for their respective sounds /j/ and /s/ unless there is a reason for possible mispronunciation. For example, *Gene* is not respelled because *g* followed by *e* is usually pronounced /j/. But *danger* is respelled with /j/ because otherwise the pronunciation might be /ng/ as in *singer* or /ng-g/ as in *anger*.

**Directed silent reading.** S. may be at the stage where he can read the whole story silently without direction. If so, have him read the complete story and do the Story Checkup before any discussion of the story. If he needs some direction, use the suggestions given here.

Ask S. to read the first six paragraphs silently to find out in what ways the two men in the story were alike and in what way they were different. After S. has read silently, discuss these points. Also, have him describe the work of a medic.

Have S. read the next paragraph to find out why it was hard for Gene and Gordon to accept war. Then have S. finish the story to find out what happened to the men. Have him summarize what happened. Then, without any discussion, have S. do the Story Checkup on page 117.

## STORY CHECKUP: Page 117

Ask S. to read the directions and do the checkup. Tell him to try to answer the questions in his own words without looking back at the story. Check his work by having him read each question and the answer he has written. Consider the content of his answers as an indication of how well he comprehended the story before you look at the way he has written the answers. Discuss any questions that he answered incorrectly. Refer him to the story to find the correct answer. The answer to number 4 is somewhat subjective but should indicate something of the author's intent to show the futility of war and how men of similar nature can be made enemies just by the act of war.

After considering the content of the answers, check them for sentence structure and spelling. If an answer is not in a complete sentence, help S. to reword it orally to make it into a sentence. Circle any words that are misspelled. Have him refer to the story for the correct spelling of any words that were in this lesson. Have him make any needed corrections. If he has many errors, defer them until the Writing Lesson.

**Reading between the lines.** Discuss these questions.

1. What shows that the personalities of the two men were similar?
2. What shows that the men were alike in their emotional reactions?
3. Do you think the men were alike in their mental ability? Why or why not?
4. What is meant by the expressions "their hearts grew heavy" and "his heart jumped"?
5. What is meant by a "gentle-hearted" person?
6. Do you think something like this could really happen? Why or why not?
7. What caused the men's deaths? Could they have been true to their beliefs if they had not gone to the river? Considering the situation they were in, do you think they could have dared *not* to shoot?

**Oral reading.** Have S. read the whole story aloud. Note his ability to interpret the mood of the story through his expression in oral reading.

**Note:** For now, skip the Practice exercise at the bottom of page 117, and go directly to the Reading for Living on page 118. The Practice exercise will be done later in the lesson, after the Writing Lesson.

## READING FOR LIVING: Page 118

Have S. read the title and new words. Call attention to the sound for *g* in *register* and *registration* and the sound for *c* in *residence* and *citizenship*.

Have S. read the two paragraphs, which include the directions, first silently and then aloud. Explain that even though he may not be qualified to vote, he should fill out the sample form as practice in filling out forms.

Call attention to the title of the form and the direction *Please Print*. Explain what is meant by the section labeled *For*

*Office Use Only* in the bottom right-hand corner. Then have S. fill out as much of the application as he can by himself. Give any needed help in spelling new words he needs to fill in the blanks. Go over with S. any parts that he doesn't understand. (If S. is a naturalized citizen, he may not have the information from his citizenship papers with him. Ask him to complete this part of the form at home.)

Check what S. has filled in, and have him make any needed corrections. If S. is qualified to register and would like to do so, help him find out where and when he can register and if he can do it by mail.

# II. Skills Practice

Have S. close his book before doing these exercises.

## PRACTICE 1: Determining the Sound for *c*

Write these new words: *fence, pencil, luck, ounce, bacon, mercy, France, connect, fancy, circus.*

T: Each of these words has a *c* in it. Look at the letter that comes after *c* so that you will know whether the sound is /k/ or /s/. Then read the word to yourself.

Have S. read the words silently and then aloud. If a word has the sound /s/ for *c*, ask him to tell how he knows the sound is /s/. If he gives the wrong sound for *c*, review the rule that *c* = /s/ before *e*, *i*, or *y*.

## PRACTICE 2: Substituting Final *ce* for *ck*

In a column, write: *slick, track, lack, rack, truck.* Have S. read each word silently and then aloud. Ask him to tell what letters stand for the sound /k/.

T: I will write a new word by each word. I will change only one letter, but notice how it changes the pronunciation of the word.

In a second column, write: *slice, trace, lace, race, truce.*

T: (Point to *slick* and *slice*.) What letter did I change? [S: You changed *k* to *e*.] How does that change the pronunciation for *c*? [S: The letter *c* is pronounced /s/ before *e*.] How does the *e* at the end of the word change the sound for *i*? [S: The *i* becomes long.]

Have S. read each pair of words.

## PRACTICE 3: Determining the Sound for *g*

Write these words: *pig, germs, brag, goat, magic, gyp, garbage, baggy, judge.* Have S. read each word silently and then aloud. If a word has the sound /j/ for *g*, ask S. how he knows the sound is /j/. If he gives the wrong sound for *g*, review the rule that usually *g* equals /j/ before *e*, *i*, or *y*.

## PRACTICE 4: Substituting Final *dge* for *g*

In a column, write: *bag, egg, bug, dog, leg, jug.* Ask S. to read each word and tell what the word would be if the sound for *g* were changed from /g/ to /j/. Write each of these words next to its corresponding word: *badge, edge, budge, dodge, ledge, judge.* Call attention to *dge* for the sound /j/. Point out that when the sound /j/ follows a short vowel at the end of a word, it is written *dge*.

Add these pairs of words: *hug, huge; rag, rage.* Point out that when the sound /j/ follows a long vowel at the end of a word it is written *ge*.

## PRACTICE 5: Unstressed Syllable *age*

Write *courage.* Have S. read it and tell which syllable is stressed. Explain that when the letters *age* are at the end of a word in an unstressed syllable, they are pronounced /ij/. Under *courage*, write these words: *bandage, manage, damage, garbage, package.* Have S. read them silently and then aloud.

## PRACTICE 6: Suffix *-ship*

Write *citizenship*, and have S. read it. Ask him what the root word is. Underline *citizen*.

T: What ending has been added to *citizen* to make *citizenship*? [S: -ship.] What does *citizenship* mean? [S: Being a citizen.] The ending *-ship* is similar to the ending *-hood*, as in *childhood*. The endings *-hood* and *-ship* both mean *the condition of being*.

In a column, write *friend, leader, owner, reader.* Have S. read each root word and tell what it would be with the ending *-ship* added. Write the new word by the root word as he says it. When the list is complete, have S. read both forms of each word.

## PRACTICE 7: Suffix *-al*

Write *political*, and have S. read it.

T: This word has a new ending. (Underline *al*.) It is spelled *al*, but it is pronounced /ul/ because it is an unstressed syllable. The root word for *political* is *politics*. (Write *politics* in front of *political*.) Read both words. [S: politics, political.] The ending *-al* means *related to*. *Political* means *related to politics*.

In a column, write *music, season, electric, person, mechanic, comic, refuse, practice, center.* Have S. read each root word and tell what it would be with the ending *-al* added. As he answers, write *musical, seasonal, electrical, personal, mechanical, comical, refusal, practical, central.* (Give help with the last three if S. is not able to supply them.) Call attention to the pronunciation of *c* in *practice* and *practical* and the reason for it. Also, point out that the *e* in *center* is dropped in *central*.

## PRACTICE 8 : Number of Syllables and Stress

Say each of the words below. Have S. tell the number of syllables it has and which syllable is stressed. (The words are divided into syllables here for your convenience.) If S. has difficulty giving the number of the stressed syllable in a long word, write the word, dividing it into syllables, and have him point to the stressed syllable.

| | |
|---|---|
| sol' dier | oc cu pa' tion |
| en roll' | e lec' tion |
| mid' dle | res' i dence |
| grad' u ate | cit' i zen ship |
| reg' is ter | po lit' i cal |
| reg is tra' tion | Dem o crat' ic |
| oc ca' sion | Re pub' li can |

## PRACTICE 9: Beginning Blends *scr, spr, str*

Write *scream, spring, strange*. Have S. read each word and tell what blend it begins with. Write *scr, spr,* or *str* under the word that begins with that blend.

Say each pair of words below, and have S. tell what consonant blend both of them begin with.

| | | |
|---|---|---|
| straw, strap | sprint, sprout | string, stretch |
| screen, scrub | scrap, scratch | strong, stroke |
| spry, spray | spread, spruce | scrawl, scrimp |

## PRACTICE 10: Ending Blends *ft, nt, pt, st*

Write *soft, present, accept, lost*. Have S. read each word and tell what the ending blend is. Underline *ft, nt, pt, st* as he answers.

Say each pair of words below, and have S. tell what blend they both end with.

| | | |
|---|---|---|
| slept, kept | front, point | different, pleasant |
| sift, left | almost, fast | raft, drift |

# III. Writing

## CHECK HOMEWORK: Page 113

Check both exercises with S., and have him correct any errors. Note his errors, and plan reinforcement exercises in writing contractions and compound words.

## WRITING LESSON (In Notebook)

**Note:** Some spelling helps are given here that may be used before S. writes in his notebook. Your student may not be interested in learning rules, but tell him that if he remembers a few points about these words, he won't have to study every word with these spelling patterns.

**Words ending in *ge* or *dge* for the sound /j/.** In a column, write *age, huge, change, large, courage, bandage*. Have S. read each word and tell how the sound /j/ at the end of the word is written. Point out that at the end of a word the sound /j/ is written *ge:*

- when it follows a long vowel, as in *age* and *huge*.
- when it follows a consonant sound, as in *change* and *large*.
- when the last syllable is unstressed, as in *courage* and *bandage*.

In another column, write *edge, bridge, dodge*. Have S. read each word and tell how the sound /j/ at the end of the word is written. Point out that at the end of a word the sound /j/ is written *dge* after a short vowel sound.

Leave these examples on the board, and dictate the words below. Ask S. to try writing them, using what he knows about the way the sound /j/ is written at the end of words.

| | | | | |
|---|---|---|---|---|
| stage | charge | manage | fudge | range |

**Words ending in *ce* or *se* for the sound /s/.** Write the following words in three columns, as shown.

| | | |
|---|---|---|
| else | horse | chance |
| false | nurse | fence |
| | | difference |
| | | residence |
| | | experience |

Have S. read the words in the first column and tell how the sound /s/ at the end is written and what letter comes before *se*. Explain that at the end of a word, the sound /s/ is always written *se* after *l*.

Have S. read the second column, telling how the sound /s/ is written and what letter comes before *se*. Explain that at the end of a word, the sound /s/ is usually written *se* after *r*. Point out that there are a few exceptions, and write *force* as an example.

Have S. read the third column, telling how the sound /s/ is written and what letter comes before *ce*. Explain that at the end of a word, the sound /s/ is usually written *ce* after *n*. Point out that there are several exceptions, and write *license* and *sense* as examples. But also point out that the spelling is almost always *nce* when the word has three or more syllables, as do *difference, residence*, and *experience*.

Have S. read the words in all three columns.

**Note:** You may want to advise S. that if he is not sure if a word is spelled with *ce* or *se* at the end, he can look it up in a dictionary. He will learn how to use a dictionary in Lesson 21.

**Word dictation.** Have S. write the titles *Lesson 18* and *Words*. Then have him number from 1 to 20 in two columns.

Help S. study these words: *occasion, graduate, wound, citizenship, occupation.* Point out that *Ginger* is written with a capital *G* only when it is a person's name; when it is used as a spice, *ginger* is written with a small *g*. Give a sentence when dictating *Ginger*.

| | | |
|---|---|---|
| 1. aid | 8. scream | 15. bandage |
| 2. animal | 9. energy | 16. courage |
| 3. army | 10. danger | 17. citizenship |
| 4. enemy | 11. accept | 18. graduate |
| 5. themselves | 12. gentle | 19. occasion |
| 6. shoot | 13. Ginger | 20. occupation |
| 7. wound | 14. bridge | |

**Sentences.** Tell S. you will dictate a paragraph from the story. He will not number the sentences. Choose any paragraph from the story. Ask S. to listen to the whole paragraph. Then read it sentence by sentence for him to write.

Check what S. has written, and have him correct any errors, including those in punctuation and capitalization. Have him write the word *Study* and any words he missed in the word and paragraph dictation.

## PRACTICE: Page 117

Have S. read the directions for the first exercise and do it. If any of his answers are incorrect, ask him to read aloud the first word in the line and tell the beginning sound. Then have him read aloud each of the other words in the line and tell its beginning sound.

Follow a similar procedure for the second exercise on ending sounds.

## HOMEWORK: Page 119

Go over the directions for each exercise with S. Encourage him to study the chart and read the story again at home and to study any words he missed in the dictation.

## CHECKING PROGRESS

**Comprehension.** Your student's responses on the Story Checkup and discussion of the story will help you evaluate his progress in interpretive reading skills, such as making inferences, interpreting the mood of the story, recognizing the author's purpose, interpreting the characters' feelings, and understanding the meaning of figurative language.

At this stage, S. should be able to do more than summarize a story and answer factual questions. If he has difficulty "reading between the lines," use some short supplementary reading selections that will invoke discussion. See the next section for suggestions.

The Reading for Living section of this lesson requires the ability to follow directions, to read details accurately, and to adjust the size of one's writing to the allotted space.

You will be able to note whether or not S. understands the exact meaning of words and which meaning is intended on the form. Let S. see his own progress by comparing this form with ones he has already filled out in this book (pages 5, 77, 98).

**Word recognition.** Most of the words on the chart in this lesson are old words. Was S. able to recognize them? Did he recognize variants of familiar words, such as *hugging, foggy, bigger?* Was he confident in trying to read longer words, such as *occasion, according, occupation?* Was he able to recognize spelling patterns as an aid in reading new words?

By this stage, S. should be able to apply word recognition skills independently. If you have to help him sound out words or remind him of letter-sound relationships that have been covered in previous lessons, his progress is not satisfactory. You will need to slow down the lessons and give an opportunity for reinforcement of word recognition skills.

**Word meanings.** New words are, for the most part, frequently used words that are probably in the speaking vocabulary of your student. Some of the words have multiple meanings, however. It is important to check your student's understanding of the meaning according to the way the word is used in context. Check his understanding of the following words as they are used in the lesson as well as other ways they can be used.

| | | |
|---|---|---|
| *longed* to | be *sick* of | the *hurt* in their hearts |
| *armed* | *heavy* heart | an *open* place |
| | | a political *party* |

Does S. recognize and understand figures of speech, word opposites, and homonyms? Use suggestions in the next section for help with these skills.

## MEETING INDIVIDUAL NEEDS

**Comprehension skills.** Use varied types of short supplementary reading selections to help S. understand the author's purpose. The selections should include these purposes: to give information, to sell something, to entertain, to explain how to do something, to convince the reader to do something, to inspire.

You may find other selections that will help S. capture the mood of a story. You may want to read some of the selections to S. Discuss the setting that helps to project the mood. Have S. identify words and phrases that make him feel a certain way. Use selections that create different moods, such as fear, excitement or suspense, joy, mystery, sympathy, sadness, despair, anger.

If you cannot find suitable supplementary reading selections to reinforce these skills, you may have S. review some of the stories and Reading for Living sections in his skill book. Have him identify the mood in a selection that clearly projects one.

**Word recognition.** Use flash cards for the words in the chart to reinforce recognition of the two sounds for *c* and *g*. You may want to add cards for a few new words, such as: *rice, slice, trace, ounce, comic, carpet, smog, stage, grocery, fudge, general, margin, magic, cigar, cream*. Write each of these key words on a card: *cup, city, go, age*. Put the key words in a row on the table. Mix up the other cards. Have S. place each card under the key word that has the same sound for *c* or *g*. (If a word has both *c* and *g*, he can choose which letter to place it under.)

In *Focus on Phonics-4*, you may use Practices 18A-18I, which cover the sounds for *c* and *g*.

**Opposites.** Make flash cards for the words below. Mix up the cards. Have S. find each pair of opposites.

| | |
|---|---|
| *enemy, friend* | *different, same* |
| *danger, safety* | *sick, well* |
| *heavy, light* | *kind, unkind* |
| *public, private* | *accept, refuse* |

**Homonyms.** Make flash cards for the sets of homonyms below. Have S. match the homonyms. Say a sentence using one of the homonyms from each pair. Have S. find the card with the right spelling for that meaning.

| | | |
|---|---|---|
| *tale, tail* | *through, threw* | *cent, sent* |
| *one, won* | *chews, choose* | *hear, here* |
| *Jim, gym* | *flour, flower* | *meat, meet* |
| *son, sun* | *their, there* | *to, too* |

spell, silent (sī' lent)

# Other Consonant Spellings

### wr = r as in write

| | |
|---|---|
| write<br>wrote<br>written | wrong | *wrap<br>*wrinkle |

### kn = n as in know

| | |
|---|---|
| know<br>knew | *knee<br>*kneel | *knob<br>*knock |

### mb = m as in climb

| | |
|---|---|
| climb<br>bomb | *dumb<br>*thumb | *crumb<br>*limb |

### ph = f as in phone

| | |
|---|---|
| phone<br>telephone | nephew<br>*elephant (el' u funt) | *physical (fiz' i cal)<br>*physician (fiz i' shun) |

### gh = f as in laugh

| | |
|---|---|
| laugh | *cough (cawf)<br>*although (awl thō') | *rough (ruf)<br>*tough (tuf)<br>enough<br>*weigh (wā) |

Note: In some words, *gh* is silent. Some examples are:
through (throo)

*New words

---

| pound | thick | bull | (buul) | Asia | (Ā′ zhu) | Africa | (Af′ ric u) | peaceful |
|---|---|---|---|---|---|---|---|---|
| skin | trunk | grown | (grōwn) | Asian | (Ā′ zhun) | African | (Af′ ric un) | unusual |
| smooth | tusk | ivory | (ī′ ver y) | | | | | |

## 1. Elephants Are Unusual Animals

The elephant is a very unusual animal. It is the largest animal that lives on land. No other animal has a nose that it uses as a hand. No other animal has ears that are four feet across and teeth that are six feet long.

Elephants may be called dumb animals. (We often call animals dumb because they cannot talk.) But elephants are not stupid. They can be trained to do many things. Some are trained to work in shows. They learn to kneel on their knees, stand on their heads, and even play baseball.

In Asia, elephants are often used as work animals. They can carry heavy loads. They can work on rough ground and in thick woods where machines cannot be used.

By wrapping its trunk around a tree, an elephant can pull up the tree by its roots. By running into a tree with its head, an elephant can knock down a tree. In this way, an elephant can knock down a tree that is 30 feet high.

The elephant's trunk may be its most unusual part. Its trunk may be six feet long and weigh 300 pounds. The elephant smells and gets food and water with its trunk. It can pick up something as small as a bread crumb or as large as the limb of a tree.

The elephant also feels with its trunk. The knobs at the end of its trunk act as fingers and thumbs. With these knobs, elephants can feel if something is rough or smooth, soft or hard.

The elephant's thick skin is very rough and wrinkled. Two of the elephant's teeth

are very long. They are the tusks. The tusks are made of ivory. These ivory tusks are strong and smooth. They can be sold for a lot of money.

There are two kinds of elephants, those that live in Africa and those that live in Asia. Elephants in Africa are larger and harder to train than those in Asia. An African bull elephant may weigh 14,000 pounds. An African elephant has two knobs at the end of its trunk.

**African elephant          Asian elephant**

An Asian elephant has a shorter trunk with only one knob at the end. An Asian bull elephant may weigh 12,000 pounds. A cow elephant weighs from 5,000 to 10,000 pounds.

Elephants are full grown at 20 years of age. They live about 60 years. They are peaceful animals and have almost no enemies. Because full-grown elephants are large and tough, other animals don't try to hurt them. Only man, who kills elephants for their ivory, is their enemy.

Countries in both Asia and Africa have made laws to protect these unusual animals. Although there are such laws, elephants are still being killed.

## 2. Having a Physical Exam

| adult | blood (blud) | chest | deep | important | medicine (med' i cin) |
| appointment | body | clinic | exam | lab | pain |
| | | | | | pressure (presh' ur) |

Having a complete physical exam is a way of checking on the health of your body.

How often should an adult have a complete exam by a physician? The answer is different for different people.

You should have a physical exam every year if:

—you take medicine for long times

—you have a long-lasting health problem

—you are over 60 years of age.

You should have a physical exam every three years if you are between 40 and 60.

You should have a physical exam every five years if you are an adult under 40.

If you are changing doctors, it is important to have a complete physical exam.

If you don't have a doctor, you can find the names of doctors in the telephone directory. Look under *Physicians* in the yellow pages.

Some cities have free or low-cost public clinics. To find out about clinics where you live, phone your city or county health department.

You will need to make an appointment for your exam at a physician's office or at a clinic. You can make the appointment by telephone. When you phone, ask if there is anything you should bring. Ask about the cost of the exam and any lab tests you will need to have.

If you have health insurance, phone your insurance company. Ask what your insurance will pay for. Although insurance doesn't usually pay for physical exams, some lab tests may be covered.

When you arrive for your appointment, a nurse will talk to you first. She will ask about any sickness you have had and any medicine you are taking. She will weigh you and measure you.

The nurse or doctor will test your blood pressure. This test is very important. About one in ten Americans has high blood pressure. High blood pressure can cause very bad problems, but a person can have it and not know it.

The doctor will ask about any health problems you are having, such as pains or coughing. It is important to tell the doctor everything about how you feel. The doctor will look into your eyes, ears, nose, mouth, and throat.

The doctor will listen to your heart and chest. He or she will ask you to breathe deeply and then to cough. As you breathe deeply and cough, the doctor will listen to sounds in your heart and chest.

The doctor will check other parts of your body. He or she will take some blood for a blood test. The doctor may want you to have other lab tests.

If you have any questions during the exam, ask the doctor. Your physician should take the time to discuss things with you.

---

**Write short answers to these questions.**

### Story 1: Elephants Are Unusual Animals

1. What are the two kinds of elephants? _African and Asian_

2. Which kind of elephant is larger? _African_

3. Which kind of elephant is easier to train? _Asian_

4. Which kind of elephant has two knobs at the end of its trunk? _African_

5. Which part of the elephant is the most unusual? _the trunk_

6. What are the elephant's tusks made of? _ivory_

7. Who is the only enemy of a full-grown elephant? _man_

8. How much may an African bull elephant weigh? _14,000 pounds_

### Story 2: Having a Physical Exam

1. Why is it important to have a physical exam?

2. According to the information in this story, how often should you yourself have a physical exam?

3. How can you find out about free or low-cost clinics where you live?

4. What should you ask when you phone for an appointment for your exam?

5. What are some of the things the doctor will do as part of the exam?

6. What are two important things for you to do during the exam?

**Underline each word that has the sound for *f*.**

| high | laugh | through | half | enough |
|------|-------|---------|------|--------|
| phone | nephew | thumb | flour | tough |
| cough | crumb | elephant | night | chef |
| weigh | physical | office | foot | although |

**Underline each word in which two letters together stand for one consonant sound.**

| write | stir | knob | phone |
|-------|------|------|-------|
| shoot | scream | cough | proud |
| wrong | chip | dumb | tusk |
| knee | slept | long | according |
| sorry | lesson | bomb | bull |
| limb | kneel | brook | wrap | accept |

**Complete the sentence with the right word.**

(know, no)    1. I _know_ the answer to the question.

(our, hour)    2. You can do the work in one _hour_.

(knew, new)    3. I bought a _new_ book today.

(right, write)    4. Gene will _write_ a letter to his wife.

(male, mail)    5. Please _mail_ the letter for me.

(their, there)    6. I have never been to _their_ house.

(road, rode)    7. Yesterday, I _rode_ home on the bus.

(through, threw)    8. They are afraid to walk _through_ the park at night.

(wood, would)    9. I _would_ like to visit Africa.

(flower, flour)    10. This cookie recipe calls for two cups of _flour_.

---

# Reading for Living

## Reading Directions on Medicines

| ache (ake) | aspirin | bite | minor (mī′ner) | direct (di rect′) |
|------------|---------|------|----------------|-------------------|
| headache | insect | case | once (wuns) | direction (di rec′ shun) |
| dose | redness | reach | taken | prescription (prē scrip′ shun) |
| overdose | tablet | soap | warn (worn) | non-prescription |
| | unless | spray | ¼ (one fourth) | |

There are some medicines that you can buy only with a doctor's prescription. There are other medicines that you can buy without a doctor's prescription. Non-prescription medicines, like the ones below, are for minor health problems. It is important to read the directions with care before you use *any* medicine—prescription or non-prescription.

### ASPIRIN

For head colds, minor headaches, and other minor aches and pains.

**Dose: (Take with water.)**
Adults: 1 or 2 tablets
Children 10 to 15 years: 1 tablet
Children 5 to 10 years: ½ tablet
Children 3 to 5 years: ¼ tablet

**For children under 3 years of age:**
Use aspirin only as directed by physician.

**For adults:**
May be taken every 4 hours, up to 6 times daily.

**For children:**
May be taken every 4 hours, up to 3 times daily.

**Warning:** Keep aspirin and all other medicine out of reach of children. In case of overdose, phone physician at once.

### COUGH MEDICINE

**Directions**

**Dose for adults and children over 12:** Take 2 teaspoons every 4 hours. Do not take more than 12 teaspoons in 24 hours.

**Dose for children 6 to 12:** Take 1 teaspoon every 4 hours. Do not take more than 6 teaspoons in 24 hours.

**Dose for children 2 to 6:** Take ½ teaspoon every 4 hours. Do not take more than 3 teaspoons in 24 hours.

**Do not give to children under 2 unless directed by physician.**

**WARNING:** Persons with high blood pressure or heart problems should not use this medicine unless directed by physician.

Do not use for more than 10 days unless directed by physician.

Keep out of the reach of children.

### FIRST AID SPRAY

**Protects skin wounds**
**Takes pain out of minor burns and insect bites**

**For minor cuts:**
First, gently clean the cut with soap and water. Dry the skin around the cut and apply First Aid Spray on the cut. May be covered with a clean bandage.

**For minor burns and insect bites:** Spray lightly onto skin.

**Warning:** Do not use on major cuts, deep wounds, bad burns, or animal bites. If redness or pain continues, stop using and see a physician. Spray should not be used on a cut for more than 10 days.

Use only on skin. Do not spray into eyes or mouth. Do not use on long-lasting skin problems.

## OBJECTIVES

To help your student

- recognize that *wr* at the beginning of a word stands for the sound /r/ as in *write*.
- recognize that *kn* at the beginning of a word stands for the sound /n/ as in *know*.
- recognize that *mb* at the end of a word stands for the sound /m/ as in *climb*.
- recognize that *ph* usually stands for the sound /f/ as in *phone*.
- recognize that in some words *gh* stands for /f/, as in *laugh*, and that in some other words *gh* is silent, as in *through*.
- read words with the consonant spellings *wr, kn, mb, ph, gh*.
- recognize the new compound words *headache, overdose*, and review other compound words.
- review the prefixes *un-* and *non-* and their meanings.
- review the suffixes *-ful, -ness, -ment*.
- recognize the root word in a word that has a prefix or suffix added.
- recognize the meaning of some words that sound alike but have different spellings (homonyms).
- read factual material to obtain information.
- take notes on factual material read in order to remember information.
- make comparisons.
- recall important details.
- distinguish between fact and fiction.
- read directions on some non-prescription medicines.
- relate reading material to own experience and values.
- write words, sentences, and numbers from dictation.
- use commas after introductory *although, because, if, since, unless, when* clauses.

## INTRODUCTION

T: In the last few lessons, you studied three single consonants and one consonant combination that can stand for more than one sound. What are the names of the single letters? [S: *s, c, g.*] What is the consonant combination? [S: *ch.*] In today's lesson, you will study some other consonant combinations.

# I. Reading

## CHART: Page 120

Have S. read the title *Lesson 19* and the two new words in the top right-hand corner (*spell, silent*). Then have him read the chart title, *Other Consonant Spellings.*

**Note:** In reading items like *wr = r* in this chart, have S. give the names of the letters before the equal sign and the sound for the letter after the equal sign.

**Section 1: *wr* = *r* as in *write***

T: Read the heading of the first section. [S: *wr* = /r/ as in *write*.] *Write* is an old word. You will remember that there is another word that sounds the same but has a different spelling and a different meaning. Say a sentence to show the meaning of *write* the way it is spelled here. [S. answers something like: *I like to write letters.*]

T: Read the words in this section to yourself. There are only two new words, and you can sound them out easily. Notice where *wr* comes in each word.

After S. has read silently, have him read each word aloud. Explain the difference in meaning between *wrap* (in the chart) and *rap*.

T: Where does the combination *wr* come in each of these words? [S: At the beginning.]

**Section 2: *kn* = *n* as in *know*.** Have S. read the section heading. Then ask him to read the words in this section, first silently and then aloud. After he has read the words, discuss the meaning of *know* and *knew*. Compare them with *no* and *new*. Have S. give a sentence for each meaning.

Ask S. to tell where *kn* comes in each word in the chart.

**Section 3: *mb* = *m* as in *climb*.** Follow the same procedure for teaching this section. Point out that *mb* comes at the end of a root word. The word may have an ending added, as in *climbed*, or it may become part of a compound word, as in *bombshell*. But if the letters *m* and *b* come in the middle of a root word, they each stand for a separate sound, as in *number*.

**Section 4: *ph* = *f* as in *phone*.** Ask S. to read the section heading aloud. Then have him study the section by himself. Encourage him to sound out each new word independently. After he has read silently, have him read each word aloud and tell where *ph* comes in the word. When he has read all of the words, have him note that *ph* may come at either the beginning or the end of a syllable or word.

**Note:** In *shepherd*, the letters *p* and *h* are in different syllables and stand for their individual sounds. In the name *Stephen, ph* stands for the sound /v/. You can mention these words to S. if you wish.

**Section 5: *gh* = *f* as in *laugh*.** Have S. read the section heading aloud. Then have him read the section silently, including the note. After he has read silently, have him read aloud the words in which *gh* = /f/. Then ask him to read the note and the examples of words in which *gh* is silent.

**Review.** Have S. read aloud each section heading and then each new word marked with an asterisk.

## STORY 1: Page 121
### (Elephants Are Unusual Animals)

Have S. read the story title and new words. If possible, have a world map or globe available, and show where Africa and Asia are.

Ask S. to read the first paragraph to himself. Tell him to note what makes the elephant an unusual animal. When S. has finished reading, explain that together you and he are going to take some notes about information in the article. Write this heading: *What is unusual about an elephant?* Ask S. to tell you very briefly some facts to write under this heading. Number the facts as you write them, and put them in sentence form. They may be similar to these:

1. It is the largest land animal.
2. It has a nose that it uses as a hand.
3. It has very big ears and very long teeth.

Ask S. to read the next five paragraphs (paragraphs 2-6) and find out what the elephant can do with its trunk. When he has finished reading, write this heading: *Things an elephant can do with its trunk.* Ask S. to tell you some facts to write under this heading. They may be similar to these:

1. It can pull up trees.
2. It can smell and get food and water.
3. It can pick up large and small things.
4. It can feel things.

Also, ask S. to tell what kinds of tricks elephants can be trained to do, some other kinds of work they can do besides pulling up trees, and why elephants in Asia are often used for work instead of machines.

Ask S. to read the next paragraph to find out about the elephant's tusks. When he has finished, write this heading: *An elephant's tusks.* Ask S. to tell some facts from this paragraph that you can write. Also, ask him to look at the first paragraph to find out how long the tusks can be. The facts you write may be similar to these:

1. The tusks are two of the elephant's teeth.
2. They may be six feet long.
3. They are made of ivory.
4. The ivory is worth a lot of money.

Ask S. to read the next two paragraphs and find out about the two kinds of elephants. When he has finished, write this heading: *The two kinds of elephants.* Under that write the subheads *African elephant* and *Asian elephant* across from each other. Ask S. to tell you facts about African and Asian elephants that can be compared. Your lists might look like this:

| African elephant | Asian elephant |
| --- | --- |
| 1. Larger and harder to train | 1. Smaller and easier to train |
| 2. Bull may weigh 14,000 pounds | 2. Bull may weigh 12,000 pounds |
| 3. Has two knobs at the end of its trunk | 3. Has one knob at the end of its trunk |

Point out that, since the story says that African elephants are larger and harder to train, you can also say that Asian elephants are smaller and easier to train. Also, point out that the story gives the size of an Asian cow elephant, but not of an African cow elephant, so it is not possible to compare them.

Ask S. to finish the story and find out if the elephant has any enemies. When he has finished, write this heading: *The elephant's enemies.* Ask S. to tell you facts you can write under this heading. Your list might look like this:

1. Other animals do not try to hurt elephants.
2. Man kills them for their ivory.
3. Laws in Africa and Asia protect elephants, but they are still being killed.

Have S. read aloud the notes you have written. Tell him he will now have a chance to see if taking the notes will help him remember the information.

## STORY CHECKUP: Page 123 (Story 1)

Ask S. to read the directions to himself and do the checkup for the first story. Tell him to answer as many questions as he can without looking back at the story in order to see how well he remembers the facts.

Check your student's work by having him read aloud each question and his answer. Make a note of the number of questions he answered correctly. Have him look back at the story to find the correct answer for any items he had wrong or did not answer.

**Discussion.** Ask S. whether this story is fact or fiction and how he can tell. Discuss what he thinks was the author's purpose in writing the story. Ask if he learned anything new about elephants from reading it and if taking notes helped him remember the information. Then discuss these questions.

1. Do you think the title is a good one for this story? Why or why not?
2. What is in the first paragraph that attracts the reader's attention? Why do you think the author began the article that way?
3. Do you think the author gave all the facts about elephants? If you wanted to know more, where could you look? (If possible, show an article from an easy encyclopedia.)

## STORY 2: Page 122 (Having a Physical Exam)

Have S. read the story title and new words. (At this point, longer words that are fairly easy to sound out are not respelled or divided into syllables.) Note whether S. is able to recognize the words *appointment* and *important* without help. If he needs help, have him find the root word and ending in *appointment* and then read the word from left to right. For help in reading *important,* cover all of the word except *im,* and have him read that much. Then, expose *por,* and have him read the first two syllables. Uncover the last syllable, and have him read the whole word. Have him tell the number of syllables in the word.

T: Do you think this story will be fact or fiction? [S: Fact.] How can you tell? [S: From the title.]

Ask S. to read the whole story to himself. Tell him to read it quickly but not to skip any parts as he will have some questions to answer about the story. Time his reading, and make a note of how long it took. Then, without any discussion, have him do the Story Checkup for story 2 on page 123.

## STORY CHECKUP: Page 123 (Story 2)

Ask S. to read the directions at the top of the page and then do the checkup for story 2. Tell him that he may look back at the story if he needs to in order to answer questions but that he should work quickly. Allow 10 minutes for him to do the checkup. If he completes it in less time, record the time it took. If he didn't finish, have him circle the number of the last question he answered and then finish the checkup.

Check your student's work by having him read each question and his answer. Make a note of the number of questions he answered correctly. If he had any wrong, have him find the part in the story that gives the correct answer. Have him read that part aloud. Note his ability to scan the page to find the correct answer. Have him make the needed corrections in his written answers.

**Reading between the lines.** Discuss these questions.

1. What do you think the author's purpose was in writing this article—to inform, to entertain, or to persuade? (In the discussion, bring out that, in addition to giving information, the author's purpose seems to be to encourage the reader to have a regular physical exam.)
2. What are some reasons a person might put off having a physical exam? [Answers might include: fear, the cost, not having a doctor, not feeling sick, not thinking it is important, other things more pressing.]
3. Do you think the author has given information that might encourage a person to have an exam? In what ways might the information encourage the person?
4. Did you learn anything new from this article? What?
5. Can you think of any other helpful information that might have been included?

**Note-taking.** If much of the information in this article was new to S., you may want to help him take some notes that would be personally useful to him. What should go in the notes depends on what the individual student already knows, what pieces of new information apply to him, and what he wants to remember. The notes may be in simple outline style under topic headings. The following is an example of some notes for a particular student.

### Having a Physical Exam

<u>How often?</u>

Every 3 years for a person between 40 and 60

<u>To find a doctor or clinic</u>

1. For doctor, look under *Physicians* in yellow pages of phone book
2. For clinic, phone health department

<u>What to do before exam</u>

1. Phone for appointment, and ask:
   a. what to bring
   b. cost of exam
   c. cost of any lab tests
2. Find out what my health insurance will pay for (any lab tests?)

<u>What to tell during exam</u>

1. Any sickness I have had
2. Any medication I am taking
3. Any health problems I'm having now

If a student is interested in preparing for a physical exam and is not reluctant to divulge personal information, you may want to expand the notes by adding facts pertinent to him, such as names of illnesses or operations he has had, medicines he is taking, and the name and address of your local health department.

If, however, a student is quite experienced with doctors and clinics, you may omit taking notes on this article.

## READING FOR LIVING: Page 124

Have S. read the title and new words, first silently and then aloud. Call attention to the compound words *headache* and *overdose* and to the prefix *non-* and its meaning.

Have S. read the introductory paragraph to himself and then tell the difference between prescription and non-prescription drugs. Then have him look quickly at the three medicine labels and tell what products they are for [aspirin, cough medicine, and first aid spray].

T: The directions given here for these non-prescription medicines are like the directions you would find on the actual products. Directions on most medicine labels are written in a similar manner. So, if you learn to read a few typical ones, it will help you to read others.

**Aspirin.** Ask S. to read this label to himself. Then discuss these questions:

1. What kinds of information does the label give? (In the discussion, bring out that the label tells what the medicine can be used for, the amount of dosage, how often to take it, and a warning.)
2. What does the label say that aspirin can be used for? Why is this information important to the user of the medicine? Why is it important to the manufacturer of the medicine to put this information on the label?
3. What does the word *dose* mean? [The amount to take at one time.] What is the dose of aspirin for an adult? What would the dose be for a child 12 years old? 9 years old? 5 years old? What does the label say about giving aspirin to children under 3?
4. How often can this dose be taken by an adult? By a child?
5. What is the warning?

6. When would it be all right to take medicine in a different dosage from what the label says? [When a doctor tells you to.]

Have S. read the aspirin label aloud. Note any words he omits or misreads. When he has finished, call errors to his attention, and point out the importance of careful and accurate reading of this type of material.

**Note:** Aspirin labels now also carry this warning: *Children and teenagers should not use this medicine for chicken pox or flu symptoms before a doctor is consulted about Reye Syndrome, a rare but serious illness.* Go over this information with S., and be sure he understands both the meaning and importance of this warning.

**Cough medicine.** Ask S. to read this label to himself. Then discuss these questions:

1. For what age groups are directions given for taking a dose of cough medicine?
2. What is the dose for a 5-year-old child? For a 10-year-old? For a 15-year-old person? For a person 80 years old?
3. What does the label say about giving this cough medicine to a child under 2?
4. How often should the dose be taken?
5. What is the *most* cough medicine that should be taken in 24 hours by a person over 12? By a child 6 to 12? By a child 2 to 6?
6. What four important points are given in the warning?

**First aid spray.** Have S. read this label to himself. Have him tell the kinds of information that are given on this label. Then discuss these questions:

1. What is this non-prescription medicine used for?
2. What is meant by *minor cuts* and *minor burns*?
3. What does the label say you should do before using this spray on a cut?
4. What five important points are given in the warning?

Have S. read the label aloud. Note how accurately he reads. Have him reread any parts where he omitted or miscalled words.

## II. Skills Practice

Have S. close his book before doing these exercises.

### PRACTICE 1: Words with *wr* and *kn*

Make flash cards for these words: *wreck, wring, wreath, wrench, wrestle, wrist,* and *knight, knit, knot, knife, knuckle, knead.*

T: (Write the words *write* and *know*.) What are these words? [S: write, know.] What sound do the letters *wr* stand for in *write*? [S: /r/.] What sound do the letters *kn* stand for in *know*? [S: /n/.] You have had several words in this lesson that begin with *kn* or *wr*. Here are some more words that begin with those spellings. Read the word on each of these cards.

Show each card, and have S. read it. (Give help with the silent *t* in *wrestle* if necessary.) When S. has read all of the words, show the card for *wring* again. Ask him to read the word. Then cover the *w*, and have him read *ring*. Ask him to tell what the word means when it is spelled *ring* and when it is spelled *wring*. Do the same thing for *knight* and *night* and for *knot* and *not*. Also, point out the different spellings and meanings for *knead* and *need*.

### PRACTICE 2: Words with *mb*

Make flash cards for these words: *crumb, numb, lamb, comb, tomb, plumb, plumber.*

Write *crumb*, and have S. read it. Have him tell the ending sound [/m/] and the letters that stand for it [*mb*]. Then show each flash card, and have S. read it. (Give help with the vowel sound in *comb* and *tomb* if necessary.) Talk about the difference in the meaning of *plum* (a fruit) and *plumb* (a metal weight attached to a line that is used to measure the depth of water or to measure whether something is straight up-and-down).

Point out that *mb* for the sound /m/ comes at the end of root words. When an ending is added to the root word, the *b* in *mb* is still silent. As examples, write *plumbing, bomber, dumbest, combed.* Have S. read each one and tell what the root word is.

### PRACTICE 3: Words with *ph* or *gh* for /f/

Make flash cards for these words: *graph, photograph, orphan, Ralph, Phillip,* and *laughed, coughing, toughest, roughly.*

Write *phone* and *laugh*. Have S. read each word and tell what letters stand for the sound /f/. Then show each flash card, and have him read it. Have S. tell how the sound /f/ is spelled in the word.

### PRACTICE 4: Compound Words

Write the compound words *headache* and *overdose*. Ask S. to read each word and tell the two words that are put together to make the compound word. Circle each of the words that are in the compound word.

Under *headache*, write the following compound words, and have S. read them: *headline, headboard, headband, headlight, headroom, headphone, headstrong, backache, toothache, earache, heartache.*

Under *overdose*, write these compound words, and have S. read them: *overcoat, overhead, overlook, overpass, overhear, overcook, overeat, oversight.*

### PRACTICE 5: Suffixes *-ful, -ness, -ment*

Write *peaceful*, and have S. read it. Have him tell the root word and the ending. Write *pain, care, beauty.* Have S. tell what each word would be with the ending *-ful* added. Write the new word by the root word. Have S. tell how the root word is changed to make the word *beautiful*. Point out that each word without the ending is a noun. When the ending -*ful* is added, the word becomes an adjective (word that describes).

Write *redness*, and have S. read it. Have him tell the root word and the ending. Write *bright, dark, sick, sore*. Have S. tell what each word would be with the ending -*ness* added. Write the new word by the root word. Point out that each word without the ending is an adjective. When the ending -*ness* is added, the word becomes a noun.

In a column, write *employment, amusement, argument, agreement, appointment*. Have S. read the words and tell what ending is in all of them. Underline -*ment* in each word. Ask S. to read each word without the ending. Have S. tell how the root word *argue* is spelled and how it is changed when -*ment* is added. Point out that each word without the ending is a verb. When the ending -*ment* is added, the word becomes a noun.

Write *disappoint*, and have S. read it. Have him tell what the word would be with the ending -*ment* added. As he says the word, add -*ment* to *disappoint*. Have S. read all of the words with the ending -*ment*.

## PRACTICE 6: Prefixes *un-* and *non-*

Write the words *unusual* and *unpleasant*. Have S. read each word, and tell the root word and prefix. Have S. tell what the prefix *un-* means. Ask him to use the words *unusual* and *unpleasant* in sentences.

Follow the same procedure for the prefix *non-*. Use the words *non-violent* and *non-prescription* as examples. Explain that in *non-prescription*, the prefix *non-* means *not with* or *without* a prescription.

# III. Writing

## CHECK HOMEWORK: Page 119

Check your student's work on the first exercise. If he has any errors, have him find the part in the story that tells whether a statement is true or false. You may also want to have S. change each false statement orally so that it is true. Check the second exercise on suffixes. Note the errors, if any, in order to plan reinforcement exercises. Then have S. make any needed corrections.

## WRITING LESSON (In Notebook)

Have S. write the titles *Lesson 19* and *Words* and number from 1 to 30 in two columns. After the dictation, check his work, and have him correct any errors by writing the whole word correctly.

**Words.** Help S. study these words: *physician, medicine, blood, ache, Asia, although, weigh*. Point out that *weigh* is an exception to the rule that *i* comes before *e*. When the vowel sound is pronounced /$\bar{a}$/, as in *neighbor* and *weigh*, *e* comes before *i*. When dictating the words, give a sentence for *wrap* and *weigh*.

| | | |
|---|---|---|
| 1. wrap | 11. although | 21. medicine |
| 2. knee | 12. weigh | 22. blood |
| 3. knock | 13. trunk | 23. body |
| 4. limb | 14. smooth | 24. peaceful |
| 5. thumb | 15. skin | 25. unusual |
| 6. elephant | 16. thick | 26. pound |
| 7. physical | 17. Asia | 27. ache |
| 8. physician | 18. Africa | 28. dose |
| 9. rough | 19. adult | 29. soap |
| 10. cough | 20. exam | 30. tablet |

**Sentences.** Write these two sentences, and have S. read them: *He phoned. I was not at home.*

Under them, write these two sentences, and have S. read them: *When he phoned, I was not at home. I was not at home when he phoned.* Point out that the two shorter sentences have been joined by adding the word *when*. Each part of the new sentence is called a clause. The *when* clause can come at the beginning or end of the sentence. When it comes at the beginning, there is a comma after the *when* clause.

Give a similar example, using these two shorter sentences: *You know the answer. Please tell me.* Show that they can be joined with an *if* clause at the beginning or end: *If you know the answer, please tell me. Please tell me if you know the answer.*

Write these words, and have S. read them: *when, if, although, because, since, unless*. Explain that when a clause with one of these words comes at the beginning of a sentence, there is a comma after the clause.

Leave the examples and the list of words on the board. Then dictate these sentences. Read the whole sentence once at a normal speed and then a second time, pausing after the introductory clause.

1. If you are over 60, you should have a physical exam every year.
2. When you phone for an appointment, ask what you should bring.
3. If you have any questions during the exam, ask the doctor.
4. Unless your doctor says so, do not take more than the dose written on the medicine.
5. Although an elephant can be called dumb, it is not stupid.
6. Because elephants are large and tough, other animals do not try to hurt them.
7. Although there are laws to protect elephants, they are still being killed.
8. Since Gordon became a citizen, he has voted three times.

Check what S. has written, and have him correct any errors in spelling, punctuation, or capitalization.

**Numbers.** Ask S. to use a numeral for the number and then write the word that follows. Dictate these items:

| | | |
|---|---|---|
| 14,000 pounds | $^1/_2$ teaspoon | $1^1/_2$ cups |
| 5,000 to 10,000 pounds | $^1/_4$ tablet | |

Have S. write the title *Study* and any words or numbers he missed in the dictation exercises.

## PRACTICE: Page 125

Have S. read the directions for the first exercise and do it. Check his work by having him read aloud the words he has underlined in each line. Have him make any needed corrections.

Ask S. to read the directions for the second exercise, first silently and then aloud. Have him do the first line to make sure he understands what to do. If he underlined *stir*, have him listen for the two sounds in the blend *st*. Contrast with other words in the line that have one sound for two consonants together (*wr, mb, ph*). Have S. finish the exercise by himself. Check his work by having him read aloud the words he underlined in each line. Have him make any needed corrections.

## HOMEWORK: Page 125

Go over the directions with S. Encourage him to reread the two stories at home and to study any words or numbers he missed in the dictation.

## CHECKING PROGRESS

Your student's responses on the Story Checkups will enable you to evaluate his ability to read factual information and remember important facts. You will also be able to determine his skill in skimming to find specific information. His work in your joint note-taking effort on story 1 will help you determine his skill in selecting facts to support main topics. His accuracy in reading and understanding directions can be evaluated from his reading of the medicine labels. You may want to have him read two or three similar labels that are reasonably easy to see if he can transfer his skills in reading new material.

**Rate of reading.** Story 2 contains about 450 words. S. should be able to read it in two or three minutes, but he may have taken somwhat longer since it is factual material. Evaluate his reading rate in terms of his accuracy of responses on the Story Checkups. In helping S. evaluate his rate of reading, help him realize the factors that may influence our rate of reading, such as the type of material, the purpose in reading it, and the time available.

**Word recognition.** Don't expect S. to master all of the words with the special consonant spellings given in this lesson. He will need many exposures to the words and most probably will need to see them in context in order to recognize them. Do, however, note his ability to recognize the difference in meaning of homonyms like *knew* and *new*, *write* and *right*, *through* and *threw*.

Note your student's ability and confidence in reading longer words. Is he able to recognize familiar word parts? Does he apply phonics skills so that he can sound out the word if it has a regular spelling? Note skills that need reinforcement.

## MEETING INDIVIDUAL NEEDS

**Comprehension.** To give S. more practice in reading to obtain information, use supplementary reading selections of a factual nature, such as articles from books in the In the Know series, the Remembering series, or easier articles from *News for You*. If the material is too difficult for him, use it for directed silent reading or even for duet reading. For more independent reading, use supplementary material that is somewhat easier than the selections in the skill book, that is, 3rd grade or lower 4th grade level.

The material you choose for supplementary reading need not be controlled to the LWR vocabulary, so long as there are not too many words that are difficult for S. Try to find some material on a subject of special interest to S. If no such material is available, you may want to simplify an article or write a paragraph or two that may be of interest to S.

Check the student's comprehension by asking questions with specific answers that can be found in the material read.

**Rate of reading.** To increase the rate of reading, use a slip strip as suggested in Lesson 17. In addition to using phrases, you may find it helpful to use short paragraphs. Expose the paragraph for a few seconds, and then ask a question about it.

You may also use short reading selections for timed readings, as described on page 86.

**Reading for living.** If S. is concerned about reading medicine labels, you may want to have him bring some medicines he uses for help in reading the directions.

**Word recognition.** In *Focus on Phonics-4*, you may use Practices 19A-19I, which cover the same consonant spellings as in Lesson 19, plus a few others.

# Words Ending in -tion, -ssion, -sion

## -tion = shun as in direction

| | | | |
|---|---|---|---|
| section | (sec′ shun) | *nation | (nā′ shun) |
| election | (ē lec′ shun) | *station | (stā′ shun) |
| direction | (di rec′ shun) | *addition | (a di′ shun) |
| contraction | (con trac′ shun) | *education | (ej u cā′ shun) |
| prescription | (prē scrip′ shun) | *recreation | (rec rē ā′ shun) |
| application | (ap li cā′ shun) | *constitution | (con sti tū′ shun) |
| information | (in for mā′ shun) | *transportation | (trans por tā′ shun) |
| registration | (rej is trā′ shun) | *pronunciation | (prō nun cē ā′ shun) |

## -ssion = shun as in discussion

| | |
|---|---|
| *discussion | (dis cu′ shun) |
| *depression | (dē pre′ shun) |
| *admission | (ad mi′ shun) |

## -sion = zhun as in television

| | |
|---|---|
| *television | (tel′ e vi zhun) |
| *decision | (dē ci′ zhun) |
| occasion | (o cā′ zhun) |

*New words

---

## The Ted Howard Show

| | | | | |
|---|---|---|---|---|
| art | | government (guv′ ern ment) | Joseph (Jō′ zeph) | they're |
| budget (buj′ et) | | guest (gest) | pronounce (prō nounce′) | we'd |
| D'Angelo (Dē An′ je lō) | | hello | reason (rea′ zun) | |
| decide (dē cide′) | | Italy (It′ u ly) | subject | |
| diploma (di plō′ mu) | | issue (ish′ oo) | | |

(This talk show takes place at public television station KRXT. It is called the "Ted Howard Show." Ted's guests are Gail Newman, Joseph D'Angelo, and Helen Baker.)

**Ted Howard:** Hello, this is Ted Howard for KRXT, your public television station. Tonight, we have a very important issue to discuss and three guests you will enjoy meeting.

Last week, we discussed budget cuts in education that our state government is planning. Tonight, we'll continue our discussion of this issue. Our three guests will tell what the budget cuts would mean to them. They are students at the Freedom Adult Education Center.

Gail Newman is on my left. Hello, Gail. Tell us your reason for enrolling at the Freedom Center.

**Gail Newman:** I decided to get my high school diploma. I never finished high school. The factory where I work was beginning to use more machines and fewer employees. I didn't know what I would do if I lost my job. The kinds of jobs that are open these days take more and more education.

**Ted:** It was a good idea to look ahead, Gail. What does an adult have to do to get a high school diploma?

**Gail:** You have to pass exams in all the important high school subjects. The admissions office at the center helped me find out what subjects I needed to study. I've passed the exams in every subject but math and writing.

**Ted:** Thanks, Gail. You seem to be moving ahead with your plans. Now let's hear from Joseph D'Angelo. Hello, Joseph. What are you studying?

**Joseph D'Angelo:** I'm studying to become a citizen. I came here from Italy about four years ago. I could not speak much English. Friends from Italy told me about the Freedom Center. I went to the admissions office. At that time, I could not even pronounce my street address, so they put me in the beginning class. My pronunciation still isn't so good. But I have learned a lot in my English class.

**Ted:** Your pronunciation sounds fine to me, Joseph. Tell us, what are you studying in addition to English?

**Joseph:** In my citizenship class, I am studying about this nation and its government. We have just started studying the Constitution.

**Ted:** That must be a pretty tough subject!

**Joseph:** Yes, but I like learning about the Constitution. In this nation, the Constitution protects our freedom.

**Ted:** That was a good speech, Joseph.

**Joseph:** It was not just a speech. I love this nation. I hope to become a citizen and vote in my first election next year.

**Ted:** Good for you! We could use more good citizens like you. Now let's meet Helen Baker. Your reason for taking classes was very different, wasn't it, Mrs. Baker?

**Helen Baker:** Please call me Helen. That makes me feel younger. Yes, my reason *was* different. After my husband died two years ago, I became very depressed. For many months, I just stayed at home, feeling sorry for myself. Then a friend brought me to her art class to get me out of my depression. The art class and being with other people did help me overcome my depression. Then I decided to take other classes just for recreation.

**Ted:** Some people say that recreation is not education.

**Helen:** Well, they're wrong. Some recreation classes, such as swimming, keep your body healthy. Others, like discussion groups, keep your mind growing.

**Ted:** Well, each of you seems to be finding something different in adult education. And the center seems to mean a lot to you. But, as you know, the future of Freedom Center is in question.

The city board of education has a hard decision to make. Next year, the state plans big cuts in the education budget. With less state money to spend on education, the school board says it may have to close Freedom Center. If that decision is made, what would it mean to you, Gail?

**Gail:** Oh, that would be awful! I would never get my high school diploma.

**Ted:** There is an adult education program at Mason County College. Couldn't you go there to study?

**Gail:** No, it costs more, and it's too far away. Transportation would be a problem. I don't have a car, and the bus would take too much time.

**Ted:** Would transportation be a problem for you, Joseph?

**Joseph:** No, I have a car. And I will be ready to take my citizenship exam soon. But I worry about my friends from Italy. Some of them cannot speak any English. It's hard for them to use public transportation. The Freedom Center is near our neighborhood, so they can walk to class now.

**Ted:** What about you, Helen? Is there a reason why you need to continue classes?

**Helen:** Yes, there *is* a reason. Older people who keep on learning live longer and enjoy life more. And they're more fun to be with.

**Ted:** We'd like to hear more from you, Helen, but we're running out of time.

My guests tonight have been speaking for the 300 students at the Freedom Adult Education Center. In addition, there are thousands of others with the same needs. Our city has 25,000 adults who, like Gail Newman, do not have a high school diploma. Joseph D'Angelo told us about his need to learn English. Each year, between two and three hundred people who do not speak English come to live in our city. And Helen Baker is only one out of 10,000 people over 60 living here.

Next year, the services that Freedom Center has for these people may be lost. I thank my guests for sharing in the discussion of this issue. Now, for television station KRXT, good night.

---

amusement

**Circle the letter of the right answer.**

1. What was the subject of the discussion on this talk show?

   a. how to get a better job by taking classes

   (b.) what cuts in the education budget would mean to some students at the Freedom Center

   c. how to become a citizen

2. Why did Gail Newman enroll at the Freedom Center?

   a. to learn how to run a computer

   b. to be on Ted Howard's talk show

   (c.) to get her high school diploma

3. Why is Joseph D'Angelo studying at the center?

   (a.) to become a citizen of the U.S.A.

   b. to study about Italy

   c. to learn how to drive a car

4. Why does Helen Baker want to continue her classes?

   a. to get a college diploma

   b. to get a better job

   (c.) to enjoy life more

**Match each word in the first list with a word in the second list that means the same thing. Write the letter in the blank. The first one is filled in for you.**

| | | |
|---|---|---|
| _C_ | 1. exam | A. doctor |
| _I_ | 2. chef | B. yell |
| _F_ | 3. tale | C. test |
| _G_ | 4. strange | D. part |
| _D_ | 5. section | E. country |
| _H_ | 6. recreation | F. story |
| _E_ | 7. nation | G. unusual |
| _A_ | 8. physician | H. amusement |
| _B_ | 9. scream | I. cook |

| | | | | | |
|---|---|---|---|---|---|
| skill | Spanish | blueprint | sew (sō) | retirement | I (one) |
| dance | process | ballroom | type (tīp) | improvement (im proov' ment) | II (two) |
| square | safety | shorthand | course (cors) | Dec./(December) | III (three) |
| history | | bookkeeping | | | |

## FREEDOM ADULT EDUCATION CENTER
### 1000 South Main Street

**Registration Sept. 6-9**

**Fall Schedule of Evening Classes**
Classes Begin Week of Sept. 12, End Week of Dec. 12

**For More Information Call 486-3500**

| COURSE TITLE | Days* | Time |
|---|---|---|
| **Language Arts** | | |
| Reading Improvement | M/W | 7:00—9:00 |
| Writing Improvement | T/Th | 7:00—9:00 |
| English as a Second Language | M/W | 7:00—9:30 |
| Public Speaking | T | 7:00—9:00 |
| Sign Language | T/Th | 7:00—9:00 |
| Spanish I | M/W | 7:00—9:00 |
| Spanish II | T/Th | 6:30—8:30 |
| Spanish III | T/Th | 8:30—10:00 |
| **Study Skills** | | |
| Speed Reading | M/Th | 7:00—9:00 |
| How to Study and Take Notes | T | 7:00—9:00 |
| How to Take Exams | W | 7:00—9:00 |
| **Social Studies** | | |
| Citizenship | T/Th | 7:00—9:00 |
| U.S. Government | M | 7:00—9:00 |
| The U.S. Constitution | T | 7:00—9:00 |
| U.S. History | W | 7:00—9:00 |
| World History | Th | 7:00—9:00 |
| **Business** | | |
| Typing I | T | 6:30—9:30 |
| Typing II | W | 6:30—9:30 |
| Bookkeeping | Th | 6:30—9:30 |
| Shorthand | M | 6:30—9:30 |
| Computer Programming | W | 7:00—10:00 |
| Word Processing I | M | 6:30—9:30 |
| Word Processing II | T | 6:30—9:30 |
| Business Math | Th | 7:00—9:00 |
| Business Writing | T | 7:00—9:30 |
| **Skill Training for Employment** | | |
| Auto Mechanics | M | 6:30—9:30 |
| Machine Shop | W | 6:30—9:30 |
| Printing | Th | 6:30—9:30 |
| Radio & TV Repairs | W | 6:30—9:30 |
| Building Repairs | T | 6:30—9:30 |
| Food Service | Th | 6:30—9:30 |
| Blueprint Reading | W | 6:30—9:30 |
| Nurse's Aide/Orderly | M/Th | 7:30—9:30 |

| COURSE TITLE | Days* | Time |
|---|---|---|
| **Art and Music** | | |
| Oil Painting | Th | 7:00—9:30 |
| Water Colors | W | 7:30—10:00 |
| Wood Carving | T | 7:00—9:30 |
| Picture Framing | M | 7:00—9:30 |
| Rug Hooking | W | 7:00—9:00 |
| Country Music U.S.A. | M | 7:00—9:00 |
| Music of Africa | Th | 7:00—9:00 |
| **Home Care** | | |
| Sewing I | M | 7:00—9:30 |
| Sewing II | T | 7:00—9:30 |
| Sewing III | W | 7:00—9:30 |
| Home Improvements | Th | 6:30—8:30 |
| Cooking to Save Money | W | 7:30—10:00 |
| Cooking Around the World | Th | 7:30—10:00 |
| Gardening | M | 7:00—9:00 |
| Care of House Plants | T | 7:00—9:00 |
| Fire Safety in the Home | Th | 7:00—9:00 |
| **Self Improvement** | | |
| Law Everyone Should Know | T | 7:00—9:00 |
| Planning for Your Retirement | W | 7:00—9:00 |
| Parenting Skills | M | 7:00—9:00 |
| Great Books Discussion Group | M | 7:00—9:00 |
| Driver Education | W | 7:00—10:00 |
| First Aid for Everyone | Th | 7:30—9:30 |
| Living with a Budget | M | 7:00—9:00 |
| **Recreation** | | |
| Basketball for Fun, Men | T | 7:00—10:00 |
| Basketball for Fun, Women | Th | 7:00—10:00 |
| Bridge Playing | W | 7:00—9:30 |
| Square Dancing I | M | 7:00—8:00 |
| Square Dancing II | W | 8:00—9:00 |
| Dances of South America | W | 7:00—8:30 |
| Ballroom Dancing I | Th | 7:00—8:00 |
| Ballroom Dancing II | Th | 8:00—9:00 |
| Body Building | M/W | 7:00—9:30 |
| Swimming | T/Th | 7:30—9:30 |
| Boating Skills & Safety | W | 6:30—9:30 |
| Fresh Water Fishing | M | 7:30—9:30 |

*Class Meeting Days: (M) Monday, (T) Tuesday, (W) Wednesday, (Th) Thursday

---

**admit, educate (ej' u cate), paragraph, (pār' u graph)**

**Fill in each blank with the correct form of the word given on the left.**

educate / education
1. Mrs. Page wants to _educate_ her children.
Their _education_ is very important to her.

admit / admission
2. City College will not _admit_ any more students this fall.
Sue will have to wait until next spring for _admission_.

decide / decision
3. I have a hard _decision_ to make.
I need to know more facts before I can _decide_.

register / registration
4. Mrs. Dawson wants to fill out a _registration_ form
so that she can _register_ to vote.

pronounce / pronunciation
5. Joseph finds it hard to _pronounce_ some English words,
but his _pronunciation_ is getting better.

apply / application
6. To _apply_ for a job at that factory,
you have to fill out an _application_.

discuss / discussion
7. Last week, our _discussion_ was about World War I.
Tonight, we will _discuss_ World War II.

depress / depression
8. Funny movies help me overcome _depression_.
Sad movies _depress_ me even more.

**Write a paragraph about one of these subjects.**
**Write the paragraph in your notebook.**

1. What does education mean to you?
2. What do you do for recreation?
3. What was the hardest decision you ever made?

## OBJECTIVES

To help your student:

- recognize that -*tion* and -*ssion* at the end of a word are usually pronounced /shun/, as in *direction* and *discussion*.
- recognize that -*sion* at the end of a word is usually pronounced /zhun/, as in *television*.
- read some common words ending in -*tion*, -*ssion*, and -*sion*.
- recognize the root word of words ending with -*tion*, -*ssion*, and -*sion*.
- recognize the suffixes -*tion*, -*sion*, -*ation*, and -*ion* that have been added to root words.
- review the suffixes -*ment* and -*hood*.
- recognize the blend *squ* as in *square* and review *scr*.
- recognize the new compound words *blueprint, ballroom, bookkeeping, shorthand*.
- recognize the new contractions *we'd, they're*, and review other contractions.
- review when to double the final consonant of a two-syllable root word before endings.
- recognize the Roman numerals I, II, III, and understand something of the system of writing Roman numerals.
- recognize words with the same meaning (synonyms).
- recognize the number of syllables in a word and which syllable is stressed.
- read dialog in the form of a script.
- read orally with expression to interpret a character's feelings.
- recognize the author's purpose.
- relate the story to personal experience and values.
- read a schedule of adult education courses.
- write words, sentences, and a business letter from dictation.
- write an original paragraph.

## INTRODUCTION

T: You have learned that some consonants stand for more than one sound and that some consonant sounds are spelled in more than one way. Sometimes, a certain combination of consonants and vowels is pronounced in a special way. In today's lesson, you will study three such combinations that come at the end of many words.

# I. Reading

**Note:** The chart respellings of *addition, discussion, depression, admission, television*, and *decision* show /sh/ or /zh/ as part of the last syllable, so that S. can clearly see the part of the word that is pronounced /shun/ or /zhun/. In dictionary respellings of these words, the /sh/ or /zh/ is grouped with the preceding short vowel in the next-to-last syllable, with /un/ as a syllable by itself. In either case, the stress is usually on the next-to-last syllable.

## CHART: Page 126

Have S. read *Lesson 20* and the chart title, *Words Ending in -tion, -ssion, -sion*.

**Note:** In reading the section headings in the chart, have S. give the names of the letters before the equal sign and the sounds for the letters after the equal sign.

**Section 1: -tion = shun as in direction.** Have S. read aloud the heading for the first section.

T: The words in the first column are old words. Each word is rewritten so that you can see how many syllables it has and which syllable is stressed. You can also see how -*tion* is pronounced.

Have S. read all the words in the first column, first silently and then aloud. Ask him to tell how -*tion* is pronounced in each word. Have him tell the number of syllables that each word has and which syllable is stressed. Point out that the stress is on the next-to-last syllable, just before /shun/, in all of the words.

Ask S. to read each word in the second column, first silently and then aloud. Encourage him to sound out each word for himself. Ask him to tell how many syllables are in each word and which syllable is stressed.

**Section 2: -ssion = shun as in discussion.** Have S. read the section heading. If he doesn't recognize *discussion*, have him look at the respelling below the heading. Ask S. to read the three words, first silently and then aloud. Have him tell the ending that is in each word and how it is pronounced. Also, have him tell how many syllables each word has and which syllable is stressed.

**Section 3: -sion = zhun as in television.** Follow the same procedure in teaching this section. If S. has difficulty pronouncing /zhun/, remind him of the sound /zh/ in *measure*. Have him listen to the difference between /shun/ and /zhun/ as you say *discussion* and *television*.

**Note:** Usually, -*sion* follows a vowel or *r* and is pronounced /zhun/. In a few words, -*sion* follows *n* or *l* and is pronounced /shun/, as in *pension* and *convulsion*. Do not bring up this exception at this time. If S. encounters such a word elsewhere, he will probably pronounce the ending /shun/ quite naturally.

**Review.** Have S. read each section heading aloud. Then ask him to read aloud each new word marked with an asterisk.

## STORY: Pages 127-128 (The Ted Howard Show)

Have S. read the story title and new words. Call attention to the sounds /f/ for *ph* in *Joseph*, /j/ for *g* in *D'Angelo* and *budget*, /s/ for *c* in *decide*. Ask S. to tell the meaning of the contraction *they're*, and explain that the contraction *we'd*, as it is used in this story, stands for the words *we would*.

**Directed silent reading**

T: This story is written in a different form than the other stories you have read. The first paragraph is an introduction. Read the paragraph to yourself, and find out what information is given.

Have S. tell what the story is about, where the talk show takes place, and who is on it. Ask him what he thinks Ted Howard's part on the talk show will be.

T: Notice the parentheses around the first paragraph. These marks show that this paragraph is for the reader's information and is not part of the talk show. The rest of the story is written as a script. A script tells who is speaking and just what the speaker says.

T: Look at the next paragraph. The speaker's name is in darker type. What is it? [S: Ted Howard.] Notice that there is a colon after his name, but there are no quotation marks. That is how a script is written. Everything after the speaker's name is what he says. Notice also that what Ted says is divided into several paragraphs, with extra space between them. But it is still Ted talking until you see the name of the next speaker in dark type.

T: Read to yourself what Ted Howard says, and find out what subject will be discussed on the talk show.

After S. has read this part silently, discuss the following questions:

1. To whom is Ted Howard speaking at the beginning?
2. How does Ted identify himself?
3. Why does Ted refer to his talk show of the previous week?
4. What does he say is the subject of discussion in tonight's show?
5. Who does he introduce as the first guest speaker?

Ask S. to read to himself what Gail Newman says and the comments Ted makes to her (the next four speeches). Then have S. summarize Gail's reason for enrolling at the center. Ask S. to tell what question Ted asks to draw more information from Gail.

Follow a similar procedure in having S. read Ted's conversation with Joseph D'Angelo and then with Helen Baker.

Ask S. to read to himself the comments that Ted Howard makes after Helen Baker finishes speaking. Then discuss these questions:

1. What issue does Ted Howard bring up?
2. Why do you think he brings up this issue?
3. What question does he ask Gail?
4. Do you think he will ask the other guests the same question? Why or why not?

Ask S. to finish reading the script to see what the guests say about the ways they would be affected if Freedom Center was closed. After S. has read silently, discuss these questions:

1. How does Gail say she would be affected? Why?
2. Does Joseph say he would be personally affected if the center were closed? Who is he concerned about?
3. Why does Helen think it is important for older people to keep on learning?
4. To whom is Ted Howard speaking in his last comments? What kinds of examples does he give of people who could use the services of the Freedom Center?

## STORY CHECKUP: Page 129

Have S. read the directions to himself and do the checkup. Check his work by having him read orally each question and the answer he circled. If an answer is incorrect, have him scan the story to find the answer. Note the number of questions that he answers correctly.

**Reading between the lines.** Discuss these questions.

1. What do you think was the purpose of the talk show?
2. Why do you think Ted Howard had three students from the Freedom Center as his guests?
3. Why do you think he chose these particular students?
4. How would what the guests said affect you if you were watching the program?
5. Does Ted Howard directly state his opinion of what should be done about budget cuts? What do you think his opinion is about closing Freedom Center? What in the story makes you think that?
6. Do you like to watch talk shows? What is your favorite? Why?
7. Do you think a script like the one you read would be written out before the talk show was given? Why or why not? Do you think a talk show is rehearsed? Why or why not?
8. Do you watch public television programs? What kind?

**Oral reading.** Have S. read the part of each guest speaker while you read the part of Ted Howard. Note your student's ability to read orally with expression that interprets the character's feelings. If you have several students, let them dramatize the talk show.

## READING FOR LIVING: Page 130

Have S. read the title and new words, first silently and then aloud. Explain that I, II, III are called Roman numerals and are sometimes used in designating beginning, intermediate, and advanced levels of courses. Ask S. to read the compound words and the words with the ending -ment. Call attention to the meaning of sew, the blend squ, and the abbreviation Dec.

Ask S. to read the four lines just under the new words—including the information at the far left and right—to find out what this Reading for Living section is about. After he has read silently, have him tell the type of material that is given here [schedule of fall courses]. Then have him answer these questions:

1. Who is offering the classes?
2. What is the address of the center?
3. When do classes begin? When do they end? (Call attention to the abbreviations for *September* and *December*.) What part of the day are they held?
4. When is registration?
5. What phone number can be called for more information?

## Column 1

T: Look at the schedule. Notice that it is divided into two main columns. Read the three headings over the first column. [S: Course Title, Days, Time.] What do you notice at the end of the word *Days?* [S: An asterisk.] An asterisk tells you to look at the bottom of the page for a note that gives more information.

Have S. read the note at the bottom of the page, first silently and then aloud. Ask S. why he thinks there are no classes offered on Friday evenings.

T: Look at the heading just under *Course Title*. What is it? [S: Language Arts.] This is a group heading to make it easier for you to find a particular course. Suppose you wanted to take a course in math. Would you be likely to find it listed under *Language Arts?* [S: No.] Might you find Spanish listed in this group? [S: Yes.] Read the titles in this group of courses to yourself. Note the dates and time that they meet.

After S. has read silently, have him answer these questions:

1. How many Spanish courses are offered? Which is the most advanced?
2. Which courses are offered on Monday and Wednesday?
3. Which course meets only on Tuesday?
4. Which courses are offered on Tuesday and Thursday?
5. For how long do most of the courses in this group meet each evening? Which one is longer? Which one is shorter?
6. Which course begins at 6:30?

Have S. read the rest of the column to himself. Then ask a few factual questions, such as the following:

1. In what group of courses is world history offered? What evening does it meet? For how long?
2. On what evening is the advanced class in typing given? For how many hours does it meet?
3. Which courses listed under *Business* meet on Thursday evening? Which ones meet on Tuesday?
4. How many evenings a week do most of the classes under *Skill Training* meet? For how many hours? Which course meets twice a week? For how many hours does it meet each of those evenings?

**Column 2.** Go over the second column in a similar way. Ask one or two factual questions about each group of courses. Have S. note the three courses offered in sewing. If there is a course title S. doesn't understand, explain what the course is probably about.

After S. has finished reading all of the course titles, ask the following questions:

1. Joseph is taking the citizenship class this spring. In the fall, he wants to take reading improvement and a course in skill training. He can go to classes four evenings a week. Which of the skill training courses would fit in with his schedule?

2. In the fall, Gail would like to take business math and bookkeeping. Can she take both?

3. Helen wants to take oil painting and the advanced class in square dancing. Which evenings will she go to class? For how many hours does each class meet?

4. If you had time to take three courses at Freedom Adult Education Center this fall, which ones would you choose? What would your schedule be for the three classes?

# II. Skills Practice

Have S. close his book before doing these exercises.

## PRACTICE 1: Distinguishing /shun/ and /zhun/

Write *direction* and *admission* in a column. Ask S. to read the words and tell how the ending is pronounced in both words. Write *shun* at the top of the column. In another column, write *television*. Ask S. to read it and tell how the ending is pronounced. Write *zhun* above *television*.

T: I will say two words that both end with either /shun/ or /zhun/. Tell me whether they end with /shun/ as in *direction* or /zhun/ as in *television*.

| | |
|---|---|
| *motion, action* | *possession, expression* |
| *notion, fraction* | *provision, explosion* |
| *vision, conclusion* | *profession, impression* |
| *position, digestion* | *confusion, division* |

## PRACTICE 2: Recognizing Roots of -tion Words

| | | -ion |
|---|---|---|
| action | act | |
| direction | direct | |
| election | elect | |
| selection | select | |
| connection | connect | |
| contraction | contract | |
| education | educate | |

| | | -ation |
|---|---|---|
| information | inform | |
| pronunciation | pronounce | |
| application | apply | |

| | | -tion |
|---|---|---|
| addition | add | |
| prescription | prescribe | |
| description | describe | |

In a column, write all of the words shown in the first column above. Have S. read the list of words. A few of them are new, but he should be able to sound them out.

T: The words in this list and most other words ending in /shun/ are nouns. The root word from which the noun comes is usually a verb. Sometimes the verb is changed somewhat before the ending is added. Look at each of these words and see if you can tell the root word it comes from.

Have S. read each word in the first column and tell the root word. Give help where needed. As he answers, write the words in the second column shown above. When the list is complete, point out that all of the root words are verbs. Then have S. read all of the verbs.

T: (Write the endings -tion, -ion, -ation.) One of these endings is added to change the verb into a noun. Look at the first seven pairs of words, and tell which of these endings was added. [S: -ion.] (Draw a line under education/educate and fill in -ion as shown above.) What letter is dropped from educate before -ion is added? [S: The final e.]

Complete the chart in a similar way. Call attention to the ending -ation in information, pronunciation, application. Then have S. tell how pronounce and apply are changed before the ending is added.

Call attention to the ending -tion in addition, prescription, and description. Then have S. note the change that is made in each verb before the ending is added.

T: All of the nouns here end in the same four letters. What are they? [S: -tion.] How are the letters pronounced? [S: /shun/.] The endings of the words look and sound the same, but you found that to change the verbs to nouns three different endings are used. What are they? [S: -ion, -ation, -tion.]

## PRACTICE 3: Recognizing Roots of -ssion, -sion Words

| | |
|---|---|
| discussion | discuss |
| depression | depress |
| admission | admit |
| permission | permit |

| | |
|---|---|
| decision | decide |
| television | televise |
| explosion | explode |

In a column, write all of the words shown in the first column above. Have S. read the list. He should be able to sound out the two new words, permission and explosion.

T: Each word in this list is a noun. Its root word is a verb. Look at each noun, and see if you can tell the root word it comes from.

Write each root word shown in the second column above as S. says it. Give help where needed. When the list is complete, have S. read all of the verbs in the second column.

T: (Underline ssion in the first four nouns.) What combination of letters do these words end in? [S: -ssion.] How are the letters pronounced? [S: /shun/.]

T: (Underline sion in the other three nouns.) What combination of letters do these words end in? [S: -sion.] How are the letters pronounced? [S: /zhun/.]

## PRACTICE 4: Suffixes -ment and -hood

In a column, write retirement, government, improvement. Have S. read each word and tell the root word and ending. As he answers, write retire, govern, improve in a second column. Then write enroll, appoint, employ under the other root words. Have S. tell the new word that can be made by adding -ment to each root word. Write enrollment, appointment, employment under the other -ment words.

Write childhood. Have S. read it and tell the root word and ending. Write adult, woman, man, girl, boy, baby, and have S. read them. Have him tell the new word that can be made by adding -hood to each root word. Write the new word by the root word.

## PRACTICE 5: Beginning Blends squ, scr

Write square and scream. Ask S. to read each word. Under square, write squ (skw). Explain that the item in parentheses is the way that the beginning blend squ is pronounced. Point out that this is a new consonant blend. Ask S. to tell what blend scream begins with. As he answers, write scr under the word.

T: I will say two words that both begin with the same blend. Tell me whether it is squ as in square or scr as in scream.

| | | |
|---|---|---|
| script, scratch | squint, squirrel | squeak, squirt |
| squash, squeeze | squad, squeal | |
| screen, scrap | scrape, scrub | |

## PRACTICE 6: Compound Words

Write *blueprint, ballroom, bookkeeping, shorthand*. Ask S. to read each compound word and tell the two words it is made up of. Circle each of the two words in the compound word as he says them. Have him use each compound word in a sentence. You may want to contrast the meanings of *shorthand* (a system of writing very quickly that uses symbols for letters, words, or whole phrases) and *longhand* (ordinary writing in which words are spelled out in full).

## PRACTICE 7: Contractions of *would, are*

Write the contractions *we'd* and *they're*. Ask S. to read each contraction and tell the two words it is made from. Then say each two words below. Have S. tell what contraction can be made from the two words and how to spell it. Write the contraction as S. spells it, putting the contractions of *would* under *we'd* and the contractions of *are* under *they're*.

| | | |
|---|---|---|
| *I would* | *we are* | *you would* |
| *he would* | *you are* | *she would* |

**Note:** You may want to explain further to S. that contractions like *we'd* can also be made from *had*, as in *We'd eaten* (*We had eaten*) *before we went to the movie* and *I'd* (*I had*) *better go now.*

## PRACTICE 8: Doubling the Final Consonant

In a column, write *forget, visit, upset, deposit, open, begin, happen, admit*. Have S. read the words. Point out that all of these words end with a short vowel and one consonant. Explain to S. that you are going to add some endings that begin with a vowel, such as *-ing, -ed, -er*. Review the rule that in words with more than one syllable, the final consonant is doubled before the ending if the last syllable is stressed. Have S. tell which syllable is stressed in each word, what the word would be with *-ing* added, and how to spell the new word. As he answers, write *forgetting, visiting, upsetting, depositing, opening, beginning, happening, admitting* in a second column.

Write these words with endings: *deposited, opener, beginner, happened, admitted*. Have S. read each word and identify the root word and ending. Also, have him tell why the final consonant of the root word is or is not doubled before the ending.

Write these words: *program, programming, programing*. Have S. read *program* and tell which syllable is stressed [the first]. Then have him read the other two words. Explain that there are a very few words in English that do not follow the rule; *program* is one of them. When an ending is added, the final consonant may be doubled or not. Both ways are correct. Have S. tell the two ways that *programmer* (*programer*) may be spelled. Write them under the *-ing* words.

## PRACTICE 9: Roman Numerals

**Note:** You may omit this exercise if you think it would be too confusing or distracting for your student.

T: (Write the Roman numerals I, II, III.) You had these Roman numerals in the Reading for Living section. What do they mean? [S: One, two, three.] Roman numerals above three are not used very often these days. But sometimes chapters in a book are numbered with Roman numerals. You may see them on some clocks and watches. A building may have the date it was built in Roman numerals. So it is a good idea to be able to read the ones that are used most often.

T: Roman numerals are really letters of the alphabet that the early Romans used as symbols for numbers. They used only a few letters. What letter is used for the number one? [S: Capital *I*.]

T: (Write IV, V, VI.) These are the Roman numerals for four, five, six. What letter is used for five? [S: Capital *V*.] Notice how four is written. Since four is one less than five, the *I* for one is put in front of the *V*. It's like saying "one from five." Now notice how six is written. Since six is one more than five, the *I* is put after the *V*. It's like saying "five and one."

Write VII, VIII. Have S. read them. If it seems helpful, explain that VII (seven) is like saying "five and two" and VIII (eight) is like saying "five and three."

Then explain that capital *X* is used for ten. Write IX, X, XI, XII, and have S. read them. If necessary, explain IX (nine) as "one from ten."

T: You can learn to read other Roman numerals if you are interested. But the ones from one to twelve are the ones you are most likely to see.

# III. Writing

## CHECK HOMEWORK: Page 125

Check your student's work. Note which homonyms he missed, and plan some extra practice on these later. S. may need to work out some memory association device that will help him relate the homonym to its particular spelling.

## WRITING LESSON (In Notebook)

Have S. write the titles *Lesson 20* and *Words* and number from 1 to 20 in two columns. After the dictation, check his work, and have him correct any errors by writing the whole word correctly.

**Words.** Help S. study these words: *sew, type, guest, budget.* When dictating, give a sentence for *sew, they're,* and *we'd.*

| | | |
|---|---|---|
| 1. square | 8. reason | 15. discussion |
| 2. dance | 9. they're | 16. direction |
| 3. sew | 10. we'd | 17. education |
| 4. type | 11. nation | 18. admission |
| 5. guest | 12. station | 19. recreation |
| 6. budget | 13. television | 20. constitution |
| 7. hello | 14. decision | |

**Sentences.** Have S. write the title *Sentences.* Have him number each sentence as you dictate it.

1. Joseph is studying English at Freedom Adult Education Center.
2. After Helen's husband died, she became depressed.
3. Gail decided to get her high school diploma.
4. Mary wants to take some courses in art and ballroom dancing for recreation.
5. I would like to take courses in typing and bookkeeping.

Check what S. has written and have him correct any errors, including those in punctuation and capitalization. Have him write the title *Study* and any words he missed in the dictation exercises.

**Writing a business letter**

T: Sometimes you may hear something advertised on TV that you would like to send for. At the time you hear the announcement, it is a good idea to write down exactly what is being offered and where to write. I will dictate a short business letter that you can use as an example. It follows almost the same form as the letter to the editor that you wrote.

Have S. write his address and the date in the heading, as shown below. Then dictate the letter for him to write. Change the date in the body of the letter to make it timely. Tell S. to underline the title of the book. Have S. sign the letter with his full name. Check his work for use of correct letter form, punctuation, spelling, and legibility of handwriting.

---

(Student's
complete address)
(Date)

ABC Oil Company
Advertising Department
1234 North Center Ave.
Dallas, Texas 75205

Dear Friends:

    I liked your TV program on WOXO in Chicago on Wednesday night, October 10.

    I would like a copy of the free book you advertised. Please send me a copy of *Safe Driving Tips.*

Sincerely,
(Student's full name)

---

## PRACTICE: Page 129

Go over the directions and example with S. Then have him do the exercise. Check his work by having him read each pair of words he has matched. Note any errors, and have him correct them.

## HOMEWORK: Page 131

Have S. read the new words and the directions for the first exercise. Ask him to read all of the pairs of words that are in the left column. Then have him read and do item 1. Check what he has written to be sure he understands the directions. Ask him to finish the others at home.

Have S. read the directions for the second exercise, a paragraph to be written in his notebook. Be sure he understands that he is to write about only one of the subjects and that he knows what is meant by a paragraph.

Encourage S. to read the story again at home and to study any words that he missed in the dictation.

## CHECKING PROGRESS

**Comprehension.** From the script for the TV show, you will be able to evaluate your student's ability to read material written in a format and style different from that of previous stories. His responses in your discussion and in the Story Checkup will indicate his ability to make inferences and relate the story to his own experiences. You can also note whether he reads fluently and with enjoyment.

**Word recognition.** There are many new long words in this lesson, but since they follow similar spelling patterns, they should not be too difficult for S. What was his attitude when he looked at the list of words in the chart? Did he recognize the old words in the first column? Did he approach the new words with confidence, or did the list discourage him? If he can read even a few of the new chart words, you can help him see his own progress by comparing this chart to the ones in earlier lessons.

Recognition of words in this lesson requires the application of phonics skills, recognition of syllables and stress, knowledge of word endings and spelling patterns. Note any of these skills in which S. needs more reinforcement.

**Oral reading.** When reading aloud the part of one of the characters, was S. able to interpret the character's feelings? Did S. read smoothly, clearly, and with expression? Did he read most of the words accurately? Did he seem to enjoy reading? Note any of these skills in which S. needs improvement. If word recognition is a problem, he should have practice to build up his sight vocabulary.

## MEETING INDIVIDUAL NEEDS

**Comprehension skills.** If S. had difficulty in understanding the main ideas in the talk show script, have him summarize in the third person what each character said. For reinforcement of character interpretation, have him describe what he thinks each of the characters was like, citing things the person said as reasons.

Try to find supplementary reading in script form for S. to read. You may want to consult bibliographies of materials for adults and teenagers with limited reading skills for plays written in easy English. But, as they are rather scarce, you and your student may want to write a short original play on a topic of interest. You might tape the dialog and then write it down, using vocabulary S. can read.

**Word recognition.** Make sets of flash cards for pairs of related words that S. can match. If you use a different color of paper—or ink—for each set of cards, it will be easier to keep them organized. The sets below will be helpful. Concentrate on those areas in which S. needs more reinforcement.

1. Homonyms: Use the ones from the Lesson 10 Practice, the Lesson 19 Homework, and *sew, so* from Lesson 20.
2. Opposites: Use the ones from the Practice in Lessons 5, 9, 11 and the Homework in Lessons 12, 16.
3. Synonyms: Use the ones from the Homework in Lessons 15 and 20.
4. Suffixes and root words: Use any from the lists below. (The starred items are new words.)

Use any of the suggestions given in previous lessons to help S. build up his sight vocabulary. Use word families, words that begin the same, words with the same vowel sound, or other skills practices that will help him remember words. Exercises in the Focus on Phonics series can be reviewed according to the needs of your student.

In *Focus on Phonics-4,* you may use Practices 20A-20E, which cover words ending with *-tion.*

| *-ful* | *-ful* | *-less* | | *-hood* | | *-ship* | *-al* |
|---|---|---|---|---|---|---|---|
| beautiful | armful | careless | noiseless | manhood | fatherhood | citizenship | central |
| careful | boxful | colorless | painless | womanhood | motherhood | *fellowship | *comical |
| forgetful | cupful | friendless | pointless | boyhood | brotherhood | friendship | electrical |
| helpful | glassful | heartless | powerless | girlhood | sisterhood | leadership | mechanical |
| hopeful | handful | homeless | speechless | babyhood | neighborhood | ownership | musical |
| peaceful | spoonful | hopeless | sleepless | childhood | parenthood | | personal |
| playful | teaspoonful | jobless | sugarless | | statehood | | physical |
| thankful | | lawless | thoughtless | | | | practical |
| wonderful | | nameless | | | | | seasonal |

| *-ment* | *-ness* | | *-ion, -ation, -tion* | | | |
|---|---|---|---|---|---|---|
| advertisement | blindness | redness | act | action | inform | information |
| agreement | darkness | roughness | contract | contraction | register | registration |
| amusement | emptiness | rudeness | direct | direction | apply | application |
| arguement | freshness | sadness | elect | election | *occupy | occupation |
| employment | gentleness | sickness | protect | protection | pronounce | pronunciation |
| excitement | goodness | smoothness | educate | education | prescribe | prescription |
| government | greatness | softness | graduate | graduation | *describe | *description |
| improvement | happiness | strangeness | *complete | completion | | |
| measurement | hardness | thickness | | | | |
| movement | kindness | toughness | *-ssion, -ion* | | *-sion, -ion* | |
| payment | loveliness | unhappiness | discuss | discussion | decide | decision |
| retirement | quickness | unpleasantness | depress | depression | *explode | *explosion |
| statement | | | *confess | *confession | *conclude | *conclusion |
| | | | *express | *expression | televise | television |
| | | | admit | admission | *confuse | *confusion |
| | | | permit | *permission | *divide | *division |

# Lesson 21

| | | | | | |
|---|---|---|---|---|---|
| noun | action | describe | (dē scribe') | alphabet | (al' phu bet) |
| verb | correct | guide | (gide) | alphabetical | (al phu bet' i cul) |
| adverb | entry | shown | (shōwn) | definition | (def i ni' tion) |
| wee | sample | weight | (wāt) | dictionary | (dic' tion ār y) |
| weed | | respell | (rē spell') | adjective | (ad' jec tiv) |

## How a Dictionary Can Help You

A dictionary is a book that tells you:

—how words are spelled,
—how words are pronounced,
—how words are used, and
—the meaning of words.

## How to Find Words

**Alphabetical listing.** In a dictionary, words are listed in order so that you can find them easily. Words are listed in the order of the letters of the alphabet. (The alphabet is shown at the bottom of this page.)

All words beginning with the letter *a* are listed in the first group of words. All words beginning with the letter *b* are listed in the second group of words, and so on, through the letter *z*.

Words beginning with the letters *a* through *e* are in the first third of the dictionary. Words beginning with *f* through *p* are in the middle third. And words beginning with *q* through *z* are in the last third of the dictionary.

All words having the same first letter are listed in order of their second letter, such as *club* and *coach*. All words with the same first and second letters are listed in order of their third letter, such as *coach* and *coin*.

Here is an example of some words listed in alphabetical order: *a, able, about, act, add, Africa, baby, back, bad, bag, band, bank, baseball.*

On the sample dictionary page shown here, you can see that the words in dark type are in alphabetical order.

**Guide words.** Two guide words are placed at the top of each page of a dictionary. The guide word at the top left shows you the first word listed on that page. The guide word at the top right shows you the last word listed on that page.

**Aa Bb Cc Dd Ee Ff Gg Hh Ii Jj Kk Ll Mm Nn Oo Pp Qq Rr Ss Tt Uu Vv Ww Xx Yy Zz**

---

## Sample Page of a Dictionary

**W**

**wedding    841    well**

**wed·ding** [wed'ing] *n.* 1 The ceremony or celebration of a marriage. 2 A special anniversary of a marriage: a golden *wedding.*

**wedge** [wej] *n., v.* **wedged, wedg·ing** 1 *n.* A tapering piece of wood, metal, etc., that can be forced into a narrow opening to split something apart, secure movable parts, etc. 2 *v.* To split or secure with or as if with a wedge. 3 *n.* Anything shaped like a wedge: a *wedge* of cake. 4 *n.* A small beginning or opening for changes, new plans, etc. 5 *v.* To crowd or squeeze (people or things) into a small or confined space.

**wed·lock** [wed'lok] *n.* The condition or relation of being married; matrimony.

**Wednes·day** [wenz'dē *or* wenz'dā] *n.* The fourth day of the week. ◆ See WODEN.

**wee** [wē] *adj.* **we·er, we·est** Very small; tiny.

**weed** [wēd] 1 *n.* Any useless or unsightly plant, especially one that grows abundantly and tends to crowd out cultivated plants. 2 *v.* To remove weeds from (a garden, lawn, etc.). 3 *v.* To eliminate what is useless, inadequate, or harmful: to *weed* out failing students. —**weed'y** *adv.*

**weeds** [wēdz] *n.pl.* The black mourning clothes worn by a widow.

**week** [wēk] *n.* 1 A period of seven days, especially such a period beginning with Sunday. 2 The days or time within a week devoted to work: The office has a 35-hour *week.*

**week·day** [wēk'dā'] *n.* Any day of the week except Sunday, or except Saturday and Sunday.

**week·end** [wēk'end'] *n.* Saturday and Sunday, or the time from Friday evening to the following Monday morning.

**week·ly** [wēk'lē] *adv., adj., n., pl.* **week·lies** 1 *adv.* Once a week. 2 *adj.* Done, occurring, computed, etc., once a week or by the week: a *weekly* wash; a *weekly* wage. 3 *n.* A publication issued once a week.

**ween** [wēn] *v.* To suppose; guess; fancy: seldom used today.

**weep** [wēp] *v.* **wept, weep·ing** 1 To show grief or other strong emotion by shedding tears. 2 To shed: to *weep* hot tears. 3 To mourn: She *wept* for her lost child. 4 To release (a liquid, as sap) slowly; ooze.

**weep·ing** [wē'ping] *adj.* 1 That weeps. 2 Having slim, drooping branches, as a willow.

**wee·vil** [wē'vəl] *n.* Any of various small beetles whose larvae destroy cotton, grain, nuts, etc.

**weft** [weft] *n.* Another name for WOOF.

**weigh** [wā] *v.* 1 To determine the weight of, as by using a scale. 2 To have as weight: That rock *weighs* a ton. 3 To measure (a substance or an amount) by weight: to *weigh* out five pounds of potatoes. 4 To consider carefully: to *weigh* an offer; to *weigh* one's words. 5 To bend or press down by weight; burden: The load *weighed* down the car. 6 To bear down; be a burden: Cares *weighed* upon her mind. 7 To have influence or be of importance: A good education will *weigh* in your favor. 8 To raise (an anchor) in preparation for sailing: to *weigh* anchor.

**weight** [wāt] 1 *n.* The heaviness of a thing; the amount a thing weighs: The *weight* of the roast is six pounds. 2 *n.* The force with which a thing presses downward, equal to its mass multiplied by the acceleration of gravity. 3 *n.* A piece of metal of known heaviness used as a standard in weighing on a balance. 4 *v.* To add weight to; make heavier. 5 *n.* A unit or system for measuring weight: troy *weight*; avoirdupois *weight.* 6 *n.* A load or burden. 7 *n.* Something like a load or burden: the *weight* of responsibility. 8 *v.* To put a load or burden on. 9 *n.* Influence or significance: His ideas carry *weight.*

**weight·less** [wāt'lis] *adj.* Having or seeming to have no weight: Objects inside a space capsule in orbit are *weightless.* —**weight'less·ness** *n.*

**weight·y** [wā'tē] *adj.* **weight·i·er, weight·i·est** 1 Of great importance, influence, or significance: *weighty* discussions; *weighty* problems. 2 Difficult to bear; burdensome. 3 Heavy.

**weir** [wir] *n.* 1 A small dam placed in a stream. 2 A fence of stakes, etc., set in a stream in order to trap fishes.

**weird** [wird] *adj.* 1 Strange in an unearthly or supernatural way; eerie. 2 *informal* Peculiar; odd: a *weird* necktie. —**weird'ly** *adv.*

**wel·come** [wel'kəm] *adj., v.* **wel·comed, wel·com·ing,** *n., interj.* 1 *adj.* Received with joy or gladness: a *welcome* visitor; a *welcome* relief. 2 *v.* To greet gladly or receive with pleasure. 3 *n.* The act of welcoming; a warm *welcome.* 4 *adj.* Under no obligation for kindness, gifts, etc.: You are *welcome.* 5 *adj.* Freely given the possession, use, etc., of something: You're *welcome* to the book. 6 *interj.* An exclamation expressing greeting: *Welcome,* friend. 7 *v.* To accept with calmness, pleasure, or courage: to *welcome* criticism. —**wear out one's welcome** To impose upon a person so much that one is no longer welcome.

**weld** [weld] 1 *v.* To unite (pieces of metal) by softening with heat and pressing together. 2 *v.* To be welded or capable of being welded. 3 *n.* A joint or seam formed by welding pieces of metal. 4 *v.* To join closely; unite: The coach *welded* them into a unit. —**weld'er** *n.*

**wel·fare** [wel'fâr] *n.* 1 The condition of being healthy, prosperous, happy, etc.; well-being. 2 Organized efforts by a community or group of people to give money and aid to those who are poor and in need. 3 *adj.* use: *welfare* work.

**welfare state** A state or community in which the government assumes responsibility for the health and prosperity of its citizens.

**well** [wel] 1 *n.* A hole or shaft dug or drilled into the earth to reach a deposit of water,

add, āce, câre, pälm; end, ēqual; it, īce; odd, ōpen, ôrder; tŏŏk, pōōl; up, bûrn; a = a in *above,* e in *sicken,* i in *possible,* o in *melon,* u in *circus;* yōō = u in *fuse;* oil; pout; check; ring; thin; this; zh in *vision.*

Guide words help you find the word you want quickly and easily. For example, on the sample page, the first word is *wedding*, and the last word is *wet*. If you're looking for *wet*, you know right away that it comes after this page.

**Entry words.** The words that are listed in the dictionary in alphabetical order are called entry words. Entry words stand out on the page because they are printed in dark type. The information about each entry word is printed in lighter type.

**Example of how to find a word.** How do you find the word *weigh* in a dictionary? You know that the first letter, *w*, is near the end of the alphabet. Open your dictionary to the last third of the pages. Turn to pages showing words that begin with *w*. Then look for pages with guide words beginning with *we*. Then choose a page with guide words that *weigh* would come between. On the sample dictionary page, *weigh* comes between the guide words *wedding* and *well*. Look down the page to find the entry word *weigh*.

**How to Spell Words**

**Letters for sounds.** To check a word for the correct spelling, pronounce the word slowly, and listen to its sounds. Think what letters stand for the sounds of the word. Then look for an entry word having those letters. Entry words are spelled correctly.

Some words sound alike, but they are spelled differently for different meanings. For example, the word *way* and the word *weigh* sound the same but have different meanings. Look for the word you want according to the way you think it is spelled. Read the meaning shown for the word. If it is not the word you want, then think of another way the word might be spelled.

**Word endings.** You may want to check the correct spelling of a word with an ending. You may not find the word with ending listed as an entry word. But you can find it on the line next to the entry word. For example, after the entry word *write* are shown *wrote, written, writing*.

**How to Pronounce Words**

**Syllables and stress.** Entry words are shown with dots between syllables. Then, each entry word is respelled to show how it sounds and which syllables are stressed.

**Pronunciation key.** At the front of most dictionaries is a pronunciation key. It tells you how each consonant and vowel sound will be shown in the respellings of entry words. The pronunciation key gives a list of short, easy words as examples of the sounds.

Also, at the bottom of every two pages there is a shorter pronunciation key. It shows how the different vowel sounds are marked.

**How to Find Word Meanings**

**Parts of speech.** A dictionary shows the way a word is used by giving its part of speech. The parts of speech used most often are:

*n.* — noun (name of person, place or thing)
*n.pl.* — noun plural
*v.* — verb (action word)
*adj.* — adjective (word that describes a noun, or name word)
*adv.* — adverb (word that describes a verb, or action word)

As an example, the word *weed* as a noun has a different meaning from the word *weed* as a verb.

**Definitions.** A definition of a word gives the meaning of the word. A dictionary gives one or more definitions for each entry word.

As an example, for the word *weight*, the sample page of the dictionary shows seven definitions for *weight* as a noun and two definitions for *weight* as a verb.

Sometimes you will need to read all of the definitions for a word to find the meaning of the word for the sentence you are reading.

**Examples of how words are used.** The dictionary helps you understand some definitions by giving examples of how the words are used. See the following:

*week, n.* — The office has a 35-hour week.

*welcome, adj.* — You're welcome to the book.

**Study the sample dictionary page, and answer these questions.**

1. What two words does *Wednesday* come between? <u>wedlock and wee</u>

2. What compound words beginning with *week* are listed as entry words?
<u>weekday</u>     <u>weekend</u>

3. What two words with endings are shown for *welcome* as a verb?
<u>welcomed</u>     <u>welcoming</u>

4. What does the word *wee* mean? <u>tiny</u>     What part of speech is it? <u>adjective</u>

5. How many meanings are there for the word *weed* as a verb? <u>three</u>
Write a sentence using the word *weed* as a verb. _____

6. What entry word has the ending *-less*? <u>weightless</u>

7. Write the words that are made by adding the endings *-er* and *-est* to *weighty*.
<u>weightier</u>     <u>weightiest</u>

8. Write the way to pronounce the word *weighty*. <u>wā´tē</u>

9. Is the word *wash* listed on the sample dictionary page? <u>No</u>
Why or why not? <u>Wash comes before the guide word wedding</u>

**These words sound alike, but they are spelled differently, and they have different meanings. Read the words. Then write the correct word in each blank.**

(weed, we'd) 1. _We'd_ like to know if this plant is a flower or a _weed_ .

(hall, haul) 2. The men took the boxes from the front _hall_ of our house.
They loaded the boxes into their truck to _haul_ them away.

(wait, weight) 3. I'll _wait_ until I've lost _weight_ before I buy a new coat.

(way, weigh) 4. A truck driver must _weigh_ his truck and its load on the
_way_ to market.

(peace, piece) 5. Ann ate a _piece_ of chocolate cake in the _peace_ and quiet
of the empty kitchen.

(threw, through) 6. Ed _threw_ the ball _through_ the basket and got the first
two points of the basketball game.

(flower, flour) 7. Joyce bought eggs, butter, milk, and _flour_ to make a birthday
cake. Then she bought some roses at a _flower_ shop.

(chews, choose) 8. Which pet would you _choose_ to have, a cat that claws your sofa
and chairs or a puppy that _chews_ on everything?

**Add re- to the beginning of each root word. Write the new word in the blank.**

Example: spell _respell_

1. read _reread_     4. pay _repay_

2. write _rewrite_     5. open _reopen_

3. turn _return_     6. marry _remarry_

**Fill in each blank with one of the new words with re-.**

1. I have to _repay_ that loan in six months.

2. My mother never wanted to _remarry_ after my father died.

3. I'll let you use my car if you _return_ it by six o'clock.

---

**Write the words in each list in the correct alphabetical order.**

| | List 1 | | List 2 |
|---|---|---|---|
| alphabet | action | describe | definition |
| adjective | adjective | dumb | describe |
| action | adult | definition | dictionary |
| adverb | adverb | does | does |
| adult | alphabet | dictionary | dumb |

**Read the guide words at the top of each list of words given below. In each list, underline the words that would be found on the same page as the two guide words.**

| face — father | safe — speed | grade — guide |
|---|---|---|
| _fact_ | _same_ | _guest_ |
| fair | sauce | gym |
| fence | _salute_ | grew |
| _fame_ | _sample_ | good |
| _false_ | save | _graduate_ |
| fault | said | gun |

**Copy the entry words that have more than one syllable from the sample dictionary page. Don't copy a word with an ending unless it is listed as an entry word.**

| _wedding_ | _weekend_ | _weightless_ |
| _wedlock_ | _weekly_ | _weighty_ |
| _Wednesday_ | _weeping_ | _welcome_ |
| _weekday_ | _weevil_ | _welfare_ |

Which syllable has the main stress in all of these words? _The first_

**Note:** Have at least one dictionary—or more—available for S. to examine. A dictionary for beginners is desirable, but if one is not available, try to find one with a simple pronunciation key. The dictionary from which the sample page in this lesson was taken is good for a new reader but somewhat expensive for S. to purchase. Other suggestions are given at the end of this lesson. Your main objective in this lesson should be to encourage S. to own and use a dictionary. Lend him one to use for the first week, but encourage him to buy one of the suggested dictionaries as soon as possible. Practice in using the dictionary will be included in the lessons that follow.

## OBJECTIVES

To help your student:

- understand the ways a dictionary can help him.
- understand the general arrangement of a dictionary.
- understand the meaning of such terms as *entry word, guide word, definition, part of speech, pronunciation key.*
- learn how to locate an entry word.
- interpret what the dictionary tells about an entry word.
- learn the meaning of some abbreviations used in the dictionary.
- review alphabetical order.
- determine the order of words that begin with the same letter.
- use the dictionary to find word meanings.
- use the dictionary to find the correct spelling of a word.
- recognize syllable divisions and stress marks.
- understand a dictionary pronunciation key, including the symbol schwa (ə) for /u/ in unstressed syllables.
- pronounce a word according to the phonetic spelling used by the dictionary.
- recognize the difference in meaning and spelling of some words that sound alike (homonyms).
- recognize the prefix *re-* as in *respell* and how to add it to the beginning of some root words.
- review the prefixes *in-* and *un-*.
- become motivated to own a dictionary and use it as an aid in his everyday reading and writing.
- review consonants that stand for more than one sound and some consonant sounds that are written in more than one way.
- arrange a list of words in alphabetical order.
- write words, sentences, fractions, Roman numerals, abbreviations, dates, addresses, and times of day from dictation.

## INTRODUCTION

T: You have studied all of the vowel and consonant sounds. You have learned about syllables, root words, endings, and some other things that help you recognize new words. But in your future reading, you'll probably come across some words that are difficult to recognize or words whose meaning you don't know. In today's lesson, you'll find out about a book that can be of great help to you in your reading and writing. It's a book that I use a lot, too.

# I. Reading

## STORY: Pages 132-135 (How to Use a Dictionary)

**Title and new words.** Have S. read the titles *Lesson 21* and *How to Use a Dictionary.* Refer him to the respelling of *dictionary* in the word list if he doesn't recognize it.

T: You have probably seen a dictionary in a school or library. Or, you may have one at home. Dictionaries come in various sizes, depending on how many words they list. A dictionary is not a book you are likely to read from cover to cover, but it is a book all of us should use often for reference.

Show the dictionaries you have brought. Let S. see the cover and a few pages of each so that he can understand what a dictionary looks like. But don't have a discussion about the dictionary at this time. Tell S. that, after he has studied the lesson, he can look at the dictionaries more closely and use one for practice.

Have S. read the new words, first silently and then aloud. Call attention to *-tion* in *action, definition,* and *dictionary.* Call attention to the sound /f/ for *ph* in *alphabet* and to the silent *gh* in *weight.*

**Surveying the article.** Point out that this factual article is divided into sections, according to the topics it discusses. The main topics are named in the large subheads in dark type that are centered in each column. (Point to *How a Dictionary Can Help You* and *How to Find Words* as examples, but do not read them.)

Some main topics are divided into subtopics. These are named in smaller subheads in dark type that are run in with the paragraphs. (Point to *Alphabetical listing* and *Guide words* as examples, but do not read them.)

Have S. look through the whole article, locate, and read aloud the subheads for the main topics that will be discussed. Then return to the beginning of the article.

## How a Dictionary Can Help You

Ask S. to read the section about the first main topic to himself and then tell in his own words the four ways a dictionary can help you.

## How to Find Words

**Alphabetical listing.** Ask S. to read the title of the next main topic, *How to Find Words*, aloud. Then ask him to read the section for the first subtopic under it to himself. After he has read silently, discuss the following points:

1. The arrangement of the dictionary in alphabetical order to make it easy to find a word.
2. What is meant by alphabetical order according to the first letter of a word. (Have S. read the alphabet at the bottom of the page aloud. Let him thumb through one of the dictionaries so that he can see that the words are in alphabetical order from *A* through *Z*.)
3. Divison of entry word section into thirds. (Divide the entry word section of a dictionary into thirds so that S. can see what is meant by the first third, middle third, and last third. Let him see what letters are covered in each third.)
4. What is meant by alphabetical order of second and third letters of a word. (Have S. look at the sample page of the dictionary shown in the skill book and tell what the first letter is in all of the words. Then have him note what the second letter is in all of the words. Point out that, since the first two letters are the same in all of the words, the third letter must be considered in arranging the words alphabetically. Point out further that if the first three letters are the same, then the fourth letter must be considered.)

**Guide words.** Have S. read this section to himself. Before he begins reading, have him notice that this section is continued on page 134. After he has read silently, ask him to point out the guide words on the sample page. Ask him how he can know just by looking at the guide words that the word *wet* will not be on this page. Ask him if the word *web* is on the page and how he can know the answer from reading the guide words.

**Entry words** and **Example of how to find a word.** Ask S. to read these two sections to himself. After he has read silently, discuss the following points:

1. What is meant by an entry word.
2. How he can tell which are entry words on a dictionary page. (Have S. point out some of the entry words on the sample page, but don't have him read them. Ask him to count the number of entry words in the first column. [There are 17.])
3. Location of the entry word *weigh*. (Ask S. if he was able to find *weigh* on the sample page. Ask him to tell how he went about finding it. Have him point to the word *weigh* on the sample page.)

## How to Spell Words

**Letters for sounds.** Ask S. to read the title of the next main topic, *How to Spell Words*, aloud. Then ask him to read the section for the first subtopic under it to himself. After he has read silently, ask him to tell if the word *way*, meaning a path or direction, is listed on the sample dictionary page. Have S. give the spelling for this meaning, *way*, and tell why it is not

on the sample page. Ask him to tell the meaning of the word /wā/ when it is spelled *weigh*.

**Word endings.** Ask S. to read this section to himself. After he has read silently, ask him to tell whether or not he can find the word *write* on the sample dictionary page. Ask him to tell why it is not there. Show him a dictionary page on which he can find *write*, and have him locate it. Then have him find *wrote, written, writing* on the line next to *write*.

## How to Pronounce Words

Ask S. to read the title of the next main topic, *How to Pronounce Words*, aloud.

**Syllables and stress** and **Pronunciation key.** Ask S. to read these two subtopics to himself. After he has read silently, have him look at the sample dictionary page. Ask him to tell how many syllables the word *wedding* has. Have him point to the dot that divides the two syllables of the entry word. Then have him look at the way the word is respelled and tell which syllable is stressed.

Show the pronunciation key in the front of one of the dictionaries that you have at hand, just so that S. will know how to recognize it. But don't explain the meaning of the symbols and markings at this time. Instead, have S. look at the pronunciation key at the bottom of the sample dictionary page.

T: In your skill book, you have been used to looking at the respelling of a new word to find out how to pronounce it. The dictionary way of respelling words is similar, but it uses more marks to show various vowel sounds. Look at the key for pronouncing words given at the bottom of the sample page.

Have S. read aloud each of the key words on the first line. Ask him to tell the vowel sound in each word and what mark indicates that sound. If he doesn't recognize the new word *palm*, explain that *a* with two dots over it stands for the sound /o/.

Ask S. to look at the second line. Explain that the symbol that looks like an upside-down *e* (ə) is called a *schwa*, and that it stands for the sound /u/ as pronounced in an unstressed syllable. Then have S. read that part of the second line, giving the sound /u/ for each vowel indicated. Point out that the schwa sound can be spelled with any one of the vowels.

Have S. read the other key words in the second line and tell the vowel sound. Explain that yo͞o is this dictionary's way of indicating the long *u* sound. Have S. read the key words in the last line and tell what sound each consonant combination stands for.

T: You don't need to memorize the dictionary markings. You can always refer to the key when you are looking at the dictionary respelling of a word. If you use the same dictionary often, you will become familiar with the key.

Ask S. to find the word *welcome* in the second column of the sample dictionary page. Have him look at the way the word is respelled. Ask him to tell the vowel sound in the second syllable and the symbol that stands for it. Do the same thing for the words *welfare* and *weep*. Point out that the dictionary respellings do not contain any silent letters.

## How to Find Word Meanings

Ask S. to read the title of the last main topic, *How to Find Word Meanings,* aloud.

**Parts of speech.** Ask S. to read this section to himself. Then ask him to find the word *week* in the sample dictionary page. Have him tell what part of speech it is. Then ask him to find the word *weekly* and tell the three parts of speech that it can be. Ask him to spell the noun plural of *weekly.*

**Definitions.** Have S. read this section to himself  Then have him find the word *weight* on the sample page. Have him note that *n.* is used seven times to indicate the different meanings of *weight* as a noun and that *v.* is used two times to indicate its meanings as a verb.

**Examples of how words are used.** Ask S. to read the last section to himself. Then have him find on the sample page under *week* and *welcome* the example sentences shown in this paragraph. Have him read aloud the definition that each example sentence goes with.

## STORY CHECKUP: Page 135

Go over the directions with S. Then have him do the Checkup independently. Check his work by having him read aloud each question and his answer. If he has an incorrect answer or has omitted one, go over the question with him to make sure he understands what it means. Then help him find the correct answer on the sample dictionary page.

## RELATING THE STORY TO EVERYDAY LIFE

Discuss some of these questions with S.

1. Have S. look at the publication date of each of the dictionaries. Ask why dictionaries need to be kept up to date. Bring out that our language is constantly changing. New words come into being, or words develop new meanings. Some words become old-fashioned. A dictionary tries to keep up with the language the way people are using it.

2. What are some of the new words that have come into our language (or have developed new meanings) since we have come into the computer and space age?

3. Who uses a dictionary? Bring out that there are so many words in English that no one can know them all. When we are reading, we sometimes have to look up a word whose meaning we don't know. When we are writing, we sometimes have to look up the correct spelling of a word, since

most of us don't know how to spell all of the words we use in speaking. Bring out that it is never a sign of ignorance to use a dictionary. It is only a sign of ignorance not to use one when unsure of the spelling, meaning, or pronunciation of a word.

4. When should you use a dictionary? Bring out the importance of looking up a word at the time you need help with it in reading or writing. If a dictionary isn't available, write it down and look it up as soon as possible. Otherwise, it will be forgotten. It is best to write down the whole sentence in which the word is used so that the correct meaning or spelling can be found in the dictionary.

5. How can you become a skillful dictionary user? Emphasize the importance of having a dictionary close at hand when reading or writing. It's a good idea to have a pocket dictionary that you can look at at any time.

Encourage S. to suggest ways that he can make use of a dictionary. Suggest that he look up a few words each day for practice. Bring out that the more he uses the dictionary, the easier it will be for him to use it.

# II. Skills Practice

Have S. close his book before doing these exercises.

## PRACTICE 1: Alphabetical Order

Have S. review alphabetical order by reciting the alphabet. Then ask him to tell you the name of the letter that comes *after* the letter you say. Say these letters: *m, d, h, s, y, w, b, q, e, j.*

Ask S. to tell the name of the letter that comes *before* each of these letters: *l, r, x, b, f, t, q, v, z, d.*

Give S. a dictionary. Have him divide the entry word section into thirds and place markers between the first and middle thirds and between the middle and last thirds. Write these headings: *A–E, F–P, Q–Z.* Tell S. that you will say a word. He should tell which third the word is in, open the dictionary to that third, and then find words that begin with that letter. For example, if you say *clinic,* he should say, "First third," open to the first third, and find the words that begin with *c.* (In this practice, do not have S. find the word, but see if he has located the proper section.) Say these words:

| | | | |
|---|---|---|---|
| *action* | *entry* | *dictionary* | *issue* |
| *welcome* | *verb* | *pronounce* | *reason* |
| *sample* | *guide* | *correct* | *history* |

List these words in a column: *passenger, body, sew, adult, cuffs, tale, medicine, government, unusual, reason.* Have S. put these words in alphabetical order by reading aloud the word that comes first, second, and so on through the list. Write the words in a second column as he gives them. When the list is complete, have him check to see if the words are in the right order.

Lesson 21   179

Follow the same procedure for these lists of words:
List 1: *bridge, budget, bandage, bought, belong.*
List 2: *gentle, gas, graduate, guest, gym.*

## PRACTICE 2: Locating an Entry Word

Tell S. that you would like for him to find the page on which the word you say is located. Remind him to look at the guide words at the top of the page. Say each word below. Have S. locate the page he thinks the word will be on by using the guide words. Have him tell the page number and the guide words on it. (If any of the guide words are very difficult, help him read them, or allow him to give the first few letters.) Then have him try to find the word on the page to see if he was correct.

If the page S. finds is not correct, say the word again, and have him tell the first three letters in the word. Write these letters for him to see and to compare with those in the guide words. Help him find the correct page.

| | | |
|---|---|---|
| *nation* | *constitution* | *elephant* |
| *television* | *diploma* | *ivory* |
| *computer* | *recreation* | *moon* |

## PRACTICE 3: Dictionary Respellings

Write these words: *syllable, opposite, accident, crumb, budget, once, character, physical.* Have S. find each word in the dictionary and note the respelling. Write the dictionary respelling by the word as he pronounces it. Bring out the following points about the dictionary respellings:

1. The respelling does not include double letters unless the two letters are pronounced differently, as in *accident.*
2. The dictionary respelling does not include silent letters, such as the *e* in *syllable* and the *b* in *crumb.*
3. The letter *c* is not used. The letter *k* is used for the sound /k/ and the letter *s* is used for the sound /s/.
4. In the respelling, the consonant that usually stands for a certain sound is given. Examples are *j* for *g* in *budget, k* for *ch* in *character,* and *f* for *ph* in *physical.*
5. The schwa symbol (ə) is used for any one of the vowels in an unstressed syllable. Have S. note the words in which the schwa is used and which syllable or syllables it comes in.

## PRACTICE 4: Prefix *re-*

Write *respell,* and have S. read it. Have him tell the root word and the new prefix. Underline *re-*.

T: The prefix *re-* can mean *back* or *again.* What does it mean in *respell?* [S: Again.] What does *respell* mean? [S: Spell again.]

T: (Write *repay.*) What does the prefix *re-* mean in this word—*back* or *again?* [S: Back.] What does *repay* mean? [S: Pay back.]

Underline *re-* in *repay.* Then, under the root words *spell* and *pay,* write *paint, marry, write, heat, turn, fill.* Have S. read each word and tell what it would be with the prefix *re-* added. As he answers, write *re-* in front of the root word. When the list is complete, have S. read all of the new words.

## PRACTICE 5: Prefixes *in-* and *un-*

Write *incorrect.* Have S. read it and tell the root word. Then have him tell the prefix and what it means. Under the root word *correct,* write these words: *experienced, complete, human, expensive, sincere.* Ask S. to read each root word (the last two are new) and then tell what new word can be made by putting the prefix *in-* in front of the root word. Write *in-* in front of the root word as he says the new word. When the list is complete, have him read all of the new words.

Follow the same procedure in reviewing the prefix *un-*. Use these root words: *welcome, safe, educated, excited, sure, healthy.*

# III. Writing

## CHECK HOMEWORK: Page 131

Check the first exercise by having S. read aloud each pair of sentences with the words he has filled in. Have him make any needed corrections.

Ask S. to read aloud the paragraph that he wrote in his notebook. First, comment on the content of the paragraph. Notice whether or not he kept to the subject of the question, how he organized his thoughts, and the clarity with which he expressed them. If he wrote the paragraph, be sure to praise him for his effort. Make constructive suggestions for any improvements needed. Then check his work for spelling, sentence structure, and punctuation. Ask him to make any needed corrections at home and to rewrite the paragraph if there are many corrections.

## WRITING LESSON (In Notebook)

Have S. write the titles *Lesson 21* and *Words.* Then have him number from 1 to 14 in two columns.

T: This time, I will dictate the new words before you have studied them. Write each word the way you think it is spelled. If you are not sure, write the word the way it sounds. When you have finished, you can check the dictionary for the correct spelling of any words you are not sure about.

**Words.** Give a sentence for *weed* and *weigh* when you dictate these words.

| | | |
|---|---|---|
| 1. action | 6. describe | 11. shown |
| 2. alphabet | 7. dictionary | 12. verb |
| 3. alphabetical | 8. guide | 13. weed |
| 4. correct | 9. noun | 14. weigh |
| 5. definition | 10. respell | |

Check what S. has written. Put a check mark by each word he has written correctly. Have him look up each of the other words in the dictionary to find the correct spelling. Have him notice which part of the word he misspelled. Then have him write the word correctly. Give help where needed in locating a word in the dictionary.

**Review words.** Have S. write the heading *Review* and then number from 1 to 16 in two columns. Dictate the words below. Or, you may substitute 16 words from his study list beginning with Lesson 17. Give a sentence for *wrap* and *gym*.

| | | |
|---|---|---|
| 1. sure | 7. knee | 13. shine |
| 2. measure | 8. elephant | 14. gym |
| 3. central | 9. cough | 15. notice |
| 4. danger | 10. although | 16. I'd |
| 5. edge | 11. gas | |
| 6. wrap | 12. doesn't | |

**Fractions and Roman numerals.** On another line, ask S. to write these fractions and Roman numerals: $^1/_2$, $^1/_4$, $^3/_4$, $^2/_3$, I, II, III.

**Abbreviations.** Have S. number from 1 to 7 in two columns. Then have him write the abbreviations for these words.

| | |
|---|---|
| 1. Avenue (Ave.) | 5. December (Dec.) |
| 2. Street (St.) | 6. Monday (Mon.) |
| 3. August (Aug.) | 7. Friday (Fri.) |
| 4. September (Sept.) | |

**Dates, addresses, times of day.** Have S. number from 1 to 10 in two columns. Ask him not to use abbreviations for months or addresses. Then dictate the following:

| | |
|---|---|
| 1. September 6, 1987 | 6. 113 East Porter Street |
| 2. December 12, 1988 | 7. 987 West Lake Avenue |
| 3. October 1, 1985 | 8. 6:30 p.m. |
| 4. 1000 South Main Street | 9. 7:20 p.m. |
| 5. 179 Park Avenue | 10. 9:00 a.m. |

**Sentences.** Have S. write the title *Sentences*. Ask him to number each sentence as you dictate it.

1. Mrs. Brown has taught all of her sons to sew.
2. The bus was so crowded that I couldn't get on.
3. Mr. and Mrs. Mitchell are going to the open house at their daughter's school.
4. They're going in their old Chevy.
5. Many parents will be there tonight.
6. We'd like to hear the chorus sing.
7. Would you like to meet me here at eight o'clock?

Check what S. has written. Make note of any errors in the spelling of words that have homonyms. Have S. make any needed corrections.

**PRACTICE: Page 136**

Go over the directions for the first exercise on homonyms with S. and have him do it. Check his work. If he has an error, have him read the sentence and tell which spelling of the word gives the right meaning. Note any pairs of words he confused so you can give extra practice.

Have S. read the directions for the second exercise on *re-*, first silently and then aloud. Ask him to read the example and then do the exercise. Check his work.

Have S. read the directions for the last exercise and then fill in the blanks in the sentences with the new *re-* words. Check his work by having him read the completed sentences aloud.

**HOMEWORK: Page 137**

Have S. read the directions for the first exercise to himself. Have him look at List 1 and tell which word would come first in alphabetical order. Then have him write the words in order. Do the same for List 2.

Have S. read the directions for the next exercise, first silently and then aloud. To make sure he understands the directions, have him underline one of the words in the first list that *would* come between the two guide words.

Have S. read the directions for the last exercise to himself. Then ask him to look at the sample dictionary page and find the first entry word that has more than one syllable [*wedding*]. Ask him to write that word on the first blank. Point out that there are just enough blanks for all of the words he should write.

Encourage S. to reread the dictionary lesson at home. If possible, lend him a dictionary to use at home. Suggest that he look up two or three new words each day in order to find the meaning, spelling, or pronunciation. Ask him to list the words he looks up in his notebook.

Suggest that, in order to find a word quickly in the dictionary, he might practice looking up a few additional words each day. These can be old words and can be chosen from any of the charts or stories in the skill book.

Ask S. to correct any spelling errors in the paragraph that he wrote in his notebook in the homework for the last lesson. He can use the dictionary to find the correct spelling for those words.

**CHECKING PROGRESS**

**Comprehension.** This lesson will help you evaluate your student's progress in reading study-type material. You can note his ability in the following skills:

1. Alphabetizing.
2. Locating specific information.
3. Following written instructions.
4. Understanding the meaning of specialized terms such as *entry word, guide word, pronunciation key.*
5. Applying to a practical situation information that was gained in reading, such as how to locate a word in a dictionary.

**Word recognition.** This lesson indirectly reviews many of the main points covered in the last five lessons. You will be able to evaluate your student's progress in the following skills:

1. Recognizing various spellings for some of the consonant sounds.
2. Recognizing root words, suffixes, and prefixes.
3. Recognizing the meaning of words that sound alike but are not spelled alike (homonyms).
4. Recognizing the number of syllables in a word and which syllable is stressed.
5. Applying phonics skills in sounding out new words in the lesson and interpreting the pronunciation key in the dictionary.

**Writing and spelling.** You can evaluate your student's progress in writing and spelling from the dictation exercises and from the original paragraph that he wrote. Note the types of errors he makes in spelling and punctuation. Note whether his writing is legible.

## MEETING INDIVIDUAL NEEDS

If S. did fairly well in this lesson, have him go on to Lesson 22. He will have an opportunity to develop more skill in using the dictionary during then next few lessons. But, if he still needs help in the main new skills covered in Lessons 17-21, then plan one or two review lessons. Note the skills with which he needs the most practice, and plan reinforcement exercises. Use any of the suggestions given in the last few lessons.

In *Focus on Phonics-4,* you may use Practices 21A-21B, which cover words ending with *-sion* and *-ssion.*

**Recommended dictionaries for student's use.** The following are paperback dictionaries (under $5) that cost considerably less than equivalent hardbound desk dictionaries.

*The Random House Dictionary* (Ballantine Books). Random House, Inc.

*Webster's New World Dictionary,* Revised (Warner Books). Simon and Schuster.

Dictionaries for beginning or intermediate level students generally have easier pronunciation keys, larger type, and more easily understood definitions than desk dictionaries. They lack information on word derivations, but most beginning students do not care about this feature, anyway. They do contain fewer words, so if your student is interested in purchasing such a dictionary, you should make sure it includes any specialized vocabulary he may need. These dictionaries are in the $9 to $15 price range. Some that are recommended are:

*The HBJ School Dictionary.* Harcourt Brace Jovanovich. (The dictionary from which the sample page in the skill book was taken.)

*Longman Dictionary of American English.* Longman, Inc. (Particularly useful for English-as-a-second-language students.)

*Random House School Dictionary.* Random House. (Intermediate level.)

*Scott, Foresman Beginning Dictionary* by Thorndike and Barnhart. Scott, Foresman and Co.

You may want to consult a school librarian about these and other beginning dictionaries. The librarian may have some of them that you can examine and may also be able to give you information about current prices and ordering.

# LESSON 22-A

**People and Places, Story 1**
**Skill Book 4, Page 138**

## OBJECTIVES

To help your student:
- use a table of contents.
- read story 1 in *People and Places* independently, understanding the main ideas.
- recognize a biography as one form of factual reading material.
- understand the author's purpose.
- recognize the sequence of events.
- recognize time relationships.
- understand cause and effect.
- distinguish between fact and fiction.
- relate the story to personal experience and values.
- interpret facts and make inferences.
- understand figurative language used in the story.
- interpret the feelings of the characters.
- recognize and understand map symbols.
- locate specific places on a map.
- recognize these new compound words: *peanut, southwest, greenhouse, cookstove, overnight, businessman, birthplace.*
- recognize the suffix *-ous,* as in *famous,* and how to add it to some known root words.
- review the suffix *-al.*
- review the ending *-er* to form agent nouns such as *rider* and recognize some other endings that form agent nouns: *-ist* as in *scientist, -ian* as in *physician,* and *-or* as in *editor.*
- recognize the pronunciation of the noun and verb forms of *use* and *excuse.*
- review words read in *Skill Book 4* by recognizing them in a new book.
- apply phonics skills in reading new words independently.
- develop further skill in using the dictionary.
- recognize the right form of an irregular verb to use in a sentence.
- write words and a paragraph from dictation.

## INTRODUCTION

T: Today you will begin a new book. It is a series of true stories about real people that you can read by yourself. Today, you will read the first story. After you finish it, you will read and answer some questions to see if you understood what you read. The questions are in your skill book.

## I. Reading in *People and Places*

Give S. his copy of *People and Places.* Have S. read the title on the cover and again on the title page. Then ask him to turn to page 3. Ask what this page is called [Contents] and what kind of information it gives [title of each story and page number it begins on]. Ask S. to look down the page and find out how many stories there are. Ask him what else is listed in this table of contents besides the titles of stories [maps].

Ask S. to give the title of the first map [North America] and then to turn to the page it is on [page 5]. Explain that this map introduces the book because the first three stories take place in North America. Some of the later maps that go with those stories show just part of one of the countries, so S. can refer back to this map any time he wants to in order to get the overall picture. Explain also that the names marked on this map include both the place names he has already learned and ones he will learn in the first three stories.

Have S. locate the countries Canada, the United States, and Mexico, and trace the borders between them. Also, have him locate these other place names he has learned: New York, Washington, D.C., Florida, Alabama, Ohio, Texas, and California.

Have S. look at the scale of miles at the bottom of the page. Discuss what this means. Have S. use the edge of a sheet of paper to mark the distance between these points, and then use the scale of miles to estimate the distance:
- from the tip of Texas to the Canadian border [about 1500 miles].
- from Washington, D.C. to the coast of California [about 2400 miles].

Have S. turn back to the table of contents and find the title and page number for the first story. Then have him turn to it.

### STORY 1: George Washington Carver

**Silent reading (pages 7-18 in *People and Places*).** Ask S. to read the story title and subtitle to himself. (Explain that the main title is in large dark type and just under it in smaller type is the subtitle). Tell S. to look at the word list if he needs help in pronouncing any of the words. Then have him read aloud the title and subtitle: *George Washington Carver: From Slave to Scientist.*

Have S. look through the story and notice that it is divided by three subheads in dark type and that there is a map on page 10. Have S. read the title of the map, *Places in George Washington Carver's Life.* Then return to the beginning of the story.

T: In the book *Changes,* you read true stories about the lives of Helen Keller and Martin Luther King Jr. This is also a true story about a person's life. We call that a *biography.*

T: As you read this biography of George Washington Carver, note the kinds of handicaps he had to overcome and what helped him to overcome them. Also, see if you can tell the author's purpose in writing this biography.

Have S. read the new words on pages 7 and 8, first silently and then aloud. Call attention to the sound for *g* in *George* and the sound for *kn* in *known*.

**Note:** In the correlated reader, all new words are listed, but respellings are given only for those that would be particularly hard for S. to sound out unassisted.

**Introduction.** Explain that the first part of the story, up to the first subhead, is an introduction to give some background about conditions at the time George Washington Carver was born. Ask S. to read this part to find out when he was born, where he was born, and how he got his name. When S. has finished, have him answer these questions. Have him find Carver's birthplace on the map on page 10.

Also discuss what Farmer Carver probably meant when he said, "I didn't get much for my best horse." Ask S. to tell what the author says that shows the farmer's words proved not to be true. Point out that in the last paragraph of the introduction, time moves ahead from 1864 to the present. Have S. summarize the facts that are given about George Washington Carver in this introduction.

T: You know something of the conditions under which George Washington Carver was born. And you know that he became a great scientist. What do you think the rest of the biography will be about? [S: How he became great.]

**Getting an education.** Have S. tell where this part of the story begins and ends. Have him read the new words first silently and then aloud. Then ask him to read this part to find out where George went to school and what difficulties he had to overcome to get an education. When S. has finished reading, have him answer these questions. Have S. locate on the map the states where George went to school. Ask S. to summarize the facts that are given about George Washington Carver in this part of the biography. Have S. figure out what George's age was at the end of this part of the story [about 32]. Point out that, except for the last paragraph in the introduction, the story is told in the order in which things happened.

**Teaching at Tuskegee.** Ask S. to read this part of the story to find out what problems Professor Carver found at Tuskegee Institute and how he overcame them. Remind S. to read any new words at the top of a page before reading that page. When S. has finished reading this part, tell him that you will have him answer the questions later. Ask him to read the new words aloud and to locate Tuskegee Institute on the map.

**Becoming famous.** Ask S. to read the rest of the story to find out what made George Carver famous. When S. has finished reading, have him answer this question. Ask him to read the new words aloud. Ask S. to tell why he thinks Carver is remembered as the "Peanut Man." Have S. locate the Carver National Monument on the map.

**Study helps (page 138 in *Skill Book 4*).** Have S. read aloud the titles *Lesson 22* and *Study Helps for People and Places*.

---

**Lesson 22**                        *Study Helps for People and Places*

### George Washington Carver

done (dun)    gone (gawn)    steal

**Discuss the answers to these questions.**

1. What handicaps did George Carver have as a child?
2. What helped him overcome these handicaps?
3. Why did George Carver accept the job offer from Tuskegee Institute?
4. What problems did George Carver find at Tuskegee Institute?
5. What did Professor Carver do to overcome these problems?
6. Why did Professor Carver think it was important to find new uses for peanuts, sweet potatoes, and pecans?
7. Why did Congress make a national monument of George Carver's birthplace?

**Write a short answer to each question.**

1. What skills did George Carver learn as a boy that helped him get through school?
   *Cooking and washing clothes*
2. In what three states did George Carver go to school?
   *Missouri, Kansas, and Iowa*
3. Where is Tuskegee Institute? *Alabama*
4. Who did George Carver turn to when he had a problem? *God*

**Circle the right form of the verb to complete the sentence.**

**Example:** I have not (do, did, ~~done~~) my homework yet.

1. Night riders (steal, ~~stole~~, stolen) George Carver's mother.
2. The Carvers were the only parents that George ever (know, ~~knew~~, known).
3. George felt that his work was never (do, did, ~~done~~).
4. The farmers were (show, showed, ~~shown~~) how to improve their soil.
5. Professor Carver (takes, ~~took~~, taken) peanuts into his lab and locked the door.
6. The farmers will (~~grow~~, grew, grown) a different crop next year.
7. Have you ever (go, went, ~~gone~~) to the Carver Museum at Tuskegee?

**138**    Lesson 22

---

Also, have S. read aloud the heading *George Washington Carver* and the new words. Ask him to read the directions for the first set of questions. Have him read each question silently and then aloud. Then have him give his answer. If he doesn't remember an answer, have him tell in which part of the story he might find the answer. Then have him scan that part to find the answer.

Have S. do the second exercise by himself. Tell him that he may refer to the story if he needs to. Check his answers, and have him correct any errors.

Go over the directions and example for the third exercise with S. Then have him do it by himself. Check his work by having him read aloud each sentence with the verb he circled. Have him correct any errors.

**Oral reading.** Ask S. to read aloud the first two paragraphs under *Getting an Education*. Discuss why the neighbors called George the "plant doctor." Have S. read the next three paragraphs aloud. Discuss what is meant by the expression "it's high time."

Have S. read aloud the first three paragraphs under *Teaching at Tuskegee*. Discuss what Professor Carver meant by "cookstove chemistry."

**Relating the story to everyday life.** Discuss the following questions:

1. What do you think is the main purpose of this biography of George Washington Carver? (Bring out that the main purpose seems to be to show the difficulties George Washington Carver faced throughout his life and how he overcame them. In order to do this, the author gives an account of the major events and turning points in Carver's life from birth to death.)

2. Does the author seem to give a realistic picture of Carver? Do you think the facts are accurate? How can you tell?

3. What help or inspiration did you get from reading this biography? Did you like it as well as the one about Helen Keller or the one about Martin Luther King? Why or why not?

4. Can there be different biographies about the same person? (Bring out that different authors may choose to emphasize different things about a person's life. You may also want to take this opportunity to explain the difference between a *biography,* written by someone else, and an *autobiography,* written by the person himself.)

5. What makes a person famous? Is being famous the same as being important? Can we always tell whether a person who is famous today will be remembered 50 or 100 years from now?

**Map study.** Have S. compare the map on page 10 with the map of North America on page 5. Have him indicate on the map of North America what part of the United States is shown on the page 10 map.

Ask S. to look at the direction marker on the page 10 map. Review what the direction marker means and what the letters *N, E, S, W* stand for. Explain that when there is *no* direction marker on a map, then north is at the top, the same as on this map. Have S. point to each direction on the map. Then have him move his finger from south to north and from east to west. Have him answer these questions.

1. Which of the states in which George went to school was the farthest north? Which one was the farthest west?

2. Is Tuskegee Institute northeast or southeast of where George was born?

3. Is Simpson College north or south of Carver's birthplace?

4. What state is directly east of Kansas?

Have S. look at the scale of miles. Review what it means. Have S. mark the distance between these points on the edge of a sheet of paper and then use the scale to estimate the distance in miles.

1. From Carver's birthplace to the nearest border of Texas [about 250 miles].

2. From Iowa State University to Tuskegee Institute [about 750 miles].

3. From the eastern border of Kansas to its western border [about 400 miles].

4. From Tuskegee Institute to Washington, D.C. [about 675 miles].

Point out that the actual traveling distance between two points on a map may be quite a bit longer. Roads zigzag to go from town to town, go around mountains, and so on, instead of going in a straight line.

**Illustrations.** Have S. look at the photographs and read their captions. Have him estimate Carver's age in each photo. Have S. tell how old Carver was when he died and how many years ago it was.

# II. Skills Practice

## PRACTICE 1: Compound Words

Write these new compound words from the story: *peanut, southwest, greenhouse, cookstove, overnight, businessmen, birthplace.* Have S. read each compound word and tell the two words that were put together to make it.

Write these words for practice in reading new compound words: *cookbook, southeast, northwest, northeast, birthmark, birthstone, businesswoman, businesslike.* Have S. read each compound word and tell the two words it is made from.

## PRACTICE 2: Suffix *-al*

Write *seasonal,* and have S. read it. Have him tell the root word and the ending. Write *season* in front of *seasonal.* Under *season,* write these words in a column: *recreation, constitution, occasion, agriculture.* Ask S. to read each root word and tell what the word would be with the ending *-al* added. As he answers, write *recreational, constitutional, occasional, agricultural.* Point out that the final silent *e* in *agriculture* is dropped before *-al* is added. Also, point out that the root words are nouns and that adding the ending *-al* changes them to adjectives. Have S. read both columns of words again.

## PRACTICE 3: Suffix *-ous*

Write *famous,* and have S. read it. Ask him to tell what he thinks the root word is. Write *fame* in front of *famous.* Ask what ending was added and what change was made in the root word. Underline the ending *-ous.*

Under *fame,* write these words in a column: *joy, danger, mountain, grace, courage.* Have S. read each root word and tell what the word would be with the ending *-ous* added. As he answers, write *joyous, dangerous, mountainous, gracious, courageous.* Explain that in *gracious,* the *e* is changed to *i.* Ask S. if he can tell why the *e* is left in *courageous* [so that we will know that *g* stands for /j/].

Point out that the root words are nouns and that the ending *-ous* is added to change them to adjectives.

Write out the exercise below for S. to do. Ask him to fill in each blank with an adjective ending in *-ous*. Have him complete the exercise by himself. Then have him read all of the sentences aloud.

1. George Washington Carver was not looking for *fame,* but his work with the peanut made him _____.
2. Molly usually spends her summer holiday in a _____ place because she likes to climb *mountains.*
3. Gene knew it would be _____ to go to the edge of the river. But he was willing to walk into *danger* to help the wounded man.
4. Gordon Chang's graduation was a _____ occasion for his family. Their *joy* did not last long, however, because Gordon soon had to go to war.

## PRACTICE 4: Suffixes -er, -or, -ist, -ian

Write *owner* and have S. read it. Have him tell the root word and ending. Write *own* in front of *owner.* Under *own* write *farm, ride, garden, labor.* Have S. read each one and tell what it would be with the ending *-er* added. As he answers, write *farmer, rider, gardener, laborer.*

T: The ending *-er* can be added to many words to make them mean *a person that does something.* The ending *-er* is the most common ending with this meaning. But there are other endings that can be added to words to make them mean a person that does something. You have already learned some words with these endings.

Write *editor,* and have S. read it. Have him tell the root word and the ending [*-or*]. Write *edit* in front of *editor.* Under *edit,* write *act, visit, govern, direct, educate.* Have S. tell what each word would be with the ending *-or* added. As he answers, write *actor, visitor, governor, director, educator.* Call attention to the dropping of final silent *e* in *educate* before *-or.* Also, point out that we have to learn which words are written with *-or* since it doesn't sound any different from *-er.* Have S. read both forms of each word.

At the head of two columns, write *science* and *scientist.* Have S. read both words. Underline *-ist,* and explain that this is the ending. Sometimes *-ist* is added directly to a root word, and sometimes the root word is changed somewhat. Under *science,* write *art, type, drug, motor, chemistry.* Ask S. to tell the word ending with *-ist* that means a person who works with each of these. As he answers, write *artist, typist, druggist, motorist, chemist.* Ask S. to tell which have *-ist* added with no change in the root word, which have final silent *e* dropped, which has the final consonant doubled, and which has the root word changed when *-ist* is added. Have S. read both forms of each word.

At the head of two columns, write *music* and *musician.* Have S. read both words. Explain that the ending *-ian* is often added to words that end with *c.* Then, *cian* at the end of the word is pronounced /shun/. Underline *cian,* and next to it write the respelling *shun.* Under *music,* write *electric, magic,*

*politics.* Have S. tell what the person is called who works with these. As he answers, write *electrician, magician, politician.* Point out that *s* is dropped from *politics* before the ending is added. Also, write *physician,* and have S. read it. Point out that we do not use the root word *physic* very much but usually add an ending like *-al* to make *physical.*

**Note:** You may want to have S. write the words in Practices 3 and 4 in his notebook as you go along so that he has a record of how they are spelled.

## PRACTICE 5: Pronunciation of use and excuse

Write sentences 1-2 below. Have S. read the first sentence. He will probably pronounce *use* correctly in context. In front of the sentence, write *use (n.).* Remind S. that *n.* is the dictionary abbreviation for *noun* if he doesn't remember. Have S. tell how *s* is pronounced in *use* when it is a noun. Write $\bar{u}s$ next to *use (n.).*

Follow the same procedure for the second sentence. Write *use (v.)* and then the phonetic respelling $\bar{u}z.$

1. The farmers thought there was no *use* to plant more peanuts.
2. Professor Carver found new ways to *use* the peanut.

Write sentences 3-4 below. Go over these sentences in the same way as the first pair of sentences.

3. There is no *excuse* for such rudeness.
4. The man did not *excuse* himself when he pushed in front of the other passengers.

Finally, point out that when the letters *use* come at the end of a verb, the *s* is usually pronounced /z/. Give as examples *refuse, confuse, abuse.*

## PRACTICE 6: Using the Dictionary

Review the steps in locating a word quickly in the dictionary:
1. Note the word's beginning letter.
2. Open the dictionary to words beginning with that letter.
3. Use the guide words at the top of the page to find the right page.
4. Glance down the page to find the word in alphabetical order.

Say each of these words for S. to find in the dictionary: *rotate, product, boll weevil, famous, acre, handicap.*

When S. finds the word, have him read the definitions to find out how many meanings the word has and what part of speech each meaning is. Then have him tell which of the meanings the word had in the story or study helps. For *handicap,* also have S. note how the word is spelled when the ending *-ed* is added [*handicapped*].

For further practice, say the following words for S. to locate: *agriculture, degree, professor, gone, gracious, steal.* Have him tell the part of speech for *steal* and read the other forms of the verb [*stole, stolen*]. Have him give the first definition. Then tell him the spelling for the word *steel* and have him locate it. Have him contrast the meanings of *steel* and *steal.*

# III. Writing

## CHECK HOMEWORK: Page 137

Have S. correct any errors in the first exercise and then read each list of words in the correct alphabetical order.

In the second exercise, go over any needed corrections with S. Have him note why any words he marked incorrectly would or would not come between the two guide words.

Then have S. read each of the entry words with more than one syllable that he copied from the sample dictionary page. If he copied a one-syllable word, read it to him, and have him listen for the number of beats. If he omitted some of the words with more than one syllable, have him look at the sample page again. Have him read each entry word aloud and note the number of syllables in each. When he finds one that he omitted, have him add it to his list.

Have S. give his answer to the last question. If it is wrong, refer him to the sample page, and have him look where the stress mark is placed in each of the respellings. *Weekday* may be confusing as it has a secondary stress. But the main stress is on the first syllable in all of the words.

## WRITING LESSON (In Notebook)

Have S. write the titles *Lesson 22* and *Words*. Then have him number from 1 to 20 in two columns.

**Words.** Dictate the words below for S. to write. Give a sentence for *steal*. When he has finished, check his work, and have him correct any errors.

| | | |
|---|---|---|
| 1. tiny | 8. known | 15. rest |
| 2. slave | 9. famous | 16. travel |
| 3. hungry | 10. soil | 17. birthplace |
| 4. offer | 11. sweet | 18. gone |
| 5. death | 12. material | 19. done |
| 6. peanut | 13. apart | 20. steal |
| 7. else | 14. use ($\bar{u}$s) | |

**Sentences.** Help S. study these words: *acre, scientist, Missouri, monument*. Then have S. write the title *Sentences*. Tell him that you will dictate a paragraph from the story and that he should write it in paragraph form, without numbering the sentences.

Dictate the last paragraph in the story. First, have S. listen to the whole paragraph. Then read it sentence by sentence for him to write. Read each sentence only once.

Check what S. has written, and have him correct any errors, including those in punctuation and capitalization. Then have him write the title *Study* and any words he missed in the word and paragraph dictation.

## HOMEWORK

Ask S. to write a paragraph about "Ways That Carver's Work Helped Farmers in the South." Help him prepare by having him look over the story and select topics he will cover, such as improving the soil, rotating crops, and increasing the market for peanuts, sweet potatoes, and pecans by finding new uses for them.

Or, you may prefer to give S. a choice of writing a paragraph about "What Impressed Me Most about the Life of George Washington Carver."

Whichever assignment you give, encourage S. also to read the story again at home and to study any words that he missed in the dictation.

## CHECKING PROGRESS

**Comprehension skills.** Your student's responses to the questions in the Study Helps for this lesson will help you evaluate his progress in comprehension skills. His responses on the first set of questions will indicate his ability in the following skills:

—recognizing main ideas.
—understanding cause and effect.
—interpreting facts and making inferences.

His responses on the second set of questions will indicate his ability to recall important facts or locate specific facts by scanning a page.

**Study skills.** You can evaluate your student's progress in using a dictionary and reading a map. When you check the homework, you will be able to evaluate his ability to organize information—no matter which assignment you gave.

**Word recognition.** The last exercise in the Study Helps and the Skills Practice exercises will enable you to note your student's progress in recognizing words outside the context of the story. His general comprehension of the story will also indicate his ability to recall old words that he should know by sight. If he had difficulty answering questions in the Study Helps, have him read several paragraphs in the story aloud, and note his accuracy in word recognition. Note the types of errors he makes. Does he omit words, confuse similar words, or substitute words? If he has many errors, plan reinforcement exercises for the recognition of the words he most frequently miscalls.

## MEETING INDIVIDUAL NEEDS

Use some of the suggestions given in Lesson 20 for the reinforcement of word recognition skills. Make flash cards for any of the words that S. miscalled when reading orally. Use these for a short practice session. Then have him reread the same paragraph orally. Note whether he has made any improvement. Use slip strips for recognition of phrases and more rapid reading of short sentences. Encourage S. to give full attention to what he is reading.

If S. needs more work on sequence of events, write the sentences below, without the numbers, on separate cards. Mix them up, and give them to S. Explain that they are sentences that summarize the events in George Washington Carver's life, as told in the story he read, but they are mixed up. Have him arrange the cards in order. Let S. refer to the story if he needs to. Also, help him understand how to use clues in the sentences themselves to put them in logical order.

1. George Washington Carver was born in Missouri in 1864 during the Civil War.

2. George and his mother were stolen from their slave owners, the Carvers.

3. The tiny baby was later returned for a horse, but he never saw his mother again.

4. As a small boy, George lived with the Carvers and did housework and gardening.

5. When he was 12, George left home to go to a school for blacks in a town eight miles away.

6. A friendly black woman let George live with her and help her with laundry and making medicines from plants.

7. After three years, George left Missouri for Kansas, where he worked his way through school as a cook and gardener.

8. At 22, George graduated with honors from a high school in Kansas.

9. After high school, George wanted to go to college in Kansas, but the college president refused to admit him because he was black.

10. George farmed by himself for three years on poor land, where he decided to study agriculture.

11. First, George went to Simpson College in Iowa.

12. George studied agriculture and plant science at Iowa State University.

13. After graduating from college, George stayed at Iowa State for two years, teaching and working on a higher degree.

14. In 1896, George Carver accepted a job offer from Booker T. Washington to be the head of Tuskegee Institute's new department of agriculture.

15. At Tuskegee, Professor Carver made a lab from things he and his students found in trash cans.

16. Professor Carver began showing farmers how to improve their soil and rotate their crops.

17. Some farmers began rotating their cotton crops with sweet potatoes and peanuts.

18. After the boll weevil killed their cotton, many more Alabama farmers planted peanuts.

19. Farmers were angry because they had raised more peanuts than they could sell.

20. In his lab, Carver found new uses for the peanut so that farmers would have a market.

21. Professor Carver spent the rest of his life at Tuskegee, finding more new ways to use peanuts, sweet potatoes, and pecans.

22. Peanuts, sweet potatoes, and pecans became important money crops in the South.

23. Before Carver's death, the George Washington Carver Museum was opened at Tuskegee Institute.

24. George Washington Carver died in 1943.

25. After his death, Congress made a national monument of his birthplace in southwest Missouri.

In *Focus on Phonics-4*, the last section of the workbook (Practices 22-24) cover irregular spellings for the sounds /ch/ and /sh/, words with the schwa sound in unstressed syllables, words with the final syllable *-le,* and compound words. You may begin using these exercises now, taking them at any pace that seems suitable for your student. Or, you may decide to finish this workbook after completing the correlated reader.

**For Lesson 22-B** ⟶

---

**Terry Fox**

**Discuss the answers to these questions.**

1. What made Terry Fox feel sorry for himself?
2. What happened to help him change his outlook on life?
3. Why do you think Terry's marathon brought in money for cancer research?
4. Why didn't Terry take the shortest way across Canada?
5. Why did Terry stop his run?
6. Do you think Terry's run across Canada was a good idea? Why or why not?

**Write a short answer to each question.**

1. What was Terry Fox's run across Canada called? *Marathon of Hope*
2. From what ocean did he start his run? *The Atlantic*
   What ocean did he hope to reach? *The Pacific*
3. How many miles did Terry try to run each day? *26 miles*
4. For about how many months did Terry run? *Five months*
5. How many miles across Canada did Terry run? *3,339 miles*
6. In what province did Terry's run end? *Ontario*
7. How much money did the Marathon of Hope raise for cancer research? *$24 million*

**Write the missing ending in each blank.**

*-ful, -less, -ly, -ment, -ness*

1. When he first learned that he had cancer, Terry felt hope *less* .
2. Terry needed cancer treat *ment* .
3. Until he learned to walk with his artificial leg, Terry felt help *less* .
4. During his training, Terry ran exact *ly* 3,419 miles.
5. Terry's running was pain *ful* to watch.
6. Terry had to stop his marathon because of pain and weak *ness* .
7. After cancer struck a second time, Terry tried to keep a cheer *ful* outlook.
8. Terry said, "Maybe the sick *ness* beat my body, but it couldn't touch my spirit."

*Lesson 22* **139**

**People and Places, Story 2**
**Skill Book 4, Page 139**

## OBJECTIVES

To help your student:

- use a table of contents.
- read story 2 in *People and Places* independently, understanding the main ideas of this factual article.
- increase the speed of silent reading.
- recognize cause and effect.
- interpret facts and make inferences.
- predict outcomes.
- understand figurative language in the story.
- distinguish between fact and fiction.
- interpret the feelings of persons in the story.
- relate the story to personal experiences and values.
- understand the author's purpose.
- recognize time relationships.
- recall important facts.
- scan the story to locate specific details.
- review words learned in *Skill Book 4* by recognizing them in a new book.
- apply phonics skills in reading new words independently.
- recognize the new compound words *outlook* and *halfway* and review other compound words.
- review the suffixes *-ful, -less, -ly, -ment, -ness, -ous, -tion*.
- recognize when the abbreviation *St.* stands for *Street* and when it stands for *Saint*.
- distinguish between homonyms, such as *whole* and *hole*.
- read orally with expression.
- develop further skill in using a dictionary.
- determine directions on a map.
- locate specific places on a map.
- write words and paragraphs from dictation.
- write a short summary of the story.

## INTRODUCTION

T: Today you will read the second story in *People and Places* and discuss the study questions in the skill book. The first story you read in this book was a biography, that is, the story of a real person's whole life. The second story is not about the person's whole life, but it is a true story about an event in his life. Look at the table of contents in *People and Places*. Find the page number for story 2, and then turn to that page.

## I. Reading in *People and Places*

### STORY 2: Terry Fox

**Silent reading (pages 19-29 in *People and Places*).** Ask S. to read the story title and subtitle to himself. Tell him to look at the word list if he needs help in pronouncing a word. Then have him read aloud the title and subtitle, *Terry Fox: Marathon of Hope*.

Have S. read the new words on pages 19-22, first silently and then aloud. Ask S. to read up to the division marked by the three asterisks and find out who the story is about and what special thing that person was trying to accomplish. When S. has finished reading, have him answer these questions. Also, have him tell why Terry Fox was running in the Marathon of Hope and what made it especially hard for him to run.

Ask S. to look at the map on pages 24-25 and locate the place where Terry began his run and the place where he hoped to finish it. Have him tell in what part of Canada each of these places is located.

Ask S. to read the rest of the story to himself to find out if Terry ran as far as he hoped to run and some of the things that happened along the way. Remind S. to read any new words at the top of a page before reading that page. Ask S. to let you know when he has finished reading the story. Time his reading. He will probably finish in 10 minutes or less. When he has finished, have him answer the questions you asked. On the map on pages 24-25, have S. trace the route of Terry's run and locate the place where it ended.

**Study helps (page 139 in *Skill Book 4*).** Ask S. to read aloud the title *Terry Fox* and the directions for the first set of questions. Have him read each question silently and then aloud. Then have him give his answer. If he gives an incorrect answer, refer him to the page in the story on which the answer is given, and have him scan the page to find it. (The answers to numbers 3 and 6 will depend on the student's own experiences and values.)

Have S. do the second exercise by himself. Let him refer to the story if he needs to. Check his answers, and have him correct any errors.

**Note:** Have S. do the last exercise on this page after the Skills Practice section of this lesson.

**Oral reading and discussion.** Have S. read aloud page 22 (beginning with the paragraph just above the asterisks), page 23, and the last page of the story, page 29. Notice his phrasing, intonation, and expression in oral reading. After class, make a written record of your evaluation, but do not comment on it now to S. except to compliment him in some way on his reading.

Discuss these questions:

1. What did the newspaper writer say Terry's run was like? Why did he use that comparison?

2. What did Terry mean by his statement, after visiting people in a cancer hospital, "I decided to do all that my body could do. I would push myself to the limit. Somewhere the hurting must stop"?
3. Why was Terry considered a hero?
4. What was the author's purpose in writing the story?
5. Did you like this story? Why or why not?
6. What in the story helps you understand how Terry felt?
7. What do you think is the best way to help someone with a physical handicap or incurable illness?
8. What has been done in recent years to make life somewhat easier for people with physical handicaps?

**Map study.** Have S. look at the map on pages 24-25. Ask him to locate these places: the Atlantic Ocean, the Pacific Ocean, the southern border of Canada, the Great Lakes, the northwestern border of Canada, and the provinces that are named on the map. Explain that provinces in Canada are something like states in the United States, that there are 10 provinces, but only those mentioned in the story are named on the map.

(You may also want to have S. locate some of these same points on the map of North America on page 5, as well as St. John's, Vancouver, and Thunder Bay.)

If at all possible, have available a map of Canada that shows at least major highways, cities, and towns. Have S. trace the approximate route of Terry's run on this map so that he gets a sense of why the distance of Terry's winding route between St. John's and Thunder Bay was much longer than a straight line between these points.

# II. Skills Practice

## PRACTICE 1: Compound Words

Write the new compound words *outlook* and *halfway*. Have S. read each compound word and tell the two words that were put together to make it.

In a column, write *line, doors, law, number, put, run, side, standing*. Ask S. to put *out* in front of each word and tell what the compound word would be. As he answers, write *out* in front of each word. Also, have S. tell which syllable is stressed in each compound word.

Make flash cards for two sets of words, using different colored paper or ink. In set 1, write *blue, short, ball, book, pea, south, green, cook, over, business, birth*. In set 2, write *print, hand, room, keeping, nut, west, house, stove, night, men, place*. Have S. match a card from set 1 with a card from set 2 to make a compound word until all of the cards are used.

## PRACTICE 2: Homonyms

Write these pairs of words: *whole, hole; week, weak*. Have S. read each pair of words and give a sentence to show the meaning of each word.

Add these pairs of words: *flour, flower; eight, ate; write, right*. Have S. read them.

T: I will read a sentence that uses one of these words. Listen for the word, and tell the right spelling for the meaning of the word in the sentence. (Read the sentences below.)
1. After I finished the marathon, I felt very *weak*.
2. George loved each *flower* in his garden.
3. The doctors had to take off Terry's *right* leg.
4. Terry Fox pulled the *whole* nation together.
5. George walked *eight* miles to town to start school.

## PRACTICE 3: Review of Suffixes

**Suffixes -ment, -ous, -ful, -ly, -less, -ness.** In a column, write *government, courageous, painful, exactly, hopeless, weakness*. Ask S. to read each word and tell the root word. Underline the root word. Have S. tell what ending has been added to each word. Write the endings in a row above the column of words.

In another column, write *real, treat, fame, cheer, sick, friend, improve*. Ask S. to add one of the endings to each of the root words. Write the new word as he says it.

**Suffix -tion.** Write the pairs of words shown below. Have S. read each pair and use each word in a sentence.

| | |
|---|---|
| *act* | *action* |
| *correct* | *correction* |
| *invent* | *invention* |
| *product* | *production* |
| *inspire* | *inspiration* |

Discuss these points:
1. The part that is the same in all the words in the second column [-*tion*] and how it is pronounced [/shun/].
2. The ending that is added to each root word [-*ion*, -*tion*, or -*ation*] and any change in the root word.
3. The way the pronunciation for *ir* changes from *inspire* to *inspiration*.
4. Which syllable is stressed in each root word and in its -*tion* form (Note that in all of the -*tion* words, the stressed syllable is just before -*tion*.)

## PRACTICE 4: Abbreviation *St.* for *Street* and *Saint*

Write *St. John's* and *Oak St.* Have S. read each item and tell what the abbreviation *St.* stands for. Point out that, in a name, it is easy to tell whether *St.* stands for *Saint* or *Street*. At the beginning of a name, *St.* stands for *Saint*. At the end of a name, *St.* stands for *Street*. Write the phrases below, and have S. read them.

| | |
|---|---|
| *at St. Mary's Church* | *from St. Joseph, Missouri* |
| *at 115 Maple St.* | *along Bridge St.* |
| *in St. Paul's Hospital* | *on South Porter St.* |

## PRACTICE 5: Using the Dictionary

Review how to find a word quickly in the dictionary. Then say each word below for S. to locate. Before he looks for the word, have him tell its first three letters. After he finds the word, call attention to the point listed below.

1. *hero*—spelling of plural form
2. *postage*—sound for *g*
3. *hospital*—number of syllables
4. *ocean*—sound for *ce*
5. *artificial*—sound for *ci*, stressed syllable

# III. Writing

## CHECK HOMEWORK

Have S. read aloud the paragrpah he wrote in his notebook. First, comment on the content. Note whether S. kept to the subject, included all the important facts, organized them well, and expressed them clearly. Praise him for what he did well, and make constructive suggestions for improvement. Then, check for spelling, sentence structure, and punctuation. Ask S. to make any needed corrections at home, rewriting the paragraph if necessary.

## WRITING LESSON (In Notebook)

**Words.** Have S. write the title *Words* and number from 1 to 20 in two columns. Dictate the words below for him to write. Give a sentence for *whole* and *weak*. Check your student's work, and have him correct any errors.

| | | | |
|---|---|---|---|
| 1. dip | 6. honk | 11. painful | 16. hospital |
| 2. twist | 7. real | 12. exact | 17. treatment |
| 3. hop | 8. lungs | 13. whole | 18. postage |
| 4. skip | 9. hero | 14. spirit | 19. inspire |
| 5. cheer | 10. weak | 15. stamp | 20. outlook |

**Sentences.** Have S. write the title *Sentences.* Tell him that you will dictate two paragraphs from the story. He will write them in paragraph form. Dictate the last two paragraphs of the story. Have S. listen to each paragraph. Then dictate it sentence by sentence.

Check what S. has written, and have him correct any errors, including those in punctuation and capitalization. Have him write the title *Study* and any words he missed in the word and paragraph dictation.

**Alphabetical order.** Write the following words in a column, and have S. write them in alphabetical order in his notebook: *Canada, Canadian, Columbia, British, Newfoundland, Vancouver, Ontario, Atlantic, Pacific, Quebec, Thunder Bay.*

## WRITTEN EXERCISE: Page 139 in *Skill Book 4*

Have S. read the directions for the last exercise on page 139 of the skill book and then do the exercise independently. When he has finished, have him read each of the sentences aloud. Have him correct any errors. Note the type of error so that you can plan a reinforcement exercise for that particular ending.

## HOMEWORK (In Notebook)

Ask S. to write a short summary of the story. Suggest that he write it like a news article. Review the Five *W's* that a news article should tell: *who, what, where, when,* and *why.* Tell him he may look at the story to make sure of facts and may use a dictionary for the spelling of words.

Also, encourage S. to read the story again at home and to study any words that he missed in the dictation.

## CHECKING PROGRESS

**Comprehension skills.** Your student's responses on the first set of questions in the Study Helps will indicate his ability in the following skills:

—interpreting the feelings of a person in the story.
—understanding the author's purpose.
—relating the story to his own experience and values.
—interpreting facts and making inferences.

His responses on the second set of questions will indicate his ability to recall important facts or to locate specific facts by scanning a page.

**Study skills.** You can note your student's progress in finding words in the dictionary, in alphabetizing, and in reading a map. When you check the homework for this lesson, you will be able to evaluate his ability to organize main ideas in a summary of the story.

**Word recognition.** Your student's ability to read the new words in the story will indicate his progress in word recognition skills. Does he apply his knowledge of phonics, syllables, word endings, and word relationships? Does he seem confident in pronouncing place names that may be new to him? Your student has learned the basic skills. Now is the time to help him realize that he can read almost any word he encounters.

## MEETING INDIVIDUAL NEEDS

If S. needed considerable help in this lesson, plan a review before going on to Lesson 23. Look over the list of skills at the beginning of this manual. Note those in which S. needs more practice, particularly in phonics and word recognition. Use any of the suggestions given in earlier lessons for reinforcing these skills. Games, crossword puzzles, and supplementary reading materials will be especially helpful.

**People and Places, Story 3**
**Skill Book 4, Page 140**

## OBJECTIVES

To help your student:

- use a table of contents.
- read story 3 in *People and Places* independently, understanding the main ideas and supporting details.
- distinguish between fact and fiction.
- recognize the sequence of events.
- understand cause and effect.
- understand time and place relationships.
- visualize the setting and main characters from descriptions given in the story.
- understand the author's purpose.
- interpret facts and make inferences.
- interpret the feelings of the characters.
- relate the story to personal experience and values.
- classify words according to similarities in meaning.
- recognize multiple meanings of words.
- review words read in *Skill Book 4* by recognizing them in a new book.
- apply phonics skills in reading new words independently.
- recognize new compound words *rowboat* and *waterfall*.
- develop further skill in using the dictionary.
- locate specific places on a map.
- understand an historical map.
- relate a route marked on a map to events in the story.
- write words and paragraphs from dictation.
- learn how to keep a simple diary or journal.

## INTRODUCTION

T: Today you will read the third story in *People and Places* and discuss the study questions in the skill book. This is also a true story. Look at the table of contents in *People and Places*. Find the page number for story 3, and turn to that page.

## I. Reading in *People and Places*

### STORY 3: Sacajawea

**Silent reading (pages 30-43 in *People and Places*).** Ask S. to read the story title and subtitle to himself. Tell him to look at the word list if he needs help in pronouncing a word. Then have him read aloud the title and subtitle, *Sacajawea: Across the Shining Mountains*.

Have S. look through the story and notice that it is divided by five subheads and that there are two maps, one on page 32 and one on pages 36-37. Then return to the beginning of the story.

Have S. read the new words on pages 30-31, first silently and then aloud. Tell him there are a number of unfamiliar names in the story and he may refer to the respellings as often as needed for help in pronunciation.

Have S. read the first part of the story—up to the first subhead—to himself to find out where and when it took place and the names of the characters. When S. has finished, have him answer those questions, plus these:

1. Where were the two white men trying to go?
2. Why could Sacajawea be of help to them?
3. What was the name of the place Sacajawea asked them to take her so that she could guide them from there?

On the map on pages 36-37, have S. locate these points, but do not have him read the captions next to them at this time:

1. Fort Mandan. (Ask S. what state this area now is.)
2. The Missouri River.
3. Three Forks.
4. The Rocky Mountains.
5. The Pacific Ocean.

**The Louisiana Territory.** Have S. read this subhead and the new words on pages 33-34, first silently and then aloud. Ask him to read the second part of the story—up to the next subhead—to himself to find out where Lewis and Clark started their journey and what its purpose was. When S. has finished reading, have him answer these questions. Also, have him tell what the Louisiana Territory was.

On the map on page 32, have S. read the title, *The United States in 1803*. Then have him identify these areas:

1. The United States in 1803 and other lands owned by the United States at that time. (Note that all U.S. land then was east of the Mississippi River.)
2. Lands owned by the British and Spanish.
3. Louisiana Territory. (Have S. tell who President Thomas Jefferson bought it from and in what year.)

Also, point out Oregon Country to S., and tell him he will learn more about it later in the story.

On the map on pages 36-37, have S. read the title, *The Lewis and Clark Expedition*. Have S. locate these points and, this time, read any captions next to them:

1. The Mississippi River.
2. St. Louis (caption).
3. The Missouri River.
4. Fort Mandan (two captions).

**Remainder of story.** Ask S. to read the rest of the story to himself to find out if the expedition was successful, what hardships were encountered, and how Sacajawea helped. When he has finished reading the story, have him tell whether the expedition was successful and tell briefly the types of hardships the expedition encountered. But do not go into detail at this time about the hardships or the ways Sacajawea helped the expedition.

**Study helps (page 140 in *Skill Book 4*).** Have S. read aloud the titles *Lesson 23* and *Study Helps for People and Places*.

Also, have S. read aloud the title *Sacajawea* and the directions for the first set of questions. Have him read each question silently and then aloud. Then have him give his answer. If he doesn't remember an answer, have him tell in which part of the story he might find the answer. Then have him scan that part to find the answer.

Have S. do the second exercise by himself. Tell him to answer as many questions as he can without looking back at the story. Check his answers, and have him scan the story to find the correct answer for any question he didn't answer or answered incorrectly.

**Note:** Have S. do the last exercise on this page after the Skills Practice section of this lesson.

**Oral reading and discussion.** Ask S. to give some words that describe Sacajawea's character and to tell something from the story that shows that trait. Some of the traits that should be brought out are: brave, friendly, resourceful, clever, observant, trustworthy, loyal.

Have S. tell the mental picture he has of each of the following episodes. After he describes the episode or setting, have him read aloud the part in the story that tells about it.

1. The Mandan Indian village (part 1, par. 1 and 7)
2. The exploring party traveling up the Missouri River (part 3, par. 1)
3. Sacajawea saves the equipment (part 3, par. 4)
4. Captain Clark saves Sacajawea (part 3, par. 5-6)
5. The exploring party reaches Three Forks (part 3, par. 7)
6. Sacajawea meets her brother (part 3, par. 9-11)
7. Climbing the Rocky Mountains (part 4, par. 1-3)
8. The first sight of the Pacific Ocean (part 4, par. 6)

As S. reads aloud, note his phrasing, intonation, and expression. Comment on what he does well.

**Relating the story to everyday life.** Discuss with S. any of these questions that seem suitable.

1. Did you like this story? Why or why not? What part did you like best?
2. Where does most of the information we know about Sacajawea come from? Do you think the conversations in this story were actually recorded by Lewis and Clark, or did the author make them up?
3. What do you think is the author's purpose in writing this story? (Bring out that the author is emphasizing how an Indian woman contributed to the success of an important expedition and why she deserves a place in American history.)

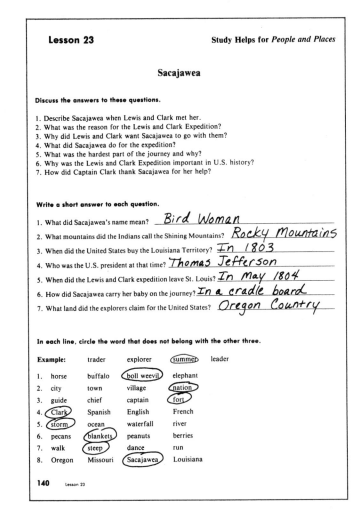

4. Why do you think there are conflicting stories about what happened to Sacajawea after the expedition? Would you like to know more about her?
5. What is meant by *history?* How are past events passed along to others? Do you think all accounts of past events are completely true? Why or why not?
6. How can a writer of history give his opinion and interpretation even if he sticks to the facts? [By selecting what he thinks is important to write about.]

**Map study.** On the map on pages 36-37, have S. trace the entire route of the Lewis and Clark Expedition, telling in his own words what happened at the points marked along the way and reading any captions he has not yet read. As he proceeds, have him also tell when the explorers were traveling by water—and the names of the rivers they were on—and when they were on land. (Note that the dotted line means they were on land.) S. should name the Mississippi, Missouri, Snake, and Columbia Rivers. He should note that the explorers had to carry their boats around the Great Falls and that they crossed the Rocky Mountains on land.

Ask S. what direction is at the top of the map. If necessary, remind him that when no direction marker is given, then north is at the top. Have him tell the general direction Lewis and Clark were going from St. Louis to the Mandan village [northwest], the direction the explorers were traveling most of the time from Fort Mandan to the Pacific Ocean [west], and in what part of the journey they travel south [from Great Falls to Three Forks].

Explain that the Lewis and Clark Expedition did not return to Fort Mandan by exactly the same route they took to the Pacific Ocean, but their return route is not shown on this map.

Have S. tell how many months the trip from Fort Mandan to the Pacific took [about seven]. Then have him look at the first paragraph on page 42 and find out how many miles long the trip Sacajawea made was [almost 7,000 miles both ways]. Have him tell about how long the trip was one way [3,500 miles], or tell him.

You may also want to have S. compare the map of the United States in 1803 with the present borders of the United States, Canada, and Mexico on the map on page 5.

# II. Skills Practice

## PRACTICE 1: Compound Words

Write the new compound words *rowboat* and *waterfall*. Have S. read each compound word and tell the two words that were put together to make it.

In a column under *rowboat*, write *sail, speed, motor, house, life*. Ask S. to put *boat* after each of these words and tell what the compound word would be. As he answers, write *boat* after each word.

Under *waterfall*, write *melon, tight, proof, ski, front*. Ask S. to put *water* in front of each of these words and tell what the compound word would be. As he answers, write *water* in front of each word.

## PRACTICE 2: Classifying Words

Write these headings, and have S. read them: *People, Places, Animals, Food*.

T: I will say a word from today's story that can be classified under one of these headings. Listen to the word, and tell which heading it should go under: *buffalo, trader, Captain Clark, Rocky Mountains, meat, St. Louis, horse, berries*. (Write each word under the heading S. indicates.)

T: This time, I will say three words. Two words belong to the same group of things. One word does not. Listen to the words, and tell which one does not belong.

1. *water, rowboat, canoe*
2. *February, April, 1805*
3. *Sacajawea, Charbonneau, Missouri*
4. *ocean, fort, river*
5. *big, strong, travel*
6. *storm, eat, sleep*
7. *Canada, United States, Three Forks*
8. *St. Louis, October, December*

## PRACTICE 3: Multiple Meanings of Words

Write these words, and have S. read them: *party, cross, run, bank, bark, claim, fork*.

T: Each of these words has more than one meaning. I will read a sentence for each word to show the way the word was used in the story. Listen for the word, and tell its meaning in the sentence. Then tell one or more other meanings for the word.

Read these sentences:

1. The exploring *party* built a fort and stayed all winter.
2. They planned to *cross* the mountains on horseback.
3. The Columbia River *runs* into the Pacific Ocean.
4. Captain Clark pushed Sacajawea up the *bank*.
5. Sacajawea ate the *bark* off the trees.
6. Some people *claim* that Sacajawea died in 1812.
7. When you come to the *fork* in the road, go to the left.

## PRACTICE 4: Using a Dictionary for Word Meanings

Have S. look up each word listed in Practice 3. When he finds the word, have him tell how many meanings it has. Then ask him to find the one that you just used in a sentence. If, in Practice 3, he was not able to give another meaning for any word, have him find one now.

## PRACTICE 5: Using a Dictionary for Pronunciations

Have S. look up the following names to note how his dictionary shows their pronunciation: *St. Louis, Missouri, Mississippi, Louisiana*.

**Note:** Some dictionaries give more than one pronunciation for these names. Have S. use the one that he usually says, or, if the name is new to him, have him pronounce it the way that is most common in his area.

## PRACTICE 6: Using a Dictionary for Plural Forms

Have S. look up each of the following words to find out how its plural form is spelled: *berry, territory, journey, society, hero, buffalo*.

Point out that, if there is no special note about how to spell the plural, you simply add -*s*, as in *journeys*. For *buffalo*, point out that the plural may be *buffalo* or *buffaloes* or *buffalos*.

# III. Writing

## CHECK HOMEWORK

Have S. read aloud the summary of Terry Fox's story that he wrote as a news article. Check to see if it covers the Five *W*'s and summarizes the events in the story reasonably well. Also check for spelling and sentence structure. Have S. make any needed corrections.

## WRITING LESSON (In Notebook)

Have S. write the titles *Lesson 23* and *Words*. Then have him number from 1 to 20 in two columns.

**Words.** Help S. study the words *built, captain, canoe, chief*. Call attention to the rule "*i* before *e*" for the word *chief*. Dictate the words below for S. to write. Check his work, and have him correct any errors.

| | | | |
|---|---|---|---|
| 1. berry | 6. canoe | 11. cross | 16. French |
| 2. berries | 7. captain | 12. explore | 17. row |
| 3. blanket | 8. chief | 13. fell | 18. set |
| 4. buffalo | 9. claim | 14. fork | 19. trade |
| 5. built | 10. cradle | 15. fort | 20. village |

**Sentences.** Have S. study these words: *Sacajawea, special, statue, honor, Oregon*. Then have him write the title *Sentences*. Tell him that you will dictate two paragraphs from the story. He will write them in paragraph form. Dictate the last two paragraphs of the story. Have S. listen to each paragraph. Then dictate it sentence by sentence. Read each sentence only once.

Check what S. has written, and have him correct any errors, including those in punctuation and capitalization (but do not worry about quotation marks around the "Shining Mountains"). Have S. write the title *Study* and any words he missed in the word and paragraph dictation.

## WRITTEN EXERCISE: Page 140 in *Skill Book 4*

Go over the directions and example for the last exercise with S. Then have him do the exercise. Check his work. If he has an error, have him read the whole line of words. Ask him what classification, or heading, most of the things could be put under. Have him eliminate the one that does not fit in that classification.

## HOMEWORK (In Notebook)

Give S. the list of phrases containing dates shown below. Explain that these are important dates in the story of Sacajawea and the Lewis and Clark Expedition. They are in the order in which they happened. In his notebook, he is to write a sentence beginning with each phrase that tells what happened on that date. He may write two or three sentences for each date if he thinks it is necessary. The first item is done for him. Tell him he may refer to the story and to the maps in it.

1. In 1803, U.S. President Thomas Jefferson bought the Louisiana Territory from the French king. Jefferson picked Captain Lewis and Captain Clark to explore it.
2. In May of 1804,
3. In October of 1804,
4. From October of 1804 to April of 1805,
5. In February of 1805,
6. In April of 1805,
7. In July of 1805,
8. On November 7, 1805,
9. During the winter of 1805-1806,
10. In the spring of 1806,
11. In August of 1806,

Also, encourage S. to reread the story and to begin keeping a diary, as suggested below.

T: In the story, you read that Captains Lewis and Clark kept records of their journey in notebooks. We call that kind of writing a *journal* or *diary*. Many people today like to keep a record of their activities or thoughts. Sometimes, these are journals of their travels, but more often they are just diaries of their everyday lives.

Discuss some ways that keeping a diary might be helpful. Ask S. to keep a diary for the next two weeks (probably the time he will complete *Skill Book 4* and the *Checkups*). Have him use the back of his notebook—or a new notebook if he prefers. Tell him to start each day's entry with the date. Discuss how often and how much you expect him to write. Tell him that you will check to see that he *has* written *something*, but you will not read what he has written unless he asks you to.

## CHECKING PROGRESS

Follow suggestions in Lesson 22B for checking progress. Also, note your student's progress in study skills. Is it becoming easier for him to find words in the dictionary and to interpret the information given? Can he locate places on a map and understand the relationship of places? Your student's progress should also be measured in terms of his own goals. Is he making use of his reading and writing skills in his everyday life? Is there something he particularly wants to be able to read? Talk with him about his plans for continuing his education after completing Level 4 of the Laubach Way to Reading.

## MEETING INDIVIDUAL NEEDS

Now is the time to make sure S. has a way to obtain additional reading material. Introduce him to the local library if you haven't already done so. (Find out if your library has a collection of high interest, low reading level books for adults.) Show S. where in the library he can find the type of material he is especially interested in and how he can locate books that he can read. Don't neglect the vertical file for pamphlets and booklets.

You may also want to encourage S. to subscribe to *News for You*. If so, you may want to prepare the order form and check or money order together in class.

There may also be books on his reading level that S. would like to order from New Readers Press or other publishers of easy materials for adults. If you can, show him some copies of some of the books, or try to get some catalogs and go over them together.

If you or another tutor will not be meeting with your student after he completes *Skill Book 4*, find out where he can attend an adult education class. Help him make plans for joining such a class. Discuss the importance of continuing to read and study.

# LESSON 23-B

## People and Places, Story 4
## Skill Book 4, Page 141

## OBJECTIVES

To help your student:

- use a table of contents.
- read story 4 in *People and Places* independently, understanding the main ideas of this factual article.
- distinguish between fact and fiction.
- understand cause and effect.
- understand time and place relationships.
- visualize the setting and main characters from descriptions given in the story.
- interpret facts and make inferences.
- understand the author's purpose.
- interpret the feelings of the characters.
- classify words according to similarities in meaning.
- recognize word opposites.
- relate the story to personal experience and values.
- review words read in *Skill Book 4* by recognizing them in a new book.
- apply phonics skills in reading new words independently.
- recognize the value of a billion as a thousand million.
- review the suffixes *-ment, -ful, -less, -ship, -ous.*
- recognize the prefixes *il-*, as in *illiterate*, and *inter-*, as in *international.*
- develop further skill in using a dictionary.
- locate specific places on a world map.
- understand the relationship of a world map and a globe.
- understand what is meant by a *continent.*
- write words and paragraphs from dictation.
- write a summary of a biographical sketch.

## INTRODUCTION

T: Today, you will read the last story in *People and Places* and discuss the study questions in the skill book. This is also a true story. Look at the table of contents in *People and Places*. Find the page number for story 4, and then turn to that page.

## I. Reading in *People and Places*

### STORY 4: Frank C. Laubach

**Silent reading (pages 45-61 in *People and Places*).** Ask S. to read the story title and subtitle to himself. Tell him to look at the word list for help in pronouncing the words. Then have him read aloud the title and subtitle, *Frank C. Laubach: Voice of the Silent Billion.*

Have S. read the new words on page 45, silently and then aloud. Then have him read the introductory paragraph, first silently and then aloud.

Have S. turn to the world map on pages 54-55 and locate the Philippines and the Pacific Ocean. Have him note where the Philippines is in relation to North America and to China. Then have S. turn to the map on page 47 and read aloud the title: *The Philippines: An island nation in the Pacific Ocean.* Have him locate Lanao Province in the Philippines and notice that the Philippines is made up of a number of islands. Then return to page 45.

**Among the Maranaos.** Have S. read this subhead silently and then aloud. Ask him to read the first part of the story—up to the next subhead—to himself to find out why Dr. Frank Laubach was in the Philippines and what problem he was facing.

Remind him to read any new words at the top of the page before reading that page. Also, point out that there are a number of new names of people and places in this story and that he may look up their pronunciation in the new words as many times as he needs to.

When S. has finished reading, have him answer the questions you asked. Then have him summarize what happened in this part of the story.

**Around the world.** Ask S. to read the next part of the story to himself to find out what parts of the world Frank Laubach visited and what he did there. When S. has finished reading, have him answer these questions.

On the world map, have him locate Asia, Africa, North America, South America, and Europe. Have him read aloud the new words that are listed for this part of the story.

**Remainder of story.** Have S. read the rest of the story to himself to find out how Dr. Laubach inspired others. When he has finished reading, have him answer this question. Have him read aloud the new words.

**Study helps (page 141 in *Skill Book 4*).** Ask S. to read aloud the title *Frank C. Laubach* and the directions for the first set of questions. Have him read each question silently and then aloud. Then have him give his answer. If he answers a question incorrectly, refer him to the page on which the answer is given, and have him scan the page to find it.

Have S. do the second exercise by himself. Tell him to answer as many questions as he can without looking back at the story. Check his answers. Then have him scan the story to find the correct answer for any question he omitted or answered incorrectly.

Ask S. to read the directions for the last exercise, first silently and then aloud. Have him note how the first item is done and then do the others by himself. Check his work by having him read each word in the first list along with the word that means the opposite. Ask him to tell the letter that he wrote on the line. Have him correct any errors.

**Oral reading and discussion.** Have S. tell the mental picture he has of each of the following episodes. After he describes the episode, have him read aloud the part in the story that tells about it.

1. Dr. Laubach tells the Maranaos that he can't pay the teachers (part 1, paragraphs 4-9).

   After S. has read these paragraphs, have him look at the quotation marks in paragraphs 6-9. Explain that, when a speech continues from one paragraph to another without interruption, there are no quotation marks at the end of the first paragraph. But there are quotation marks at the beginning of the new paragraph to remind you that the person is still speaking. And there is a quotation mark at the very end of the person's speech.

2. The Maranao chief talks to the people about what they can do to keep the literacy program going (part 1, par. 11-20).

   After S. has read these paragraphs, go over the way quotation marks are used in the chief's speech of several paragraphs.

3. The Maranaos tell Dr. Laubach good-by as he gets on the ship (part 2, par. 5).

4. Dr. Laubach speaks about the silent billion to a large group of North Americans (part 4, par. 2-7).

As S. reads aloud, note his phrasing, intonation, and expression. Comment on what he does well.

**Relating the story to everyday life.** Discuss these questions.

1. Did you get any inspiration from this story? If so, in what way did the story inspire you?
2. What qualities about Frank Laubach do you admire the most?
3. What motivated Frank Laubach to spend his life helping the "silent billion"?
4. Do you think Dr. Laubach was successful in what he was trying to do? Are there still many illiterate people in the world? What is success?
5. What do you think was the author's purpose in writing this story? Is it a complete biography? What part of Frank Laubach's life is emphasized? How old was Dr. Laubach when the "each one teach one" plan began in the Philippines?

**Note:** You may want to point out that this story was written by Dr. Frank Laubach's son, Dr. Robert Laubach. If your local library has any books by or about Frank Laubach, you may want to check them out to show to S.

**Map and globe study.** On the world map, have S. locate again Asia, North America, South America, Europe, and Africa. Explain that these are continents and that a continent is a huge land area surrounded or almost surrounded by water. Ask S. to tell the name of a country in the continent of Asia and the name of a country in the continent of North America.

---

### Frank C. Laubach

**Discuss the answers to these questions.**

1. Why was Dr. Laubach's literacy program in Lanao in danger?
2. How did the Maranao people keep their literacy program going?
3. How did the literacy program help the Maranao people?
4. Why was Dr. Laubach called the "Apostle to the Illiterates"?
5. How did Frank Laubach find inner peace and strength?
6. What problems of illiterates of the world did Dr. Laubach describe in his speeches?
7. What did Frank C. Laubach do to help the illiterates of the world?

**Write a short answer to each question.**

1. In what country did Each One Teach One begin? _The Philippines_
2. In what year did Each One Teach One begin? _In 1930_
3. Whose idea was it? _A Maranao chief_
4. Who did Dr. Laubach call the "Silent Billion"? _Illiterate people_
5. Give the title of a book by Frank Laubach. _Forty Years with the Silent Billion_
6. What group named for him carries on his work in the country where you live? _Laubach Literacy International_

**Match each word in the first list with a word in the second list that means the opposite. Write the letter in the blank. The first one is done for you.**

| | | | |
|---|---|---|---|
| D | 1. soft | A. | toward |
| G | 2. birth | B. | remember |
| F | 3. tiny | C. | peace |
| C | 4. war | D. | hard |
| B | 5. forget | E. | minor |
| J | 6. weak | F. | huge |
| I | 7. literate | G. | death |
| L | 8. friendly | H. | smooth |
| K | 9. apart | I. | illiterate |
| A | 10. away from | J. | powerful |
| H | 11. rough | K. | together |
| E | 12. major | L. | unfriendly |

Lesson 23  **141**

---

Show S. a world globe. On the globe, have S. locate North and South America, Africa, Europe, and Asia. Explain that Europe and Asia are part of the same land mass, but they are considered two continents because Europe is somewhat set off from Asia by mountain ranges and seas. Explain that there are seven continents in the world. On the globe, point out Australia and Antartica. Explain that Antartica is extremely cold and only a few settlements for scientific study are located there. Write the heading *Continents* and under it the names of the seven continents. Have S. copy these in his notebook.

On the globe, have S. locate the areas that Frank Laubach probably marked with black and white stripes to show where most of the illiterates of the world were. (Let him refer to the book if he doesn't remember.)

Also on the globe, have him trace two round-the-world trips, one from California, west across the Pacific Ocean to China, across the rest of Asia, Europe, and across the Atlantic Ocean to New York. For the other trip, have him start at the Philippines and go east across the Pacific Ocean to South America, then to Africa, across the Indian Ocean to Australia, and then north to the Philippines again.

## II. Skills Practice

### PRACTICE 1: Meaning of *billion*

Write the following numbers and number words, and have S. read them. Explain that a million equals a thousand thousands.

| 1,000 | one thousand |
| 10,000 | ten thousand |
| 100,000 | one hundred thousand |
| 1,000,000 | one million = a thousand thousands |

Then add the following numbers and number words, and have S. read them. Explain that a billion equals a thousand million. Also, point out that a million has six zeroes and a billion has nine zeroes.

| 10,000,000 | ten million |
| 100,000,000 | one hundred million |
| 1,000,000,000 | one billion = a thousand million |

### PRACTICE 2: Suffixes *-ful, -less, -ous, -ment, -ship*

Write these endings, and have S. tell what they are: *-ful, -less, -ous, -ment, -ship*. Then write the sentences below, and have S. fill in each blank with one of the endings.

1. Everyone jumped up and down with excite_____.
2. Dr. Laubach had a close friend_____ with the Maranaos.
3. The Maranao literacy program was saved by their power_____ chief.
4. Dr. Laubach went into many danger_____ places to carry on his literacy work.
5. Dr. Laubach said that the illiterates of the world were poor and help_____.

Have S. read his completed sentences aloud. Have him make any needed corrections.

### PRACTICE 3: Prefixes *il-* and *inter-*

Write *illiterate*. Have S. read it and tell the root word. Underline *literate*. Ask S. what he thinks the prefix *il-* means. Explain that *il-* is another form of the prefix *in-*, meaning *not*. The prefix *il-* is used only in front of root words beginning with *l*.

In a column, write *legal, legible, legitimate, logical*. Ask S. to read each root word and tell what new word can be formed by putting the prefix *il-* in front of the root word. If S. doesn't know the meaning of a root word, have him look it up in the dictionary. Write the new word by the root word. Have S. read both columns of words.

Write *international*. Have S. read it and tell the root word. Underline *national*. Ask S. to tell what he thinks the prefix *inter-* means [between or among]. If he doesn't know, have him look up *inter-* in the dictionary.

In a column, write *state, section, locking, marry, view*. Ask S. to read each word and tell what new word can be formed by putting the prefix *inter-* in front of it. Write the new word by the root word. Have S. read both columns of words.

### PRACTICE 4: Classifying Words

Write these headings: *Persons, Languages, Countries, Qualities*. Give an example of a quality, such as *honesty, truth, courage*. Say each word below, and have S. tell which heading it should go under. As he answers, write the word under the heading he indicates. Say these words: *English, chief, missionary, peace, strength, French, Spanish, apostle, kindness, Canada, Philippines, United States*.

Say each group of three words below. Have S. tell which one does not belong in the group.

1. *ship, airplane, apartment*
2. *leader, friend, chief*
3. *Lanao, Asia, Africa*
4. *island, continent, ocean*
5. *magazine, book, television*
6. *knife, dagger, belt*
7. *pain, sickness, literacy*
8. *several, billion, million*
9. *English, Muslim, Christian*

### PRACTICE 5: Using the Dictionary

Say each word listed below, and have S. find it in the dictionary. When he finds the word, have him tell how it is spelled, how it is pronounced, the number of syllables, the stressed syllable, and the meaning of the word that is most likely the way it was used in the story. Say these words: *apostle, billion, inspire, dagger, meant, tears, international, Muslim* (may be listed as *Moslem*).

Also, have S. look up *equip* and find out how the forms with *-ed* and *-ing* are spelled. Have him tell why the *p* is doubled in *equipped* and *equipping* [because the last syllable of *equip* is stressed].

Note your student's progress in using the dictionary. Does he know in which third of the dictionary to look for the word? Does he make use of the guide words? Does he glance down the page to find the word in the right alphabetical order? Is he able to interpret the information given about the word? Compliment him on the skills he is using. Give help where needed, and plan reinforcement exercises if necessary.

## III. Writing

### CHECK HOMEWORK

Check the sentences S. wrote in his notebook for the dates having to do with the story of Sacajawea and the Lewis and Clark Expedition. If any information is incorrect, refer him to the story and the map of the expedition. Then check sentence structure, spelling, and punctuation. Have S. make any needed corrections and then read his sentences aloud.

Also, check to see if S. has started keeping a diary and if he has written about as much as you asked. Do not read what he has written unless he gives you permission to do so. Encourage him to continue making entries in his diary.

## WRITING LESSON (In Notebook)

Have S. write the title *Words* and then number from 1 to 20 in two columns.

**Words.** Have S. study the words *meant, Laubach, literacy*. Then dictate the words below for him to write. When he has finished, check his work, and have him correct any errors.

| | | | |
|---|---|---|---|
| 1. flash | 6. meant | 11. simple | 16. powerful |
| 2. belt | 7. inner | 12. sudden | 17. strength |
| 3. wipe | 8. forgot | 13. several | 18. tears (tērz) |
| 4. buzz | 9. globe | 14. prayer | 19. Laubach |
| 5. ship | 10. Bible | 15. prison | 20. literacy |

**Sentences.** Have S. study the words *Maranao* and *Lanao*. Then have him write the title *Sentences*. Tell him you will dictate some paragraphs from the story. He will write them in paragraph form. Dictate the last four paragraphs in the first part of the story. Have S. listen to a whole paragraph. Then dictate it sentence by sentence.

Check what S. has written, and have him correct any errors, including those in punctuation and capitalization. Have him write the title *Study* and any words he missed in the word and paragraph dictation.

## HOMEWORK (In Notebook)

Ask S. to write a summary in one or two paragraphs to tell the main points about Frank C. Laubach. Tell him he may refer to the story.

Also, have S. look at the word list that begins on page 142 of *Skill Book 4*. Point out that this list includes the 708 words that were introduced in this book. Suggest that he might like to review one page each day and see how many of the words he can recall. Ask him to put a pencil mark by any that he is not sure of, and you will help him study them in the next session. Also, have him look at the word list at the back of *People and Places*. Point out that it is usually easier to recognize a word when it is used in a sentence than when it is in a list. He shouldn't feel discouraged if he doesn't remember all of the words. Going over the word list is one way to review, but he may prefer to reread some of the stories for review.

Tell S. that there will be one or two sessions for review and then he will have a checkup on the main reading and writing skills that he has covered in this book. Or, if you feel that S. is ready, you may give him the *Checkups* in the next session.

Remind S. to write in his diary and to study any words he missed in the dictation.

## CHECKING PROGRESS

If S. has been able to read the story in *People and Places* without much help from you and has been able to answer most of the questions in the Study Helps, his progress is satisfactory. You may want to have one or two review lessons not only to reinforce needed skills but also to allow more time for supplementary reading on this level. Give the *Checkups* within a few class sessions of the student's completion of *Skill Book 4*, however, so that he has a feeling of accomplishment. The *Checkups* will help you and your student evaluate his progress and plan for his next program of study.

## MEETING INDIVIDUAL NEEDS

Plan for any review sessions you will have with S. Include reinforcement of word recognition skills through the use of slip strips, word wheels, and flash cards, as suggested in earlier lessons. Have S. complete any sections of the skill book that he has not done. Review spelling words.

Use at least half of each period for supplementary reading, using any of the titles suggested on the inside front cover of this manual or earlier manuals. If you have not already done so, this might be a good time to have S. start one of the short novels in the Sundown Books collection so that he has the experience of reading a longer work and not just short selections that can be read in one sitting.

Help S. to see his own progress. If he will not be continuing with you beyond completion of *Skill Book 4*, discuss with him ways that he can continue his education, either on his own or in a class situation.

# CHECKUPS for Skill Book 4

To evaluate the student's progress in reading and writing skills, use the separate booklet *Checkups for Skill Book 4*, available from New Readers Press.

## OBJECTIVES

The objectives of the evaluation are:
- to measure the student's progress in relation to the learning objectives of *Skill Book 4*.
- to diagnose the student's strengths and weaknesses in phonics, word recognition, reading comprehension, and study skills.
- to develop the student's confidence in taking a test.

## ADMINISTERING THE CHECKUPS

*Checkups for Skill Book 4* consists of 10 parts. You may give the Checkups in two sessions if you feel that would be desirable for your student. In that case, it is suggested that the first six checkups be given in one session and the other four in another session.

Simple written directions are given for each part, and most parts have one or two sample questions. Go over the directions and samples with S. before he does each part. Help him correct any errors he makes in the samples but do *not* correct his errors in the actual test items.

## INTRODUCTION

T: Today you will do some checkups on *Skill Book 4*. They will help you find out if there are any sounds or words you need to study more. Some of the checkups will show how well you understand what you read and your skill in following directions.

T: Most of the checkups are like exercises you have done in your skill book. There are a few new words in the stories, but you will be able to sound them out easily. There will be no certain score that you need to make in order to go on to another book. But the checkups will help us plan your next program of study and choose books you can read independently.

Give S. his booklet. Have S. read the title *Checkups for Skill Book 4*. Have him read the word *Name* and write his name. Have him read the word *Date* and write today's date.

## Checkup 1: Sounds (pages 1-2)

This checkup has two parts. In the first exercise, S. circles the words in each line that have the same vowel sound as the first word. The sounds and their regular spellings are those taught in *Skill Book 4*.
1. The sound /ū/ as in *music*, written *u-e, ue, ew*.
2. The sound /oo/ as in *food*, written *oo, u-e, ue, ew*.
3. The sound /uu/ as in *book*, written *oo*.

4. The sound /ou/ as in *mouth*, written *ou, ow*.
5. The sound /aw/ as in *lawn*, written *aw, au*.
6. The sound /oy/ as in *boy*, written *oy, oi*.

In the second exercise, S. circles the words in each line that have the same consonant sound as the letter or letters underlined in the first word. Items 1-11 check knowledge of consonants that stand for more than one sound, as taught in *Skill Book 4*.
1. Two sounds for *c*, as in *cup* and *city*.
2. Two sounds for *g*, as in *go* and *age*.
3. Four sounds for *s*, as in *snake, eggs, sure, measure*.
4. Three sounds for *ch*, as in *child, Chris, machine*.

Items 12-15 check knowledge of other consonant spellings: *wr* as in *write*, *kn* as in *know*, *mb* as in *climb*, *ph* and *gh* as in *phone* and *laugh*.

Items 16-17 check knowledge of how to pronounce *-tion, -ssion*, and *-sion* at the end of words.

**What to do.** Have S. read aloud the title *Checkup 1: Sounds*. Have him read the directions silently and then aloud. Have him read the first word in the example and tell the vowel sound. Then have him circle the words with that vowel sound. If he has an error, have him read the word aloud and tell the vowel sound or sounds he hears in the word. Have him correct any errors. Then have him do the six items in this exercise by himself.

Have S. read the directions for the second exercise silently and then aloud. Have him read the first word in the example and tell the sound for the letters underlined. Then have him circle the words that have that sound. If he has an error, have him read the word aloud and listen for the sound /ch/. Have him correct any errors. Then have him do all of the items in this exercise by himself. Point out that the exercise is continued on page 2.

## Checkup 2: Compound Words (page 2)

S. puts together words from two lists to make compound words. There are eight items, one of which is to be done with the student as an example.

**What to do.** Have S. read aloud the title *Checkup 2: Compound Words*. Have him read the directions silently and then aloud. Ask him to look at List 1 and read the first word, *side*. Have him look down List 2 to find the word that can go with *side* to make a compound word. Ask him to say the compound word aloud. If he says *sidewalk*, have him write it after number 1. If he doesn't, tell him what the word should be, and have him write it. Then have him do the other items by himself.

## Checkup 3: Plurals (page 2)

S. writes the plural form of each word. There are eight items and two examples, including irregular plurals.

**What to do.** Have S. read aloud the title *Checkup 3: Plurals*. Have him read the directions silently and then aloud. Ask him to read each example and write the plural form. If he doesn't write *men* and *loaves*, tell him what these plurals should be, and have him write them correctly. Then have him do the eight items by himself.

## Checkup 4: Contractions (page 3)

This checkup has two parts. In the first exercise, S. reads a contraction and writes the two words it comes from. In the second exercise, S. reads two words and writes the contraction for them. There are eight words and two examples for each exercise.

**What to do.** Have S. read aloud the title *Checkup 4: Contractions.* Have him read the directions for the first exercise silently and then aloud. Ask him to read the first example, *I'd,* and tell the two words it is made from. Have him write the words *I would.* Go over the second example, *you're,* in the same way. Then have S. do the eight items in this exercise by himself.

Follow the same procedure for the second exercise.

## Checkup 5: Syllables and Stress (page 3)

S. reads a word that is rewritten with syllable divisions. Then he puts a stress mark after the stressed syllable. There are 10 items and two examples.

**What to do.** Have S. read aloud the title *Checkup 5: Syllables and Stress.* Have him read the directions silently and do the two examples by himself. If he has an error, have him say the word aloud—or say it for him—and have him listen for the stressed syllable. Have him correct any errors. Then have him do the 10 items by himself.

## Checkup 6: Word Parts (pages 4-5)

This checkup has four parts:

1. Write the missing ending (one example, six items).
2. Add prefixes to root words (two examples, six items).
3. Fill in blanks in sentences with the new words with prefixes (no examples, six items).
4. Write the root word (two examples, 12 items).

**What to do.** Have S. read aloud the title *Checkup 6: Word Parts.* Have him read the directions for the first exercise to himself and do the example. Check his work, and have him correct his answer if it is wrong. Then have him do the six items in this exercise by himself.

Have S. read the directions for the second exercise silently and then aloud. Give help with the new word *prefix* if necessary. Have S. do the examples. Check his work, and have him correct any errors. Then have him do the six items in this exercise by himself.

Have S. read the directions for the third exercise silently and then aloud. Be sure he understands that he is to use words from the second exercise to fill in the blanks here. Then have him do the six items.

On page 5, have S. read the directions for the fourth exercise about root words to himself and do the two examples. If he has an error in the examples, go over the words with him. Explain that, in a word like *education,* it is necessary to change the spelling for the root word *educate.* And, for a word like *unfriendly,* it is necessary to drop both the prefix and the ending to find the root word, *friend.* Then have S. do the 12 items in this exercise by himself.

## Checkup 7: Word Meanings (pages 5-6)

This checkup has three parts, each of which has one example and six items:

1. Words that mean the same (synonyms).
2. Opposites.
3. Words that sound the same but are spelled differently (homonyms).

**What to do.** Have S. read aloud the title *Checkup 7: Word Meanings.* Tell him there are three parts to this exercise. Ask him to read the directions for the first part to himself and do the example. Have him read aloud the first word and the word he has circled. If it is not right, have him read all of the words in the example and circle the right one. Then have him do the six items.

Follow the same procedure for the other two parts.

## Checkup 8: Dictionary Skills (page 6)

This checkup has two parts. In the first part, S. writes three lists of words in alphabetical order to check his skill in alphabetizing to the second, third, and fourth letters. In the second part, S. circles the words in each of three lists to show which ones would come between two given guide words.

**What to do.** Have S. read aloud the title *Checkup 8: Dictionary Skills.* Ask him to read the directions for the first exercise silently and then aloud. Have him do the exercise independently. An example is not given and should not be required.

Have S. read the directions for the second exercise silently and then aloud. An example is not given, as understanding what the directions mean is part of the dictionary skill being checked. Ask him to do the exercise by himself.

## Checkup 9: Understanding Stories (page 7)

This checkup has two parts. In the first part, S. reads a short news story and answers *who, what, where, when,* and *why* questions to check his ability to understand factual material.

In the second part, S. fills in the missing words in a passage taken from the correlated reader, *People and Places.* This cloze exercise requires S. to fill in every fifth word. The first two words are filled in for him as examples. The cloze exercise integrates word recognition skills with the skills of using context and grammatical clues in the reading material. There are 21 blanks to fill in.

**What to do.** Have S. read aloud the title *Checkup 9: Understanding Stories*. Tell him there are two parts to this checkup. Have him read the directions for the first exercise silently and then aloud. Ask S. to read the news story and then answer the questions. Tell him that he will have 10 minutes in which to do this exercise. Have him stop at the end of that time. If he has not finished, mark the question he is on, and then allow five more minutes for him to finish. If he finishes in less time, record the time at the top of the page.

Have S. read the directions for the second exercise silently and then aloud. Also, have him read the first two sentences silently and then aloud as an example of what to do. Explain that, although this is a passage from the story of Sacajawea, he doesn't have to fill in the exact words that were used in that story. He may fill in each blank with any appropriate word that makes sense. But he is to use only *one* word in each blank. Tell him to read ahead in the paragraph to make sure what word will best fit the meaning. He should spell the word the best he can. Spelling errors will not be counted against him if the word can be recognized. Allow about 15 minutes for completion of this exercise.

### Checkup 10: Following Directions (page 8)

This checkup has two parts. In the first part, S. studies a simple neighborhood map and answers some questions about it. In the second part, S. fills in an application for credit, using information given.

**What to do.** Have S. read aloud the title *Checkup 10: Following Directions*. Tell him there are two parts to this checkup. Point to the map, and have him read aloud its title, *Map Made by Roy to Show How to Get to His House*. Have S. read the directions for the first exercise silently and then aloud. Explain that he is to study the map and then answer the questions about it.

For the second exercise, point to the application form, and explain to S. that he is to fill in this application with the information given below the form. He is not to write any information about himself. Have him read the application and the information to himself and then fill in the form.

### Concluding the Lesson

Collect the student's booklet when he has completed all he can. Praise him for his effort and concentration. If he has done the whole booklet, tell him that you will go over the checkups together at the next lesson. If there is time, have him read aloud from *People and Places* or some other supplementary material. If he is doing the checkups in two sessions, tell him he will finish next time.

## SCORING AND EVALUATING THE CHECKUPS

On the student's booklet, mark his *correct* answers rather than his wrong answers. Answer keys are given after the Teacher's Evaluation Form. Use the Teacher's Evaluation Form to record your student's scores. Do not count the answers to the sample questions. The suggested satisfactory score is about 75% of the perfect score for each part. If you want to translate the student's score into a percentage, divide his score by the perfect score and multiply by 100. The student's scores are for *your* use. The numbers would be of little use to the student.

The scores for each part of the *Checkups* will give you an informal diagnosis of the student's strengths and weaknesses. If he made less than the suggested satisfactory score for a particular checkup, analyze the type of errors he made. List the items that he needs to review the most. If needed, try to have one or two review sessions with S. before he studies a new book or enters a new class. If this is not possible, then some suggestions may be helpful for the next tutor or teacher.

## REVIEWING CHECKUPS WITH THE STUDENT

At your next session, go over the *Checkups* with S. Be sure to point out his correct answers so that he receives some encouraging news about his work. Help him correct his wrong answers, as you have done with skill book exercises, so that he has a chance to learn from the *Checkups*. Be sure to give S. some encouraging report about his progress.

The next section of this manual is the Writing Checkups for Skill Book 4. You may want to give the writing checkups in two sessions, spending the rest of each session on review of reading skills that the *Checkups* in the booklet have shown need reinforcement.

# CHECKUPS FOR SKILL BOOK 4: Teacher's Evaluation Form

Student's Name _____

Date of Enrollment _____ Date Checkups Given _____

| | Perfect Score | Satisfactory Score | Student's Score |
|---|---|---|---|
| **1. Sounds**<br>Count 2 points for each line in which *all* of the right words and *only* the right words are circled.<br>Count 1 point for each line in which there is only one error.<br>(6 vowel lines + 7 consonant lines = 23 × 2 = 46 points) | 46 | 34 | |
| **2. Compound Words**<br>Each correct answer counts 1 point.<br>The compound word must be written correctly.<br>(7 compound words = 7 points; consider item 1 as an example) | 7 | 5 | |
| **3. Plurals**<br>Each correct answer counts 1 point. The word must be spelled correctly.<br>(8 plurals = 8 points) | 8 | 6 | |
| **4. Contractions**<br>Each correct answer counts 1 point.<br>Words and contractions must be written correctly.<br>(2 parts × 8 items each = 16 points) | 16 | 12 | |
| **5. Syllables and Stress**<br>Each correct answer counts 1 point.<br>(10 items = 10 points) | 10 | 7 | |
| **6. Word Parts**<br>Each correct answer counts 1 point.<br>(8 endings + 6 prefixes + 6 fill-ins + 12 roots = 32 points) | 32 | 24 | |
| **7. Word Meanings**<br>Each correct answer counts 1 point.<br>(6 synonyms + 6 opposites + 6 homonyms = 18 points) | 18 | 14 | |
| **8. Dictionary Skills**<br>Count 5 points for each list of words in correct alphabetical order.<br>(3 lists × 5 = 15 points)<br>Count 1 point for each correct word circled.<br>(3 lists × 3 correct words in each = 9 points) | 24 | 18 | |
| **9. Understanding Stories**<br>Count 3 points for each question answered correctly.<br>(6 questions × 3 = 18 points)<br>Count 2 points for each correct word filled in the blanks.<br>(21 blanks × 2 = 42 points) | 60 | 45 | |

| 10. Following Directions<br>Count 2 points for each correct answer about the map.<br>(5 questions × 2 = 10 points)<br>In the application, count 1 point for each of the following items filled in correctly (17 points).<br>Line 1: Name, married, number of children<br>Line 2: Address, telephone<br>Line 3: Employer, position, income<br>Line 4: Employer's address, how long employed<br>Line 5: Bank, branch, account no., savings/checking<br>Line 6: Signature, Social Security no., driver's license no. | 27 | 20 | |
| --- | --- | --- | --- |
| **Total Score** | 248 | 185 | |

## WRITING CHECKUPS FOR SKILL BOOK 4: Teacher's Evaluation Form

| | Perfect Score | Satisfactory Score | Student's Score |
| --- | --- | --- | --- |
| **1. Words**<br>Count 1 point each. | 30 | 23 | |
| **2. Numbers**<br>Count 1 point each. | 15 | 11 | |
| **3. Sentences**<br>Count 5 points each (see directions for scoring). | 50 | 37 | |
| **4. Paragraphs**<br>Count 25 points total (see directions for scoring):<br>— 15 points for content<br>— 5 points for form<br>— 5 points for spelling | 25 | 19 | |
| **5. Letter Writing**<br>Count 25 points total for the letter (see directions for scoring):<br>— 15 points for content<br>— 5 points for form<br>— 5 points for spelling | 25 | 19 | |
| **Addressing an Envelope**<br>Count 5 points total. | 5 | 4 | |
| **6. Handwriting**<br>Count 20 points total. | 20 | 15 | |
| **Total Score** | 170 | 128 | |

The publisher hereby grants permission to reproduce this Teacher's Evaluation Form for the purpose of evaluating student performance.

# ANSWER KEYS

## 1. Sounds

### Vowel sounds
1. argue, cure, few, huge
2. chew, pool, blue, school
3. cook, could, good
4. down, house, found
5. haul, crawl, taught, fall, bought
6. point, toy, noise

### Consonant sounds
1. cat, music, cut, back, cool
2. icy, face, citizen
3. game, fog, grade, bigger
4. gym, Ginger, gentle, edge
5. see, miss, yes
6. jobs, noise, visit
7. sugar, issue
8. usual, pleasure
9. chair, teach, kitchen
10. chorus, school, mechanic
11. Chicago, chef, Charlotte
12. write, wrap, rest, wrong
13. know, knee, now, knob
14. game, limb, storm, climb
15. laugh, phone, cough, nephew
16. election, mission, discussion, section.
17. decision, occasion

## 2. Compound Words
1. (example)
2. overnight
3. southwest
4. birthplace
5. headache
6. rowboat
7. peanut
8. waterfall

## 3. Plurals
1. feet
2. teeth
3. women
4. leaves
5. wives
6. speeches
7. heroes
8. taxes

## 4. Contractions

### Write the two words
1. could not
2. they will
3. we would
4. do not
5. will not
6. is not
7. we are
8. that is

### Write the contractions
1. they're
2. aren't
3. haven't
4. wouldn't
5. doesn't
6. I'm
7. I've
8. here's

## 5. Syllables and Stress
1. oc ca' sion
2. oc cu pa' tion
3. ac cept'
4. di plo' ma
5. pro nounce'
6. chem' is try
7. me chan' ic
8. pas' sen ger
9. re mark'
10. reg' is ter

## 6. Word Parts

### Endings
1. childhood, hardship
2. improvement
3. dangerous
4. painful
5. National
6. kindness, helpless

### Prefixes
1. repay
2. nonstop *or* non-stop
3. unusual
4. international
5. illiterates
6. injustice

### Fill in words with prefixes
1. nonstop *or* non-stop
2. injustice
3. unusual
4. international
5. repay
6. Illiterates

### Root words
1. enemy
2. power
3. citizen
4. fame
5. discuss
6. person
7. decide
8. fill
9. pay
10. literate
11. employ
12. admit

## 7. Word Meanings

### Synonyms
1. permit
2. arrive
3. journey
4. lead
5. say
6. kind

### Opposites
1. below
2. weak
3. incorrect
4. carelessly
5. right
6. unusual

### Homonyms
1. whole
2. sew
3. weak
4. You're
5. there
6. rowed

## 8. Dictionary Skills

| List 1 | List 2 | List 3 |
|---|---|---|
| bandage | fact | stairs |
| belong | fail | stamp |
| billion | fair | star |
| blanket | fame | station |
| buffalo | fault | statue |
| **remark— rest** | **mean— medicine** | **war— water** |
| rescue | measure | wash |
| report | mechanic | warn |
| remove | medic | watch |

## 9. Understanding News Stories

### News story
1. Rosa Gomez
2. Her grandchildren, Carla and Pablo
3. At 989 West Carlos Ave.
4. Thursday morning at about 11 o'clock
5. The children made a fire to roast hot dogs.
6. A neighbor

### Fill in missing words
Accept any answer that makes sense and is grammatical even if it is not shown here. Spelling need not be correct if the word is recognizable.

At, the, wild, the, of, As, much, for, baby, on, for, had, which, eat, also, men, their, men, dangers, She, with.

## 10. Following Directions

### Map
1. South
2. 6 blocks
3. East (or, left)
4. S. 6th St.
5. 16 blocks

### Application
Answers should match information given in the directions.

To evaluate your student's progress in writing and spelling, use the checkups given here. Have S. write on lined notebook paper.

## OBJECTIVES

To evaluate the student's progress in these skills:
- spelling words that follow regular spelling patterns and rules taught in *Skill Books 1-4*.
- spelling some known irregular words.
- writing numerals, prices, addresses, and dates.
- using correct punctuation and capitalization.
- writing an original paragraph.
- writing a short letter, using correct letter form.
- addressing an envelope.
- writing legibly in cursive writing.

## ADMINISTERING THE CHECKUPS

The five parts of the writing checkups can probably be done by your student in one long session. If you feel that two sessions would be less tiring for him, however, give the dictation in one session and the rest of the checkups in the next session.

**Checkup 1: Words.** Explain to S. that the writing checkups are much like the writing lessons he has been doing in his notebook. On a sheet of lined paper, have him write the titles *Checkup 1* and *Words*. Then have him number from 1 to 30 in two columns. Give a sentence when you dictate *through*.

| | | |
|---|---|---|
| 1. music | 11. crawled | 21. walking |
| 2. few | 12. football | 22. usual |
| 3. room | 13. noise | 23. through |
| 4. grew | 14. sure | 24. machine |
| 5. book | 15. because | 25. strange |
| 6. house | 16. taught | 26. knocked |
| 7. town | 17. employer | 27. false |
| 8. Tuesday | 18. continue | 28. energy |
| 9. amusing | 19. decide | 29. accident |
| 10. mouth | 20. thought | 30. discussion |

**Checkup 2: Numbers.** Have S. write the titles for this checkup and number from 1 to 15 in three columns. Ask him to write numerals for the numbers you dictate.

| | | |
|---|---|---|
| 1. 2,000 | 6. $25 (or, $25.00) | 11. ½ |
| 2. 7,500 | 7. $50.15 | 12. ¼ |
| 3. 12,125 | 8. $17.35 | 13. ¾ |
| 4. 60,550 | 9. $660.10 | 14. 10:30 p.m. |
| 5. 250,000 | 10. $39.99 | 15. 8:45 a.m. |

**Checkup 3: Sentences.** Have S. write the titles for this checkup. Have him number each sentence as you dictate it. Tell him to write out all of the words in full instead of using abbreviations.

1. My niece and nephew will graduate from Central High School in June.
2. Jake bought sugar, flour, and fish hooks at the store. (*Fishhooks* may also be written as one word.)
3. "You and the boys are my jewels," said Judy.
4. I have a doctor's appointment at 2:30 on Wednesday.
5. The winter months are December, January, and February.
6. Do you know how long the Browns have lived in Howard County?
7. Freedom Adult Education Center is at 1000 South Main Street.
8. "Each one teach one or die!" shouted the chief.
9. Frank Laubach was born September 2, 1884.
10. Terry Fox ran 3,339 miles across Canada to raise money for cancer research.

**Checkup 4: Paragraphs.** Write these topics on the board or on a sheet of paper:

1. The story in *Skill Book 4* I liked best and why
2. The kind of job I would like to have and why
3. A place I have visited
4. A person who has inspired me

Have S. read the topics and choose one to write about. Or, substitute a topic of more interest to him. Ask S. to write the titles *Checkup 4* and *Paragraphs*. Under these, have him write the topic he chose. Tell him to write one or two paragraphs about the topic—about 15 sentences in all—and that he will have a time limit of 30 minutes. He should spell the words the best he can without help.

**Checkup 5: Letter Writing.** On a sheet of unlined paper, have S. write the titles *Checkup 5* and *Letter Writing* at the top. Just under the titles, have him draw a line across the paper. Then give these directions:

T: On this page, you are to write a thank you letter. It may be about a real incident, or you may make it up. Write a short letter to a friend or relative whom you have visited recently. Tell some of the things you enjoyed about the visit. Use the correct form for writing a personal letter. You will have about 20 minutes to write the letter.

When S. has finished, have him fold the letter in thirds to form an envelope. Have him address the envelope to the person he wrote to. If he doesn't know the address, he may make up one. He should put his own return address in the proper place on the envelope.

## SCORING THE CHECKUPS

Record the student's scores on the Teacher's Evaluation Form, in the section at the end.

**Checkup 1: Words.** Score one point for each word spelled correctly. On the student's paper, underline any word he misspelled.

**Checkup 2: Numbers.** Score one point for each item written correctly. Underline any items with errors.

**Checkup 3: Sentences.** Score each sentence as suggested below. A total of 5 points is possible for each sentence.

- 2 points if all words are spelled correctly and no words are omitted or added, *or* 1 point if there is only one misspelled word.
- 2 points for correct punctuation, *or* 1 point if there is only one error in punctuation.
- 1 point for correct capitalization.

Underline any word that is misspelled. If a word that should begin with a capital letter is not capitalized, count that only as a capitalization error and not also as a spelling error. But underline the letter that should have been capitalized. If any capital letter is omitted or used needlessly, do not give a point for capitalization. Any word omitted from the sentence or added to it is an error. Any incorrect punctuation omitted from or added to a sentence is an error.

**Note:** A helpful way to keep track of the points for each sentence is to put a check mark in front of the sentence for each point given.

**Checkup 4: Paragraphs.** In this section and the next one on letter writing, you will have to use your own judgment in deciding how many points out of the total to give S. in each skills area. Keeping that in mind, score the paragraphs as suggested below:

- up to 15 points for content. Note the following: Is each paragraph written about a main idea? Do the sentences flow along in some logical order? Has S. expressed his thoughts clearly? Is there too much repetition in order to fill up space?
- up to 5 points for form. Is each paragraph indented? Is sentence structure used correctly enough to express the thought? Is correct punctuation used for the most part? Are sentences capitalized?
- up to 5 points for spelling. If all the words are spelled correctly, score 5 points. If most of the regular words are spelled correctly, score 4 points. Underline any irregular words that are misspelled, and have S. look them up in the dictionary later. Deduct more points for words that are definitely spelled carelessly or so poorly that you can't tell what they are supposed to be.

A total of 25 points is possible for the paragraphs.

**Checkup 5: Letter Writing.** Score the letter and the envelope as suggested below:

- up to 15 points for content. Did the student write several sentences that show that he understands what is meant by a thank you letter? Did he express himself clearly?

- up to 5 points for form. Score 1 point each for correct heading, greeting, and closing. Score 1 point if paragraphs are indented correctly and 1 point if the correct punctuation is generally used.
- up to 5 points for spelling. Follow suggestions for scoring spelling in Checkup 4: Paragraphs.
- up to 5 points for addressing the envelope correctly, including the return address.

A total of 25 points is possible for the letter, and 5 points are possible for the envelope.

**Handwriting.** Score up to a total of 20 points for legibility of cursive writing throughout the writing checkups. See the introduction to the *Teacher's Guide* for the *Laubach Way to Cursive Writing* for criteria to help evaluate legibility.

## EVALUATING THE WRITING CHECKUPS

The scores for each part of the writing checkups will give you an informal diagnosis of the student's strengths and weaknesses in such writing skills as spelling, written expression, and handwriting. The suggested satisfactory score is about 75% of the perfect score for each part. If S. made less than the suggested satisfactory score for a particular checkup, analyze the type of errors he made. List the items he needs to review the most. The words selected for the word and sentence dictation cover most of the sound/letter relationships taught in *Skill Book 4*. Note which patterns gave him the most trouble, and review those. Also, note whether he was able to apply his knowledge of phonics and spelling rules in spelling new words that he may have used in his original writing. If his handwriting is poor, review some of the lessons in the *Laubach Way to Cursive Writing*.

## REVIEWING CHECKUPS WITH THE STUDENT

At your next session, go over the writing checkups with your student. Give praise and encouragement where possible. Have him correct errors in spelling and punctuation, following the procedure used in his writing lessons. He may want to make a list of the words he needs to study in his notebook. Discuss the original paragraphs and letter that he wrote. Help him see ways that he may make any needed improvements in his written expression. Give emphasis to the content of his writing, and praise him for what he has done well. Encourage him to write original stories and letters at home.

Give S. some encouraging report about the progress he has made in reading and writing. Assure him that the checkups he has done are only one way to measure progress. The use he makes of his reading and writing in daily life are even more important. Discuss with S. the possiblities for his next program of study.

# Word List

Skill Book 4 and its correlated reader *People and Places* introduce the 882 words and 7 symbols listed below. Variants with -s, -es, -'s, -s', -ed, -ing, -er, -est, -y, and -ly are not listed, even when y is changed to i before an ending. New words are listed in their root form when they are used with these previously taught endings. Italics indicate that a word taught earlier is reintroduced at this level as a key word for a particular sound and spelling. A hyphenated word made from two previously taught words is not listed as new.

In the list below, the number indicates the lesson in which the word is introduced. The abbreviation *cr* stands for the correlated reader, and the number following it refers to the story number in the correlated reader.

| | | | | | | | | | |
|---|---|---|---|---|---|---|---|---|---|
| 9 | about | 12 | awful | cr.2 | Canadian | 5 | cool | 10 | down |
| 5 | above | 13 | ball | 7 | cancer | 21 | correct | 15 | downtown |
| 18 | accept | 20 | ballroom | cr.3 | canoe | 19 | cough | 10 | drove |
| 12 | accident | 18 | bandage | cr.3 | captain | 8 | could | 4 | drum |
| 16 | according | 2 | barbecue | 8 | carve | 12 | couldn't | 6 | Duke |
| 19 | ache | 12 | bark | cr.1 | Carver | 9 | council | 19 | dumb |
| cr.1 | acre | 13 | baseball | 19 | case | 10 | county | 15 | during |
| 12 | across | 13 | basketball | 8 | catch | 20 | course | cr.4 | earn |
| 21 | action | cr.2 | bay | 14 | caught | 9 | courthouse | 9 | east |
| 20 | addition | 17 | beat | 12 | cause | 2 | cousin | 10 | easy |
| 21 | adjective | 17 | beaten | 17 | central | 10 | cow | 18 | edge |
| 20 | admission | 8 | beautiful | 13 | chance | 13 | crack | 16 | editor |
| 20 | admit | 12 | because | 18 | Chang | cr.3 | cradle | 16 | editorial |
| 19 | adult | 1 | become | 8 | chapter | 12 | crawl | 20 | educate |
| 21 | adverb | 3 | bedroom | cr.3 | Charbonneau | 5 | crew | 20 | education |
| 16 | advertise | 3 | begin | 17 | Charles | cr.3 | cross | 18 | election |
| 1 | afraid | 6 | believe | 17 | Charlotte | 10 | crowd | 19 | elephant |
| 19 | Africa | 16 | belong | cr.2 | cheer | 19 | crumb | cr.1 | else |
| 19 | African | cr.4 | belt | 17 | chef | 17 | cuffs | 5 | emergency |
| 3 | afternoon | cr.3 | berry | 17 | chemistry | 1 | cure | 15 | employ |
| 10 | against | 14 | between | 19 | chest | cr.4 | dagger | 15 | employee |
| cr.1 | agriculture | cr.4 | Bible | 17 | Chevy | 7 | daily | 15 | employment |
| 18 | aid | cr.4 | billion | 5 | chew | cr.3 | Dakota | 18 | enemy |
| 16 | aide | 6 | birthday | 17 | Chicago | 12 | damage | 18 | energy |
| 1 | airplane | cr.1 | birthplace | cr.3 | chief | 20 | dance | 15 | enjoy |
| 10 | alike | 19 | bite | 17 | chip | 20 | D'Angelo | 18 | enroll |
| 13 | all | 1 | blank | 17 | chocolate | 18 | danger | 21 | entry |
| 11 | allow | cr.3 | blanket | 2 | choke | 14 | daughter | cr.3 | equipment |
| 15 | almost | 19 | blood | 17 | choose | 12 | Dawson | cr.4 | Europe |
| 12 | along | 4 | blue | 17 | chorus | 4 | daytime | 1 | everywhere |
| 21 | alphabet | 20 | blueprint | 17 | chose | cr.1 | death | cr.2 | exact |
| 21 | alphabetical | 7 | board | 17 | Chris | 20 | Dec. | 19 | exam |
| 13 | also | 19 | body | 13 | Christmas | 13 | December | 1 | example |
| 19 | although | cr.1 | boll | 18 | citizenship | 20 | decide | 10 | excite |
| 15 | always | 8 | book | cr.3 | claim | 20 | decision | cr.4 | excitement |
| 14 | American | cr.1 | Booker | cr.3 | Clark | 19 | deep | 17 | excuse (v.) |
| 1 | amuse | 20 | bookkeeping | 16 | classified | 21 | definition | 12 | exit |
| 20 | amusement | 16 | bottom | 14 | classroom | cr.1 | degree | cr.3 | expedition |
| 7 | animal | 14 | bought | cr.3 | Clatsop | 18 | Democratic | 15 | experience |
| 15 | annoy | 15 | *boy* | 12 | claw | 3 | deposit | cr.3 | explore |
| cr.1 | apart | 13 | Branch | 7 | climb | 16 | depress | 1 | fact |
| cr.4 | apostle | 2 | breathe | 19 | clinic | 20 | depression | 10 | fair |
| 15 | apply | 18 | bridge | 10 | clown | 21 | describe | 13 | fall |
| 19 | appointment | cr.2 | British | 4 | club | 14 | desk | 13 | false |
| 1 | aren't | 8 | brook | 6 | coach | 15 | destroy | 13 | fame |
| 2 | argue | 13 | Brooklyn | 15 | coin | 21 | dictionary | cr.1 | famous |
| 18 | army | 14 | brought | cr.2 | Columbia | 16 | different | 13 | fan |
| 9 | around | 10 | Brown | 7 | company | 18 | difference | 12 | fault |
| 20 | art | 11 | Brunoski | 12 | complete | 12 | dig | 13 | February |
| cr.2 | artificial | 20 | budget | 13 | compound | cr.2 | dip | 10 | feet |
| 19 | Asia | cr.3 | buffalo | 1 | computer | 20 | diploma | cr.3 | fell |
| 19 | Asian | 4 | bugle | 4 | concert | 19 | direct | 16 | female |
| 17 | aspirin | cr.3 | built | cr.1 | Congress | 19 | direction | 12 | fence |
| cr.2 | Atlantic | 19 | bull | 17 | consonant | 5 | dirt | 2 | few |
| 16 | Aug. | 8 | Bush | 20 | constitution | 15 | disappoint | 9 | fifth |
| 13 | August | 1 | business | 8 | contents | 9 | discuss | 4 | fireworks |
| 2 | aunt | cr.1 | businessmen | 10 | contest | 20 | discussion | 2 | fist |
| 12 | auto | cr.4 | buzz | 2 | continue | 13 | Dodgers | 4 | flag |
| 12 | automobile | 8 | cabin | 6 | contraction | 17 | doesn't | cr.4 | flash |
| 9 | Ave. | 6 | calendar | 8 | cook | 12 | dog | 17 | flour |
| 6 | avenue | 13 | call | 17 | cookie | 22 | done | 10 | flower |
| 15 | avoid | 13 | California | cr.1 | cookstove | 19 | dose | | |

| | |
|---|---|
| 4 | flute |
| 12 | fog |
| 3 | food |
| 8 | foot |
| 13 | football |
| 12 | Ford |
| 3 | forever |
| cr.4 | forgot |
| cr.3 | fork |
| 1 | form |
| cr.3 | fort |
| cr.2 | Fox |
| 14 | fought |
| 9 | found |
| cr.4 | Frank |
| cr.3 | French |
| 16 | Fri. |
| 12 | front |
| 10 | frown |
| 8 | full |
| 3 | furnished |
| 1 | game |
| 17 | gas |
| 18 | Gene |
| 18 | gentle |
| cr.1 | George |
| 18 | Ginger |
| 7 | given |
| 11 | Gladys |
| cr.4 | globe |
| 4 | goes |
| 22 | gone |
| 8 | good |
| 18 | Gordon |
| 20 | government |
| 18 | Grace |
| 15 | grade |
| 18 | graduate |
| 16 | grand |
| 16 | grandchildren |
| 2 | grandfather |
| 2 | grandmother |
| cr.1 | greenhouse |
| 5 | grew |
| 9 | ground |
| 7 | group |
| 5 | grow |
| 19 | grown |
| 20 | guest |
| 21 | guide |
| 17 | gym |
| cr.2 | halfway |
| 13 | hall |
| 12 | haul |
| 2 | haven't |
| 19 | headache |
| 7 | headline |
| 16 | health |
| 4 | heart |
| 3 | heat |
| 10 | held |
| 20 | hello |